Developing an Annuity Market in Europe

Developing an Annuity Market in Europe

Edited by

Elsa Fornero

Professor of Economics, Faculty of Economics, and Director of CeRP, Center for Research on Pensions and Welfare Policies, University of Turin

Elisa Luciano

Professor of Mathematical Finance, Faculty of Economics, University of Turin

Edward Elgar
Cheltenham, UK • Northampton, MA, USA

Published by
Edward Elgar Publishing Limited
Glensanda House
Montpellier Parade
Cheltenham
Glos GL50 1UA
UK

Edward Elgar Publishing, Inc.
136 West Street
Suite 202
Northampton
Massachusetts 01060
USA

A catalogue record for this book
is available from the British Library

Library of Congress Cataloguing in Publication Data

Developing an annuity market in Europe / edited by Elsa Fornero, Elisa Luciano.
p. cm.
Includes bibliographical references and index.
1. Annuities—Europe. 2. Pensions—Europe. I. Fornero, Elsa. II. Luciano, Elisa.

HG8790.D48 2004
368.3'7'0094—dc22

2004040555

ISBN 1 84376 476 8

Printed and bound in Great Britain by MPG Books Ltd, Bodmin, Cornwall

Contents

Figures

Tables

Contributors

Laura Ballotta	Faculty of Actuarial Science and Statistics, Cass Business School, City University London
Margherita Borella	Center for Research on Pensions and Welfare Policies (CeRP)
Monika Bütler	Départment d'économétrie et d'économie politique (DEEP), Université de Lausanne and Centre for Economic Policy Research (CEPR)
Edmund Cannon	Department of Economics, University of Bristol and Centre for Research in Applied Macroeconomics
E. Philip Davis	Department of Economics and Finance, Brunel University, UK and National Institute of Economic and Social Research
Elsa Fornero	Department of Economics, University of Turin and Center for Research on Pensions and Welfare Policies (CeRP)
Steven Haberman	Faculty of Actuarial Science and Statistics, Cass Business School, City University London
Michael D. Hurd	RAND
Elisa Luciano	Department of Statistics and Applied Mathematics, University of Turin
David McCarthy	Department of Insurance and Risk Management, The Wharton School, University of Pennsylvania
Olivia S. Mitchell	Pension Research Council, The Wharton School, University of Pennsylvania
Constantijn W.A. Panis	RAND
Ermanno Pitacco	Faculty of Economics, University of Trieste, Italy
Giacomo Ponzetto	Center for Research on Pensions and Welfare Policies (CeRP)

Reinhold Schnabel	Department of Economics, University of Essen, and Zentrum für Europäische Wirtschaftsforschung (ZEW), Mannheim
James P. Smith	RAND
Chris Soares	US Treasury Department
Ian Tonks	University of Bristol and Centre for Market and Public Organisation
Mark Warshawsky	US Treasury Department
Julie M. Zissimopoulos	RAND

Acknowledgments

This volume is a collection of the papers presented at the CeRP[1] third annual conference, 'Developing an Annuity Market in Europe' (Turin, 20–21 June, 2002).

This work – and before it, the conference – would not have been possible without the funding of the Compagnia di San Paolo, which supports all the activities of the Center.

We wish to express our gratitude to all contributors for their enthusiasm towards this project and their cooperation during the realization of the volume. We are also grateful to the conference participants for helpful comments and suggestions and to the CeRP researchers for precious encouragement.

In addition to the acknowledgments contained in each chapter, many thanks go to Silvia Maero for her brilliant coordination of the editing process and to Giacomo Ponzetto and Serena Trucchi for excellent editorial assistance.

Elsa Fornero and Elisa Luciano

[1] CeRP (Center for Research on Pensions and Welfare Policies, Turin; http://cerp.unito.it) is an independent research Center within CORIPE Piemonte (www.coripe.unito.it).

1. Introduction

Elsa Fornero and Elisa Luciano

1. Pension provision in Europe will change dramatically over the next decades, mainly as a consequence of:

- the reforms of the public pay-as-you-go (PAYG) systems, aimed at reducing their overall generosity and restoring financial equilibrium;
- the efforts to build a substantial funded component;
- the shift from defined benefit (DB) to defined contribution (DC) schemes.

This book concentrates on the funded component of pension wealth, and specifically on annuities, namely financial products that allow the conversion of wealth into a lifelong stream of guaranteed income. By their very nature, annuities protect households from the risk of outliving their wealth or, on the contrary, of leaving undesired bequests.

The analysis presented in this book builds upon two premises, respectively normative and descriptive in nature. The first is the belief that, in order to effectively improve the allocation of pension wealth, the funded pillar needs to be based on efficient annuity markets, where pricing, hedging and risk monitoring are aligned with the current best practice in financial markets. The second is the observation that in most European countries these markets are very thin, characterized by imperfect and incomplete information, on one side, and by significant disparities in risk assessment and in pricing with respect to other financial assets, on the other.

Many issues in the field of annuity markets have attracted increasing attention from scholars and policy makers alike, starting from the apparent contradiction between the theoretical prediction, derived from a life-cycle model of savings, of annuities as the dominant asset, and the above mentioned observation that annuity markets are very thin, or simply non-existent. This contradiction has, of course, many possible explanations and most of them have already been investigated:

- social security pensions are high enough to satisfy the demand for annuitized wealth;
- insurance markets are plagued by various kinds of 'imperfections' and the market for annuities is no exception; adding to this the substantial financial and demographic risks that are involved, the pricing can be such as to make annuities a dominated, instead of a dominant, asset;
- considering household behavior, it is quite possible that individuals do not choose according to either an intertemporal optimization model in general or a strict life-cycle model in particular; various impediments limit their ability to optimize with respect to the long run; or various factors can justify their reluctance to annuitize and their preference towards capital; finally, the theoretical framework itself may be too restrictive to capture even perfectly rational motives behind the unwillingness of households to buy annuities.

Policies are generally adopted to overcome these difficulties in establishing a mixed pension system. By limiting the generosity of the public pension system – a measure required to increase sustainability – they also make room for private pensions; by an appropriate regulation of the market they can reduce and redistribute risks; by granting fiscal incentives they increase the attractiveness of the products with respect to other financial instruments.

Policies can also be adopted within the 'industry' itself, such as innovation in the products and cost reduction leading to greater competition.

2. Within this broad framework, this volume collects the papers presented at the third CeRP Conference, with the title: 'Developing an Annuity Market in Europe' (Turin, June 2002).

The conference aimed at providing:

i. a survey of recent research on the role of annuities in helping households to finance retirement and decumulate wealth;
ii. an overview of regulatory issues, such as prudential provisions, and risk measurement and mitigation by annuity suppliers, that is, insurance companies;
iii. a discussion of demand-side issues, such as the variability of the first annuity payment, the exposure to inflation, and their relationship with the willingness to annuitize;
iv. an analysis of longevity risk and the resulting difficulties in pricing, both as determinants of individual demand and as fundamental issues for annuity provision;
v. an examination of the development of annuity markets in Europe.

The contributions to the present collection reflect the above goals, as follows.

The second chapter, by **David McCarthy and Olivia Mitchell**, introduces the fundamental economic role of annuities as asset decumulation tools: annuitizing, that is, exchanging an initial premium for a steady income stream which lasts as long as the annuitant (or the longer-lived of two joint annuitants) lives, allows the latter to avoid the symmetric problems of consuming too aggressively or too conservatively. Annuitants are thus protected from the so-called longevity risk arising from the uncertain length of their lives.

The insurance company who sells the annuity, in turn, pools the longevity risk of retirees with similar *ex ante* life expectancies but different *ex post* survival outcomes.

In a world in which households and insurance companies invest their wealth in the same portfolio, and the latter do not apply any loading factor, annuitization should be the exclusive instrument used to finance consumption in retirement. From an empirical point of view, the authors argue that, in spite of possibly different portfolio allocations and the existence of fees, there is still a significant advantage to be gained from annuitization. They motivate this result by computing, for selected OECD countries, the so-called 'money's worth ratio (MWR)', that is, the ratio of the expected present value of annuity benefits to the corresponding premium, as well as the 'equivalent wealth measure (EWM)', that is, the amount of wealth which a retiree would require if he had no access to annuities if he were to attain the same utility level as with annuities. By so doing, they demonstrate that, at least in developed countries, annuities provide good value: computed MWRs are higher than 80 per cent for the overall population, and close to or even higher than unity for actual annuitants; correspondingly, the EWM measures range from 1.3 to 2.0.

Given these figures, which indicate a very positive evaluation of annuities, on the one hand, and the limited demand, on the other, the authors discuss a number of factors which could be responsible for the modest size of annuity markets, even in developed countries. On the demand side, these include possible wrong perceptions of the cost of annuities and the preference for being financially liquid in old age. On the supply side, mention is evidently made of the crowding out by generous PAYG systems, whose importance is however expected to decrease in the future because of sustainability problems. Aside from reducing the size of social security systems, a number of ensuing new roles for government intervention and regulation, aimed at increasing the overall efficiency of annuity markets, are finally discussed, such as the collection and provision of accurate mortality data and the promotion of consumer education on the various forms of retirement provision.

These references to public intervention open the way to the third chapter, by **E. Philip Davis**, which discusses regulation of annuities markets from three perspectives: prudential regulation of insurance companies; regulation of their conduct of business, and regulation of annuities in the overall pension system.

To begin with, Davis introduces the economic rationale supporting regulation versus the simple reliance on market discipline. Given the existence, in annuity markets, of various forms of imperfections, ranging from information asymmetry, adverse selection and moral hazard to externalities, such as counterparty risk and contagion among insurance or reinsurance firms, imperfect competition and market power, there is scope for government intervention based on the need to enhance the equity, adequacy and security of retirement income.

Within the perspective of insurance company regulation, Davis presents the case for appropriate reserving and capital adequacy rules, as well as for portfolio regulation, in the form of appropriate quantitative portfolio restrictions complementing a general 'prudent person rule'.

Within the perspective of the conduct of business regulation, he focuses on the usefulness of the provision of accurate information to consumers and of product design regulation, which could help in making the market more transparent and presumably, at a second stage, more liquid.

Within the third and last perspective, that of annuity regulation in the overall context of pension design, Davis discusses taxation and timing issues, as well as the possibility of compulsory annuity purchase, meant to overcome the adverse selection problem mentioned above, even suggesting that only inflation-protected annuities should be mandated. These aspects, however, should arguably be considered in the light of the characteristics of social security promises: in countries characterized by generous PAYG systems, where the typical replacement rate is high (up to 80 per cent) and the pension level is indexed to prices, the case for introducing additional constraints, such as compulsory annuitization, within the private component is, in our view, much weakened.

In addition to regulatory interventions on a company-by-company basis, Davis highlights the market-wide importance of accurate risk assessment. This concerns not only mortality and interest rates, needed to price annuities and to estimate their value (for instance according to the MWR, as in the chapter by McCarthy and Mitchell), but also credit and systemic risks, which increasingly involve all financial institutions. Insurance companies, as the natural annuity providers, face a particularly challenging task of asset-liability management, and are confronted with evolving market conditions, which cannot exclude disquieting prospects of potential insolvency due to system-wide shocks, as exemplified by the recent Japanese experience. Credit and market risks should therefore come to the forefront, as is already the case for financial firms other than insurance companies, especially when developing innovative products.

While Davis focuses his attention on the risks faced by insurance companies, **Chris Soares and Mark Warshawsky** concentrate on two risks which mainly concern the annuitant: the variability of initial annuity payments over subsequent calendar years, which is a consequence of the DC formula, and the lack of inflation protection in the time profile of payments, characterizing the products typically sold in the market.

They wonder whether DC pension plans excessively expose participants to these risks, whether they are worth bearing and whether they are avoidable. To answer these questions, the authors analyse US data on fixed nominal, nominally increasing and inflation-adjusted annuities, as well as phased purchases of the first type, using projected mortality tables and interest rates implicit in the term structure. Given that the last two categories of annuities prove to be much less volatile than the first, the authors conclude that risk-averse households should:

- buy inflation protected annuities and/or
- phase the purchase of fixed annuities over a period of time or, equivalently, obtain a group annuity whose price is based on moving averages of interest rates.

Since the market, however small, is currently dominated by fixed nominal annuities, whose purchase is not phased over time, questions remain regarding the true appeal of annuities and their understanding by households. The authors recognize that there is room for further research on annuity risks, as defined above, and more generally on investment diversification for retirement provision. A better management of both the supply-side risks, as discussed by Davis, and the demand-side ones, analysed by Soares and Warshawsky, could probably increase the households' propensity to annuitize.

This propensity is shown to be currently quite limited in the following chapter, by **Michael Hurd, C. Panis, J. Smith and J. Zissimouplos**. The authors use data from the Health and Retirement Study to assess households' willingness to annuitize.

They infer its magnitude from two different empirical exercises. One estimate is derived from the disposition of pension rights by workers who left a job and could choose between a lump-sum payment, an annuity, or continued participation in a pension plan; the other from the timing of the claim to social security retirement benefits, which in the US can be delayed one year, in exchange for an 8 per cent increase in the resulting annuity. Both indicators suggest that most people prefer not to annuitize, when given the choice.

When analyzing the characteristics of the selected sample, mixed evidence is found on the possible determinants of annuitization. Overall, the evidence does not lead to any meaningful and consistent relationship between the subjective survival assessment – which in theory should have an important role on the decision to annuitize – and the above-mentioned indicators. Other possible theoretical determinants of annuitization, such as the level of bequeathable wealth or the education level, have an explanatory power only for one indicator but not for the other.

Thus the authors are led to conclude that simple versions of the life-cycle hypothesis are not a good predictor of actual annuitization behavior, and that innovation to the theoretical framework might be required.

Annuity demand could probably be fostered, on the other hand, by more accurate risk measurement and management by insurance companies. In this spirit, the next chapter, by **Ermanno Pitacco**, presents a thorough investigation of the primary risk which annuities are meant to pool, that is, longevity risk.

The chapter discusses uncertainty in mortality and disability trends, presenting a moving mortality scenario from which the longevity risk in living benefits arises. Recently, projected mortality tables have been used to take into account the evolution of mortality; however, the future trend of survivorship is inherently random. This introduces in all pension and annuity computations, both for pricing and reserving purposes, a model risk: in particular, when we think of the changes in the 'tail' of life tables, the term 'longevity risk' is used.

The author, using a comprehensive stochastic approach and a number of examples, analyses the financial impact of longevity risk, focusing on solvency requirements and reinsurance arrangements. Finally, he concentrates on the fact that actuarial aspects must be carefully considered when designing new insurance products involving living benefits, such as annuities and long term care policies.

Life insurance products provide an important example of the need for new ideas consistent with a rapidly evolving demographic setting, but also with an accurate financial evaluation. The latter should be aimed at avoiding the so-called pricing risk, that is, the risk of mispricing insurance products.

Pricing risk is the main focus of the chapter which follows Pitacco's, contributed by **Laura Ballotta and Steven Haberman.**

Their analysis evaluates a common feature of UK pension policies in the late 1970s and 1980s: the guaranteed annuity conversion option (GAO), that is, the option to convert a cash benefit at retirement, equal to the reference portfolio value, into an annuity computed at a guaranteed rate. The correct evaluation of these options, embedded in some unit-linked pension contracts, such as the Equitable ones, should be the basis for the commercialization of these contracts and could have prevented the troubles suffered by some UK companies in the past.

Apart from the specific option at hand, Ballotta and Haberman's chapter provides an interesting example of how the tools of modern finance can be fruitfully applied to insurance products. The authors indeed resort not only to the classical Black-Scholes formula, but also to the Heath-Jarrow-Morton model for interest rates, enriching it with a thorough modeling of stochastic mortality. They do not simply provide the needed pricing formulae, but also offer some guidance on hedging and test the price sensitivity with respect to key financial and mortality variables.

Finally, they provide a historical analysis of the solvency problems experienced by UK insurance companies, by examining a hypothetical contract issued in 1970 to a policyholder then aged 20, and monitoring the evolution of its GAO value up to the present. The option was brought 'in the money' by the halving of interest rates in the early 1990s and its value kept rising as interest rates kept falling. Changes in mortality assumptions, from the original deterministic life table to a stochastic scenario add to the increase in the GAO value, but a much more substantial effect results from the use of projected mortality.

3. The final part of the book examines aspects of private pension markets in specific European countries, trying to provide a meaningful sample of countries where the three pillars have markedly different weights, and private schemes attract different degrees of confidence and familiarity on the part of households: UK, Switzerland, Germany and Italy.

The British case is examined, under a specific perspective, in the chapter by **Edmund Cannon and Ian Tonks**. The UK is a country with a relatively small social security system and mature private pension schemes, including the most developed annuity market; one would theoretically predict annuity demand to be significant, especially with regard to inflation-indexed and possibly investment-linked products. On the contrary, traditional nominal annuities are prevalent and the market remains rather thin. The government introduced compulsory annuitization of pension plan balances, but this measure has been widely criticized by the public and the press, which perceive annuity rates as unfairly low.

To assess the credibility of this claim, Cannon and Tonks construct a time-series of UK annuity prices since 1972. They find that, while prices naturally fluctuate with interest rates, the MWR is high, and obviously increasing with life expectancy. Nonetheless, it could be claimed that interest rates themselves are distorted, because pension funds and annuity providers demand more long-term securities than the government is willing to supply.

The authors therefore consider the replacement rate which can be obtained by retirees annuitizing at current prices a fund previously invested in the stock market. Due to the correlation of asset values with interest rates, this replacement rate is steady over time and adequate, dispelling the doubt that annuity prices might be excessively high.

The Swiss system, analysed by **Monika Bütler**, is also characterized by a limited social security program and a surprisingly thin third pillar, but also by the fundamental role played by a long-established second pillar.

Private occupational pension funds are heavily regulated in Switzerland, with compulsory participation and pervasive government intervention: despite being fully funded, these schemes have a notional nominal rate of return and a guaranteed annuity conversion rate, both predetermined by law. Paradoxically, this tends to replicate some of the defects usually associated with the public PAYG system of other European countries.

Concerning annuity provision, in particular, the conversion rate is higher than any private insurer could afford, unsurprisingly leading retirees to prefer annuitization. Along with this overall generosity come idiosyncratic disparities of treatment, based on outdated notions of the labor market and of the family, which favor in particular married men with children (and their widows, at the expense of widowers).

Finally, as for the accumulation phase, the system suffers from a lack of transparency, and potential unsustainability of pension promises, notwithstanding the reduction of guaranteed returns introduced after the recent market downturn.

As for Germany, as shown in the chapter by **Reinhold Schnabel**, private pensions and annuities have so far had a marginal role, while public pensions, indexed to average earnings, have usually provided incomes exceeding the average consumption of the elderly.

This situation is set to change as first-pillar replacement rates are progressively reduced, while new rules provide fiscal incentives and subsidies for private pension plans as well as for annuitization. The 2001 reform represents, however, no more than a very partial reduction in the generosity of the social security system.

The same law introduced a subsidy for occupational and individual pension plans meeting certain conditions, the so-called 'Riester-plans'. This combines with a complex system of preferential tax treatments, dependent partly on pension-plan characteristics, partly on workers' choices.

Pension funds have also been created as a vehicle for retirement savings, but they are overburdened by regulation, making them more expensive and less flexible than the pre-existing alternatives (internal pension plans and *Pensionskassen*). Arguably the most important provision is that each employee is entitled to demand some sort of pension scheme from her company, independently of its size. The government has also mandated full transferability of account balances between pension plans, and is trying to discourage traditional DB schemes, so far with limited success.

Riester-plans have not proved very popular: average contributions are very low, exactly matching the minimum requirement for the full tax advantage. Surveys show that workers neither feel nor are well informed about pension products, tax treatment and personal eligibility. German workers do increasingly think that private savings are required to supplement public pensions, but they do not necessarily want to channel their saving into specific products.

Finally, Italy, as illustrated in the chapter by **Margherita Borella, Elsa Fornero and Giacomo Ponzetto**, is also characterized by a very generous public pension system and an extremely limited private funded component. The reforms enacted in the 1990s aimed both at ensuring the long-term sustainability of the social security system and at developing the demand for private pension plans.

The intense legislative action undergone during the decade had, however, only a limited impact on the demand for private pensions, both in the second and in the third pillar. The authors show, through an analysis conducted on Italian micro-data, that the decrease in public pension wealth experienced by Italian families during the 1990s helps in explaining the observed increase in participation in the market for contractual savings for retirement. Nevertheless, private accumulation for retirement is still modest by international standards, and participation in formal pension schemes is even more limited.

This may be partly explained by the complexity of regulation, with respect to market segmentation, fiscal advantages and constraints imposed on participants. The single most important factor, however, is probably the overwhelming role of the first pillar: although the reforms have reduced future benefits, the contribution rates are still very high (33 per cent for employees), leaving scarce room for the financing of supplementary pensions. Law makers meant to solve this problem by earmarking the annual flow of contributions destined to the accumulation of severance pay (TFR for *Trattamento di fine rapporto*) as the ideal candidate to finance the funded component of pension wealth. The chapter investigates the reasons why the devolution of TFR to supplementary pension plans has not proved the preferred option for employees, mainly explained by the precautionary-saving nature of TFR.

4. The overall picture which emerges from the (albeit limited) analysis of European countries provided in the book confirms a modest level of development of annuity markets, except for those countries where the second pillar, made up of occupational pension plans, is strong, possibly compulsory, and such as to constitute a significant integration with social security benefits.

We are thus left with the apparent contradiction of an important risk-sharing tool, potentially very relevant for the intertemporal savings decision of households, and also empirically granting 'good value for money' – as shown, right from the beginning of the book, by the money's worth ratios provided by McCarthy and Mitchell – being scarcely demanded.

A number of factors have been discussed which can account for this contradiction. A rationale for the limited role of annuities in households' portfolios comes first of all from the high level of public pensions, which inevitably crowd out the demand for private provision; a second kind of explanation can easily be found in the many imperfections of the insurance sector which burden supply.

The country studies thus bring us back to one of the main questions addressed by this volume: what can be done, in terms of policy measures and product design, to help the development of an annuity market in Europe. The answers which emerge from this collection of papers can be summarized as follows.

On the **demand** side, while making annuitization compulsory, as advocated by those who fear the adverse-selection effect, is of course the most direct way to achieve the goal, the drawbacks of this solution should not be underrated; the resulting welfare costs would not necessarily be offset by the ensuing reduction in prices. In fact, the analysis by McCarthy and Mitchell shows that – in those countries where it can be measured – the difference in longevity between self-selected annuitants and the average individual is of the same order of magnitude as the one between the average man and the average woman; the impact of adverse selection on MWRs is thus rather limited, ranging from 5 to 10 percentage points, as confirmed by Soares and Warshawsky.

Without resorting to compulsory annuitization, an obvious spur to the development of annuity markets could consist, as recalled by many contributors, in limiting the generosity of the social security system, and possibly in introducing, or reinforcing, fiscal incentives to the funded component. European countries are increasingly committed to improve the long-run sustainability of their social security systems, threatened by population ageing, by further reducing the current overall generosity of the public benefits. Even if these will very likely remain the most important source of income for the elderly in most countries, this strategy places a greater role on private provision.

To trigger the development of the private sector, however, the mere reduction of the first pillar is not sufficient; an appropriate and sound regulatory framework is also required, capable of ensuring a high degree of efficiency, affordability and security of the funded component, whether of the second or the third pillar, and both for the accumulation and the payout phase, where annuities come to the forefront. In defining the regulatory framework, the European Union has an important role, mainly because the consequences of the present differences in the national regulations impact on various aspects relevant at Union level (such as the portability of pensions, which affects labor mobility). (See European Commission, 2003.)

Together with these traditional forms of market spur, the present collection of papers has also suggested improving consumers' awareness of:

- their survival prospects and disability probabilities (Pitacco);
- the value of annuities, as measured by the MWR (McCarthy and Mitchell, Soares and Warshawsky, Cannon and Tonks), their utility value (McCarthy and Mitchell), the replacement ratio (Cannon and Tonks) and, last but not least, the value of embedded options, such as GAO (Ballotta and Haberman);
- the range of legally available private pension options (Schnabel, Borella et al.).

Furthermore, the contributors have proposed increasing the appeal of annuities by

- packaging different benefits in a single contract for retirees (McCarthy and Mitchell, Pitacco);
- providing financial flexibility, for example through the 'with profits' clause, or the guarantee of a minimum income with a variable bonus, or protection from inflation risk (Davis, Soares and Warshawsky).

Nevertheless, further research on the determinants of households' choices and their apparent reluctance to annuitize is clearly warranted, as stressed by Hurd et al.

On the **supply** side as well the collected papers have put forward both traditional and innovative proposals. On the one hand, the country studies underlined the importance of the classical advice such as:

- to improve transparency, liquidity and competition (as stressed in particular by Bütler);

- to reduce costs, as stressed by Borella et al.;
- to enhance the matching of legal rules and incentive structures to actual individual preferences (cf. the case of Riester-plans in Germany, as described by Schnabel, and that of TFR devolution in Italy, presented by Borella et al.).

On the other hand, the following suggestions have emerged, which, paying attention to risk factors not limited to those concerning mortality, also reflect innovative views coming from the financial markets:

- prompt insurance companies to diversify not only mortality risk (through an appropriate liability choice), but also market risk (by an appropriate asset allocation, or choice of the assets which back annuities);
- induce insurance companies to reduce mortality risk through annuity guarantee pools, reinsurance, or risk sharing between different cohorts of annuitants, as well as market risk through financial hedging techniques such as duration matching;
- prevent excessive credit-risk acceptance, inherent in defaultable bonds;
- enforce accurate reserving rules (Davis, Ballotta and Haberman).

The attainment of these goals could go hand in hand with the attempt to increase the attractiveness of annuities from the point of view of insurance companies: inflation-linked bonds could help them back annuities (Soares and Warshawsky); their awareness of reinsurance policies and solvency requirements could be improved (Pitacco); they could profit, for diversification reasons, from packaging benefits together (Pitacco).

At a higher level, however, we agree with Davis that macro prudential indicators – such as the ones adopted for the banking sector in the Basle Committee proposals – are a very promising tool to measure and regulate the various risks incurred by annuity providers, and therefore to foster the development of an annuity market in Europe.

In any case, much work remains to be done both in theoretical research and at empirical level. In this light, we consider this book as a useful preliminary contribution.

REFERENCES

European Commission (2003), *Joint Report by the Commission and the Council on Adequate and Sustainable Pensions.*

2. Annuities for an ageing world*

David McCarthy and Olivia S. Mitchell

The recent passing of the British Queen Mother at age 101 has brought home to many observers the very real possibility that living to be quite old is a risk to which many of us are increasingly exposed. Longevity patterns throughout the developed world indicate that many more of us will live beyond what was once considered the 'normal' retirement age, surviving to celebrate our 100th birthdays and beyond. One long-term consequence of global demographic ageing is that it will become increasingly challenging to maintain a decent standard of living during such a long retirement period. Planning ahead for retirement requires confronting and managing a host of risks that threaten to undermine our prospects of retirement well-being.

Over the next half-century, global ageing trends will imply that more of the world's population will attain the age of 60 and over than ever before, amounting to a higher fraction than children under 15. By 2050, there will be several million centenarians alive on earth, more than at any prior time in human civilization (Desai, 2002). This dramatic global ageing process represents an historical 'first' by world standards, and it prompts a fundamental question for retirement systems experts: namely, how can societies finance longevity risk, in the light of ever-longer-lived populations?

In this light, the appeal of life annuities is that they offer retirees an opportunity to protect against the risk of outliving their assets, by exchanging these assets for a lifelong stream of guaranteed income (BMPW, 2001). That is, life annuities are financial products, which, in exchange for an initial premium, pay beneficiaries a periodic benefit as long as the annuitant lives. Contracts protecting people from outliving their life expectancies have been

* The research was supported in part by the Pension Research Council at the Wharton School, the National Bureau of Economic Research, and the Economic and Social Research Institute of Japan. This chapter was written in part during Dr. Mitchell's time as the Metzler Visiting Professor to the Johann Wolfgang Goethe Universitat, Lehrstuhl fur Investment, Portfolio Management und Alterssicherung. Helpful comments were provided by E. Philip Davis. Opinions and errors are solely those of the authors and not of the institutions with which they are affiliated.

around since at least the 1300s (Jennings and Trout, 1982). Insurance companies have taken on the task of pooling annuity purchasers with similar life expectancies but different longevity realizations, to help protect them against longevity risk. In many countries, however, life annuity products have tended to be sold as retirement *accumulation* vehicles, rather than as *decumulation* products. This may explain why annuity markets in the OECD countries have been relatively underdeveloped to date.[1]

Nevertheless, global interest in annuity markets is beginning to grow. In Latin America, for instance, more than a dozen countries have recently converted their unfunded national defined benefit (DB) pension plans into funded defined contribution (DC) pensions.[2] With the new models well in place, these nations have now begun to consider how the payout phase of these benefit programs will be handled.

Many European countries have also begun moving toward funded pension systems and these reforms are focusing attention on European annuity markets.[3] This chapter identifies factors shaping annuity markets in the past, with a primary focus on longevity protection in developed nations. We then identify developments that promise potential growth for annuity markets, over the near term as the baby boom generation retires.

2.1 IS LONGEVITY INSURANCE A GOOD DEAL?[4]

In a world with no uncertainty, it would be straightforward for a retiree to allocate their wealth at retirement by spreading payments over their remaining life years. If no formal retirement system were in place, the life-cycle model predicts that rational decision makers would save optimally; at retirement, they would merely divide their assets over years remaining, so as to ensure optimal retirement consumption (and cover bequest motives, if any).[5]

In reality, of course, many sorts of uncertainty make it far more difficult to decide how much to consume in old age. One risk is that associated with unknown longevity: retirees could outlive their expected lifespans, and run the risk of exhausting assets before passing away. Retirees can reduce this risk by consuming less per year, but such a tactic then boosts the chance that they might die with *too much* wealth left unconsumed. In other words, dying with too little wealth is undesirable, but having too much wealth is also undesirable since it represents forgone consumption opportunities.

Retirement security can potentially be enhanced with the purchase of a life annuity which provides a steady income stream until the insured party's death. The annuity thus involves a premium paid to an insurer, who then pools retirees with similar *ex ante* longevity expectations but different *ex post* survival outcomes (MPWB, 1999; Warshawsky, 1998a).

To illustrate these issues, data from 2000 indicate that 65-year-old US males could have anticipated a life expectancy of age 81, but some 18 per cent would anticipate living to age 90 or older. Analogously a 65-year-old female expected 19.6 more years of life, but she had a 31 per cent chance of living to age 90 or older (Table 2.1). The high probability of living to very old age underscores the important degree of uncertainty facing people as they allocate their retirement assets. An alternative approach is depicted in Figure 2.1, where we illustrate alternative consumption profiles generated by alternative wealth drawdown rules. The profile labeled '1/LE' assumes that the retiree draws down his/her retirement wealth completely by the time he/she has reached his/her life expectancy at age 65. The individual consumes a level amount each year, which takes into account any investment earnings on his/her retirement wealth (here assumed to earn 4 per cent p.a. fixed). Clearly this strategy has the retiree running out of money if he/she outlives his/her life expectancy (probability = 43 per cent). A smoother but declining consumption path is represented by the profile labeled '1/Rem LE', which assumes that each year the retiree recomputes the level fraction of retirement wealth he/she can consume based on his/her updated life expectancy. For comparison, the profile labeled 'Life Ann' assumes the retiree's entire wealth is used to purchase an actuarially fair life annuity which smoothes consumption from 65.

Table 2.1 Life expectancy remaining and probabilities of survival to selected ages: men and women at age 65 (in 2000)

	Men	Women
Remaining life expectancy (years):	16.4	19.6
Probability of surviving to age:	(%)	(%)
70	88	92
75	74	82
80	56	69
85	36	51
90	18	31
95	6	14
100	1	4

Source: Brown (2000).

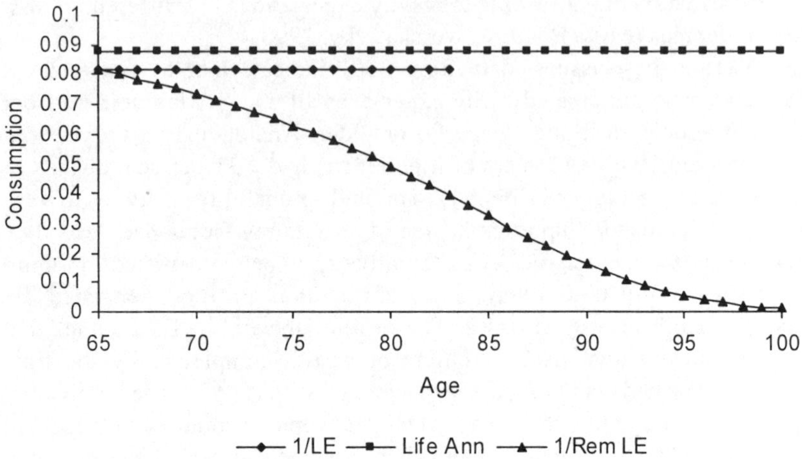

Note: Figure assumes worker attains retirement age with assets normalized at 1.0, and draws down fractional amounts of remaining assets over his/her remaining lifetime. The '1/LE' profile assumes that the retiree consumes a level proportion of his/her retirement wealth each year, at a rate sufficient to completely draw down all his/her wealth (and investment earnings) by the time he/she reaches his/her life expectancy (as of age 65). The 'Life Ann' profile assumes that the retiree's entire wealth is converted into an actuarially fair life annuity payable from 65. The profile labeled '1/Rem LE' assumes that the retiree recomputes the level consumption that will draw down his/her wealth over his/her remaining life expectancy each year, based on annually updated life expectancy. All profiles assume retirement at 65 and a real investment return of 4 per cent.

Source: Authors' computations using US male population cohort table from McCarthy and Mitchell (2002).

Figure 2.1 Alternative consumption profiles as a function of age

2.1.1 Alternative Payout Profiles

Recent research has sought to explore the pros and cons of alternative wealth drawdown patterns in retirement, to determine whether higher returns on non-annuitized investments might offset the value of the longevity insurance (which also must take into account insurance loads and fees).

Some might think that an older person would do better by holding onto his/her assets and investing them directly early in retirement, and waiting to buy an annuity later. This perception arises because annuity payouts are higher for those who purchase them later in life, reflecting higher expected mortality of older purchasers. But as Figure 2.2 shows, this is not necessarily a good strategy. Buying an annuity implies that survivors share the assets of those who died prematurely – essentially pooling the mortality risk of longer and shorter-lived people. As individuals age, mortality increases, implying that this effect becomes relatively more important. Consequently, the rate of return that a surviving retiree who had not annuitized his/her wealth would have to 'beat' in order to be at least as well off as if he/she had annuitized his/her wealth rises with age. In other words, older people's money must work harder 'if they are not to lose by delaying buying an annuity' (Inland Revenue, 2002).

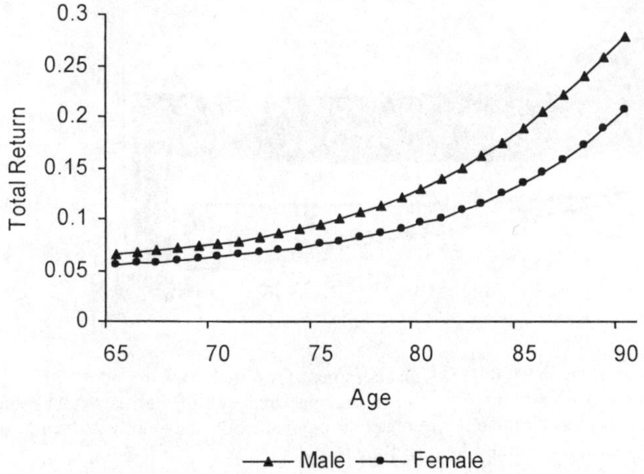

Note: Figure shows the return required to be earned on privately invested capital to compensate for the risk pooling aspect of annuities (which increases with age). Figure assumes a real annual interest rate underlying annuity prices and US male population cohort mortality from McCarthy and Mitchell (2002).

Source: Authors' calculations.

Figure 2.2 Return benchmark on residual capital that would have to be earned to compensate for 'mortality drag'

As an alternative approach, Albrecht and Maurer (2002) using German data demonstrate that the probability of exhausting one's assets prior to death without an annuity can be quite substantial, though how likely this is will depend on the asset allocation of the retiree's non-annuity wealth. Not only does the volatility of the self-insurer's investment portfolio matter, but also so does the interest rate assumed on the annuity asset. In this case an actuarially fair annuity is used as a benchmark (see Figure 2.3). In the German case, holding some equities provides higher expected returns as compared to annuities, depending on the assumed interest rate (AIR) used in pricing the annuity product.

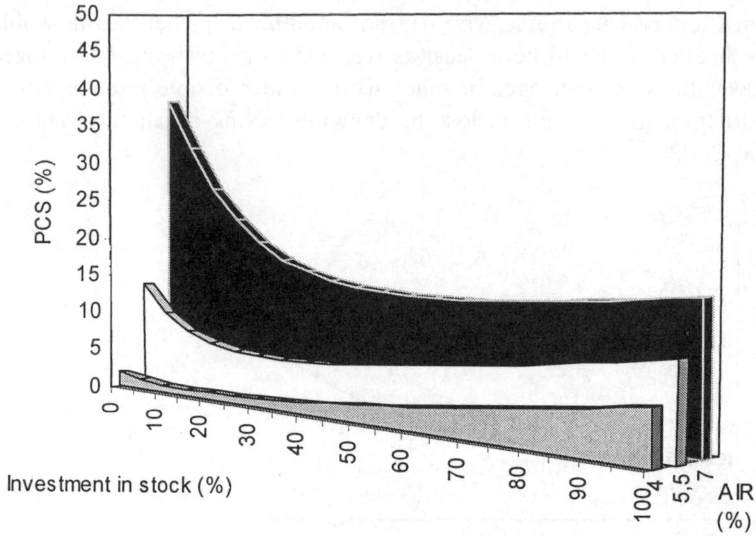

Note: Probability of consumption shortfall (PCS) in retirement for a male retiring at age 60 who does not annuitize, but instead invests his portfolio in the specified mix of German stocks and bonds. The shortfall is computed compared to consumption that could be purchased with an annuity priced using the specified Assumed Interest Rate (AIR).

Source: Albrecht and Maurer (2002).

Figure 2.3 Shortfall risk from self-insuring

2.1.2 Assessing Payoffs from Life Annuities

One way to assess the value of annuities to purchasers is to measure the 'money's worth' (MW) of life income products. This is facilitated by computing the expected present discounted value (EPDV) of the lifelong benefit stream paid out to the annuitant, and comparing this discounted cashflow to the annuity premium. In the economics literature, the MW is most easily understood in the instance of an immediate single-life annuity which pays out $A per period for life, in exchange for an initial purchase price (for example, $100 000).

For a nominal annuity, MPWB (1999) specifies that $q_{a,t}$ is the probability that an a-month-old individual alive at the beginning of month t will die during that month. P_j is the probability that a 65-year old retiree survives for at least j months after he/she purchases a lifelong annuity:[6]

$$P_i = (1-q_{780,1}) \times (1-q_{781,2}) \times .... \times (1-q_{780+j-1,j}) \qquad (2.1)$$

In this context, the EPDV of a life annuity with monthly payout A purchased by an individual of age b is $V_b(A)$, which can depend on a term structure of interest rates, i_k, expressing the nominal short rate k periods into the future:

$$V_b(A) = \sum_{j=1}^{600} \frac{A \times P_j}{\prod_{k=1}^{j} (1 + i_k)} \tag{2.2}$$

In much annuity research, the term structure of yields on Treasury bonds is used to estimate the time series of expected future nominal short-term interest rates.[7] For inflation-indexed, or real annuities, equation (2.2) incorporates the fact that payout is fixed in real terms (but varies in nominal terms). As BMP (2002) illustrates, this is easily expressed by letting A_r represent the real annual payment (and nominal interest rates in the denominator of equation (2.2) are replaced with real interest rates r_k). Then the EPDV of the real annuity becomes:

$$V_b(A_\tau) = \sum_{j=1}^{600} \frac{A_\tau \times P_j}{\prod_{k=1}^{j} (1 + r_k)} \tag{2.3}$$

Irrespective of the payout format, an annuity product's 'money's worth' is then defined as the ratio of the EPDV of the annuity's payout stream to its purchase price. For instance, a nominal annuity selling for $100 000 has a money's worth defined as $V_b(A_n)/100\ 000$. Such a money's worth ratio represents a currency-independent metric for comparing annuities across different groups, over time, and across countries.

2.1.3 Annuity Prices and Benefit Flows

In practice, constructing MW measures requires that the analyst obtain data on several key parameters, some of which are difficult to obtain and complicated to understand. Most importantly, data are needed regarding the payout stream and the premium charged by the annuity issuer. These are not always simple to model, since many products are on the market taking many different payout forms and structured with a wide range of premium payment paths. For example, a buyer may pay for the annuity with one lump sum or in many payments over a long period of time. Further, the benefit payments may be fixed in nominal terms for the life of the annuity contract, or they may rise at a predetermined rate over time. In yet other cases a retiree may receive dividends that vary with the value of the underlying assets in which the premium is invested, and/or an annuity policy may include a feature guaranteeing a death benefit to one's heirs.

The complexity of the annuity product market and the fact that products are not widely advertised makes it relatively difficult to compare them around the world. In some countries, such as the US and Singapore, prices and structures of annuity products are available on the internet; in other countries, however, it is more difficult to compare annuity benefit and cost structures (Doyle et al., 2001). The simplest product is a *single premium immediate annuity,* for which data appear in Table 2.2 for men and women at alternative ages in the US. Several sensible conclusions emerge from a scan of these data. First, monthly payouts are higher for older people, given the same immediate premium, due to the higher expected mortality of the older buyers. Second, men receive higher payouts than women, due to their higher anticipated mortality. Third, the dispersion across insurance companies indicates that it would pay to shop around, and fourth, payout levels are not closely correlated with the strength of the insurer.

Table 2.2 Immediate monthly annuity payouts per $1000 premium, by age and sex

	Age 55	Age 65	Age 75
All companies, average:			
Men	6.64	7.94	10.52
Women	6.24	7.17	9.22
Ten highest payouts, average:			
Men	7.38	8.72	11.61
Women	6.88	7.76	9.99
Ten lowest payouts, average:			
Men	5.98	7.25	9.45
Women	5.59	6.56	8.63
Twenty highest rated firms, average:			
Men	6.50	7.78	10.35
Women	6.09	7.07	9.09
Ten largest annuity firms, average:			
Men	6.72	7.98	10.43
Women	6.31	7.21	9.14

Note: Each entry indicates the monthly income payable as a life annuity, based on the purchase of a $100 000 single premium immediate policy at the ages specified. The $100 000 purchase price is inclusive of policy fees but exclusive of annuity premium taxes. Data are for 1995.

Source: MPWB (1999).

2.1.4 Mortality Tables

To convert annuity payout data of this sort into money's worth measures, it is critical to obtain high-quality information on mortality tables depicting a particular group's distribution of expected remaining lifetime. Many developed nations have their own mortality tables,[8] having invested in the substantial effort and cost of collecting data on the incidence of deaths by age and sex. Then experts convert these raw data into projection tables by estimating the probability that a group member aged x will die in the next year of life by fitting hazard models to observed distributions of deaths, or by applying a smoothing algorithm to the raw maximum likelihood estimates (McCarthy and Mitchell, 2002). Of course mortality rates tend to be low except at the oldest ages, so obtaining reliable estimates of small probabilities depends on observing a large number of lives. It is also important to recognize that these tables are not fixed, but rather change due to improvements in life expectancies. Particularly among older people, mortality experiences have declined rapidly in developed countries, and this trend is expected to carry over to the future (Executive Committee, 1999). Consequently, those seeking to value future annuity payouts must take this into account by developing forward-looking cohort mortality tables, generally based on past trends.

Not only do mortality patterns change over time; there are important cross-country differences as well.[9] Inasmuch as US and UK data-collection efforts are relatively consistent, these tables have been adopted by numerous other developed and developing countries: we have observed that US mortality tables tend to be used in the Western hemisphere, while UK tables are often adopted in former British colonies or where British influence was strong. Frequently local actuarial adjustments are applied to the tables so as to make them more reflective of local conditions, though without good mortality data it is probably impossible to know whether the adjustments are adequate. Unfortunately uncertainty regarding mortality tables can also cause insurance companies to raise prices, with adverse consequences for annuity markets in general.[10] Conversely, countries seeking to develop annuity markets may find there is a strong public good aspect to the development and dissemination of mortality data.

There is no single metric to assess such mortality differences, but the A/E ('A over E') method expresses the number of deaths anticipated in a given group with a specified age structure using one mortality table, and compares these to the expected number of deaths in a population of the same size using a second mortality table. This is equivalent to a ratio of the weighted average probabilities of death for the two mortality tables, using a specific population structure for the weights (McCarthy and Mitchell, 2003):

$$A/E = \frac{\sum_x w_x q_x^*}{\sum_x w_x q_x} \times 100 \qquad (2.4)$$

where q_x^* is the probability that an individual of age x dies according to the table in question, and q_x is the probability that an individual of age x dies according to the base table. The weights, w_x, are set so that $w_{65} = 100\ 000$, and $w_x = w_{x-1}\,(1 - q_{x-1})$.

Two examples of A/E measures are provided in Figures 2.4 and 2.5. Figure 2.4 represents mortality trends for US men age 65+ over time, using the 1991 male population table as the benchmark. The trend shows clearly that men's mortality has fallen by just under one-third since 1965, a rather remarkable achievement; results are similar for women. A/E population metrics that can be computed across the OECD appear in Figure 2.5. All statistics assume a benchmark of US age 65+ male population tables using the US 1991 tables as a benchmark. These data show that Canada and Australia have very similar mortality patterns to the US, whereas Japan has much lower male population mortality rates. Results for Italy as well as Germany indicate substantially higher mortality patterns (among others).

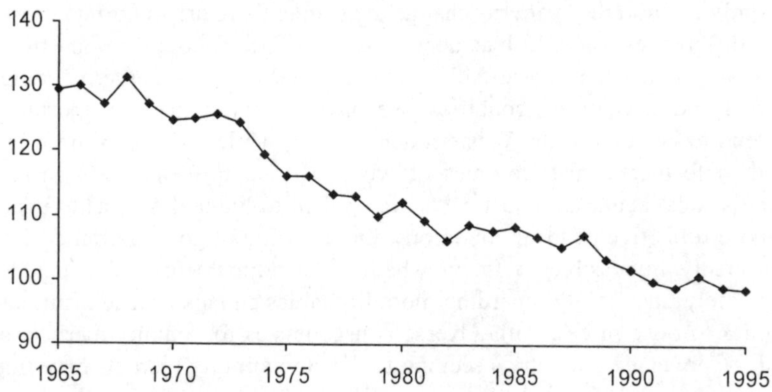

Note: Data represent Actual/Expected death rates for US males, standardized so the 1991 table is equal to 100.

Source: Social Security Administration, Male Population Mortality, reported on Berkeley Mortality Database, http://demog.berkeley.edu/wilmoth/mortality

Figure 2.4 Time series decline in US male mortality: 1965–95

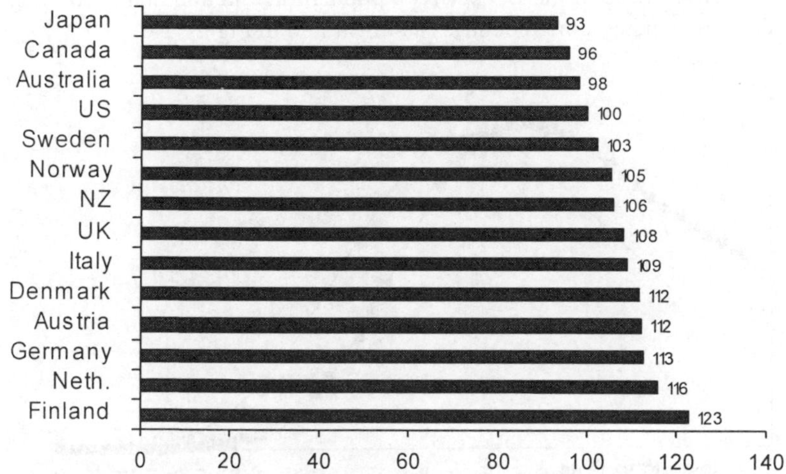

Notes: The following male mortality tables from ~1991 were used for these computations (in some cases these were extended to age 111):

Finland	Central Bureau of Statistics 1986–90
Netherlands	Central Bureau of Statistics 1985–90
Germany	Federal Statistics Office 1990–92
Austria	Statistische Zentralamt 1990–92
Denmark	Danmarks Statistik, Statistical Yearbook 1990–92
UK	Government Actuaries Department 1999
NZ	Statistics New Zealand, 1990–92
Norway	Statistics Norway, 1993
Sweden	National Central Bureau of Statistics, 1993
Australia	Statistics Australia 1990–92
Canada	Statistics Canada Life Tables, 1990–92
US	Social Security Administration, 1991
Japan	Japanese Ministry of Health, Labor and Welfare, Statistics Division, 1990
Italy	National Institute of Statistics, 1991

Source: Authors' computations; see McCarthy and Mitchell (2002).

Figure 2.5 A/E metrics for selected OECD countries

An additional, and key aspect of cross-national mortality table comparisons for annuity purposes pertains to the role of *adverse selection*. This arises in the present context if buyers of annuities prove to be longer lived than average, prompting actuaries to devise separate mortality tables for annuitants versus the general population. Whether adverse selection is quantitatively important may depend on whether annuitization is optional or mandatory: for example, in the US, purchase of annuities has become increasingly a matter of personal choice, since defined benefit pension plans are in decline (Brown and Warshawsky, 2000). As a result there are substantial differences in the US between population and annuitant mortality tables, as well as many other countries as illustrated in Figure 2.6.

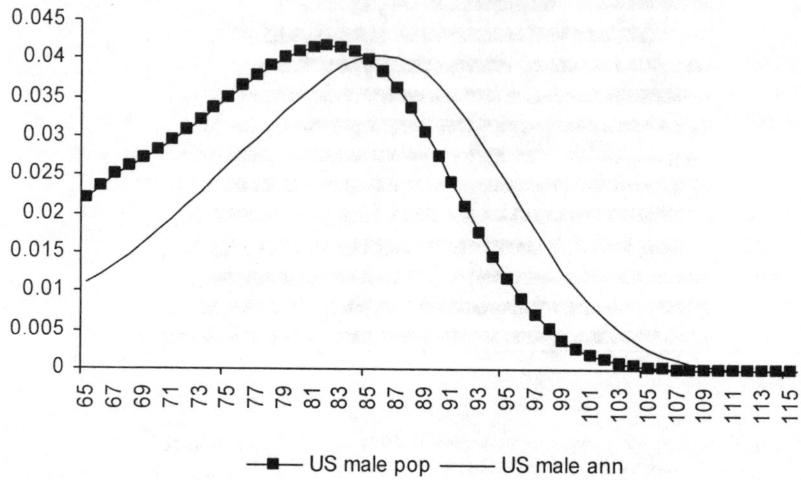

Source: Mitchell (2002).

Figure 2.6 Distribution of US male population versus annuitant age at death, conditional on survival to age 65 (US male)

Measuring the extent of adverse selection among annuity purchasers as compared to the population is critical for proper annuity pricing, but some countries lack the data necessary to do this with care. Table 2.3 presents A/E results for men and women age 65 in the US, UK, and Japan, for voluntary as well as compulsorily purchased annuities (where available). In the UK, for example, a portion of retirement benefits is subject to mandatory annuitization, with other benefits voluntarily annuitized. As a result, insurers have generated separate UK mortality tables for both voluntary and compulsory-purchase annuitants, each of which differs from that of the general population (Finkelstein and Poterba, 2002; Murthi et al., 1999). In this case, the reference or 'base' table is the population table for that country. Patterns for men, in the top panel, as well as women, in the bottom panel, indicate that voluntary annuitants experience much lower mortality than do compulsory annuitants. Results for Japan are markedly different, with male insurance purchasers having apparently *heavier* mortality than voluntary annuitant holders, but rates equalizing for women.

Table 2.3 Comparative data on actual/expected (A/E) mortality measures for purchasers of voluntary and compulsory life annuities versus population: age 65 by sex

	Voluntary Annuities	Compulsory Annuities	Population
Males			
UK	67.5	82.6	100
US	65.3	84.0	100
Japan	81.8	na	100
Females			
UK	73.5	84.9	100
US	73.6	90.8	100
Japan	100.7	na	100

Notes: na means not available. Base table (=100) is population table for each country and gender.

Source: McCarthy and Mitchell (2003).

Next we use available population and annuitant mortality data from a range of developed countries, to measure the empirical degree of adverse selection in annuitant mortality tables internationally.[11] The derived average measure of adverse selection then becomes a benchmark that can be held up against results for specific countries, to evaluate whether and how far a particular country may deviate from the standard.[12] The dependent variable in this analysis is the A/E value for each table relative to the US male population period table (=100). The model relates this to the degree of selection associated with annuitants, controlling on regressors including country-specific indicators (the US is the omitted category), indicators of whether the table was for male or female (male is the omitted category), for period or cohort (period is the omitted category), and whether the table was a population or compulsory or voluntary annuitant table (population is the omitted group). Other cross-country effects are assumed to be uncorrelated and captured in a disturbance term in the following regression model:

$$Y_{ijkl} = \alpha + \boldsymbol{\beta}'\mathbf{C}_i + \boldsymbol{\chi}'\mathbf{S}_j + \delta G_k + \zeta T_l + \theta(S * G) + \lambda(T * G) + \varepsilon_{ijkl} \qquad (2.5)$$

where Y_{ijkl} refers to the A/E metric for the mortality table in question; $\mathbf{C}_i$ is a vector of indicator variables representing country; $\mathbf{S}_j$ is a vector representing the degree of selection; G_k is a scalar representing gender; and T_l is a scalar representing table type (cohort or period). Remaining noise is summarized in the error term ε_{ijkl}, modeled as independent, identically distributed random variables.[13] If mortality tables display no additional statistically significant adverse selection, after controlling on the country-specific effects as well as table and gender differentials, χ will equal $\mathbf{0}$. Our alternative hypothesis is that $\chi \neq \mathbf{0}$; the coefficient magnitude is then an indication of the extent of predictable adverse selection in annuitant mortality tables.

Regression results appear in Table 2.4, based on data on over 60 population and annuitant mortality tables for ten countries including Australia, Austria, Canada, Chile, Germany, Israel, Italy, the United Kingdom, and the US, representing more than half a billion lives.[14] Estimated results show the model fits very well overall with an adjusted R-squared of 98.8 per cent. Turning to specific coefficients, we find that the 'female effect' turns out to be negative and statistically significant for the A/E measure, and implies that mortality rates for women are 35 per cent lower than the benchmark US male population rates. This is comparable to the 33 per cent and 26 per cent lower relatively mortality experienced for voluntary and compulsory annuitants, versus the population. Only one of the interaction terms is statistically significant, indicating that selection between female voluntary annuitants and the population is one-third lower than among men.

The results also show no significant difference between estimated coefficients for the voluntary versus compulsory selection variables. This implies that the extent of compulsory and voluntary selection overlaps in different countries to some extent. The data series are consistent with an average degree of adverse selection for annuitants versus the general population, of at least 25 per cent. This difference in mortality is on the order of the difference between males and females in the population at large. The cohort effect is much smaller, on the order of 12 per cent relative lower mortality. Another factor to emphasize is that many of the country-specific effects are statistically significant, with the exception of Italy and Germany. Some countries, such as Austria and Israel, have substantially higher (12–13 per cent) mortality than the US benchmark, while Japan, Switzerland, and Canada have 10–14 per cent lower mortality than the US.

Predicted male A/E cohort values derived from this regression analysis are provided for male population and annuitant mortality in Figure 2.7. The results indicate that according to our model, Italy and Germany both have higher annuitant mortality than US tables, but Switzerland, Australia, Canada and Japan appear well below the US benchmark.

Table 2.4 Regression of A/E metrics on type of mortality table, country effects, and interactions

	Coeff.	Std Err
Female	-34.68**	2.79
Comp Ann	-26.17**	3.47
Vol Ann	-32.95**	3.01
Cohort	-12.33**	2.85
FxCompAnn	6.88	4.65
FxVolAnn	11.48**	4.14
FxCohort	3.33	3.79
UK	7.79**	2.91
Canada	-9.93**	3.35
Chile	7.57*	4.31
Australia	-8.95**	3.67
Israel	11.68**	4.31
Italy	6.14	5.66
Austria	13.94**	4.17
Germany	6.49	4.19
Switzerland	-9.10**	3.72
Japan	-13.91**	5.66
Intercept	106.97**	2.94
Adj R-square	98.8%	
N of Obs	64	

Notes:
* = significant at 10 per cent;
** = significant at 5 per cent.

Source: Authors' computations following McCarthy and Mitchell (2003).

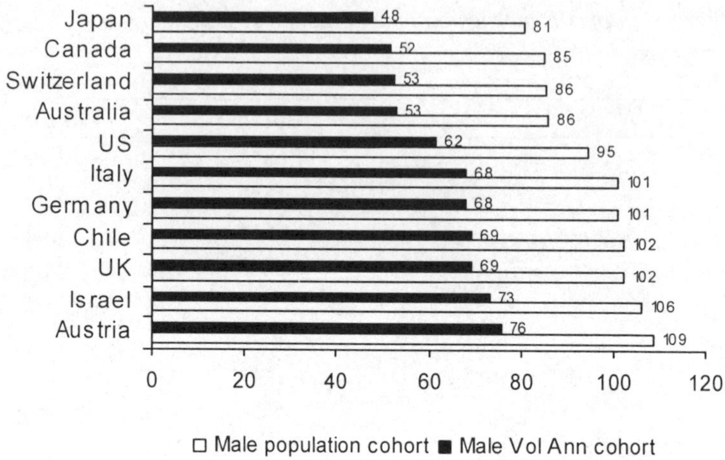

Notes: Figure derived from A/E values predicted using regression estimates in Table 2.4.

Source: Authors' computations.

Figure 2.7 Predicted male cohort A/E values for variety of countries; male population mortality and annuitant mortality

While some countries have the necessary mortality data needed to produce annuitant tables for voluntary versus compulsory annuities, others do not. For instance, Italy does not – the 1995 RG48 annuitant mortality table used in our analysis was constructed by applying an estimate of adverse selection obtained from UK annuitant tables.[15] Therefore in Figure 2.8 we use the results of the regression analysis to generate predicted values of the A/E metric, and also we represent male and female voluntary annuitant tables for Germany and Italy, as well as Japanese compulsory and voluntary annuitant tables. The vertical axis represents the A/E measure, while the vertical bars represent confidence intervals for predicted levels of the A/E metric. The points show where we calculated that these tables actually lie. Examination of the results indicates that predicted values for the German annuitant tables are well within estimated confidence intervals. However, results for Italian male annuitants fall outside the confidence intervals, as do the results for Japanese male and female tables (circled in the figure). In other words, these findings indicate excess mortality as compared to what international norms would suggest for tables of this type.

The fact that annuitant tables differ so much in Japan and Italy from the international norms could indicate either that these countries have annuity markets that are unusual in an international context, or that there is some problem with the way the annuitant mortality tables are computed. In fact, in both cases, these mortality tables are derived without reference to the mortality of actual annuitants, suggesting a possible reason why they fall outside our predicted confidence intervals. Of course, these results need not imply that annuity prices or liability estimates are incorrect for the annuity business in those countries. This is because actuaries use many different assumptions to value annuities, and it is not uncommon to alter one or more other assumptions to compensate for a mortality assumption known to be inaccurate. But there is a chance that using offsetting assumptions can lead to inaccurately estimated reserves, distort sensitivity estimates, and complicate analyses of insurer surplus/strain. In general, such practice is best avoided.

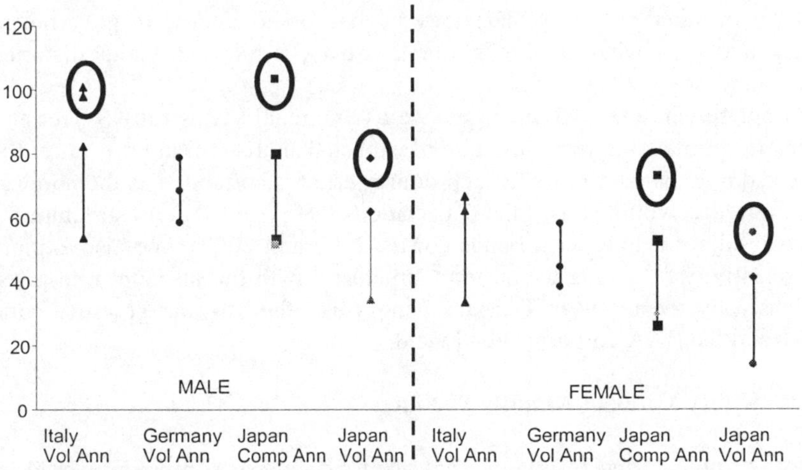

Note: A/E values for male and female annuitant mortality computed from RG48 tables for Italy (estimated from MacDonald, 1997), DAV1994R tables for Germany (MacDonald, 1997), EPF and TQPP mortality tables for Japan compulsory annuitants (data kindly provided by the Ministry of Health, Labor and Welfare) and the Japan Institute of Actuaries for Japan annuitants. Figure shows actual A/E values and 95 per cent confidence intervals for predicted A/E values from model described in Table 2.4. Circled values fall outside the 95 per cent confidence intervals; see text.

Source: Authors' computations following methodology described in McCarthy and Mitchell (2002).

Figure 2.8 Cross-national predicted values: actual and predicted values of A/E metrics

2.1.5 Discount Rate Assumptions

As with all economic assumptions, there is no single and clear-cut rule about what discount rates to use when deriving annuity valuation formulas. One approach uses term structures for yields on government bonds, on the argument that the annuity payoff depends on an individual's mortality, which is essentially uncorrelated with market risk. Yields closer to those on government bonds may be appropriate if insurers are backed by government bonds or mutual solvency funds, as is often the case. Another tactic uses riskier corporate bond yields to proxy for expected future interest rates, on the view that insurers often hold such instruments to back their annuity promises. Others argue that discount rates for annuity computations should recognize that governments frequently regulate insurance company investment practices. For instance, the fraction of annuity assets that insurers can hold in equities is capped at 30 per cent in Peru and 40 per cent in Chile; no real estate investment is permitted in Argentina (Palacios and Rofman, 2001). In other countries there may be few or no long-term government bonds, and even when they exist, markets may be thin and yields distorted (James and Song, 2001).

In our research on US annuities, we use nominal yields on US Treasury bonds to estimate the term structure of expected short-term interest rates; the expected nominal short rate in each future period is computed as the nominal short rate that would satisfy the expectations theory of the term structure for the two adjacent long-term bonds (BMP, 2000 and 2002). We also explore the sensitivity of results to flat term structures, with the discount rate given variously by the ten-year Treasury bond yield, the 30-year Treasury bond yield, and the BAA corporate bond yield.

2.1.6 Utility Value of Annuity Products

Before turning to the results, we note that risk-averse consumers would be expected to value annuities more highly than the simple financial money's worth ratio, since the insurance component provides additional utility against the shortfall risk. It is not surprising that the economics literature shows that annuities should appeal most to risk-averse consumers,[16] while less risk-averse retirees, and people seeking to provide their heirs with bequests, will be likely to want to self-insure with some portion of their assets.

A commonly used metric for the utility value of annuities is the *equivalent wealth measure*. Specifically, this concept identifies the additional wealth a consumer would require, if he/she did not have longevity protection, to achieve the same lifetime utility as with that annuity (MPWB, 1999). This approach assumes that the consumer elects an optimal consumption path $\{C_t\}$ from time 0 to time T (the maximum possible lifespan), given his/her rate of time preference ρ and a vector of cumulative survival probabilities

$\{P_t\}$ to maximize an expected utility function V: $\underset{\{C_t\}}{Max}\sum_{t=0}^{T}\frac{P_t U(C_t)}{(1+\rho)^t}$. The consumer's budget constraint depends on whether he/she has access to a fair annuity market. If he/she does not, the present value of future consumption, discounted using the riskless interest rate *r*, must equal to his/her initial wealth, W_0: $W_0=\sum_{t=0}^{T}\frac{C_t}{(1+r)^t}$. If he/she can purchase actuarially fair annuities, the budget constraint then becomes: $W_0=\sum_{t=0}^{T}\frac{P_t C_t}{(1+r)^t}$. The difference between the two budget constraints is due to survival probabilities. That is, lacking access to annuity markets, a retiree's future consumption cannot exceed his/her initial wealth; by contrast, with an annuity, his/her *expected* future consumption cannot exceed his/her initial wealth. In other words, access to annuity markets reduces the relative price of future consumption and lowers the amount of precautionary saving that he must undertake.

To actually measure how much a consumer might value an annuity requires that the researcher specify the functional form for the utility function, along with the relevant risk-aversion parameters. In much economic research, a one-period utility function, U(C_t), is assumed to exhibit constant relative risk aversion: $U(C_t)=\frac{C_t^{1-\beta}}{1-\beta}$, where β is the Arrow-Pratt coefficient of relative risk aversion, and $1/\beta$ is the elasticity of intertemporal substitution in consumption. The indirect utility function V(.) which corresponds to the budget constraint permits evaluation of the maximum utility that an individual might attain by following their optimal consumption path. Finally, it is possible to evaluate the utility gain in financial terms by computing how much additional wealth the retiree would require if he/she lacked access to annuities, if they were to be made as well off as with annuities. This computation requires solving for α such that:

$$V_0(\alpha W_0)^{no\ annuities}=V_0(W_0)^{annuities}.$$

In this formulation, α is the 'Annuity Equivalent Wealth'.[17]

2.1.7 Illustrative Money's Worth and Annuity Equivalent Wealth Computations[18]

Panel A of Table 2.5 presents money's worth calculations for annuities offered across a range of developed countries, specifically, for Australia,

Canada, Switzerland, the UK, and the US.[19] These results were developed using both *annuitant* and *population* mortality tables, in order to indicate the extent to which adverse selection may play a role.

Table 2.5 Comparisons of annuity values: money's worth and annuity equivalent wealth

A: Money's worth of nominal annuity payouts: single premium nominal life annuities offered to 65-year-olds across countries

	UK		Australia		Canada		Switzerland		US		Italy	
	Pop	*Ann*	*Pop*	*Ann*	*Pop*	*Ann*	*Pop*	*Ann*	*Pop*	*Ann*	*Pop*	*Ann*
Men	0.897	0.966	0.914	0.986	0.925	1.014	0.965	NA	0.814	0.927	NA	0.958
Women	0.910	0.957	0.910	0.970	0.937	1.015	1.115	NA	0.852	0.927	NA	0.965

Note: Computations use country Treasury yield curve. *Pop* refers to population mortality table while *Ann* refers to annuitant mortality table.

Source: James and Vittas (1999) for UK, Australia, Canada, and Switzerland; MPWB (1999) for US; Cardinale (2002) for Italy.

B: Annuity equivalent wealth values: US male age 65

	(I)			(II)		
	Annuity equivalent wealth for real and nominal annuities					
Coefficient of relative risk aversion (CRRA)	Consumer with no pre-existing annuity wealth			Consumer with half of initial wealth in pre-existing real annuity		
	Real annuity	Nominal annuity: i.i.d. inflation	Nominal annuity: persistent inflation	Real annuity	Nominal annuity: i.i.d. inflation	Nominal annuity: persistent inflation
1	1.502	1.451	1.424	1.330	1.304	1.286
2	1.650	1.553	1.501	1.441	1.403	1.366
5	1.855	1.616	1.487	1.623	1.515	1.450
10	2.004	1.592	1.346	1.815	1.577	1.451

Note: The annuity equivalent wealth calculation for the nominal annuity assumes inflation takes one of six possible values, roughly capturing the distribution of inflation outcomes over the 1926–97 period. Inflation shocks are assumed independent across periods in the i.i.d. case and follow a stylized AR(1) process in the persistent inflation case.

Source: Mitchell (2002).

These estimates indicate that annuities computed in each of these countries using population tables prove to have very high money's worth ratios. Estimates are at 0.90 or better in all countries but the US. This implies that a typical member of the population could anticipate receiving at least 90 per cent of their premium from the single life annuity. The results also imply that adverse selection as well as loadings and administrative charges must be below 10 per cent of the purchase price.[20]

Results are even more consumer-favorable using the figures computed with annuitant mortality tables. In the US, for instance, the MW ratio with annuitant survival rates stands at around 93 per cent for both men and women, versus figures of 81–85 per cent using population tables. The difference between these numbers, 8–11 per cent, is indicative of the extent of adverse selection. That is, the difference is a measure of how much longer annuity buyers live than people in the general population. The remaining load of 7 per cent indicates relatively low charges and fees levied by US insurers; this number is half what it was in the previous decade (BMP, 2000). Panel A also implies that annuity products are exceptionally good investments in a few countries – perhaps too good to be believable. In Canada, for instance, the estimated values using annuitant tables are above 1.0, meaning that an annuitant could anticipate receiving more than his money back on this financial asset. This may be the result of using overly conservative discount rates to compute the expected present values. In any event, a financial assessment of these life annuity products indicates that (a) adverse selection explains a substantial portion of the load perceived by potential purchasers in the general population, and (b) these products would be expected to be quite valuable to annuitant purchasers.

Panel B moves from a strict financial computation to the broader utility-based measure of annuity values. Specifically we report computations on annuity equivalent wealth for the US case, which it will be recalled represents the amount of wealth that a consumer would need *if he did not have access to an annuity market,* in order to achieve the same lifetime expected utility level that he could achieve by using that wealth to purchase a nominal annuity.[21] To illustrate the results, we employ a logarithmic utility function to represent the consumer's utility and assume a relatively low level of risk aversion (CRRA = 1). For such a person, a real (inflation-protected) single annuity would be valued at 1.5, assuming the retiree had no other annuitized wealth. This signifies that such a consumer lacking access to an annuity, would be willing to give up half of their investment to obtain a real lifetime annuity with the same investment. At higher levels of risk aversion, the annuity equivalent wealth value rises to 2, meaning that access to a real annuity is worth double the wealth than the same value invested in a nominal annuity.

Evidently, an annuity would be valued much more highly in utility terms, than in money's worth terms.

Results in Panel B also show that an inflation protected annuity is more valuable to the risk-averse consumer than is a nominal annuity. The CRRA=1 consumer, for instance, finds the real annuity worth 5–8 cents more per dollar invested versus a nominal annuity, and the value rises with higher risk aversion (at CRRA=10, the gap is 40–60 cents). Our results do show that the valuation depends on how inflation is expected to move, however, since a real annuity is valued at 1.451 with i.i.d. inflation and 1.424 in the case of persistent inflation.[22] It is also critical to take into account the fact that the AEW measure depends on whether a retiree has some portion of their wealth already annuitized. The leftmost subsection of Panel A (labeled I) assumes no other annuities, while the rightmost (II) section assumes that half of retiree wealth is already annuitized, perhaps through social security or occupational pensions.[23] In this case, the AEW associated with annuities is still substantial, but its value is reduced. For instance, the half-annuitized consumer with CRRA=1 would need only one-third more wealth to be made as well off as if he/she had a real annuity, compared to 50 per cent in the case where he/she lacked an annuity altogether. Clearly having a pre-existing real annuity provides retirees with insurance against very low consumption values, and it drives down the value of additional privately-purchased annuities.

2.2 FUTURE DETERMINANTS OF ANNUITY MARKETS

The economics literature over the last decade underscores the conclusion that annuities deserve an important role in retiree portfolios of the future. Though annuity markets in the past might have been underdeveloped, there are several reasons for optimism about their future potential.[24] We discuss these next in terms of demand-side factors, pertaining to reasons that retirees might find them more attractive in the future, and supply-side factors, relevant to the enhanced role that providers might play. Public policy factors that could foster stronger annuity markets are also mentioned.

2.2.1 Demand-side Factors

Some have claimed that retirees have shied away from annuities in the past because they were perceived to be 'too expensive'. But the evidence presented above indicates that this is not true at present in many countries, and other information implies that it is even less valid now than in the past (BMPW, 2001). Our finding of relatively moderate adverse selection and relatively low administrative loadings relative to the past, as well as relative to the value of the premium paid, suggests that such charges can be and are being moderated over time. In addition, the research shows that retirees should reap substantial utility benefits from insurance protection against longevity risk. Thus well-managed annuity markets with charges of the magnitudes seen should be appealing to purchasers. Competition among insurers in Europe and Asia should also hold down costs. Along the way, of course, it will still be essential to understand that consumers will expect reasonable money's worth from the products.

Retirees' decisions are also driven by people's perceptions about the appeal of alternative retirement investments. For instance, some financial planners have advised retirees to avoid annuitizing, on the grounds that they can manage their money better than institutional pension managers. Others propose that annuitization decisions be delayed to older ages, on the grounds that young retirees can then benefit from the upside potential of investment portfolios (Milevsky, 1999). Still others argue that retirees should invest in financial assets since these may keep up with inflation better than annuities. This is an area of substantial ongoing research, though the prediction has been inaccurate for the US at various times (BMP, 2000), but may be better supported in Europe (Albrecht and Maurer, 2002).

A different reason that older people might avoid buying annuities is that some might wish to remain somewhat financially liquid in old age, whereas the traditional immediate annuity does not provide this option. For instance, the risk of perhaps having to pay large medical bills or cover nursing-home costs could induce many elderly to hold on to the assets they have, instead of annuitizing them. This concern may be mitigated in the future for several reasons. One is that some insurers have brought to market new financial products that merge life annuities with nursing-home insurance (Warshawsky et al., 2002). Related to this point is the finding that improved health among older people may actually reduce the need for nursing-home care, as a consequence curtailing the demand for long-term care (Lakdawalla and Philipson, 2002). Yet another factor that can enhance the demand for annuities is that financial products are being devised to help meet liquidity requirements, affording older people the chance to consume the net equity in their homes (Caplin, 2002). This of course may conflict with older people's desires to leave bequests, but economic research has no clear answer regarding just how a bequest motive can best be incorporated into models of annuity demand (Gale and Slemrod, 2001). Brown (2001) argues that most specifications imply that full annuitization is no longer optimal, and Blake et al. (2000) explore a range of possible and interesting alternative formulations.

Yet a further concern regarding the future demand for annuities is the possibility that retirees might seriously underestimate their survival prospects, which, if true, would lead them to downvalue longevity insurance.

An interesting survey on this point finds, however, that older people in the US at least are in fact very well informed about their survival probabilities. That is, their expected survival patterns track actuarial tables quite closely (see Figure 2.9). Whether this is more of a problem in Europe would be worth investigating empirically. It is our impression that recent discussion of plummeting fertility and population ageing in Europe would likely imply that many older people are reasonably well informed about future survival patterns.

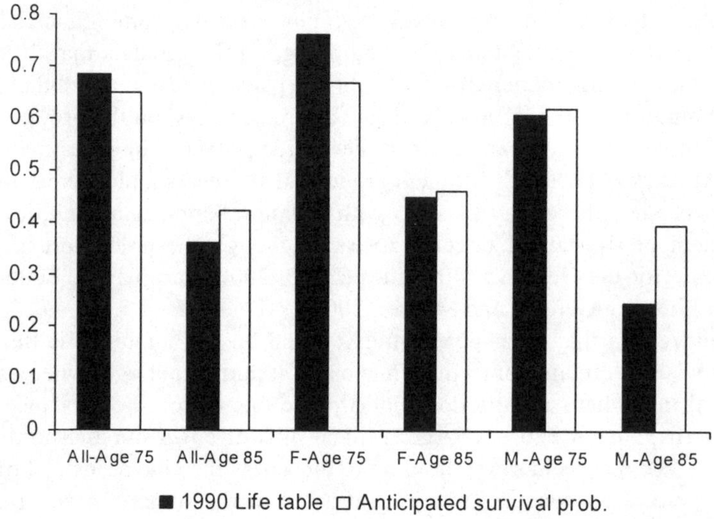

Note: Subjective probabilities of survival to age 75 and 85 reported by Wave 2 respondents in the Health and Retirement Study, born 1931–41 and interviewed in 1994. Responses weighted by sample weights.

Source: Hurd and McGarry (1997).

Figure 2.9 Objective and anticipated survival probabilities to ages 75 and 85

Looking ahead, there are a number of other reasons that one might anticipate growth in demand for annuities in the European market. One is that mortality patterns are continuing to decline, and in many countries, actual longevity may be even higher than reported in official government statistics (Schieber and Hewitt, 2000). This is tied up with major changes forecasted in the role and function of traditional old-age retirement systems in the European region. Paralleling a movement that began in the US two decades ago, many countries have recently witnessed a trend toward company-sponsored defined benefit plan termination (Mitchell, 2003). Furthermore, in much of Europe, state-financed public pensions will be forced to moderate benefit promises going forward. Both these factors imply a drop in the fraction of retirees' retirement wealth that is a mandatory annuity, and in turn, they suggest that insurance-based and privately purchased annuity products will be in increasing demand as substitutes.

2.2.2 Supply-side Considerations

In many ways, the successful development and growth of annuity markets must depend on supportive public policy.

In the past, large government social security systems may have crowded out annuity demand in many European countries. This may explain why there is a small market for private annuities in European countries with the largest social security systems. Figure 2.10 and Table 2.6 report after-tax replacement rates for selected OECD countries in 1995, divided by source of income. Germany, Sweden, and Italy have the highest proportion of retirement income coming from government transfers, over 55 per cent, and it is probably no coincidence that in these countries, the private annuity market is fairly small. Nevertheless, as these countries' populations age, their PAYG systems will have to be reformed. Consequently the proportion of retirement income coming from government transfers will likely decrease, implying potential for growth in annuities markets.

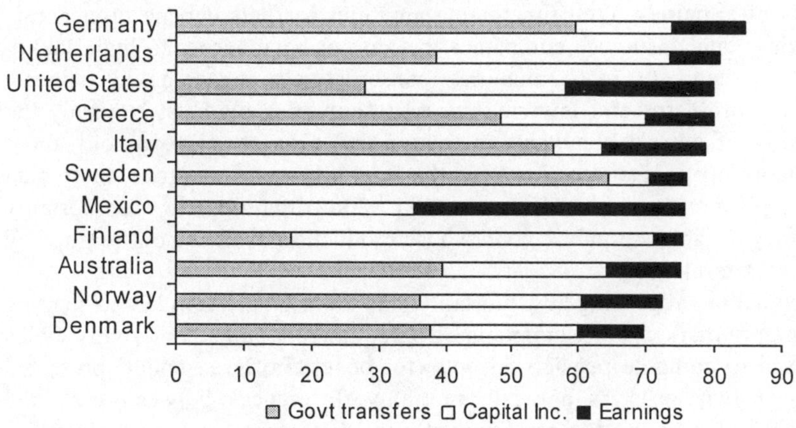

Note: Figure shows show disposable income for persons aged 65–74 as a percentage of those aged 55–64.

Source: Table 2.6.

Figure 2.10 Old age replacement rates for selected OECD countries

Table 2.6 Old age replacement rates for selected OECD countries

Country	Govt Tsfr	Capital/SEInc.	Earnings	Total
Denmark	37.6	22.3	9.6	69.4
Norway	36.1	24.5	11.7	72.3
Australia	39.5	24.7	10.9	75
Finland	17.1	54	4.4	75.5
Mexico	9.7	25.6	40.3	75.6
Sweden	64.6	6	5.5	76.1
Italy	56.2	7.2	15.3	78.7
Greece	48.3	21.6	10	79.9
United States	28	30.2	21.7	79.9
Netherlands	38.6	35	7.2	80.8
Germany	59.6	14.4	10.4	84.4
Average	39.57	24.14	13.36	77.05

Note: Table reports show total disposable income for persons aged 65–74 as a percentage of those aged 55–64.

Source: OECD data from Feldstein and Siebert (2002).

The need for better mortality information and clear supervision

Regulatory policy regarding mortality tables can drive both the demand and supply of annuities. Well functioning annuities markets depend on accurate mortality data. Insurance companies that do not have access to high quality data will tend to price annuities conservatively, exacerbating adverse selection problems and lowering access to annuities markets. Not only the mortality of current annuitants is needed, but also good projections about how mortality is likely to change in the future. In most countries, these data are simply not available. Cardinale et al. (2002) hypothesize that mortality data may in fact be a public good whose production costs are outweighed by positive externalities.

Regulations regarding how mortality data are used are also key to shaping the annuity market. For example the UK requires that unisex mortality tables are used to compute pension payouts (for benefits offered under 'protected rights' legislation). As a result, mortality differences between men and women cannot be used to price payouts, which generates cross-subsidization between male and female retirees on average. The common mortality table combined with mandatory annuitization thereby restricts the potential for adverse selection that otherwise might occur in voluntary annuitizations. By contrast, unisex tables are required for employer pension calculations in the US but are not imposed on individual purchases; moreover many workers are permitted to take lump-sum cashouts from their company pension. This structure implies that informed and rational workers anticipating shorter-than-average life expectancies have incentives to cash out rather than take life annuity streams. The policy issue, then, is how to integrate pension and insurance regulations so as not to detract too strongly from the appeal of annuities (Mitchell, 2000b). Prior to the introduction of the Third Life Directive of the European Union in 1994, many European countries regulated the tariffs that insurance companies were able to charge, often specifying out-of-date mortality tables or unisex tables (Davis, 2002). MacDonald (1997) reports that, since this time, many countries in Europe have started to collect and use annuitant mortality data in pricing, although this practice continues in countries such as Japan and Mexico.

2.2.3 New Roles for Government Provision of Financial Products

One supply-side explanation for thin annuity markets in some countries may be that insurers lack assets with which to back the long-term promises represented by annuities. Standard theory suggests that, in order to immunize themselves from small changes in interest rates, insurance companies would do well to back their annuity portfolios with assets whose duration equals the duration of the annuity liabilities. This is difficult to do in practice if long-term bonds are not available in national markets.

Figure 2.11 shows the term of the financial instruments needed to back actuarially fair annuities priced using US male voluntary annuitant cohort mortality tables. As is evident from the figure, the term varies with the bond interest rate. This is due to so-called 'convexity risk', which results from the fact that the incidence of payments on an annuity portfolio and that of a coupon-bearing bond portfolio are necessarily different.[25] The figure indicates that in the US market, at least, insurers would require 12-year par bonds to exactly immunize themselves from interest rate changes, at zero interest rates. If the company wished to sell annuities to females, it would require 13-year bonds trading at par (results not shown). Should interest rates rise, the implied bond terms required fall somewhat, but only slowly.

While the US does have a relatively well developed long-term bond market, many other countries lack long-term assets. This implies that annuity markets would likely benefit from the issuance of longer-term government bonds than are currently available. In addition, if real annuities are to be provided, real long bonds will have to be provided as well. At present, only a select handful of countries currently offers inflation-linked bonds, including the US, UK, Israel, and most recently France. Down the road, European insurers may therefore benefit from the recent entry by France into the Euro-denominated inflation-protected bond market.

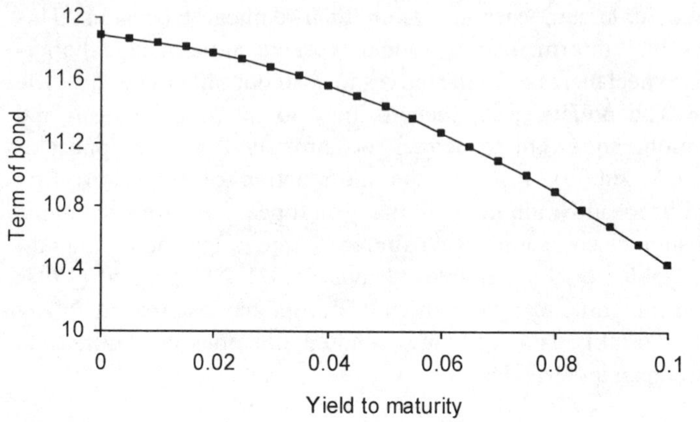

Notes: Bonds assumed to trade at par with coupons paid continuously.

Source: Authors' computations using US Male Voluntary Annuitant Cohort Mortality (see McCarthy and Mitchell, 2002).

Figure 2.11 Term of bond required to match mean duration of life annuity, as a function of the interest rate

Insurers, and customers purchasing the insurance products, should also consider the quality of the assets concerned. Recent events in Argentina and Russia have shown that it is possible for governments to default on their debt. The risk increases with the term of the bond, implying that insurers in emerging economies may be unwilling to sell annuities even if assets of sufficient term are available. It is worth noting in this context that the debt rating of the Japanese government was recently cut by Moody's to the same risk class as Cyprus, Greece, Latvia and South Africa, indicating that this problem may not be confined to emerging markets.[26]

There also remains a very real concern over cohort mortality risk. This is due to the chance that entire cohorts live longer than anticipated, which is of grave concern to those selling the products since substantial changes in mortality patterns could seriously challenge their profitability. Some contend that governments will have to issue cohort 'survivor bonds' (Blake et al., 2002). On the other hand, this problem may be resolved in the private market, by annuity providers which hedge longevity risk with offsetting life insurance contracts. Initial research on this topic using international data suggests, however, that this may be difficult to do in practice (McCarthy and Mitchell, 2003), though more research is needed on this point.

A related argument was made by financial experts and economists seeking to encourage the US government to issue inflation-linked bonds

(Brynjolfsson and Fabozzi, 1999). Retiree demand for these products in the US has been modest, though inflation rates have been quite low of late. In other pension markets, including the UK and Israel, inflation-linked bonds have become a mandatory component of the retiree portfolio and demand for these assets has been more substantial.

2.2.4 Regulatory Policy Toward Annuities

Insurers' long-term liquidity and solvency should also be important factors to consider when individuals purchase annuities. In an environment where the liquidity position of insurance companies is sometimes in question due to the lack of an effective regulatory environment – as is the case in many emerging and developed countries – workers and retirees may be deterred from participating in the annuities market (Mitchell, 2000a). In some cases, individual policyholders are protected by solvency funds in the event of insurance company insolvency. In turn, this highlights the importance of effective solvency regulation, because it introduces the possibility of moral hazard on the part of the annuity seller. In some cases, the regulation of reserves can be a barrier to sellers because it imposes a large or highly variable need for capital or onerous reporting or valuation requirements (Lemaire, 1997).

A key policy level influencing the future shape and form of annuity offerings is how governments encourage or discourage the growth of annuity products via tax incentives. Across Europe and around the world, the range of tax programs is so extensive and complex as to be bewildering, most likely the result of tax law accretion over many years, and often producing conflicts with sensible social policy. In Italy and France, for example, tax policy discourages companies from building up collateral assets that back pension promises, and also it encourages workers to take lump-sum withdrawals of deferred earnings instead of periodic payments or annuities (Cardinale, 2002; Wadsworth et al., 2001). In the US, tax policy favors funding and provision of employer-sponsored annuity promises (to a limit), but it also establishes a rather undesirable profile of taxation on private annuity payouts that taxes people more heavily after retirees attain life expectancy (BMPW, 1999). In Australia, tax and transfer policy favors purchase of fixed nominal annuities, but inflation-linked payouts and variable annuity programs are not similarly tax-favored.

Other regulations also apply to annuity products, and it is fair to say that in general, these are often complex and differ widely across countries. Yermo's (2001) review of annuity regulation across OECD countries illustrates for example that Italy requires mandatory annuitization of half workers' accumulated pension balances while Portugal requires annuitizing two-thirds of the balance; and Spain offers free choice between lump sum, term and life annuities. Germany's new Riester-reform law permits workers to take 20 per cent of their accumulated assets at retirement in a lump sum, another 20 per cent as a graduated withdrawal payment, and the remainder can be paid out in periodic payments with the stipulation that at age 85, the retiree must annuitize their balance and the benefit cannot be less than the periodic payment received before that age (Maurer and Schlag, 2002). Similarly, retirees at age 75 in the UK are required to annuitize their pension assets. However, Cantor and Sefton (2002) point to the fact that accumulated funds in voluntary individual DC pension arrangements in the UK (called 'personal pensions') might be a factor underlying the poor demand for these products among lower earners.

2.2.5 The Need for Consumer Education

Some countries have taken the perspective that it is the government's responsibility to promote public education and understanding regarding annuity products. Thus, for instance, the Financial Services Authority (FSA) in the United Kingdom was recently charged with statutory responsibility for enhancing consumer understanding and protection regarding annuity products (Inland Revenue, 2002). This is to take the form of internet and paper explanations of terms and pricing, as well as annuity types. Not only will this agency help new purchasers, but it will also take on the task of helping people contemplating switching providers, with a focus on fees and switching costs. As a different approach, the Italian government requires that annuity payouts be explicitly described to purchasers using real returns of 1 per cent and 3 per cent, so that buyers can compare payouts across products (Cardinale, 2002). In Mexico and several other Latin American countries, annuity providers must submit competitive bids to workers as they draw near their retirement dates, so as to enhance comparability and competition across insurers (Palacios and Rofman, 2001).

2.3 CONCLUSION

As the world ages, it will become increasingly critical to develop and offer new financial products that help protect economic security during the retirement period. This chapter demonstrates that several factors will drive modernization of global annuity markets in the future, particularly in European nations which are among the most challenged by rapid population ageing.

Our review suggests several conclusions. First, the demand for annuities is likely to rise in the future, even for risk-averse elders who want to keep some portion of their assets liquid. This will be driven by increased longevity, diminished public and corporate pensions, and the availability of new annuity-linked products. Second, the supply of annuities is likely to grow, but here, thoughtful public policy can play a beneficial role. Specifically, there are important ways in which governments can play a potent role in strengthening annuity markets. These include developing and disseminating high-quality data on mortality tables, enhancing consumer education and awareness of longevity insurance, standardization of cost reporting, and streamlining tax policy to make it more attractive to invest in sensible products. It may also be useful for governments to mitigate the potential problems caused by adverse selection, including encouraging group annuities and possibly requiring some minimum level of annuity provision. Finally, there may be a new role required for oversight groups, if annuity markets are to thrive. Specifically, they can serve as sponsors of new financial products that can help insurers provide annuities more efficiently. These could include longer-term government bonds that can be used to match annuity liability patterns, inflation-indexed bonds, and possibly, survivor bonds.

NOTES

1. See for instance BMPW (2001); Bodie et al. (2002), Doyle, Mitchell and Piggott (2001); Finkelstein and Poterba (2002); Murthi et al. (1999); Sheshinski (2002) and Tonks (1999).
2. See Mitchell and Barreto (1997) and Palacios and Rofman (2001) for a discussion of the Latin reforms.
3. See Cardinale (2002 and Cardinale et al. (2002); Blake (1999); Disney (2000); Disney and Johnson (2000); European Commission (1997), and Maurer and Schlag (2002) among others, for discussions of the European reforms.
4. This discussion draws on BMPW (2001).
5. The classic references are Ando and Modigliani (1963), and Modigliani (1986).
6. To compute the EPDV of an annuity purchased by a 65-year-old, one must forecast future mortality probabilities, discussed below. Computations also assume that no one lives beyond age 115 years; our calculations are insensitive to this upper limit on lifespan.
7. In addition we evaluate the responsiveness of conclusions to taxes; in the US, federal tax treatment of annuities is quite complex (BMWP, 1999). A useful comparison of tax treatment for annuities across Europe is provided in Wadsworth et al. (2001).
8. The Society of Actuaries maintains an excellent database of international mortality tables on its website www.soa.org. Recent European population, insured lives, and annuitant mortality tables may be obtained from MacDonald (1997). The Berkeley Mortality Database (http://demog.berkeley.edu/wilmoth/mortality) is an invaluable resource for those investigating population mortality in developed countries.
9. This discussion draws on McCarthy and Mitchell (2003).
10. Of course errors in the other direction may lead to insolvency.
11. This section draws on McCarthy and Mitchell (2002).
12. Our work acknowledges that the distinctions between population versus compulsory and voluntary annuitant tables may not be precisely identical across countries. Selection is

defined here as 'compulsory' if the mortality table relates to annuitants of pension plans, and 'voluntary' if it refers to voluntary individual annuitants. Countries may have different voluntary or compulsory selection effects, even within these categories, due to different labor force demographics (including participation rates), compensation packages, tax codes, and legislation.

13. Our earlier work also explored results in which 'table type' was treated as a random effect with non-zero mean and variance σ_T^2, to allow for the possibility that cohort mortality tables may be based on period mortality tables. We reject the null hypothesis that $\sigma_T^2 = 0$ using a likelihood ratio test and coefficient estimates are virtually unchanged. We also estimated standard errors robust to heteroskedasticity and found these to be lower than OLS standard errors; here we report the more conservative OLS results.
14. For sources see McCarthy and Mitchell (2002 and 2003).
15. In fact, when we performed this analysis we did not have the actual RG48 table. We used life expectancies of individuals on the RG48 tables, obtained from MacDonald (1997) and the fact that life expectancy is very closely related to the A/E measure to derive confidence intervals for the actual A/E metric for the RG48 tables.
16. See, for instance, Albrecht and Maurer (2002); Milevsky (1998, 1999); Blake (1999); Blake et al. (2001 and 2002); and Warshawsky (1998a and b).
17. The derivation requires dynamic programming algorithms described in MPWB (1999) for the case of a single individual; Brown and Poterba (1999) discuss the case of couples: and BMP (2002) discuss the case with uncertain returns and/or inflation.
18. This discussion draws on Mitchell (2002).
19. For other countries see Cardinale et al. (2002), Doyle et al. (2001), Finkelstein and Poterba (2002), James and Song (2001), James and Vittas (1999), and Murthi et al. (1999).
20. The Swiss money's worth figures may be overly high, the result of quite conservative discount rates; see James and Song (2001).
21. This section draws on MPWB (1999) and Mitchell (2002).
22. BMP (2002) note that risk aversion and annuity equivalent wealth are not linearly related for nominal annuities in the presence of uncertain inflation, because risk aversion works in opposing directions in the face of inflation uncertainty. On the one hand, higher risk aversion makes the consumer value an annuitized payout more highly since he/she avoids the risk of outliving their resources, and this is all that matters in the case of the real annuity. On the other hand, a risk-averse consumer dislikes the uncertainty introduced into the nominal annuity stream by stochastic inflation. Increased variability in the real value of the nominal annuity payouts reduces utility, and this effect is larger for those with the highest degree of risk aversion. At low levels of risk aversion, the first effect dominates, and the annuity equivalent wealth for a nominal annuity rises with risk aversion.
23. For instance, the median US older household holds about three-fifths of its retirement resources in the form of expected future social security and pensions benefits, payable only as life annuities (Moore and Mitchell, 2000).
24. For further discussion of these points see Mitchell (2002) and BMWP (2001).
25. Of course, an insurer could exactly match the outgo of an annuity portfolio and the income of a bond portfolio by investing in zero-coupon bonds of varying terms. However, zero-coupon bonds of the term and quality required (>35 years, AAA+) currently exist in no bond market.
26. Standard and Poor's (2002) also warns that the sovereign credit ratings of the majority of highly rated European Union members (EU–15) could fall to non-investment grade unless governments bring debt and deficit burdens under control.

REFERENCES

Albrecht, P. and R. Maurer (2002), 'Self-Annuitization, Consumption Shortfall in Retirement and Asset Allocation: The Annuity Benchmark', Pension Research Council Working Paper 2002–6, Wharton School, Philadelphia, PA.

Ando, A. and F. Modigliani (1963), 'The Life Cycle Hypothesis of Saving', *American Economic Review*, **53**(1), 55–74.

Blake, D. (1999), 'Annuity Markets: Problems and Solutions', *Geneva Papers on Risk and Insurance*, **24**, July, 358–75.

Blake, D., W. Burrows, and J.M. Orszag (2002), 'Survivor Bonds and Compulsory Annuitization: Helping Reduce the Cost of Pension Provision', in Z. Bodie, B. Hammond, O.S. Mitchell and S. Zeldes (eds), *Innovations in Retirement Financing*, Pension Research Council, Philadelphia, PA: University of Pennsylvania Press, 222–33.

Blake, D., A. Cairns, and K. Dowd (2000; revised 2001), 'Pensionmetrics: Stochastic Pension Plan Design During the Distribution Phase', Proceedings of the 3rd Annual BSI Gamma Foundation Conference on Global Asset Mgmt, Lugano, November; BSI Working Paper No. 19.

Blake, D., A. Cairns, and K. Dowd (2001), 'Pensionmetrics: Stochastic Pension Plan Design and Value-At-Risk During the Accumulation Phase', *Insurance: Mathematics and Economics,* **29**, 187–215.

Bodie, Z., B. Hammond, and O.S. Mitchell (2002), 'A Framework for Analyzing and Managing Retirement Risks', in Z. Bodie, B. Hammond, O.S. Mitchell and S. Zeldes (eds), *Innovations in Retirement Financing*, Pension Research Council, Philadelphia, PA: University of Pennsylvania Press, 3–19.

Brown, J. (2000), 'How Should We Insure Longevity Risk in Pensions and Social Security?,' *Issue in Brief*, **4**, August, Center for Retirement Research, Boston College, Boston, MA.

Brown, J. (2001), *Redistribution and Insurance: Mandatory Annuitization with Mortality Heterogeneity*, JFK School, Harvard, Cambridge, MA.

[BMP 2000] Brown, J., O.S. Mitchell, and J. Poterba (2000), 'The Role of Real Annuities and Indexed Bonds in an Individual Accounts Retirement Program', in J.Y. Campbell and M. Feldstein (eds), *Risk Aspects of Investment-Based Social Security Reform*, NBER, Chicago: University of Chicago Press, 321–60.

[BMP 2002] Brown, J., O.S. Mitchell, and J. Poterba (2002), 'Mortality Risk, Inflation Risk, and Annuity Products', in Z. Bodie, B. Hammond, O.S. Mitchell and S. Zeldes (eds), *Innovations in Retirement Financing*, Pension Research Council, Philadelphia, PA: University of Pennsylvania Press, 175–97.

[BMPW 1999] Brown, J., O.S. Mitchell, J. Poterba and M. Warshawsky (1999), 'Taxing Retirement Income: Nonqualified Annuities and Distributions from Qualified Accounts', *National Tax Journal*, **LII**(3) September, 563–92.

[BMPW 2001] Brown, J., O.S. Mitchell, J. Poterba, and M. Warshawsky (2001), *The Role of Annuity Markets in Financing Retirement*, Cambridge, MA: MIT Press.

Brown, J.R. and J.M. Poterba (1999), 'Joint Life Annuities and Annuity Demand by Married Couples', NBER Working Paper No. 7199, June.

Brown, J.R. and M.J. Warshawsky (2000), 'Longevity-Insured Retirement Distributions from Pension Plans: Market and Regulatory Issues', Working paper prepared for the Brookings/SIEPR/TIAA-CREF Institute Conference on Public Policies and Private Pensions, Washington, DC, September 21–22.

Brynjolfsson, J.B. and F.J. Fabozzi (eds) (1999), *The Handbook of Inflation-Indexed Bonds,* F.J. Fabozzi Associates, New Hope, PA.

Cantor, A.C.M., and J.A. Sefton (2002), 'Personal Pensions and Future Rates of Return', http://www.actuaries.org.uk/files/pdf/sessional/sm0110.pdf

Caplin, A. (2002), 'Turning Assets into Cash: Problems and Prospects in the Reverse Mortgage Market', in Z. Bodie, B. Hammond, O.S. Mitchell and S. Zeldes (eds), *Innovations in Retirement Financing*, Pension Research Council, Philadelphia, PA: University of Pennsylvania Press, 234–53.

Cardinale, M. (2002), 'Annuities in Italy', Watson Wyatt Working Paper, April.

Cardinale, M., A. Findlater and M. Orszag (2002), *Paying Out Pensions: A Review of International Annuities Markets*, Watson Wyatt LLP, London, May.

Davis, E.P. (2002), 'Ageing and Financial Stability', in H. Herrmann and A. Auerbach (eds), *Ageing and Financial Markets,* Berlin: Springer Verlag - Deutsche Bundesbank, 191–227.

Desai, N. (2002), Press Conference, 'World Assembly on Ageing, Second World Conference on Ageing', United Nations, www.un.org/ageing.

Disney, R. (2000), 'Crises in Public Pension Programmes in OECD: What are the Reform Options?', *Economic Journal,* **110**, (461): F1–F41.

Disney, R. and P. Johnson (2000), 'Pension Systems and Retirement Incomes Across OECD Countries', Institute for Fiscal Studies Working Paper, London.

Doyle, S., O.S. Mitchell and J. Piggott (2001), 'Annuity Values in Defined Contribution Retirement Systems: The Case of Singapore and Australia', NBER Working Paper No. W8091.

European Commission (1997), *Supplementary Pensions in the Single Market: A Green Paper*, http://europa.eu.int/comm/internal_market/pensions/docs/com-1997-283/com-1997-283_en.pdf/

Executive Committee of the Continuous Mortality Investigation Bureau (1999), *Continuous Mortality Investigation Reports no. 17*, London and Edinburgh: Institute and Faculty of Actuaries.

Feldstein, M. and H. Siebert (eds) (2002), *Social Security Pension Reform in Europe*, Chicago: The University of Chicago Press.

Finkelstein, A. and J. Poterba (2002), 'Selection Effects in the United Kingdom Individual Annuities Market', *The Economic Journal*, **112**(476), 28–50.

Gale, W.G. and J. B. Slemrod (2001), 'Overview', in W. Gale, J. Hines and J. Slemrod (eds), *Rethinking Estate and Gift Taxation,* Washington, DC: Brookings, 1–64.

Hurd, M.D. and K. McGarry (1997), 'The Predictive Validity of Subjective Probabilities of Survival', NBER Working Paper No. W6193.

Inland Revenue (2002), *Modernising Annuities*, Consultative Document, Department for Work and Pensions.

James, E. and X. Song (2001), 'Annuities Markets Around the World: Money's Worth and Risk Intermediation', www.estellejames.com/downloads/aea_annuities.pdf

James, E. and D. Vittas (1999), 'Annuities Markets in Comparative Perspective', presented at the World Bank Conference on 'New Ideas About Old Age Security', Washington, DC.

Jennings, R.M. and A.P. Trout (1982), *The Tontine: From the Reign of Louis XIV to the French Revolutionary Era*, Huebner Foundation Monograph, Number 12, Wharton School, University of Pennsylvania, Philadelphia, PA.

Lakdawalla, D. and T. Philipson (2002), 'The Rise in Old-Age Longevity and the Market for Long-Term Care', *American Economic Review*, **92**, March, 295–306.

Lemaire, J. with the assistance of K. Subramanian (1997), *Insurance Regulation in Europe and the United States*, Huebner Foundation Monograph, Number 16, Wharton School, University of Pennsylvania, Philadelphia, PA.

MacDonald, A.S. (1997), *The Second Actuarial Study of Mortality in Europe*, Groupe Consultatif des Associations d'Actuaires des Pays des Communautés Européennes, London.

Maurer, R. and C. Schlag (2002), 'Money-Back Guarantees in Individual Account Pensions: Evidence from the German Pension Reform', Paper presented at the Wharton School's Pension Research Council Conference on Risk Transfers and Retirement Income, April (prc.wharton.upenn.edu/prc/PRC/WP/WP2002-11.pdf).

McCarthy, D. and O.S. Mitchell (2002), 'Estimating International Adverse Selection in Annuities', *North American Actuarial Journal*, October, 38–54.

McCarthy, D. and O.S. Mitchell, (2003), 'International Adverse Selection in Life Insurance and Annuities', NBER Working Paper No. 9975.

Milevsky, M. (1998), 'Optimal Asset Allocation Toward the End of the Life Cycle' *Journal of Risk and Insurance*, **65**, 401–26.

Milevsky, M. (1999), 'Optimal Annuitization Policies: Analysis of the Options', *North American Actuarial Journal*, http://www.soa.org/library/naaj/1997-09/naaj0101_4.pdf

Mitchell, O.S. (2000a), 'Building an Environment for Pension Reform in Developing Countries', in Z. Bodie and E. P. Davis (eds), *Foundations of Pension Finance*, Cheltenham and Northampton, MA: Edward Elgar, 480–503.

Mitchell, O.S. (2000b), 'Developments in Pensions', in G. Dionne (ed.), *Handbook of Insurance*, Boston, MA: Kluwer Academic Publishers, 873–99.

Mitchell, O.S. (2002), 'Developments in Decumulation: The Role of Annuity Products in Financing Retirement', in A. Auerbach and H. Herrman (eds), *Ageing, Financial Markets and Monetary Policy*, Berlin: Springer-Verlag, 97–125.

Mitchell, O.S. (2003), 'New Trends in US Pensions', in O.S. Mitchell, D. Blitzstein, M. Gordon and J. Mazo (eds), *Benefits for the Future Workplace*, Philadelphia, PA: University of Pennsylvania Press, 110–36.

Mitchell, O.S. and F. Barreto (1997), 'After Chile, What? Second-Round Social Security Reforms in Latin America', *Revista de Analisis Economico*, **12**(2) November, 3–36.

[MPWB 1999] Mitchell, O.S., J. Poterba, M. Warshawsky and J. Brown, 'New Evidence On the Money's Worth of Individual Annuities', *American Economic Review*, December, 1299–318.

Modigliani, F. (1986), 'Life Cycle, Individual Thrift, and the Wealth of Nations', *American Economic Review*, **76** (3), 297–313.

Moore, J. and O.S. Mitchell (2000), 'Projected Retirement Wealth and Saving Adequacy', in O.S. Mitchell, B. Hammond and A. Rappaport (eds), *Forecasting Retirement Needs and Retirement Wealth*, Pension Research Council, Philadelphia, PA: University of Pennsylvania Press, 68–94.

Murthi, M., M. Orszag and P. Orszag (1999), 'The Value for Money of Annuities in the UK', Economics Department Working Paper, Birkbeck College, London, August.

OECD, Tables and Figures on Aging, http://www.nber.org/pensioncrisis/oecd-toc1.doc

Palacios, R. and R. Rofman (2001), 'Annuity Markets and Benefit Design in Multipillar Pension Schemes: Experience and Lessons for Four Latin American Countries', World Bank, *Pension Reform Primer*.

Schieber, S. J. and P. S. Hewitt (2000), *Demographic Risk in Industrial Societies: Independent Population Forecasts for the G-7 Countries*, an Analysis for the Global Aging Commission, *World Economics*, **1**(4), 27–72.

Sheshinski, E. (2002), 'Equilibrium and Optimality In Annuity Markets', four lectures given at the Stockholm School of Economics, February, http://www.hhs.se/secs/MiniCourses/RefListSheshinski.doc

Standard and Poor's (2002), *Western Europe Past Its Prime: Sovereign Rating Perspectives in the Context of Aging Populations,* Ratings Direct Report, London, January.

Tonks, I. (1999), 'Pensions Policy in the UK', November, http://www.bris.ac.uk/Depts/CMPO/workingpapers/wp12.pdf

Wadsworth, M., A. Findlater and T. Boardman. (2001), 'Reinventing Annuities', Staple Inn Actuarial Society, http://www.sias.org.uk/papers/reinvann.pdf

Warshawsky, M. J. (1998a), 'The Optimal Design of Minimum Distribution Requirements for Retirement Plans', *Benefits Quarterly*, **14**(4), 36–53.

Warshawsky, M. J. (1998b), 'Private Annuity Markets in the US', *Journal of Risk and Insurance*, **55**(3), 518–29.

Warshawsky, M.J., B. Spillman and C. Murtaugh (2002), 'Integrating the Life Annuity and Long-term Care Insurance: Theory, Evidence, Practice, and Policy', in Z. Bodie, B. Hammond, O.S. Mitchell and S. Zeldes (eds), *Innovations in Retirement Financing*, Pension Research Council, Philadelphia, PA: University of Pennsylvania Press, 198–221.

Yermo, J. (2001), 'Private Annuities in OECD Countries', in *Insurance and Private Pension Compendium for Emerging Economies*, book 2, part 1:5 Paris: OECD, http://www.oecd.org/dataoecd/7/37/1815951.pdf

3. Issues in the regulation of annuities markets*

E. Philip Davis

3.1 INTRODUCTION

When an individual retires in a defined contribution pension scheme, there are three ways in which the tax-privileged assets can be released. One is a lump-sum payment – which of course may be dissipated leaving the individual destitute. The second is programmed withdrawals over the retirement period, which also involves longevity risk if the individual lives longer than expected. And the third is the annuity from an insurance company, the only contract which guarantees income right up to the point of death. The key role played by annuities in the assurance of retirement income in defined contribution pension schemes is placing an increased focus on the appropriate regulation of such instruments. This is particularly the case in Europe, in the light of ongoing and prospective reductions in social security pensions and progressive withdrawal of companies from provision of defined benefit pensions in many countries.

This chapter seeks to address issues underlying the pattern of regulation both for individual annuities (in the context of insurance regulation) and the rules for annuitization (in the context of pension systems). Some general and longer-term risks affecting annuities and insurance companies are also addressed. We focus in particular on lessons from the situation in the UK, one of the most advanced annuities markets (Yermo, 2001), but also address broader European and EU issues, while wider country experience, notably from countries outside the EU with mandatory funded pension schemes, is

* The author thanks Graham Bishop, David Blake, Monika Bütler, Chris Daykin, Mitsuhiro Fukao, Robert Holzmann, Estelle James, Olivia Mitchell, Mike Orszag, Michael Winkler, and Juan Yermo as well as participants in the Turin conference and a seminar at the London School of Economics for helpful provision of material and suggestions. They are of course not responsible for the author's errors.

also drawn upon where appropriate. We begin, however, by assessing the functioning of annuities markets abstracting from regulation.

3.2 BACKGROUND – ANNUITIES IN A FREE MARKET

3.2.1 Annuities' Characteristics

It is useful to begin by outlining the characteristics of annuities as financial instruments. Annuities are contracts sold to individuals by life insurance companies to provide a guaranteed income from the point of purchase (or coming into effect for deferred annuities) until death. They thus provide insurance against the non-diversifiable risk of outliving assets, which is feasible given the operation of the 'law of large numbers' in a pool of annuitants. Investment risk is also eliminated in traditional level annuities, and even inflation risk can be removed by indexed annuities (if suitable price-indexed bonds are available). The trade-off is losses in terms of missed opportunities to invest freely. Annuities, if fairly priced, allow maximization of income over the pensioner's lifetime compared with other ways of releasing assets, since alternatives would always require excess assets at death (Mitchell, 2002). They also can provide a smooth income consistent with what is typically assumed to be a desired pattern of consumption (Blake and Hudson, 2000). They may thus also be the optimal way to invest, unless there is a bequest motive.

Correspondingly, for the provider, risk in annuities is related to two main aspects, the degree to which returns from the financial instruments chosen to back the claim match the income stream precisely, and the accuracy of the mortality assumption. If either of these is inaccurate in favor of the annuitant, the company can make unexpected losses. Ultimately, such losses may threaten solvency and hence the income stream to the pensioner. Equally, if the insurance company becomes insolvent for other reasons arising from liabilities (such as losses on life or general contracts) or assets (such as credit risk on corporate bonds), the annuity payment stream may again be threatened.

The conventional form of annuity, notably in Anglo Saxon countries, is a nominal-fixed contract, but in countries where inflation-indexed bonds are available, such as the UK and Chile, there can be real annuities. Variants on these basic annuities are available in some markets, such as survivor annuities, which effectively cover a couple rather than solely one person, and continue to function, usually at a lower income, if one partner dies. A further hybrid is with-profits annuities, where the income stream increases with the returns on the underlying investments, and the increase once granted may in some cases (so called reversionary bonuses) not be removed. Such annuities often have a high element of discretion to the insurance company in how much of its profits on investments it chooses to allot to policy holders. A variant on this structure, with a guaranteed rate and the remainder paid as a bonus, is common in Continental Europe (see Section 3.5.2).

Variable annuities transfer the market risk (usually of equities) to the annuitant, and hence they lack the guarantee element on income, while the insurance company still bears mortality risk. This is achieved by promising the payment of a number of shares in an underlying portfolio, with the number being recalculated annually and evolving over time according to a fixed formula. The actual money value of the pension varies according to the difference between the actual return on the assets and the assumed interest rate set out in the contract. If the pool of pensioners die more slowly than assumed, then the insurer bears the risk. Note that the name 'variable annuities' is also applied in the US to pension-savings contracts, which merely give the option to buy a true variable annuity (an option which, as noted by Cardinale et al. (2002), few consumers take).

CREF annuities promise the payment of a number of annuity units in the underlying portfolio, whose price is recalculated annually with a fixed formula, accounting for the difference between the actual rate of return on the underlying portfolio and the projected interest rate, the difference between mortality experience of the pool of annuitants and the expected mortality of that group; and changes in expected mortality. A danger is that the insurance company, if so permitted, may offer new clients more favorable mortality tables, thus cross-subsidizing from existing members.

3.2.2 Annuities and Pension Systems

How do annuities fit into pension systems? During retirement, guaranteed cash flows are offered by pay-as-you-go pension schemes (out of taxation) and defined benefit funds (usually out of the fund itself), albeit subject to wide discretion in respect to inflation indexation (Valdes Prieto, 1998). Both these types of schemes typically spread the risks at the income stage among pensioners, between pensioners and those of working age, and between members of the scheme and the sponsors of the arrangement.

In defined contribution pension schemes, such risk-sharing mechanisms are not automatically available. Nevertheless, if defined contribution schemes are to provide a substitute for social security and occupational defined benefit funds, as typically sought in pension reforms, they will also need to provide guaranteed cash flows in a risk-sharing context. Annuities fulfill this objective by pooling the risk of living longer among all the pensioners who purchase them. As noted, annuities are the only form of financial contract that can provide the beneficiary with a guaranteed income till he/she dies. Of course, if substantial social security and/or defined benefit funds are retained, then defined contributions could justifiably provide only lump sums (see Section 3.6).

To gain a guaranteed retirement income, each individual in a defined contribution scheme may (or must, in the case of mandatory systems) invest his/her own accumulated pension savings in the form of an annuity with an insurance company. As noted, the use of an insurance company entails certain financial risks, which justify financial regulation in the interests of retirement income security, as well as for the other objectives regulation may pursue.

3.2.3 Financing of Annuities

In order to evaluate regulation, it is essential to outline how annuities are financed. Focusing on level annuities, if suitable assets are available as reserves, there can be matching of assets and liabilities, with cash flows precisely equal to the expected payments in the annuity. Immunization leading to duration matching would allow a wider range of assets to cover the liabilities, with changes in market yields not affecting the coverage of liabilities by assets. Government bonds would in turn provide risk-free backing for such strategies.

However, although a strategy of matching or immunization would cover the liabilities, James and Song (2002) note that owing to the narrow margins inherent in it, it would not account for the high money's worth ratio (MWR) typical of most developed annuities markets, where the MWR is the expected discounted present value of cash flows from the annuity divided by the initial premium cost. Discounting at the risk-free rate, they find MWRs of 95 per cent or more for the annuitant population in a variety of countries. The difference in payout across countries is closely related to the differences in government bond yields, and the difference in MWR is related to mortality prospects.

The issue arises as to how insurers cover their administrative costs, risk premia and profits given such high MWRs based on risk-free rates. James and Song suggest, supported by discussions with industry players, that insurers actually invest the initial lump sum on an annuity in riskier instruments, notably corporate bonds, mortgages and some equities. Blake and Hudson (2000) add that the menu may also include private placements and foreign bonds plus currency swaps. They may also duration-mismatch, not holding short-term assets to cover initial annuity payouts, but using net cash inflow from new business and maturating old investments, current interest and dividend receipts to pay them. This raises the average return with an upward-sloping yield curve and reduces reinvestment risk. (The lack of bonds longer than ten years in most markets, and the cessation of issuance at 30 years in the UK and US, mean that in most cases maturity mismatching is inevitable.) Life insurers may thus earn a return that exceeds the guaranteed risk-free rate by over 130 basis points, and thus cover their costs. Underpinning this argument, in their sample, excluding most EU countries, James and Song note that the lowest MWRs are for UK indexed annuities, for which higher-yielding substitute assets are not readily available. They also point to life insurance company portfolios, which include sizeable proportions of risky assets (see Table 3.1), although as discussed below, riskier assets may link mainly to products such as variable or unit-linked policies where investment risk is passed on to the consumer.

Table 3.1 Life insurers' portfolio composition (per cent) 1998

	Liquidity	Loans	Domestic bonds	Domestic equities	Property	Foreign assets
UK	5	1	25	48	6	13
US	6	8	52	26	0	1
Germany	1	57	14	17	4	0
Japan	5	30	36	10	0	9
Canada	7	28	55	26	7	3
France	1	2	74	15	7	0
Italy	0	1	75	12	2	0
Netherlands	1	29	24	24	5	10
Sweden	4	2	35	27	5	27
Finland	1	61	0	21	12	0
Average	**3**	**22**	**39**	**23**	**5**	**6**
Prudent person	**4**	**13**	**33**	**33**	**4**	**8**
Restrictions	**3**	**26**	**41**	**18**	**5**	**6**

Source: Davis and Steil (2001).

The means whereby risky portfolios are transformed to risk-free outflows include risk reduction and risk-shifting approaches. Such methods are important to spell out here, as they constitute a key part of internal risk management by the firm, which underpins and complements regulation. Risks arising from failure of such risk management methods are discussed in Section 3.7. In terms of risk reduction, insurers employ investment diversification, including foreign assets (Davis, 2002c); use of derivatives for hedging (if permitted) such as swaptions, which should provide a cheaper way of covering these risks (Blake, 1999; Rule, 2001); sharing of risk across product lines whose risks are orthogonal, such as annuities and life insurance; lower information costs than for individual consumers owing to specialization, as for any financial intermediary; and using cash inflows to provide liquidity and thus reducing market timing risk. In terms of risk shifting, there is reinsurance; annuity guarantee pools; risk sharing between cohorts of annuitants or different products (if competition is imperfect) notably in with-profits policies; using shareholders as residual claimants; and bankruptcy laws giving annuitants high priority.

3.3 INSURANCE COMPANIES, ANNUITIES AND FINANCIAL REGULATION

3.3.1 Why is Financial Regulation Needed?

Given that annuities offer benefits to retirees, and insurers have various risk-spreading and risk-reduction methods at their disposal, why does a free market solution not suffice to ensure security of retirement incomes? Abstracting from issues of redistribution, a case for public intervention in the operation of markets arises when there is a market failure, that is, when a set of market prices fails to reach a Pareto optimal outcome. When competitive markets achieve efficient outcomes, there is no case for regulation. There are three key types of market failure in finance, namely those relating to information asymmetry, externality and monopoly. Moral hazard and adverse selection may also play a role.

As regards information asymmetry, if it is difficult or costly for the purchaser of a financial service to obtain sufficient information on the quality of the service in question, they may be vulnerable to exploitation. This may entail fraudulent, negligent, incompetent or unfair treatment as well as failure of the relevant institution per se. Such phenomena are of particular importance for retail users of financial services such as annuities, because clients are seeking investment of a sizeable proportion of their wealth, contracts are one-off and irrevocable and involve a commitment over as much as 40 years. Innovative annuity products, while offering potentially desirable income streams, may be particularly difficult to evaluate by consumers (FSA, 2002a). Equally, consumers are unlikely to find it economic to make a full assessment of the risks to which life insurance companies are exposed across their entire asset and liability portfolios, which may nevertheless affect their ability to pay annuities. Such asymmetries are clearly less important for wholesale users of financial markets such as life insurers themselves, which have better information, considerable countervailing power and carry out repeated transactions with other financial institutions. However, a partial protection against exploitation, even for retail consumers, is likely to arise from desire of financial institutions such as life insurers offering annuities to maintain reputation.

Externalities arise when the actions of one individual in the economy have a consequence for other individuals which are not taken into account by the price mechanism. The most obvious type of potential externality in financial markets relates to the risk of contagious bank runs, when failure of one bank leads to a heightened risk of failure by others, whether due to direct financial linkages (such as interbank claims) or shifts in perceptions on the part of depositors as to the creditworthiness of certain banks in the light of failure of others. Given the matching of long-run liabilities and long-run assets, such externalities are less likely for life insurance companies. But on the other hand one can point to the possibility of contagion due to common ownership of different insurance firms; contagion from a failing bank to an insurance company in a conglomerate; counterparty risk in the over-the-counter derivatives market; failure of a reinsurance company that had accepted risks from a large number of other firms; and a weakening of other insurance companies by an insurance company failure that leads to a decline in purchase of insurance products, given the key role played by new inflows and commissions in insurers' profitability.

A third form of market failure may arise when there is a degree of market power. This may be of particular relevance for life companies *vis-à-vis* consumers who have saved in a personal pension and are seeking to purchase annuities at the time of retirement. The consequence for consumers who are, or consider themselves to be, locked in, is that they may receive worse terms on an annuity that is available in the open market. Also there is a need for more general competition regulation to ensure that prices are not artificially boosted by monopoly. But as discussed in this chapter, stringent prudential regulation may also be needed to prevent such competition from becoming destructive (externality case) or leading to abuse of consumers (the information asymmetry case).

Justifications for regulation may also include attempts to overcome problems of adverse selection – a situation common in insurance markets such as for annuities in which a pricing policy induces a low average quality of sellers in a market, while asymmetric information prevents the buyer from distinguishing quality. Basically, the annuity provider may face bad risks; those who know that they will live a longer time than the population average. When adverse selection is sufficiently severe, the market may cease to exist. For example, making annuities compulsory should reduce adverse selection in that market. Moral hazard considerations may also enter, in that individuals that are not forced to provide retirement income via annuities purchase could deliberately become destitute and a burden on the state.

Some would argue that annuities should be regulated independently of these standard justifications, notably as a component of the overall pension system, for example to ensure tax benefits are not misused, and that the goals of equity, adequacy and security of retirement income are achieved – correcting the market failures in annuities markets that necessitate pension funds and social security.

One may distinguish a number of aspects of annuities regulation that are covered below. One is the prudential regulation of insurance companies – ensuring insurers have the financial resources to pay all claims as they fall due. The second is their conduct of business regulation – ensuring they treat consumers in an equitable manner. The third is the overall regulation of annuities in the context of the pension system, with the aim that a secure retirement income is available. It will be seen there are overlaps, notably owing to prudential and pension regulations affecting annuity product design. In Sections 3.4–3.6, we discuss these aspects in turn. But first we consider whether market discipline could obviate the need for regulation, or whether incentives generated by market processes rather underpin the case for regulation.

3.3.2 Market Discipline and Incentives to Risk Taking

It was pointed out above that individual consumers are unlikely to have sufficient information to discipline insurance companies by avoiding their products – though insurance companies will still be concerned to maintain reputation. This puts an onus on monitoring by wholesale financial markets for ensuring market discipline.

Disclosure of current balance sheets and profit and loss as well as other material facts affecting life companies are essential if market discipline is to be effective. It hence places a premium on sound accounting and the independence of the actuary, as well as on rating agencies. As noted in Financial Times (2002a), there is a wide diversity in insurance accounting standards internationally, which weakens market discipline by making it difficult to compare performance of companies cross-country. Often insurers use book value accounting, there is a problem of 'opacity of often subjective actuarial assumptions' and off-balance-sheet exposures are rarely reported in accounts (IMF, 2002c). There is ongoing work at the IASB towards a standard. Further work will seek to introduce fair value accounting for insurers, valuing all assets and liabilities at current market value. This would imply for example that financial guarantees and onerous options on life policies such as annuity rate guarantees would be valued consistently with traded options in the market.

Credit-rating agencies play an important role in informing policy holders and investors about financial risks. Standard and Poor's assess risk-based capital for insurers based on their own capital adequacy model. Indeed rating agencies are widely seen as private market supervisors (European Commission, 2002). Insurance companies may also monitor one another in a free market if they fear loss of reputation for the industry arising from company failure or if there is mutual insurance.

One may also consider the differing influence of market discipline depending on instruments outstanding. Market discipline will clearly have an independent effect on insurance companies that have debt outstanding, as risky behavior will lead to a higher cost of debt via loss of credit rating. In practice insurers are typically not heavily levered, but this is a consideration for counterparties in derivatives transactions such as credit derivatives, which as discussed in Section 3.7 are becoming increasingly important. Outside equity means that equity holders may exert corporate governance over managers, either directly or via takeovers (Davis, 2002d). However, the market discipline exerted via equity is ambiguous, since equity holders lose from bankruptcy, but may gain from a high but volatile rate of profits. There may be a particular danger of risky behavior where equity values are low. Here it is useful to recall the contribution of Keeley (1990) to banking theory, which we suggest is applicable to insurance also. He showed that deregulation may lead directly to incentives for risk taking by financial institutions, even abstracting from the safety net. In a structurally regulated market, for example with controls on new entry, where institutions have a degree of market power, the charter is a capital asset. Then banks/insurance companies have incentives not to risk failure by reducing capital or increasing asset risk. Deregulation that facilitates new entry, or that liberalizes pricing or mortality assumptions reduces the value of the charter. Risk taking becomes more attractive, as the potential loss from bankruptcy is lower, and hence a higher mean and variance of profits may be sought. Such incentives will of course be increased by mis-priced safety net protection, as for US Savings and Loans institutions (Davis, 2001a).

Mutual insurance companies, which typically have neither debt nor equity outstanding, have made some of the worst errors in risk control. This points to the importance of management and its own incentives. If they seek to increase market share regardless of rate of return, there may be a particular risk of insolvency. In this context, we shall see in sections below how regulation seeks to enforce prudence, as well as failures of risk control in the case of the mutual insurer Equitable Life and the Japanese life company sector.

3.4 PRUDENTIAL REGULATION

Prudential regulation of insurance companies affecting annuities is directed in particular at regulation of solvency and asset regulation, as well as compensation schemes, and these are the focus of this section. We note that entry regulation is also usually a feature – which in Europe entails acceptance of entry by firms from other EU countries on the basis of home country recognition. This of course entails a need for confidence in foreigner countries' regulatory standards, which is underpinned by the harmonized solvency and asset standards set out in the relevant Directives.

3.4.1 Reserving and Solvency Regulation

The key protection for insurance companies against insolvency, and hence protection for annuity holders, is reserving and capital adequacy. The need for such solvency regulation for insurance companies in general is underlined by the argument of Finsinger and Pauly (1992), that given the technical properties of claims that insurers usually face, there are often two possible equilibria, in one of which the insurer will not put up any capital but rely on premium income and investment returns to meet claims. Then the risk of insolvency is very high; the insurer merely declares bankruptcy if claims exceed premium income and asset returns, having invested funds equivalent to capital separately in the securities markets. Following the argument above, this case may be particularly likely if the penalty from losing reputation or licence is low, in other words the franchise value of insurance is small due to intense competition and deregulation. Moreover, as noted in Rees et al. (1999), if there are restrictions on portfolio composition, making it costly to hold capital in an insurance company as opposed to investing in the open market, the risk that insurers put up no capital in the absence of regulation increases. An argument against is that consumers would rapidly lose any illusion that insolvency is ruled out in an insurance market where zero capital were feasible.

As an introduction to solvency regulation, one may distinguish several parts of an insurance company's asset portfolio (Dickinson, 1998a). First, there are assets that are held to cover obligations to policy holders, including annuities, called reserves or assets held against guaranteed liabilities (technical provisions). These are generally purchased with inflows of premium income and are expected to be repaid in the future. Second, there are assets that correspond to the capital funds of the company, in other words the surplus over policy-holder liabilities. Besides these two categories, there are also fixed assets (such as buildings) and current assets (forms of trade credit or other receivables). The main focus of solvency regulation is on reserves and investments held against the capital base. Assets held as reserves are or should be constrained by the risk characteristics of the liabilities, derived in turn from the guarantees inherent in the contracts that have been sold. Reserves are also the part of the portfolio which is most commonly subject to investment regulation, discussed in the following section.

Daykin (2002) outlines the main issues in reserving for annuities, using as background the UK regulatory regime – itself conditioned by EU Directives. He points out that there are multiple reasons for reserving, first ensuring sound and prudent management of the insurer (that is, internal risk management); second, ensuring accounts give a true and fair view of the insurance company; third, providing information to the tax authorities on which profits tax may be based, and, fourth, for prudential supervisory purposes. There are potential conflicts between these different reasons. While the supervisors would like very conservative approaches to ensure the firm can meet future liabilities, tax authorities would prefer a low level of reserves, so as to maximize the tax 'take' on profits. The accounting and internal risk-management approaches are intermediate, although generally firms prefer lower reserves than the supervisors, in the interest of profitability. The chosen level of reserves should feed directly to the price of policies, given a desired return on capital.

In theory, life business may offer a hedge against mortality *vis-à-vis* annuities, since life business becomes more profitable when life expectancy increases.[1] It may be added that the larger the annuities business is relative to the total, the less such hedging is feasible, and the more the insurance companies represent a concentration of risk. Furthermore, any with-profits policies on an insurer's books, where the terminal bonus is provided with discretion, provide an additional buffer. This is, however subject to the right of policy holders to challenge for their 'reasonable expectations' to be upheld in court, as witness the Equitable Life case discussed below. Particularly given these caveats, from a prudential point of view, Daykin suggests that the annuities business should be stand-alone and not dependent on other business of the firm. Although hidden reserves or excess profitability in other parts of the business may cover losses on annuities temporarily, they should not be relied upon.

Prudential supervision of reserves requires a focus on prospective liabilities based on existing contracts. The main issues, as for the companies themselves as outlined in Section 3.2, are the mortality assumptions, the discount rate (based on the investments backing the contract) and future expenses. Mortality is not readily judged by the current mortality of the entire population. Allowance needs to be made for the likely self-selection of annuitants (especially if annuitization is voluntary, see below), for the likely future improvement in mortality and the fact that those with larger annuities tend to have a higher life expectancy. Using UK data, Daykin (2002) notes that the current trend is for life expectancy to rise one year every 4–5. This would justifiably raise the value of an annuity at age 60 – and hence appropriate reserves – by 10 per cent above that based on current mortality experience, while the annuity-size adjustment may imply a 5 per cent rise in the value. Since annuitization in the UK is compulsory, the annuitant population is actually close to that of the population as a whole – this is not the case in countries such as the US where annuitization is voluntary. Further increases in reserves would be justified to allow for prudence.

The rate of interest should be related to the returns on assets to back the annuity, and precisely so if there is matching or immunization. Reserves can then be calculated on the basis of market value and the interest rate on the annuity taken from their redemption yield. However, the issue is more complex in the case of private bonds, when allowance has to be made for default risk and possible call provisions, and for the case of asset and liability mismatching, due for example to lack of long-term government bonds. In the latter case allowance has to be made for reinvestment risk in terms of larger reserves. This may be done by dynamic cash flow modeling, reducing the interest rate on the liabilities or, when equities are used, by stochastic asset and liability modeling. The suggestion in Section 3.2.3 that mismatching and consequent exposure to default and reinvestment risk is very common in order even to cover costs lends considerable weight to this issue. Meanwhile, even if long-term government bonds exist, UK experience in the 1990s has shown the bond market can be significantly distorted by the demands of insurance companies and pension funds, leading to low annuity rates.

An additional policy implication of this point is that if governments wish to reduce the cost of annuities, they may be able to help by issuing long-term bonds allowing insurers to match or immunize – contrary to the current situation. A more radical suggestion (Blake and Burrows, 2001) is for governments to issue survivor bonds, which would be indexed to the mortality of a cohort, and would thus help insurers to hedge demographic risks.

Expenses need to be allowed for also in reserves, to cover the full expected cost of administering the payments on the annuity. The firm itself would naturally do this on a going-concern basis, whereby new business helps finance overheads, but supervisors typically insist on a closed-fund basis. This assumes no more business is written and that the firm makes a transition from a going concern to a firm that is running off all its accrued liabilities, thus requiring extra margins for reserving, given the lack of inflows from new business.

Besides reserves per se, the firm must also hold capital and surplus assets in sufficient quantities to cover unexpected shocks and thus minimize solvency risk. The process of assessment must be made frequently (dynamic financial analysis) to assess how the firm's position is evolving. Stress testing may be combined with regulation, as well as being an internal risk management tool, to assess how the firm would cope with adverse scenarios affecting the above factors (mortality, interest rates and expenses). For example in the UK, reserves must be sufficient to cover a change in interest rates of 3 percentage points or a 25 per cent fall in equity prices. Immunization or matching would mean that such tests have no implication, but they will highlight the dangers of a mismatched position. More recently, risk-based supervision in the UK has been extended to formally cover a range of risks to insurance companies, namely financial risks (capital adequacy and valuation of assets and liabilities), external environment risks (economic developments) and control risks (how firms organize and manage risks) (FSA, 2001). Further progress is mooted in FSA (2002b). In practice there has been some easing of solvency tests (making some allowance for recent price falls) given the context of the severe decline in share prices (Davis, 2003).

The EU Life Directives set out a minimum harmonized level of capital for insurance companies. However, as reported in Financial Times (2002a), the formal minimum solvency requirements (for example, 4 per cent of reserves for annuities with matching assets) are only part of the solvency margin, with the rest hidden in accounting reserves. There is a great deal of discretion to actuaries of life firms. In times of stress, hidden buffers may be 'eaten into or effectively mortgaged by using devices such as reinsurance, that erode solvency in ways invisible to the outside world' (Financial Times, 2002a). Also IMF (2002c) suggests that a weakness of EU solvency regulation is that no account is taken of risk on the asset side but only the volume of business underwritten. In Australia, Canada, Japan and the US regimes include capital charges for risks on the assets side of the balance sheet, although even in those countries there is doubt whether the weights are adequate to reflect risks (see Section 3.7.4 on Japan).

The EU council of ministers has adopted two improvements to solvency regulation of insurance companies. Solvency I will give regulators extra powers to intervene when an insurer's financial position is deteriorating, as well as mandating higher capital overall and allowing member states to impose tougher solvency requirements. Solvency II will examine in greater detail the rules on valuing liabilities and the corresponding assets, asset-liability matching, treatment of reinsurance cover and double gearing within financial conglomerates, where life companies and banks in a group hold loans or shares in each other (see also Section 3.7.4).

3.4.2 The Equitable Life Case

The case of Equitable Life may justifiably be mentioned in this context, resulting as it does from failure of reserving and pricing of annuities. It would appear that the company gave the option of deferred guaranteed annuities (promising a minimum return on retirement) during the period 1957–88 to a large number of personal pension savers. This was apparently done without extra charge and with no specific reserves held to cover the cost of the guarantees. It also disregarded the history of the long-term bond market, when bond yields were often below the rates promised – a particular paradox given Equitable itself was the oldest life company dating back several centuries.

Over this period the embedded option was never 'in the money' since market rates were always above the guaranteed rates. However, in 1993 the market rate fell below the guaranteed rate, and the guarantees began to have an intrinsic value. Other insurance companies that had sold such policies dealt with the implicit mortality and interest rate risks in the guarantees in various relatively prudent ways. For example, they reserved for them, reinsured them, bought them out, capped them or put them in an orphan fund to run off. Instead, Equitable sought to manage them by discretion, by paying a smaller final bonus to those with-profits investors who sought to retain their guarantee, as compared to those willing to give it up.

Challenged in court, this policy was abandoned, and the company claimed that as a mutual company with no shareholders and a small capital base, its only recourse was to use for reserves the general with-profits fund (including assets held for non-guaranteed policy holders) to pay the guarantees. This was feasible because there was no separation between the guaranteed and non-guaranteed policy holders' funds, although the appropriate investment was entirely different – bonds for the former and equities for the latter. Effectively, the burden of the guarantees was transferred to the non-guaranteed policy holders (who were forced to issue implicit interest rate put options), many of whom had bought contracts well after the guarantees ceased to be sold. Indeed, Blake (2001) argues that the process of attracting new policy holders after 1988 was akin to a Ponzi scheme, while the closure of the fund to new members in 2001 reduced investment flexibility by making the fund one that is winding up. It can be argued that the non-guaranteed policy holders are suffering from a number of adverse effects resulting from inadequate pricing, reserving, illegitimate combinations of types of liability in the same pool and asymmetric information.

Lessons for regulation are in particular to monitor closely the reserving against embedded options in annuity contracts, whether in or out of the money. Separation of guaranteed and non-guaranteed funds may also be required. Similar, albeit broader, issues arising from life policies rather than annuities are raised by the insolvency of the bulk of the Japanese life insurance sector (Section 3.7.4).

3.4.3 Portfolio Regulation of Insurance Companies

Since the assets held to back the annuities will be subject to portfolio regulation, it is relevant to probe the nature of overall asset regulation faced by life insurers.

Background is provided by the overall business mix of life insurers. Life insurance company liabilities tended historically to be defined in nominal terms, which besides those arising from level annuities as outlined above include term policies (purchased to provide a certain sum in the event of death), and whole-life policies (term policies with a saving element). Guaranteed investment contracts (GICs) – a form of zero-coupon bond typically sold to pension funds – are a modern variant. Insurers may also offer nominal, insured defined benefit pension plans. All of these require forms of matching or immunization, with bond finance predominating. As noted above, the introduction of financial derivatives such as swaptions should provide a cheaper way of covering the associated interest rate risks (Blake, 1999; Rule, 2001), while insurance companies are also increasingly accepting credit risk per se in search of higher yields.

Life companies nowadays are also offering variable policies such as variable life policies, variable annuities (invested in equities), with-profits endowment and unit (mutual fund)-linked life or annuity policies. As noted in Section 3.2.1, the life policies typically combine a term policy with a saving element aimed at capital appreciation, where for the latter there is no explicit guarantee regarding the rate of return. The annuities may still have a guarantee element overall, as shown in the examples given in Section 3.2.1, but much of the investment risk is passed to the consumer. Some policies may have option features, with, for example, variable returns but a guaranteed floor (as in Equitable's guaranteed polices). Variable policies may offer higher returns – and also risks – to policy holders, while posing less shortfall risk to the surplus of the life insurer. Unlike traditional policies, variable policies imply active investment in equities, real estate and international investments which may be expected to keep pace with inflation. The related assets may often be held in the form of mutual funds. A life insurer's overall liabilities will reflect the chosen balance between these different types of policy, which can change over time as insurers choose which markets to serve. The desired asset portfolio will change in a corresponding manner, from mainly bonds for nominal-fixed products (including level annuities) to a greater share of equities (for variable and unit-linked annuity and life products, especially when the element of guarantee is small).

The surplus over guaranteed liabilities is intended to protect the firm against insolvency over time, and to finance future growth. Not held explicitly to back liabilities, it is likely to be aggressively invested for return to shareholders and development of reserves. The size of the surplus has an independent effect on investment from the nature of liabilities. This is because its size will affect the prudent degree of investment risk, that is, the appropriate degree of mismatching of the embedded risks of liabilities and the assets held to cover them (Dickinson, 1998b). In order to protect insurance firms from insolvency in the shorter term, supervisory rules typically impose stricter regulations on reserve assets backing technical provisions (that is, guaranteed liabilities) than for the surplus (Dickinson, 1998a). For example, a number of asset types are often forbidden to be held against technical provisions, but these restrictions typically do not apply to the surplus. This is also the case for the quantitative restrictions on asset holdings. Hence, the assets backing technical provisions are more likely to be invested in bonds, with only the surplus including a share of equities.

On the other hand, the size of the surplus is itself affected by the degree of conservatism of the regulatory and accounting framework. For example, surplus calculations are affected by valuation methods (such as whether assets are valued at market value or book value) and discount rates used to calculate the present value of future liabilities. Undervaluation of the capital base may significantly increase the leverage of investment restrictions. Life company sectors having low discount rates and book value accounting for the assets tend to have smaller surpluses and correspondingly lower allocations to equities than those with high discount rates and market value accounting. The German case used[2] to be an extreme, with 'lower of cost and market' accounting leading to aversion to equities well beyond limits imposed by portfolio restrictions.

The choice in regulation of insurance (and pension fund) asset portfolios is between prudent person rules and quantitative asset restrictions (Davis, 2002a). A quantitative asset regulation is simply a quantitative limit on the portfolio share of a given asset class. Typically, those instruments whose holding is limited are those with high price volatility and/or low liquidity. Meanwhile, a prudent person rule stipulates that investments should be made in such a way that they are considered to be handled 'prudently' (as someone would do in the conduct of his or her own affairs). The aim is to ensure adequate diversification, thus protecting the beneficiaries against insolvency of the sponsor and investment risks. Evaluation of the risk management as well as reserving of the insurance company are essential aspects of this approach.

Compared to pension funds, the case in favor of quantitative portfolio restrictions may be quite strong for life insurance companies which have nominally fixed liabilities such as level annuities (Davis, 2002a). For such institutions, matching with assets of similar duration may indeed be a desirable portfolio strategy. Hence, portfolio regulations (which usually do not restrict bond holdings) may not strongly distort free-market portfolios. On the other hand, as argued by Dickinson (1998a), restrictions may make it more difficult to cope with some of the underlying risks of traditional life insurance business, notably interest rate risk on annuities and term policies, arising from the interest rate guarantee implicit in the price of the contract. He suggests that this can only be evaluated in the context of the asset and liability composition (immunization characteristics) of the whole portfolio and not asset-by-asset. If there are strict investment restrictions, combined with restrictions on minimum premia, these may also give rise to economic inefficiency, as resulting low competition perpetuates a fringe of high cost firms (Rees and Kessner, 1999). It is notable that the German annuity market is still less concentrated than other EU markets (Cardinale et al., 2002), suggesting this critique still holds.

More generally, a competitive insurance market will involve firms seeking to earn higher rates of return on their financial assets in order to develop new products and compete with alternatives. They may then seek to have a wider and more flexible choice of financial assets than regulations may allow, including taking advantage of the risk diversification offered by international investment. Even traditional liquidity and interest rate risks can be handled at lower cost by use of derivatives. It can be argued that prudent-person-based diversification plus solvency rules,[3] as well as comprehensive conduct of business rules to protect consumers, are sufficient protection for policy holders without the overlay of asset restrictions. This will be so especially if the restrictions are imposed on an annual or more frequent basis.

This may be a particularly relevant argument for long-term policies, including annuities to some extent, where any mismatched position can be corrected well before liabilities are due, and where appropriate asset-liability management techniques are undertaken. Strict portfolio regulations could limit scope for innovative product design. It applies even more strongly for the surplus over and above the level of technical provisions (EU rules only apply to reserves). Furthermore, assets corresponding to non-guaranteed liabilities (such as the bulk of variable or unit-linked policies, which may include annuities as well as life policies) are subject to inflation risk, as policy holders will anticipate a positive real rate of return on the policy. Such risks are minimized by investment in assets with real returns (indexed bonds,

Table 3.2 Portfolio regulations for life insurance companies

	Prudent person rule/diversification rules	Quantitative restrictions on domestic assets	Self investment and ownership concentration	Foreign asset restrictions
Canada (maxima applied to all assets)	No PPR	5–25% in real estate and stocks combined; 10% in non-mortgage loans	Self investment banned, localisation rules apply	No currency matching rules
Finland (maxima applied to investments against technical provisions only)	No PPR, EU diversification rules (10% maximum of technical reserves in one piece of real estate, 5% shares and 5% loans of one borrower), maturity matching rules apply	Maximum 50% in domestic shares, 10% unquoted shares, 40% real estate, 40% mortgage loans, 50% in secured non-mortgage loans or corporate bonds, 3% cash	Self investment banned, EU localisation rules apply	80% currency matching limit, non-OECD shares limited to 25%, technical reserves must be covered by real estate in Finland, securities issued by residents or assets guaranteed by residents
Germany (maxima applied to investments against technical provisions only)	No PPR, EU diversification rules (10% maximum of technical reserves in one piece of real estate, 5% shares and 5% loans of one borrower)	Maximum 30% quoted shares, 10% unquoted shares, 25% real estate, 50% in loans, 30% mutual funds and 50% bonds	Self investment banned, localisation rules apply	80% currency matching limit overall; 5% of premium reserve and 20% of other restricted assets
Italy (maxima applied to investments against technical provisions only)	No PPR, EU diversification rules (10% maximum of technical reserves in one piece of real estate, 5% shares of one borrower and 5% loans of one borrower)	Maximum 20% quoted shares, 20% unquoted shares, 50% real estate, 50% mortgage loans. Non-mortgage loans prohibited	Self investment banned, localisation rules apply	80% currency matching limit overall; 20% may be held in foreign shares and 50% in other foreign securities
Japan (maxima apply to all assets)	No PPR, 10% limit on debt or equity exposures to one borrower	Maximum 30% shares, 20% real estate, 10% non-mortgage loans, 10% corporate bonds, 30% mutual funds (mortgage loans prohibited for life companies)	Self investment banned, localisation rules apply for foreign companies	No matching rules, 30% limit on foreign currency assets

	Prudent person rule/diversification rules	Quantitative restrictions on domestic assets	Self investment and ownership concentration	Foreign asset restrictions
Netherlands (maxima applied to investments against technical provisions only)	PPR, EU diversification rules (10% maximum of technical reserves in one piece of real estate, 5% shares of one borrower and 5% loans of one borrower); maturity matching rules apply	Maximum 8% in unsecured loans, 10% in real estate and 3% in cash	Self investment banned, EU localisation rules apply	80% currency matching
Sweden (maxima applied to investments against technical provisions only)	No PPR, Maximum 5% in a single item of real estate and for exposures to a single borrower	Maximum 25% in shares, 25% in real estate and mortgage loans together, 50% in corporate bonds and 3% in cash	Self investment banned, EU localisation rules apply	80% currency matching, maximum 20% of technical reserves in foreign currency and foreign securities; overall 25% limit on foreign shares
UK	PPR, maturity matching required	Maximum 3% in cash		80% currency matching
US (maxima apply to all assets)	PPR, per-issuer limitation of 3–5% of issues other than US government	Imposed at state level, e.g. Delaware 250% of capital and surplus in shares, 25% in real estate, 50% in mortgage loans New Jersey 15% in shares, 10% real estate, 60% mortgages		No currency matching rule; aggregate limits on foreign assets of 0–10% imposed at state level. Canadian investment more liberalised

Source: Davis (2002a)

or in their absence international equities and real estate), which are often restricted by regulations.

If long-term rates fall sharply and the regulations enforce holdings of bonds, while maturities are relatively short, then the regulations can pose a danger to insurance companies. This appears to be the case in Japan, where guaranteed rates tended in the 1990s to exceed actual rates, leading initially to insurers cashing in gains on securities, but later to actual solvency problems (Section 3.7.4).

As regards experience, the portfolio regulations of life insurance sectors are summarized in Table 3.2 (source: Davis, 2002a). The bulk of life insurance sectors, notably in Europe, have quantitative restrictions, drawing on EU rules set out in the relevant Directives, with the UK being the clearest exception. Davis (2002a) shows that the restrictions come at a cost in terms of average real or nominal returns on the asset portfolio (around 100 basis points), see Table 3.3, and although risk as measured conventionally with the nominal standard deviation is reduced, this is not the case for the standard deviation of real returns, which is identical for both kinds of regulation. The superiority of prudent person rules for investment-linked products is underlined.

Table 3.3 Returns on life company portfolios, seven OECD countries, 1980–95

	Nominal return	Standard deviation	Real return	Standard deviation
UK	14.5	7.4	8.7	8.4
US	11.4	8.4	6.7	9.8
Germany	10.8	3.8	7.8	3.7
Japan	7.5	6.4	5.5	6.7
Canada	11.9	6.5	6.9	6.6
Netherlands	9.9	4.9	7.1	5.1
Sweden	12.8	13.9	6.1	14.4
Average	**11.2**	**7.3**	**7.0**	**7.8**
Prudent person	**11.9**	**6.9**	**7.5**	**7.8**
Restrictions	**10.7**	**6.1**	**6.6**	**7.9**

Source: Davis (2002a).

3.4.4 Insurance and Compensation Schemes

Within the insurance industry, the process of reinsurance helps to spread risk across a variety of insurance companies, both at a national and global level.

On the other hand, reinsurance only functions well in cases where companies face differing risks, giving scope for intra-industry risk sharing.[4] This is not the case for annuities, where longevity and market return risks are common. This and the possibility of insolvency of (re)insurance companies leads to the issue of whether some form of a compensation fund for their claims is also appropriate. Many countries have set up mutual arrangements whereby insurance companies' policies may be honored even when they become insolvent.

The danger is that such a fund may lead to moral hazard and excessive risk taking by firms, as is the case for the 'safety net' in banking (Davis, 1995). Such an effect is intensified by a weakening of consumer discipline, in that a compensation fund would reduce the incentive for the public to deal only with strong and well managed companies. Firm prudential supervision as well as market discipline (notably insurers monitoring each other in their own interests) is needed to prevent this taking place. Managers and equity holders must lose their jobs and stakes in the case of insolvency, while consumers may be given less than their guaranteed returns to ensure market discipline operates to the extent possible.

3.5 CONDUCT OF BUSINESS REGULATION

We now turn to conduct of business regulation. In this section, we focus mainly on information aspects and the design of products. We note, however, that conduct of business links to other aspects, to the extent that regulators insist insurance products should have standard specification of 'fine print', and also regulate, inter alia, use of language, grievance redressal, dispute resolution and licensing of intermediaries.

3.5.1 Information Provision to Consumers

At retirement with a defined contribution pension, the individual is faced with a plethora of choices, which will have an important influence on retirement income. Taking the example of what is feasible in the UK, first, the duration or term of the annuity must be selected. The highest income comes with 'single life' annuities, which cease to be paid at the time of death. But some protection against the risk of early death (offset by a lower annuity) may be obtained by a 'joint life' annuity, paid till both holder and spouse die, or a temporary annuity which lasts for a fixed period whether the individual dies or not. 'Capital protection' may allow for return of outstanding funds when the annuitant dies.

Second, the type of annuity must be selected. In the UK, options besides a 'level annuity' are 'index linked' where the income rises with inflation; 'with profits' where income grows in line with an assumed annual bonus rate, 'unit-linked' which fluctuates in line with unit prices; and an 'escalating annuity' which rises at a fixed rate. Note that the actual return on a level annuity itself depends on the current yield on government bonds, less any charges the insurance company levies and the costs of any of the variants outlined above.

Of course, besides cost, the risks of the various annuities differ; inflation is the main difficulty in the case of level annuities and market crashes for unit-linked and with-profits annuities. These may be hedged by a combination of annuities. It is also possible to stagger purchase over time, so that the pension fund is converted to annuities in stages. This reduces the 'timing' risk of retiring when annuity rates are low, owing to low yields on government bonds. It may also maximize the remaining assets, which stay in the pension trust. But there is an offset in terms of higher loadings for mortality improvements, the longer purchase is delayed. The third choice is frequency and timing of annual payments. The less frequent and later the payment, the higher the annuity. There is also the question whether individuals are able to assess in any way the solvency of a life company. In principle, access to credit ratings may help with such understanding, but in practice the degree of understanding of such information is likely to be low.

In this context, FSA (2002a) comments that consumer understanding of annuities is very low and people do not fully understand the risks of the decisions they are taking. In the UK, there is an open market option to buy an annuity from a different provider, but not many individuals are aware of it, although shopping around could gain a 35 per cent increase in income. Second, there is money illusion with falls in rates due to lower inflation seen as a fall in the value of annuities, whereas if it reflects lower inflation the value is less likely to be eroded, while increases in longevity have to be balanced by lower annuity rates also. Often individuals delay purchase of an annuity, although such a strategy is vulnerable to 'mortality drag' where lower mortality at a later date implies lower annuity rates, as well as high commission rates. Finally, very few individuals were buying impaired life annuities, which could offer a higher income, although 40 per cent were eligible (due to health conditions, smoking history and so on).

In response to these concerns, the FSA is introducing consumer advice literature and also obliging firms selling annuities to inform consumers of their open market rights. Stringent qualifications are required of salesmen, in the light of earlier mis-selling scandals in the personal pensions field. Best advice must be offered for the circumstances of the individual, and cooling off periods during which the individual may change their mind. Only specially trained individuals may conduct such analysis; and all such advice must be double checked within the insurance company. Equally, the government has imposed increasingly tough disclosure rules for commissions. Since 1990 providers have had to declare commissions earned by salespeople, as a proportion of contributions. Since 1995 commissions have had to be declared in cash terms. Also affecting UK advice is the current controversy over with-profits life insurance policies, a variant of which is available in annuitized form. Following Equitable Life and poor returns on such policies sold to back house purchase loans, they are widely criticized for lack of transparency and exposing investors to unanticipated risks. Accordingly, a severe tightening of the regulatory regime is underway.

As noted by Cardinale et al. (2002), the regulatory regime is so severe that many annuities are sold execution-only with individuals receiving little or no financial advice. Given the tough regime and low commissions arising from the small size of maturing personal pensions, the level of interest among advisers in getting such business is low. Again this helps to explain why most individuals take annuities from their pension saving provider. And a larger proportion of these go for level annuities (90 per cent compared to 80 per cent who buy in the open market), which may not, as noted, be the best option.

The open market option is not present in some other markets. In Swiss occupational pension funds, the annuity is generally provided by an insurance company chosen by the pension fund or employer. And more generally, the practice of group annuities purchased by a firm entails a lack of choice by definition. Whereas there are clear dangers that a monopoly provider will give poor terms, in fact analysis (James and Song, 2002) suggests that group annuities are superior in terms of money's worth to individual ones, with the benefit of risk pooling and reduced adverse selection, as well as lower administrative and marketing costs to the insurance company more than offsetting any potential for higher monopoly profits and lower consumer choice. It is suggested that very low average commission on annuities in the UK stems from the weight of group annuities. It may be added that corporate firms seeking providers of group annuities on behalf of their workers may have superior information and bargaining power to an individual.

3.5.2 Product and Product-Design Regulation

The basic choice in terms of regulation of product design is between strict controls of products, maintaining a standard design and even pricing by regulation, and allowing innovation freely as long as consumers are provided with appropriate information. This is not, however, solely an issue for regulators. Tax authorities are typically vigilant in limiting the range of annuity products to ensure tax benefits to retirement income accumulation are actually used for that purpose. In the UK for example, the criterion is that the income provided should be regular, stable and throughout life. We may add that although this section is grouped as a regulation of insurance company conduct of business, aspects of prudential regulation (Section 3.4) and pension system regulation (Section 3.6) are also present under this heading. Moreover, idiosyncratic control of product design can be an important barrier to entry preventing cross-border competition in the EU.

At one extreme, in Germany until recently, only products approved by the regulator could be sold and prices were strictly regulated (Rees and Kessner, 1999). There remains a degree of regulatory control over product design, with little variety and controls imposed on profit sharing. In countries such as the US and France, firms are free to design innovative products for voluntary annuity purchasers, although as noted below prices are not entirely free.

Pricing regulations apply in a number of EU countries, where traditional with-profits annuities are priced according to supervisory guidelines on a 'guaranteed rate basis', with the guaranteed rate being equal to only 60 per cent of the government bond yield and changed infrequently (Blake and Hudson, 2000); any excess over this is paid in the form of a revaluation of the initial annuity.[5] This is the case for example in Belgium, France, Germany and Italy, while there is also a separate ceiling on guaranteed interest rates of 3.5 per cent in France and 4 per cent in Italy (Cardinale et al., 2002). The Netherlands permit insurers to offer higher guaranteed rates for 15 years, before reverting to the guaranteed rate. Besides 'consumer protection', this system provides a prudential safety margin since it cuts rates with bond yields, arguably at a cost in terms of lower incentives to maximize returns. Competition may be limited to second order aspects such as expenses – as well as bonus record. On the other hand, if rates change markedly and the administered rate is fixed, there can be solvency risks for firms, as is the case in Japan (Section 3.7.4). In this context, Bank of England (2002) suggests that some EU insurers suffer from an overhang of older policies with higher guaranteed rates.

Regulation of prices may also arise for pure consumer protection reasons. It can be argued that ceilings prevent exploitation of uninformed consumers. For example, in the US, the assumed interest rate on variable annuities is not permitted to be over 5 per cent per year, thus seeking to limit aggressive sales tactics by salesmen promising high returns. This in itself tends to limit the size of the market, since consumers typically consider such returns to be inadequate. More generally according to Mathur (2001) US state laws typically require that 'policy benefits are commensurate with premiums charged'.

The advantages of a liberal approach to design and pricing are clear in a system of voluntary annuitization, as there is a need to attract savers who would otherwise choose uninsured products, by offering appropriate income streams. Where annuitization is compulsory, the case for free pricing remains clear, while the case for a liberal approach to design is more balanced. Plain vanilla products allow readier comparison of prices across providers and may thus help to stimulate price competition that benefits consumers, where this is permitted. Competition is for example intense in the UK, where most annuities are level annuities, even though the market is dominated by five firms (Cardinale et al., 2002). More complex products may facilitate price dispersion, and indeed James and Song (2002) note that dispersion is high in the US, where there are few regulations on product design.

Marketing expenses are also boosted by a wider range of products, as witness distribution costs in the US of around 5–6 per cent of the initial premium compared with a reported 4 per cent in Singapore, where products are standardized, and only 1–1.5 per cent in the UK, where there is a sizeable mandatory sector but the product range is limited and, as noted above, a strong role for group annuities.

More generally, there is a close relation between restrictions and the mandating of annuities, discussed further below, which directly limits the freedom to sell differentiated products. As noted by James and Song (2002), governments often place restrictions on the type and price of annuities in mandatory systems. For example, in Switzerland, the pension at retirement is annuitized in a form and price closely regulated by the government, with the government insisting on joint annuities. Whereas this reduces the initial payment relative to an individual annuity, it does help to prevent old age poverty among dependent spouses. (Single men can avoid cross-subsidizing the married by lump-sum capital withdrawal.) The Swiss also impose an actuarial factor to be used in transforming savings into such a joint annuity, namely 7.2 per cent.[6] This is actually 20 per cent higher than average rates available in the voluntary market. But it also prevents provision of new types of products. (Pension funds can deviate from the actuarial factor in some conditions, especially for the excess over the mandatory part.)

As noted, tax authorities may also play a role in limiting product design. In the UK, Wadsworth et al. (2001) note that the Inland Revenue is likely to oppose new products if it appears that the aim of the product is to provide 'excessive income' in the early years, or to find a way of preserving the member's capital on death to an extent greater than is allowed for in the income protection permitted by legislation.

Mandatory use of certain mortality tables is another aspect of regulation affecting annuity products. Unisex tables of mortality are commonly mandated to prevent low income among older women retirees. In the UK, unisex mortality tables using a mixture of male and female rates are mandated, while in the US, tax rules require that unisex tables be used in the taxable part of the benefit. As argued by Mitchell (2002) this implies governments are introducing cross-subsidization if product purchase is mandatory, or may be worsening adverse selection if the product purchase is voluntary, leading mortality pools to be increasingly female.

James and Vittas (1999) note that in many countries, detailed mortality tables by cohort are not available, and reliance is placed on those from other countries, such as the UK, arbitrarily adjusted (for example, Australia and Portugal). The US, by contrast, has a wide range of estimates that could be abused for competitive purposes by insurance companies. In many Continental countries, such as Belgium, risk is limited by the government mandating mortality tables, although this could leave the government implicitly responsible for the errors in longevity projections. In Switzerland it is the industry association that mandated (till recently) the common mortality table, thus reducing this risk.

In Sweden, the defined contribution pensions derived from social security contributions will be provided by the government itself, which will also index the pensions to mortality trends. While the government is more financially sound than insurance companies, it is, as pointed out by James and Song (2002), not able to access the risk-shifting and risk-reducing methods of insurance companies and this may make annuities more costly.

We now turn to considerations relating to the regulation of annuities in the context of pension systems.

3.6 ANNUITIES REGULATION WITHIN THE PENSION SYSTEM

3.6.1 Compulsion in Annuities Purchase

Whether to encourage annuities or lump-sum withdrawals is a key issue. Lump sums are less desirable for a number of reasons, such as the fact they may be dissipated and not used for pensions, thus imposing a burden on the state (a form of moral hazard); they have an adverse effect on the cost of annuities, as those buying annuities will be assumed to be bad risks; and they undercut protection for survivors as compared to joint annuities. Individuals may well be myopic about their prospective life expectancy, which justifies mandating annuities. On the other hand, compulsory annuity purchase on the day of retirement for defined contribution funds exposes the retiree to market timing risk. Such risks can be reduced by allowing staggered purchase, variable annuities or defined benefit pensions.

In general, the practice in countries that tax-exempt pension savings is to severely restrict lump sums. Lunnon (2002) notes that of a range of countries, annuities are compulsory for all of defined contribution funds in Austria, Brazil, France, Germany, the Netherlands and Sweden, while a mix of annuity and lump sum (where there may also be differences in regulation between types of pension fund) is permitted in Canada, Denmark, Ireland, Israel, Italy, Norway, Portugal, South Africa, Spain, Switzerland and the UK. Only in Australia, Belgium and the US, among countries which tax-exempt contributions and interest income, are payouts mainly or entirely lump-sum. In contrast, countries where pensions are accumulated from taxed income, such as Hong Kong, Israel and New Zealand, rely mainly on tax-free lump sums. See Table 3.4, derived from Yermo (2001) for a summary of practice in selected OECD countries.

Related to compulsion is the issue of controls over the way in which funds that are not available as a lump sum may be released. Lunnon (2002) suggests that there are several criteria for judging systems of release, such as whether they ensure pensioners have a secure income; whether they ensure money saved for retirement is actually used for it; the extent to which such controls inhibit asset allocation; and administrative ease. The conventional level annuity scores well on all these criteria except possibly asset allocation. But even in this case, pensioners would be likely to invest cautiously even if free to do so. Alternatives, such as investment-linked annuities and 'pseudo annuities' (where investment risk is held by the pensioner, and there is only partial insurance of mortality risk) score less comprehensively in terms of income security and administrative complexity, while allowing more freedom in asset allocation.

This is even more the case for pure income drawdown, even if there are controls based on age or interest rates or both (as in Chile). These do not offer protection against either fund depletion or over funding by wealthy individuals. Some combinations can be envisaged. These include a requirement to secure a minimum income with an annuity, while allowing income drawdown on the rest; income drawdown with the requirement to annuitize if the fund falls below a given level, or requirement to annuitize before a certain age, with a possibility of drawdown before that age (the current UK approach). But again these score poorly on the criteria relative to complete annuitization. Similar conclusions are reached by Doyle and Piggott (2000), after more systematic calculations. See also Blake and Hudson (2000) and Wadsworth et al. (2001) for an assessment of issues in the UK.

In practice, as pointed out by James and Song (2002), when there is free choice between these options, people frequently prioritize investment choice over longevity assurance (usually involving scheduled withdrawals – or lump sums). This is the case, for example, in the US, Canada and Australia, as well

Table 3.4 Regulation of retirement income from defined contribution plans

	Occupational pension funds	Personal pension funds	Memo: tax treatment of funded pensions
Canada	No specific regulations – lump sums as well as annuities possible	Option of programmed withdrawals or annuities	EET
Finland	Annuities most common – lump sums subject to tax penalties	Annuities most common – lump sums subject to tax penalties	EET
Germany	No specific regulations	'Riester' individual pensions must provide an annuity or capital withdrawals guaranteeing payments also in very old age	TET/EET
Italy	Annuitization required of at least 50% of the balance	Annuitization required of at least 50% of the balance	EET
Japan	No regulations, DC funds just being introduced	No regulations, DC funds just being introduced	ETT
Netherlands	Full annuitization at retirement mandatory	Full annuitization at retirement mandatory	EET
Sweden	Full annuitization at retirement mandatory	Full annuitization at retirement mandatory of new compulsory individual accounts	ETT
UK	Pension fund must be annuitized by age 75, subject to 25% tax-free lump sum, and scheduled withdrawals from retirement till 75	Pension fund must be annuitized by age 75, subject to 25% tax-free lump sum, and scheduled withdrawals from retirement till 75	EET
US	Lump sums as well as annuities possible	Lump sums as well as annuities possible	EET

Source: Yermo (2001), updated.

as many EU countries. Underlying factors may be the high level of annuitization provided by social security and defined benefit funds, underestimation of life expectancy based on current experience, bequest motives (Bernheim, 1991), and confidence in families substituting for annuities. Tax aspects may play a role (Section 3.6.4). Also, there may be a desire for a higher rate of return than the risk-free rate, due to liquidity constraints or the rest of the wealth portfolio, which leads to application of a discount rate to annuities in excess of the risk-free rate. To the extent these issues are incorrectly perceived, a role for consumer education is indicated. On the other hand findings in Switzerland (Bütler and Teppa, 2002) contradict the James and Song result, in that given the choice most individuals choose annuities, although the first pillar provides a subsistence level of annuitization and although the lump sum is treated in a preferential way by the tax authority (the tax on the lump sum is up to three times smaller than on the annuity).

3.6.2 Inflation Indexation

Defined contribution funds have inherent problems with indexation, as indexed annuities are not available in many countries, partly due to lack of indexed instruments, or are priced prohibitively. Where indexation of annuities is optional, it is common for retirees to avoid it. This is risky in the sense that even low inflation of 2.5 per cent could erode the value of a level annuity by more than half over a 30-year retirement, thus contributing to financial difficulties. Individuals may commonly underestimate their life expectancy, enhancing this bias. In principle, real values of indexed and conventional annuities should be identical, as long as there is no unanticipated inflation (or unanticipated increase in longevity). It is the time path of real income flows that differs. In practice 'preferred habitats' of investors in the bond market may hinder this equilibrium.

The UK is one exception, in that indexation is mandated for part of a personal pension. Social security regulations require the division of such personal pensions into two parts, first the national insurance rebate, which is used to buy a so-called 'protected rights pension' equivalent to the state second pension, and the remainder, the so-called 'personal fund' including employees' and employers' contributions. Regulations state that the protected rights pension has to be uprated by Limited Price Indexation (that is, inflation capped at 5 per cent) and is taken at state retirement age at the earliest (60 for women, 65 for men). The disposition of the remainder is more flexible in terms of timing and type of annuity; 25 per cent of the value of the fund at retirement (excluding the protected rights) can be obtained as a tax-free lump sum.

3.6.3 Timing of Annuitization

Market timing risk is commonly viewed as applying to the purchase of an annuity with an entire pension fund at a given point in time, when market conditions may be adverse. In the UK, annuities may be purchased at the date of retirement but may also be delayed until the age of 75. Income drawdown is also permitted, at a rate equivalent to that of a corresponding annuity or less, since the government changed the rules in 1995 in response to a fall in annuity rates. It is widely argued that UK government bond yields are artificially low due to regulations obliging pension funds to hold significant assets in long-term UK instruments, see Davis (2001b) and Bishop (2002). (In Ireland the liberalization in 1999 went further, shifting from compulsory annuitization to no requirement at all other than income drawdown.)

The UK rule is widely considered to reduce the timing risk of purchasing annuities on the date of retirement, when the market conditions may be adverse. On the other hand, as pointed out by Valdes Prieto (1998), the risk actually arises from a change in the allocation of the portfolio. If the retiree had already switched to bonds prior to retirement, as recommended by so-called lifestyle investment, the risk would not arise.

3.6.4 Taxation of Annuities

Rather than being viewed in isolation, the taxation of income annuities is an integral part of overall pension taxation, which we summarize briefly here. (For a comprehensive analysis of the economics of pension fund taxation, see Dilnot and Johnson (1993).) The basic choice in taxation of savings such as pensions, assuming there is not to be double taxation of contributions and pensions, is between a regime where asset returns are tax-free (expenditure tax treatment) and where they are taxed (comprehensive income tax treatment).

The choice between income and expenditure taxes rests on contrasting views of the appropriate form of neutrality to aim for. Is it neutrality between consumption and saving (implying returns are taxed) or between consumption at different points in time (in which case they are tax-free)? On balance, the former seems more objectionable, since saving is not a commodity like any other, but an intermediate good, which is carried out as a means to future consumption. So an expenditure tax treatment, which taxes consumption at the same rate at all times and does not distort the equality between pre- and post-tax returns, seems more appropriate.

The other key issue in pension taxation is whether to treat pensions more favorably, thus leading to greater flows of saving being directed through this channel. Under a pure expenditure tax treatment of saving, all forms of saving would be equally tax-advantaged. In OECD countries, reasons for taxing pensions relatively leniently are, first, the need to assist people to save enough to maintain post-retirement living standards; second, a desire to encourage people to save and thus cut the cost to the state of means-tested social security benefits; and third, that annuitized pension funds are in some way superior to other types of financial institution. The first is the most important, and is largely paternalistic; it suggests the government knows best and accordingly should distort choices to ensure adequate retirement saving. The argument suggests that people are generally myopic and do not foresee their needs in old age, and/or that there is a form of moral hazard, in that they assume they will be cared for by the state even if they do not save. Moreover, a tax system based on income taxation makes postponement of consumption expensive, as noted above, and thus promotes inadequate retirement saving. The argument of encouraging saving and thus reducing social security is applicable where opting out of part of social security is possible, as in the UK and Japan.

A subsidiary argument in this context focuses on the different characteristics of different types of saving. Forms of saving other than pensions may be decumulated at will, or used as security for a loan,[7] whereas in the UK (and for defined benefit funds elsewhere) pension funds are unique in being contractual annuities. Thus they are on the one hand most appropriate for retirement income provision, but on the other hand are a priori less attractive to individuals. They may thus need some privileges to appear equally attractive, in the interests of ensuring that saving for retirement is adequate and not dissipated. The tax privilege underpins the need for compulsory annuities, so that pension assets are not used for other purposes, as well as to ensure wealthy people do not take undue advantage of pension saving privileges. Accordingly, in expenditure tax systems where contributions as well as asset returns are tax-free (EET), the income from the annuity is taxed as current income (and annuitization is usually compulsory), while in expenditure tax systems where contributions are from taxed income (TEE), the income from the annuity is exempt (and lump sums are usually permitted).

Corresponding to this argument, the taxation of annuities may often lead to them being avoided if they are not compulsory, as is for example the case in Belgium, where taxes on lump sums are lower (Cardinale et al., 2002), and also in France where the tax treatment is identical to lump sums. Differential tax treatment of annuities is an important aspect of market fragmentation, for example in the EU, limiting or preventing cross border sales of annuities products.

3.7 LONGER-TERM RISK

We noted in Section 3.2 above that there may be errors in risk management by insurance companies in a free market, and this underlines the need for regulation. There may be errors in mortality assumptions and competitive conditions leading to inadequate premia being charged, as well as risks incurred on the asset side. History, particularly of banking, suggests that 'company-by-company' regulation alone may not be sufficient to prevent such errors. This is the case even though externalities among insurers are less than for banking. It is suggested that regulators need to be sufficiently aware of incentives faced in companies, monitor the market structure and competition and take a long-term view of potential risks.

3.7.1 Current Issues

As pointed out by the UK insurance regulator FSA (2002a), one of the key risks for annuities for insurance companies is that owing to market-share competition or simple errors, they underestimate the average age to which people live. This could in turn lead to insolvency of an insurance company heavily reliant on annuities. Indeed, Blake (1999) suggests that UK insurance companies have already underestimated life expectancy of their annuitants by two years or more, which could lead to major losses. Similar losses were made by US firms in the 1930s (Poterba, 1997). This resulted from lower than expected nominal interest rates during the deflation of the Great Depression, and underestimation of longevity (companies still used mortality tables from 1868, till 1938). Whereas well capitalized life insurers could charge such losses to shareholders, the Equitable Life case shows grounds for caution for mutuals when capital is low and liabilities are underestimated. Blake (1999) adds that uncertainty about mortality in the future makes the deferred annuities market very thin, despite the fact that such products limit adverse selection compared to immediate annuities. There are clearly great difficulties in forecasting mortality, especially given the possibility of cures for cancer and heart disease in coming years. This leads some commentators to suggest that government intervention is the only answer to the uncertainty in this area, either by direct provision of annuities as in Sweden or via 'survivor bonds'.

Section 3.2.4 highlighted the fact that risks linking annuities and insurance companies may be aggravated by taking on of increased credit risk, if it is not properly priced and reserved for. A number of credit risk concerns are emerging for life insurance companies at the time of writing, exposure to which has been prompted by a desire for higher yields than are available on government bonds. In particular, defaults on corporate bonds are expected to impact on insurance companies that have sought low-rated high-yield bonds in the search for sufficient return (Financial Times, 2002b). Background to this includes increased competition, lower inflation reducing market yields and the current shortage of government bonds. There remain questions whether insurers' credit risk assessment is adequate, with simple reliance being placed on fallible credit ratings (IMF, 2002d) or inappropriate application of actuarial approaches to volatile credit risks.

Furthermore, credit risk has been transferred from banks to insurance companies via securitized claims (such as collateralized debt obligations) and credit derivatives at an unprecedented rate (Bank of England, 2001). Such a process is widely seen as driven by regulatory arbitrage, whereby insurance companies are seen as less regulated than banks and so are willing to hold credit risk at prices banks cannot afford (IMF, 2002a). Such a situation where banks transfer credit risk to insurers may leave the banks also vulnerable if the insurers fail, in other words they enhance systemic risks arising from insurance company failure (Financial Stability Forum, 2000). There is another avenue of contagion within bancassurance groups, which are common in Europe.

Falling equity prices have also hit insurance sectors which hold significant proportions of shares in their portfolios. As noted in Bank of England (2002) this includes the UK, Irish, Nordic and Benelux countries' life sectors. Falling equity prices (Davis, 2003) have put pressure on life companies' solvency, requiring them to raise extra capital or sell shares. There is a risk of a vicious circle in equity markets whereby solvency concerns lead to equity sales, pushing down prices and aggravating related solvency issues. The German insurance association has set up a rescue fund to take over any insurer unable to meet contractual obligations – but with a risk of moral hazard.

3.7.2 Financial Instability and Competition among Financial Institutions

In this context, it is helpful to outline three approaches to the theory of financial instability, originally devised to address banking competition, that we maintain may be relevant to market dynamics of annuities and insurance, notably where price competition is liberalized and franchise values of insurers are low (for a more comprehensive survey see Davis (1999)). Given the duration of many life products, the phenomena noted may have more profound consequences than the classic 'insurance cycle' of property and casualty insurance premia.

First, there is the issue of uncertainty (Shafer, 1986). Following Knight (1921), uncertainty is defined as pertaining to future developments that cannot be reduced to objective probabilities (such as financial crises – or changes in longevity), and also providing opportunities for profit in competitive markets. It thus contrasts with risk, which refers to events for which in principle probability analysis can be employed. Behavior of markets for new financial instruments, such as new types of annuities or forms of credit risk transfer, which have not yet been present in adverse market conditions, may be particularly subject to uncertainty in this sense. Systemic crises relating to insurance in Korea and Jamaica have related to losses on the innovation for insurance companies of offering deposit like instruments (IMF, 2001).

Responses to uncertainty, for example by insurance underwriters, may be to apply subjective probabilities to uncertain events (such as the enhanced credit risk, interest rate risk and mortality trends in the light of medical advances) and add a risk premium. But agents often tend to judge such probabilities by the actions of others ('herding'[8]), which can collectively lead to errors affecting the entire industry. (One feature of herding is that individually low-risk strategies may collectively raise system fragility.)

Developing this point further, Guttentag and Herring (1984) note that bankers are prone to disregard low-frequency, high-impact risks. Again this may be applicable to insurance companies. Their example distinguishes between systematic market risks, such as recession and financial crises – which are subject to much greater uncertainty. In the case of recession, it is suggested that ex ante risk pricing is generally accurate as such events occur frequently and are generally well understood. But for financial crises and other uncertain events, there is no such presumption; competition may drive prudent creditors from the market, as they are undercut by those disregarding the likelihood of financial crisis, because of ignorance or hope of competitive advantage.

In addition to competition, various psychological factors underlying this pattern of 'disaster myopia'[9] may be identified, notably a tendency to calculate probabilities by how easily past occurrences are brought to mind, which declines with time, as well as institutional factors such as short periods over which loan officers are assessed, and asymmetry of outcomes for managers and shareholders. These tendencies, which imply declining expectations of financial crises during periods of calm, may lead to declining capital positions, loosening of 'equilibrium' price and quantity rationing of credit, and hence increased vulnerability of creditors to shocks, since the actual probability distribution of shocks has not changed. Expectations and reality may thus drift apart during a period of calm, until a financial shock leads to an abrupt increase in credit rationing, as lenders become aware of their imprudence triggering a crisis. There is an obvious extension of this point to annuities pricing and in particular long-term shocks to mortality, as well as possible market crashes and their impact on the asset portfolio, sharp increases in credit risk, and permanently lower interest rates affecting guaranteed annuity rates. There is also an extension to the behavior of regulators, who often have accepted conventional market judgments, when those proved to be over optimistic in retrospect.

Third, Davis (1995) notes financial crises have frequently followed changes in market structure and suggests that changes in entry conditions in financial markets can provide a supplementary set of underlying factors and transmission mechanisms for excessive risk taking and subsequent financial instability. Again we consider it applicable to insurance companies selling annuities. Note that EMU, following on from the Single Market, generates considerable scope for changes in market structure in insurance, with in particular formerly oligopolistic markets being subject to new entry either directly or cross-border, albeit subject to fiscal and regulatory barriers. Indeed, as shown in Mathur (2001), even the US has a fairly concentrated market for life products, with 41 per cent provided by the top 15 firms, a figure Europe may well tend to.

Easing of entry barriers may be caused by deregulation (such as the Single Market), technical progress (such as innovative product design) or market developments reducing the comparative advantage of incumbents over new entrants (such as loss of reputation due to mis-selling). Note that such a framework does not require actual new entry – rather, the key is that the sunk (irrecoverable) costs of market entry should decline. This may be reflected in more competitive behavior by incumbents, in order to protect themselves from the threat of entry. It is commonly observed that such changes in entry barriers typically do not merely entail reductions in profits and/or smooth elimination of excess capacity, but rather that reductions in risk pricing go beyond the equilibrium level (that is, the level at which intermediaries can make normal profits in the long term), leaving the institutions involved vulnerable to financial instability.

It is argued that the following mechanisms, *inter alia*, may play a role. First, if new entrants to financial markets can induce clients to switch away from established relationships, information-based linkages will be weakened and existing information devalued. For example adverse selection of annuitants could increase. Second, uncertainty may be increased by new entry. Incumbents may be unable accurately to predict the responses of new entrants to changing conditions, and their existing knowledge of market dynamics will be rendered less useful. Entrants, inexperienced in the market, will face even greater uncertainty. Unaware of the dynamics of supply and demand in the market, they may be prone to herd-like behavior. Third, as above, competition may cause firms to make inadequate provision for uncertain events such as sharp falls in mortality, because firms that make adequate provision are undercut by those disregarding such possibilities for reasons of ignorance or competitive advantage. New entrants may be particularly prone to such undercutting. Sufficiently short time-horizons may even make firms disregard standard risks such as those on reinvestment in their risk appraisals, and so again, via the process of competition, help to reduce the prudential standards for the whole market. Hit-and-run entry as predicted by the theory of contestable markets must by its nature have a short-time horizon.[10] Finally, competition for market share, as stressed by managerial theories of the firm – an approach frequently adopted by entrants, or in new and developing markets – may lead to cumulative reductions in market prices until it is checked by losses for participants, and withdrawal or retrenchment. Such competition may persist if participants can cross-subsidize their operations from others making excess profits (in other words there is a market failure elsewhere) and they are relatively immune to take-overs, as is the case for mutuals.

3.7.3 Ageing of the Population, Insurance and Annuities

Further perspectives on risks are provided by the consequences of population ageing. As discussed in Davis (2002b), the prognosis among forecasters is for a major build-up of aggregate retirement funds in OECD countries owing to saving by workers in the large 'baby boom' prime saving cohort up to around 2010, followed by decumulation, including a switch from pension funds to annuities.

As regards the build-up phase, Davis (2002b) points out that even if funds are invested in life insurance companies, avoidance of systemic risk is not guaranteed. Owing to the nature of their liabilities, as well as regulations (Section 3.4.2), life insurers tend to invest heavily in domestic bonds. As noted, a shortage of government bonds that may continue for some time ahead, as well as competition in asset management driving life insurers to increase returns, are already prompting more investment in higher-risk assets such as high-yield bonds and low-rated securitized loans. Besides their general effect on credit expansion, which could generate fragility in the non-financial sectors, such funds may feed a property boom. This could leave insurers as well as banks vulnerable to a downturn in the property cycle, as was the case in the Jamaican insurance crisis of 1996 (IMF, 2001). Following Allen and Gale (1999, 2000), if insurers become significantly involved in property investment and related credit finance, the massive inflows to pension funds as well as insurance companies could generate expectations of ongoing boosts to credit flows into property. There may also be increasing uncertainty about future such flows as ageing progresses. These in the past have tended to foreshadow asset bubbles generated by such credit flows.

Externalities in property lending are significant, owing to the effect of new construction on the profitability of contiguous buildings.

When insurance companies focus increasingly on debt claims as members approach retirement, competition may lead insurance companies and their investment managers again to be willing to take heightened credit risks in order to maximize their return on assets (Bishop (1998), Allen and Gale (1999)). This suggests again that insurers could increasingly invest in high-yield bonds and EME sovereign and corporate debt, and thus be vulnerable to credit risk to a greater extent than was the case in the past. Credit cycles could, in other words, affect them as well as banks. Solvency could be threatened directly for life insurance companies if a significant proportion of their assets defaulted.

A further key issue is whether asset prices will also be put under general downward pressure in coming decades by declining saving in OECD countries affecting the real interest rate or the risk premium. Schieber and Shoven (1994) note that given the correlation of ageing in OECD countries, and the likely decumulation of defined benefit pension fund assets, there could be widespread falls in asset prices, linked to high real interest rates. Supporting this, Erb et al. (1997) find a positive correlation in the US between the fraction of the population aged 25–45 and 65+ to stock returns,[11] while those aged 45–65 have a negative effect. Looking at a range of OECD and EME countries, they find a positive relation of stock returns to the average age of the population. Davis and Li (2003) show that there has been an impact from the demographic structure on equity and bond returns as well as the equity premium in the major industrial countries over the past 50 years. Brooks (2000) focuses on the relation between ageing and the demand for equities and bonds, and suggests that there will be excess demand for bonds and excess supply of equities in coming decades, with a marked decline in the returns on the retirement savings of baby boomers. Arguably the current low level of bond yields in countries such as the UK is a harbinger of these effects, exacerbated by misdirected regulation and accounting.

It should be noted that not all researchers agree that a meltdown is likely, see Poterba (1998). Changes in issuance, for example, might smooth equity returns. Nevertheless, the possibility means prudence is warranted. In this context, solvency could be threatened for life insurance companies and defined benefit pension funds that had made undertakings based on expected returns on assets formed during the bull period (as has been the case recently for the Japanese life insurers and pension funds and for UK insurers such as Equitable Life). Mismatched balance sheets could have particularly adverse consequences. There are obviously also implications for the need to only institute partial funding, retaining elements of pay-as-you-go as a form of insurance.

3.7.4 Issues Raised by Experience in Japan

We have already discussed the issue of Equitable Life. A key ongoing policy issue in Japan is the negative net worth of life insurance companies (and a number of pension funds). The pattern shows the downside of life insurance when there are guarantees on returns to beneficiaries in combination with poor risk management, restricted investment of assets, low levels of competition in asset management, and poor returns on the assets available. Although it resulted largely from life policies, the Japanese crisis is relevant both because failure will also affect any annuities and also because the regulatory lessons are applicable to annuities.

As was the case for Equitable Life, Japanese life insurers basically offered forward rate agreement options to their clients (mainly on life policies rather than annuities), at prevailing rates such as 5.5 per cent up to 1992 (Fukao, 2002). There was no duration matching of assets and liabilities, partly because most Japanese bonds are ten-year maturity. Average duration on the asset side has been five years and liabilities 15 to 20 years. As Japanese long-term interest rates have now fallen to 1–2 per cent, the firms have been unable to make returns sufficient to meet guarantees to policy holders. The life insurers also faced huge bad debts on loans. Accordingly a number have become insolvent. Indeed, since the failure of Nissan Life in April 1997, seven life insurance companies of the 20 traditional firms have failed, of whom five were mutual. The paradigm of 'disaster myopia' outlined above is germane.

Firms that failed went through a legal reorganization procedure to cut promised interest rates on their insurance policies, thus leading to major losses by consumers. Policy holders lost 10 per cent of their savings directly and had guaranteed rates reduced from 4 per cent to 1–2 per cent. A further 20 per cent would be charged on early withdrawal. The best strategy according to Fukao (2002) was to cancel a policy before bankruptcy and get a new one with a sound company – a form of 'run', from which unhealthy policy holders were excluded. Clearly, it is likely that uncertainty caused by these patterns may also have affected overall consumption.

Fukao (2002) points out also that the firms that failed had declared satisfactory solvency margins before closure, and more generally that the crisis was worsened by forbearance by the supervisory authorities. Assets may be included in solvency calculations that have no liquidation value, and also deferred tax liabilities and future profits can be included in net assets. Risk weights for equities are one-third of those for US insurance and real estate and foreign currency assets one-half. Due to this lenient solvency margin and slow closure, firms tended to be massively insolvent at the time of closure, worsening the losses of policy holders.

There is massive double gearing between Japanese banks and life insurers, with banks providing subordinated credit and surplus notes (non-voting redeemable preference shares) of Yen 2.3 trillion in 2000, and life insurers providing Yen 6.7 trillion in subordinated loans to banks, as well as owning Yen 7.7 billion in bank stocks. This sharply increases systemic risk, since failure of a bank or a life company impinges directly on the other sector. Also it weakens corporate governance. When Chiyoda Life failed in October 2000, Tokai bank lost Yen 74 billion.

Earlier on in the crisis (Clark, 1994), book value accounting[12] obscured poor performance of life insurers and prevented a clear assessment of solvency. It has also prevented institutions from selling poorly performing shares and prevented switching of asset managers (as both would entail realization of losses).

These difficulties may not be unique to Japan. As noted by IMF (2002c) life companies in Switzerland are unable to earn the guaranteed returns of 4 per cent on occupational pensions, given a market rate of 3.6 per cent. They had also not taken advantage of previous high returns to accumulate sufficient reserves (Bütler and Teppa, 2002). There has been comment on possible difficulties of life insurers in southern European countries such as Italy, Spain, and Portugal as well as Belgium and France.

Besides lessons for regulation in respect of capital adequacy supervision, forbearance, accounting, price controls and portfolio restrictions applicable also to annuities, the Japanese case highlights the difficulties of life companies when bond yields fall sharply, as may occur in the accumulation phase of ageing. Whereas the main focus of losses was on life insurance and not annuities, it is relevant to note that the life companies made partially offsetting gains from errors in mortality assumptions, because life policies benefit when longevity is underestimated. Had the focus been annuities, the losses owing to underestimation of longevity would have rather aggravated the asset problems.

3.8 CONCLUSION

This chapter has covered the main issues in regulation of annuities, from three sides: prudential regulation of insurance companies, conduct of business regulation of insurance companies and the regulation of annuities within the overall pension system. We have also discussed forms of industry-wide risk that could be missed by detailed company-by-company regulation. Regulation of annuities is a vital part of a number of reformed pension systems around the world. Given the substantial risks highlighted as arising from inadequate pricing, regulation, 'disaster myopia', ageing and heightened competition, more research in these areas is needed.

Some aspects of regulation have been neglected in this chapter. One is organization of regulation; whether there should be a pillars approach to regulation, treating insurance, banking and securities as separate, a conglomerate approach with a lead regulator on the predominant business, or a single regulator (see the discussion in Mathur (2001)). There are also some issues relating to defined benefit occupational systems, where for example if a sponsoring firm of a defined benefit fund in the UK becomes insolvent, then the fund is used to buy deferred annuities for the members. Competition regulation may also be important, where in countries with concentrated insurance sectors, prices may become artificially high.

The structural analysis of Section 3.7 suggests that regulators should seek to develop 'macroprudential indicators' for insurance along the lines of those developed for banking (IMF, 2002b). For example, MWRs themselves could be monitored as a possible warning signal of intense competition, besides the portfolios and the mortality and interest rate assumptions made by life companies. Changes in market structure could be used as signals for possible increases in competition. Lack of government bonds of matching maturity – or very low yields on them – may be another danger signal, since they prompt mismatching and taking on of credit risk. Recent results suggesting that equity prices give useful warning signals of failure of banks via the 'distance to default' derived from the Black Scholes option pricing formula may also be valid for insurance companies (Gropp et al., 2002).

Finally, some EU issues may be highlighted. The advent of EMU will be an interesting case study in respect of market structure, since it facilitates cross-border purchase of annuities in a common currency (although fiscal and other restrictions prevent such competition being fully expressed as yet, and such barriers need to be eliminated in the interests of market efficiency). Harmonization of accounting standards becomes more urgent in an integrated market. As for banking, the issue arises whether and when transnational regulation of insurance companies becomes appropriate, especially as conglomerates operating on a cross-border basis become more common. As noted, pension reform makes resolution of issues relating to competition and stability all the more urgent.

NOTES

1. In fact the mortality experiences of the two pools are unlikely to be similar, due for example to age-specific shocks such as those due to AIDS affecting life policies taken out at a younger age and not annuities taken out at an older age. This limits the scope for hedging by this means.

2. This system was abolished after the potential impact of the 11 September 2001 attacks on New York led to asset price shifts entailing potential insolvency of insurers and pension funds. According to IMF (2002c) German insurers are now subject to an impairment rule whereby 'permanent' declines in asset values affect solvency calculations.
3. Where the latter may include suitable stress tests, conservative valuation methods and/or risk based capital requirements.
4. Reinsurers would need vast reserves to cover such risks. An example of difficulties in practice is in Switzerland where there is a national reinsurance company, called the 'security fund', whose reserves are quite low at 0.1 per cent of capital. To cover its own obligations, the fund would need to raise contribution rates when individual funds themselves face difficulty in meeting obligations.
5. Note that such guaranteed rates only apply to the promised return on traditional policies – variable annuities have technical rates that differ from the guaranteed rates and are not subject to explicit regulation, while the with-profits element of traditional policies may also use technical rates.
6. The rate is set to be reduced to 6.8 per cent shortly, owing to lower yields and higher longevity.
7. In practice, personal pensions in countries such as the UK – but not occupational pensions – may also be used as security for a loan or mortgage.
8. 'Herding' may be defined as willingness of financial institutions to imitate each other's portfolios and pricing strategies, even if this is contrary to long-run profit maximization.
9. 'Disaster myopia' may be defined as a tendency to disregard uncertain, low-probability, high-risk hazards.
10. Besides the features outlined above, which are of particular importance in financial markets, several more general features of competitive processes may cause overshooting of competitive equilibrium. Firms earning normal profits on their existing products may all be simultaneously attracted to situations offering potential for growth, but individual firms are unable to predict in advance whether rivals will follow. Such tendencies will be particularly marked if there is no clear ordering of firms in terms of likelihood of success. Once investments are sunk, entry decisions may be difficult to reverse. Moreover, if there are sunk costs, firms may find it optimal to stay in the market for some time even if they make losses, as they will lose sunk costs of reputation and so on if they leave. During this period, they may be vulnerable to adverse conditions in financial markets.
11. And thus a negative effect on prices.
12. A reform in the late 1990s shifted towards market value accounting (Pensions and Investments, 1997).

REFERENCES

Allen, F. and D. Gale (1999), 'Bubbles, Crises and Policy', *Oxford Review of Economic Policy*, **15**(3), 9–18.

Allen, F. and D. Gale (2000), 'Bubbles and Crises', *Economic Journal*, **110**, 236–55.

Bank of England (2001), *Financial Stability Review*, December 2001, London: Bank of England.

Bank of England (2002), *Financial Stability Review*, December 2002, London: Bank of England.

Bernheim, D. (1991), 'How Strong Are Bequest Motives?; Evidence Based on Estimates of the Demand for Life Insurance and Annuities', *Journal of Political Economy*, **99**, 899–927.

Bishop, G. (1998), 'Securitizing European Saving', Salomon Smith Barney, 1 December 1998.

Bishop, G. (2002), 'UK Defined Benefit Pension Funds; the Trustees' Nightmare', Salomon Smith Barney, 3 October 2002.

Blake, D. (1999), 'Annuities Markets; Problems and Solutions', *Geneva Papers on Risk and Insurance*, **24**, 358–75.

Blake, D. (2001), *An Assessment of the Adequacy and Objectivity of the Information Provided by the Board of the Equitable Life Assurance Society in Connection with the Compromise Scheme Proposal of 6 December 2001*, London: The Pensions Institute, Birkbeck College.

Blake, D. and W. Burrows (2001), 'Survivor Bonds; Helping to Hedge Mortality Risk', *Journal of Risk and Insurance*, **68**, 339–48.

Blake, D. and R. Hudson (2000), *Improving Security and Flexibility in Retirement; Full Technical Report*, London: Retirement Income Working Party.

Brooks, R. (2000), 'Life Cycle Portfolio Choices and Asset Market Effects of the Baby Boom', IMF Working Paper WP/00/18.

Bütler, M. and F. Teppa (2002), 'The Personal Discount Rate; Evidence from Swiss Pension Funds', Working Paper, University of Lausanne and University of Tilburg.

Cardinale, M., A. Findlater and M. Orszag (2002), *Paying Out Pensions; a Review of International Annuities Markets*, Watson Wyatt research report 2002–RU07.

Clark, R.L. (1994), *The Impact of Market Access and Investment Restrictions on Japanese Pension Funds*, Employee Benefit Research Institute Special Report SR-26, Washington, DC.

Davis, E.P. (1995), *Debt, Financial Fragility and Systemic Risk, Revised and Expanded Version*, Oxford: Oxford University Press.

Davis, E.P. (1999), 'Financial Data Needs for Macroprudential Surveillance: What Are the Key Indicators of Risk to Domestic Financial Stability?' Lecture Series No 2, Centre for Central Banking Studies, Bank of England.

Davis, E.P. (2001a), 'Financial Stability in the Euro Area – Some Lessons from US Financial History', in M. Balling, E.H. Hochreiter and E. Hennessy (eds), *Adapting to Financial Globalisation*, London and New York: Routledge.

Davis, E.P. (2001b), 'Regulation of Private Pensions – A Case Study of the United Kingdom', Occasional Paper No. OP15, London: Financial Services Authority.

Davis, E.P. (2002a), 'Prudent Person Rules or Quantitative Restrictions? The Regulation of Long-term Institutional Investors' Portfolios', *Journal of Pension Economics and Finance*, **1**, 157–91.

Davis, E.P. (2002b), 'Ageing and Financial Stability', in A. Auerbach and H. Herrmann (eds), *Ageing, monetary policy and financial markets*, Berlin: Springer.

Davis, E.P. (2002c), 'Pension Fund Management and International Investment – a Global Perspective', Discussion Paper 02–05, London: Pensions Institute, Birkbeck College.

Davis, E.P. (2002d), 'Institutional Investors, Corporate Governance and the Performance of the Corporate Sector', Discussion Paper 02-05, London: Pensions Institute, Birkbeck College; forthcoming in *Economic Systems*.

Davis, E.P. (2003), 'Comparing Bear Markets, 1973 and 2000', *National Institute Economic Review*, **183**, 78–89.

Davis E.P. and C. Li (2003), 'Demographics and asset prices in the major industrial economies', Brunel University Department of Economics and Finance, Discussion Paper No. 03-07.

Davis, E.P. and B. Steil (2001), *Institutional Investors*, Cambridge, MA: MIT Press.

Daykin, C. (2002), *Reserving for Annuities*, UK Government Actuary's Department, mimeo.

Dickinson, G. (1998a), 'Issues in the Effective Regulation of the Asset Allocation of Life Insurance Companies', in H. Blommestein and N. Funke (eds), *Institutional Investors in the New Financial Landscape*, Paris: OECD.

Dickinson, G. (1998b), 'The Impact of the Euro on the Investment and Treasury Management Policies of European Insurance Companies', Paper presented at the SUERF conference, Frankfurt.

Dilnot, A. and P. Johnson (1993), *The Taxation of Private Pensions*, London: Institute for Fiscal Studies.

Doyle, S. and J. Piggott (2000), 'Mandatory Annuity Design in Developing Countries', Research Paper No. 18, Retirement Economics Group, University of New South Wales.

Erb, C.B., C.R. Harvey and T.E. Viskanta (1997), 'Demographics and International Investment', *Financial Analysts Journal*, **53**, July/August, 14–28.

European Commission (2002), *Studies into the Methodologies to Assess the Overall Financial Position of an Insurance Undertaking from the Perspective of Prudential Supervision*, Study prepared by KPMG for the EC.

Financial Stability Forum (2000), *Report by the Study Group on Insurance Issues and Developments*, Basel.

Financial Times (2001), 'Equitable Debacle', by A. Bolger, 18 October 2001.

Financial Times (2002a), 'A Fair Value Approach', by A. Bolger, 14 March 2002.

Financial Times (2002b), 'Where the Risk Falls; Debt Mountain Threatens Avalanche', by V. Boland and S. Fidler, 31 May 2002.

Finsinger, J. and M.V. Pauly (1992), 'Reserve Levels and Reserve Requirements for Profit-Maximizing Insurance Firms' in G.H. Dionne and E. Scott (eds), *Foundations of insurance economics: Readings in economics and finance*, Huebner International Series on Risk, Insurance, and Economic Security, Norwell, MA and Dordrecht: Kluwer Academic, 685–704.

FSA (2001), *Memorandum to the Treasury Committee: Inquiry into the Regulatory Environment and the Management of Risk in the Life Assurance Sector Following the Equitable Life Affair*, London: Financial Services Authority, 9 February 2001.

FSA (2002a), *Financing the Future: Mind the Gap!*, London: Financial Services Authority.

FSA (2002b), *The Future Regulation of Insurance*, London: Financial Services Authority.

Fukao, M. (2002), 'Barriers to Financial Restructuring; Japanese Banking and Life Insurance Industries', Paper presented at the NBER conference on 'Structural impediments to growth in Japan', Tokyo, 18–19 March 2002.

Gropp, R., J. Vesala and G. Vulpes (2002), 'Equity and Bond Market Signals as Leading Indicators of Banking Fragility', Working Paper No. 150, Frankfurt: European Central Bank.

Guttentag, J.M. and R.J. Herring, (1984), 'Credit Rationing and Financial Disorder', *Journal of Finance*, **39**, 1359–82.

IMF (2001), *Experience with the Insurance Core Principles Assessments under Financial Sector Assessment Programs*, IMF/World Bank 21 August, 2001.

IMF (2002a), *Global Financial Stability Report, March 2002*, Washington DC: International Monetary Fund.

IMF (2002b), *Financial Soundness Indicators: Analytical Aspects and Country Practices*, Occasional Paper 212, Washington DC: International Monetary Fund.

IMF (2002c), *Global Financial Stability Report, June 2002*, Washington DC: International Monetary Fund.

IMF (2002d), *Global Financial Stability Report, December 2002*, Washington DC: International Monetary Fund.

James, E. and X. Song (2002), 'Annuities Markets around the World; Money's Worth and Risk Intermediation', Expanded version of paper presented at the American Economic Association meeting, January 2001.

James, E. and D. Vittas (1999), 'The Decumulation (Payout) Phase in Defined Contribution (DC) Pillars', Policy Research Working Paper No 2464, Washington DC: The World Bank.

Keeley, M.C. (1990), 'Deposit Insurance, Risk and Market Power in Banking', *American Economic Review*, **80**, 1138–99.

Knight, F.H. (1921), 'Risk, Uncertainty and Profit', Boston, No. 16 in a series of rare texts in economics, republished by the LSE.

Lunnon, M. (2002), *Annuitisation and Alternatives*, UK Government Actuary's Department, mimeo.

Mathur, S. K. (2001), 'Insurance Regulation; Some Issues', *Geneva Papers on Risk and Insurance*, **26**, 54–70.

Mitchell, O. S. (2002), 'The Role of Annuity Products in Financing Retirement', in A.J. Auerbach and H. Herrmann (eds), *Ageing, Financial Markets and Monetary Policy*, Heidelberg: Springer.

Pensions and Investments (1997), *Japan Dumps Fund Investment Restrictions*, 14 April, 1997.

Poterba, J.M. (1997), 'The History of Annuities in the United States', NBER Working Paper No. 6001.

Poterba, J.M. (1998), 'Population Age Structure and Asset Returns – an Empirical Investigation', NBER Working Paper No. 6774.

Rees, R., H.S.E. Gravelle and A. Wambach (1999), 'Regulation of Insurance Markets', *Geneva Papers on Risk and Insurance*, **24**, 55–68.

Rees, R. and Kessner E. (1999), 'Regulation and Efficiency of European Insurance Markets', *Economic Policy*, October 1999, 365–97.

Rule, D. (2001), 'Risk Transfer Between Banks, Insurance Companies and the Capital Markets; an Overview', *Bank of England Financial Stability Review*, December 2001, 137–59.

Schieber, S.J. and J. Shoven (1994), 'The Consequences of Population Ageing on Private Pension Fund Saving and Asset Markets', NBER Working Paper No. 4665.

Shafer, J. R. (1986), 'Managing Crises in the Emerging Financial Landscape', *OECD Economic Studies*, **8**, 56–77.

Valdes Prieto, S. (1998), *Risks in Pensions and Annuities; Efficient Designs*, Human Development Network, The World Bank.

Wadsworth, M., A. Findlater and T. Boardman (2001), 'Reinventing Annuities', Paper presented to the Staple Inn Actuarial Society, 16 January 2001.

Yermo, J. (2001), 'Private Annuities in OECD Countries', in *Insurance and Private Pension Compendium for Emerging Economies*, book 2, part 1:5 Paris: OECD, http://www.oecd.org/dataoecd/7/37/1815951.pdf

4. Annuity risk: volatility and inflation exposure in payments from immediate life annuities*

Chris Soares and Mark Warshawsky

4.1 TRENDS IN RETIREMENT PLANS: DEFINED BENEFIT TO DEFINED CONTRIBUTION

Over the last two decades, there has been a steady movement, gathering speed, around the world, in both public and private sectors, toward the defined contribution type of retirement plan and away from the defined benefit type. Much research has been done on the reasons for this shift; the primary causes have been identified as increased labor mobility, the possibility of higher returns on assets held in a defined contribution plan account, fewer distortions in work incentives, reduction in regulatory burden, and the flexibility usually gained in the distribution of assets during the working and, especially, retirement years. The defined benefit plan type generally offers the promise of lifetime (annuity) benefit payments during retirement, closely related to the level of earnings experienced during the working years (most typically, in the years just before retirement).[1] Defined contribution plans, on the other hand, offer market returns on contributions and broader options for distribution of accumulated balances.

In the face of the strong forces leading to the dominance of the defined contribution plan type, a legitimate set of questions can be posed: are certain types of risks being assumed, perhaps unknowingly, by holders of defined contribution retirement plans? Are these risks, in some measurable sense,

* The authors are with the US Department of the Treasury. Any views expressed, however, are those of the authors alone and not necessarily those of the Treasury Department. We appreciate helpful comments from conference participants and John Ameriks, Jeffrey Brown, James Duggan, and Kent Smetters, and assistance with data from Norman Carleton and Ron Koenecke at Treasury, and Stephen Goss, Alice Wade and Felicitie Bell at the Social Security Administration.

unduly large? Are there mechanisms available, at reasonable cost-benefit ratios, to control or modify these risks? Are the risks acceptable in light of the additional flexibilities obtained?

This short chapter focuses on the volatility, over time, of simulated initial monthly payments from individual immediate life annuities, as well as the inflation risk experienced after annuitization. Such annuities are those most relevant and available to participants in defined contribution pension plans and individual retirement accounts. We examine a recent time horizon, 1983 through 2002, as relevant to current and likely future economic and policy conditions. We also record high frequency results – monthly since the beginning of 1983 through December 2002 and daily since the beginning of February 2002 through December 2002 – in order to get a better sense of the volatility of income from life annuities that might be experienced by households timing their retirement and purchase of life annuities, or who are aware of the outcomes of other similarly situated individuals. The daily simulations are also compared to actual daily payments over the period from a AAA-rated life insurance company, which provides a rough gauge of how well our model tracks actual market outcomes.

We examine fixed nominal annuities, fixed increasing annuities (whose payments increase with the rate of inflation expected at the time of annuity issue), and since 1998, inflation-adjusted annuities. The latter two products do not currently widely exist in the United States, but certainly are within the realm of practical and technical possibility, and are shown to illustrate methods of handling post-retirement inflation risk. We also consider a phased purchase of fixed nominal annuities over a three-year period prior to retirement. Volatility is measured primarily by the standard deviation of monthly payments, and their percentage change over one-year periods.

It should be noted that the evaluation of risk for the defined contribution plan type is relative because, despite its notional stability, the defined benefit plan type is also subject to risk. In the case of private plans, insolvency or inadequate prefunding can reduce pension payments. In the case of government plans, demographic and political risk could result in reductions to expected benefits. In either case, contributions to a defined benefit retirement plan that are made prior to vesting or retirement can be lost in the event an individual dies or no longer works. By contrast, in most defined contribution plans, contributions are generally quickly vested and bequeathable.

There is a strong public policy interest in retirement plans, whether those directly sponsored by public sector entities for all workers and families or their employees, those sponsored by private sector entities for their employees, or those purchased by individuals and households for themselves. The public interest can be stated as a desire to assure financial security in retirement, at a reasonable cost and level of risk, with the maximum possible flexibility. This public interest is implemented in the form of direct sponsorship, tax incentives, insurance guarantees, and regulatory restrictions, guidelines, and oversight.

4.2 DEFINED CONTRIBUTION PLANS: THE DISTRIBUTION PHASE AND IMMEDIATE LIFE ANNUITIES

The defined contribution plan type is subject to certain risks, potentially borne by the plan beneficiary, in both the accumulation and distribution phases. In the accumulation phase, these risks include the possibility of poor investment performance and, depending on plan rules, the use of assets for purposes other than the fundamental one of a primary pension plan: financial security in retirement.

The distribution phase is less studied and understood. Most defined contribution plans in the United States offer little structure to the distribution of assets. Although life annuities are sometimes offered by the plan, they are almost never mandated. Clearly this state of affairs offers maximum flexibility, but it also exposes the retired household to the risk of outliving its assets if the household is not otherwise covered by a defined benefit plan or does not have a significant stock of asset holdings. As has been formally demonstrated by Mitchell et al. (1999) and by Ameriks et al. (2001) using expected utility and asset return simulation methodologies, respectively, longevity risk is substantial and the insurance value of a life annuity is significant compared to the alternate strategy of phased withdrawals of assets.

Moreover, there is a potential moral hazard problem in old age: if the retired household mistakenly employs its assets in excess spending or poor investments, it will have to fall back on a social safety net provided by government welfare programs or private charity. In fact, largely to prevent these problems and to reduce adverse selection (explained below), life annuities are mandated in primary defined contribution pension plans in the United Kingdom. In discussions of reforming of the United States social security system by establishing personal accounts, annuities are prominently mentioned as a distribution mechanism (President's Commission Report, December 2001, p. 56).

Whether made available in a defined contribution pension plan or purchased as an individual product sold in the voluntary market, two specific areas of concern have been highlighted about fixed immediate life annuities: they are costly for many potential annuitants, and they are risky.

The first concern has been investigated intensively in a series of published articles, many collected in the volume by Brown et al. (2001a). These authors confirm that immediate life annuities sold in a voluntary market are subject to adverse selection: that is, the tendency of individuals in poor health (with impaired longevity prospects) to avoid life annuities. This tendency leads to an increase in annuity prices of about 10 per cent as insurers must anticipate annuitants with a longer expected lifespan than average individuals in the general population. In addition, there are administrative and sales costs embedded in annuity prices, particularly for those annuities sold in the individual (as opposed to the group) market. Yet the authors also find that an index of actuarial fairness (or money's worth as they call it) of individual annuities improved substantially over the decades of the 1980s and 1990s. A recent finding on this score, in Poterba and Warshawsky (2000), indicated that, using projected annuitant mortality and government bond rates as the benchmark, life annuities issued in the individual market in the United States, by some hundred insurance companies, in 1998 have had an average money's worth of nearly one.[2]

Burtless (2000) has expressed the second concern. The risk referred to here is not that, once a fixed life annuity is purchased, regular income payments will not be paid. Rather, it is the risk that at the point in time they retire, workers may find it expensive to purchase nominal fixed annuities because annuity prices will be, in some sense, too high (owing to interest rates being, in some sense, too low). Also, if they purchase fixed nominal annuities, workers will be exposed to the risk of uncertain future inflation. Burtless claims that these risks, combined with the more conventional investment risk in the accumulation phase, are so significant and daunting that 'they challenge the ability of a pension system based solely on individual accounts to deliver reliable income replacement in old age' (p. 9).

To back up this claim, Burtless produces calculations of account balances and annuity income, based on certain assumptions and annual data on asset returns, interest rates, and price inflation over the period from 1871 through 1999. In his empirical work, Burtless emphasizes the variability of asset returns, and hence the variability of account balances at the point of retirement. He also mentions, however, the importance of fluctuations in long-term interest rates which determine annuity prices. He notes that the simulated account balance/labor earnings ratio was about the same for a worker who retired in 1982 as one who retired during the Great Depression. Yet Burtless found that the replacement rate provided by the defined contribution plan of the 1982 retiree was about two-thirds larger because interest rates (and hence, annuity income) were so much higher in the early 1980s than in the early 1930s.

4.3 EMPIRICAL EVIDENCE: SIMULATED AND ACTUAL, MONTHLY AND DAILY

In return for a single premium to the insurance company, the fixed nominal annuity pays a constant stream of payments, generally monthly, to an individual, or, in the case of a joint-and-survivor annuity, a couple. An increasing annuity is also a nominal annuity, but its payments increase at a fixed rate determined at the time of purchase. Finally, an inflation-adjusted annuity has payments that increase with the rate of inflation actually experienced. Obviously, increasing and inflation-adjusted annuities will have lower initial payments than the fixed annuity for a given premium.

Our simulated annuity payments are produced by a model which considers the annuitant mortality rates projected using social security cohort tables and the full-term structure of implied spot interest rates based on Treasury securities at the end of every month (or day) during the period of our analysis. (See the Appendix for more details.) For the most part, we use simulated annuity payments because data on actual prices on life annuities issued to 65-year-olds are not available for most of the time horizon for the frequencies we desire, nor for the annuity types (increasing and inflation-adjusted) we imagine for the United States. The simulated annuity payments reflect the factors determining the changes in annuity prices over time – interest and mortality rates. For the monthly simulations shown below, we consider only straight life annuities, that is, those annuities whose payments stop when the annuitant dies. In the daily simulations, because of the nature of the product for which we have actual payment data, we consider annuities with guarantee periods; that is, annuities whose payments continue for the length of the guarantee period if the annuitant dies before the end of the period and for life if the annuitant dies after the end of the guarantee period.

4.3.1 Monthly Simulations: Volatility in Initial Payments

Figure 4.1 shows the monthly payment per $100 000 single premium for nominal immediate fixed life annuities, simulated over the period 1983 through 2002, issued to 65-year-old male and female individuals and couples. We focus on the joint-and-survivor annuity because most households enter retirement as married couples. For example, the payment was as high as $1148 for a joint-and-survivor annuity issued to a 65-year-old couple in May 1984, and as low as $535 in September 2002. Over the entire time period, the monthly nominal initial payment for a joint-and-survivor annuity averaged $742 and had a standard deviation of $131.

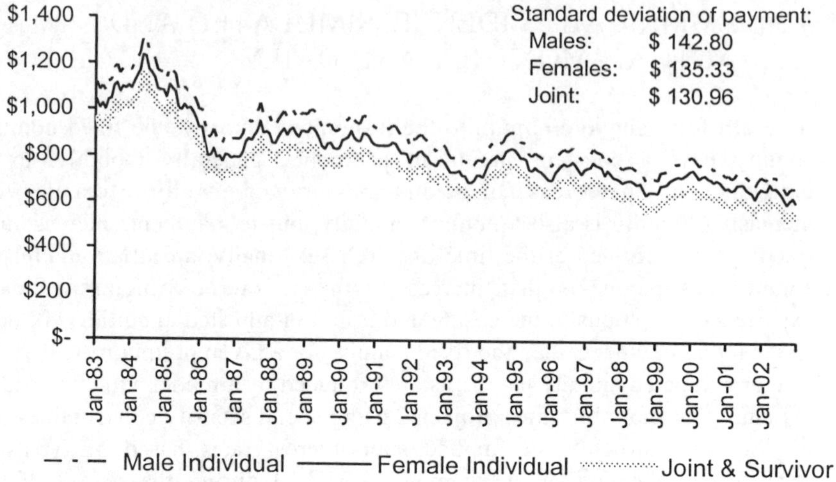

Figure 4.1 Monthly payment per $100 000 single premium nominal immediate fixed annuity: 1983–2002 simulations

Besides range and deviation, another way of showing the volatility of annuity payments is to calculate one-year differences in monthly payments from nominal immediate fixed joint-and-survivor annuities simulated over the 1983–2002 period. This statistic might also be considered a measure of envy or regret resulting from the ill-timed purchase of a life annuity. As seen in Figure 4.2, one-year differences are volatile and can be large – as high as +21 per cent in September 1994 and as low as -28 per cent in March 1986.

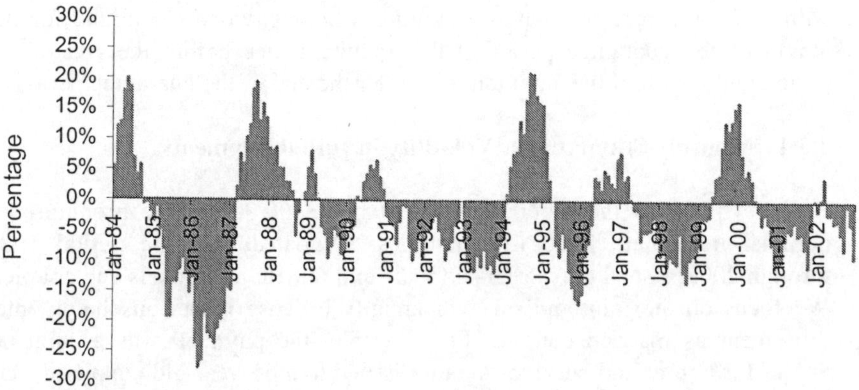

Note: Because the graph contains first differences, it is based on simulations beginning in 1983, but showing data beginning in 1984.

Figure 4.2 One-year differences in monthly payments nominal immediate fixed joint-and-survivor annuity: 1983–2002 simulations

Figure 4.3 shows the source of the volatility of annuity payments – interest rates. Although in our simulated pricing for nominal and increasing annuities we employ the entire horizon of implied spot interest rates derived from the full maturity spectrum of Treasury securities traded at the end of the month over the period 1983–2002, in the figure we only show one illustrative rate – the implied spot rate for a bond maturing in the twentieth year. Here we convert the annuity payment from monthly to annual to achieve comparability with interest rates. Clearly, annuity payments track interest rates fairly closely, and show similar volatility.

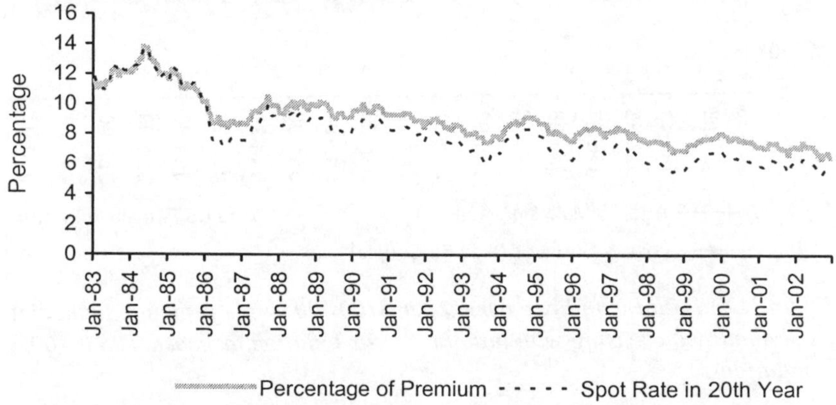

Figure 4.3 Interest rates and annual payment as percentage of single premium nominal immediate fixed joint-and-survivor annuity: 1983–2002 simulations

The volatility in nominal interest rates can come from many sources, including changing inflation expectations. Hence, we decided to investigate whether a nominal fixed annuity with monthly payments increasing based on a forecast of experts of long-range (ten-year average) inflation at the time of purchase would exhibit less volatility.[3] In addition, we wanted to see whether this increasing annuity would adequately address inflation risk during the retirement period, another aspect of annuity risk.

Figure 4.4 shows the initial monthly payment per $100 000 single premium for nominal immediate life annuities increasing with an initial ten-year inflation forecast, simulated over the period 1983 through 2002, issued to 65-year-old male and female individuals and couples. We again focus on the joint-and-survivor annuity because most households enter retirement as married couples. For example, the initial payment was as high as $779 for a joint-and-survivor annuity issued to a 65-year-old couple in May 1984, and as low as $406 in September 2002. Over the entire time period, the monthly nominal initial payment for a joint-and-survivor annuity averaged $526 and had a standard deviation of $72.

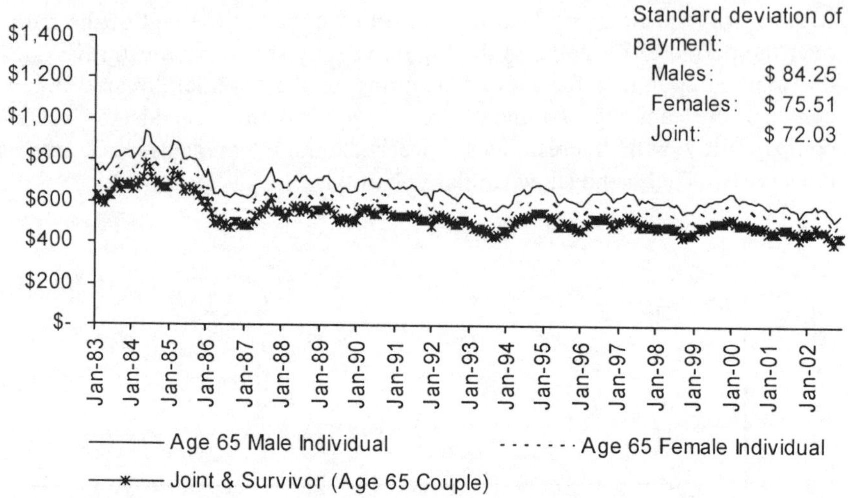

Figure 4.4 Initial monthly payment per $100 000 single premium immediate fixed annuity increasing with initial ten-year inflation forecast: 1983–2002 simulations

The increasing annuity does not reduce the volatility of initial payments. As indicated above, the range and standard deviation of payments are large. Also, as shown in Figure 4.5, the one-year differences in monthly initial payments from immediate fixed increasing joint-and-survivor annuities simulated over the 1983–2002 period exhibit considerable volatility. The one-year differences can be large – as high as +26 per cent in September 1994 and as low as -33 per cent in March 1986 – actually greater volatility than the nominal fixed annuity. Of course, the increasing annuity has longer duration than the nominal fixed annuity.

Finally, we consider an alternate strategy to reduce volatility in initial payments from nominal fixed (and increasing) annuities, namely, phased purchases over a short time period. In particular, we consider a three-year purchase period, represented here by averaging the simulated nominal payments over the same month in three consecutive years. In Figure 4.6, we show one-year differences in initial monthly payments from a three-year phased purchase of nominal joint-and-survivor immediate fixed annuities. The volatility is reduced considerably – the worst observation is about -13 per cent in June 1987, and, more recently, one-year differences were rarely over 6 per cent in either positive or negative directions.

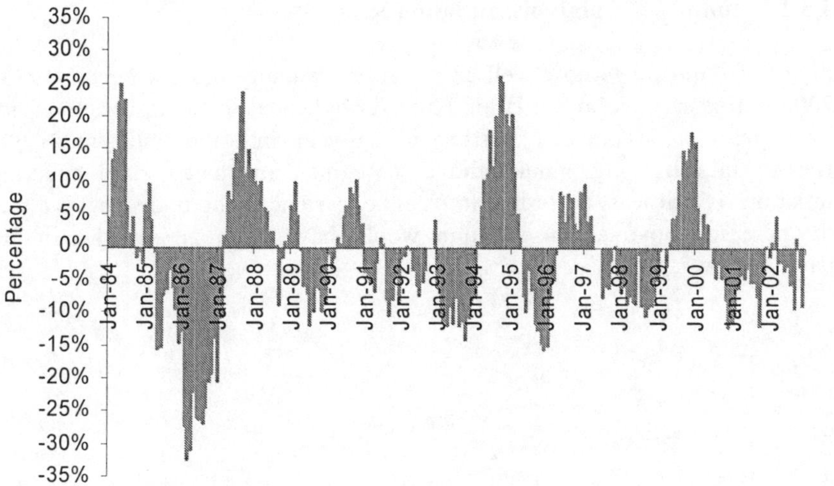

Note: The graph is based on simulations beginning in 1983, but showing data beginning in 1984.

Figure 4.5 One-year differences in initial monthly payments immediate increasing joint-and-survivor annuity:1983–2002 simulations

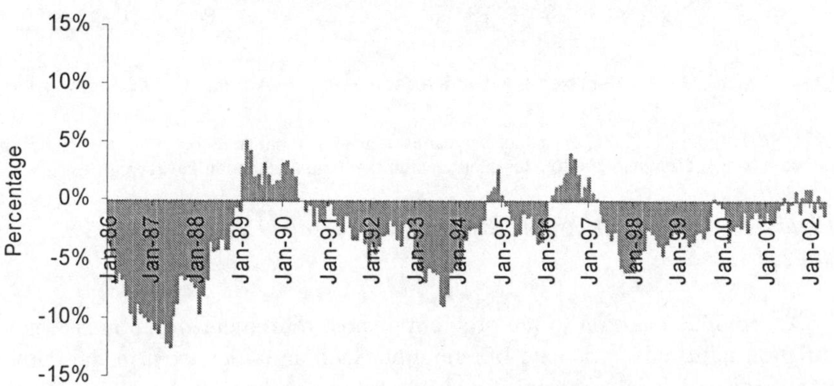

Note: The graph is based on simulations beginning in 1983, but showing data beginning in 1986.

Figure 4.6 One-year differences in initial monthly payments nominal fixed joint-and-survivor annuities purchased over three years: 1983–2002 simulations

4.3.2 Monthly Simulations: Inflation Risk

Figure 4.7 illustrates how well an increasing annuity did during the 1983–2002 period in covering inflation risk.[4] As indicated in the figure, forecasts by experts consistently overestimated ten-year inflation until late 1998. Hence, an increasing annuity did a more than adequate job of covering inflation risk, at least according to recent experience. The trade-off for a rate of increase above actual inflation would have been an initial monthly payment lower than necessary.

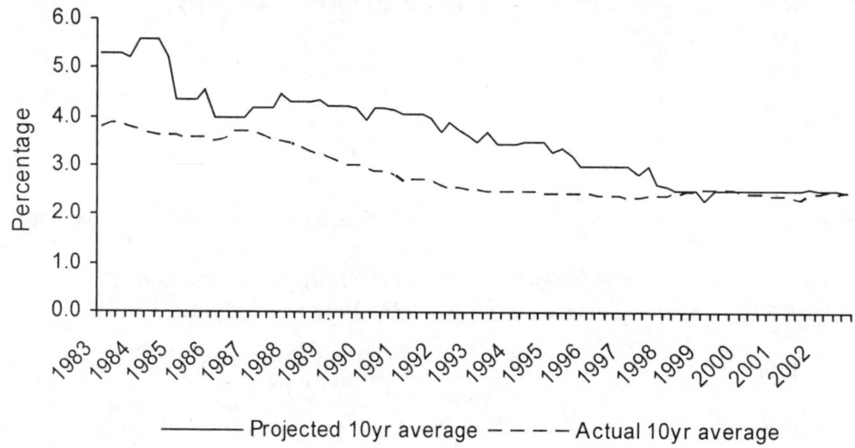

Note: Beginning in 1992Q3, the actual 10-year average shown above incorporates the long-range inflation forecast made in 2002Q2 for quarters after that date included in the average.

Figure 4.7 Actual versus forecast ten-year average CPI inflation: 1983–2002 simulations

An obvious solution to the problem of post-retirement inflation risk is an inflation-adjusted immediate life annuity. Such annuities exist in the United Kingdom and it is technically possible to issue them in the United States owing to the existence since 1997 and 1998 of Treasury inflation-protected securities (TIPS). Nevertheless, these annuities are not widely issued in the United States.[5] Moreover, evidence produced by Brown et al. (2001b) from the United Kingdom indicates that the money's worth of inflation-adjusted annuities is worse than that of nominal annuities. This is likely owing to the absence of inflation-protected corporate securities, whose yields would be higher than those of Treasury securities. Inflation-adjusted corporate securities would be the natural preference of insurance companies skilled in investing in the corporate bond and mortgage markets and issuing such insurance products.

It should be noted that our annuity pricing methodology is more limited in the inflation-adjusted case than in the nominal cases, because the time period of analysis only begins in 1998 when 30-year TIPS were first issued, and a full-term structure of implied real spot rates is impossible to calculate. Also the current TIPS market has somewhat limited depth. Several important caveats result: our estimates of prices of inflation-adjusted annuities are probably lower (payments higher) than would obtain in an actual market, and the volatility of our simulation results might differ from that of an actual inflation-adjusted annuity.

In Figure 4.8, the initial monthly payment per $100 000 premium is compared with the payment on a nominal fixed annuity. Obviously, the initial payment for the inflation-adjusted annuity is lower, but it covers inflation risk and it is also substantially less volatile, at least over the period for which we have data. This lower volatility is also exhibited in Figure 4.9, where the one-year differences in initial monthly payments are shown for the inflation-adjusted annuity. The maximum one-year difference is under 10 per cent in either a positive or negative direction, a reduction of over 45 per cent relative to the maximum one-year differences for the nominal fixed or increasing annuity over the same time period.

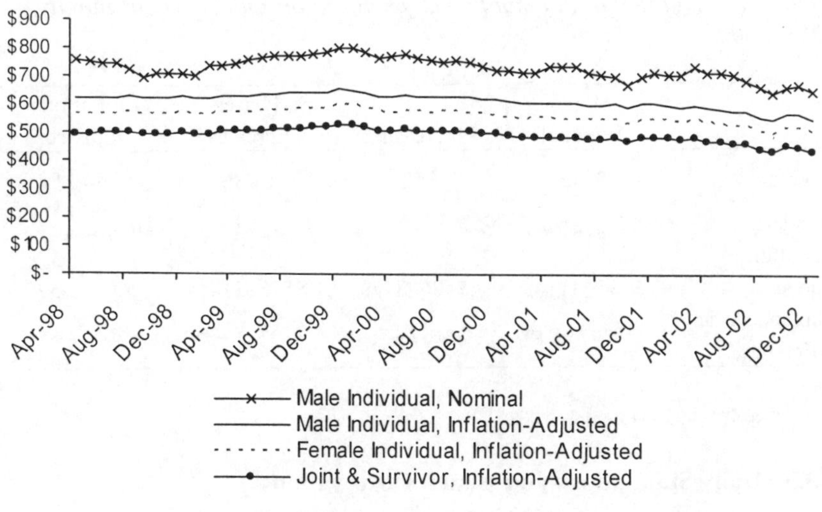

Figure 4.8 Initial monthly payment per $100 000 premium inflation-adjusted annuity: 1998–2002 simulations

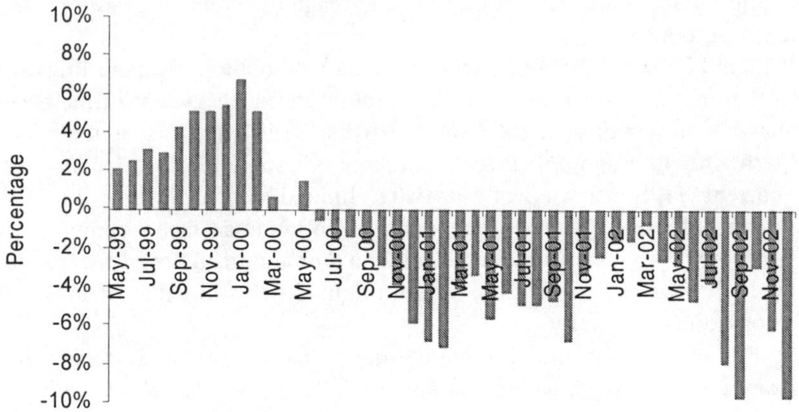

Note: The graph is based on simulations beginning in 1988, but showing data beginning in 1989.

Figure 4.9 One-year differences in initial monthly payment inflation-adjusted joint-and-survivor annuity: 1998–2002 simulations

Table 4.1 summarizes the main results of our monthly simulations.

Table 4.1 Simulated initial monthly payments, joint-and-survivor annuity, 1983–2002

	Nominal	Increasing	Phased purchase	Inflation-adjusted*
Average	$742	$526	$736	$492
Standard deviation	$131	$72	$104	$21
Range	$535–$1148	$406–$779	$578–$1014	$437–$529
Max. one-year difference	−28% / +21%	−33% / +26%	−13% / +5%	−10% / +7%

Note: * April 1998 to December 2002.

4.3.3 Daily Simulations and Actual Observations

To get a rough idea of how well our model simulates payment amounts, we compare our results to actual annuity payment data. In Figure 4.10, we show simulated monthly payment rates from annuities issued on a daily basis. In particular, we show the monthly initial payment per $100 000 single premium for nominal immediate fixed life annuities, simulated over the period 1 February 2002 through 31 December 2002, issued to 65-year-old male and female individuals and couples. Unlike the monthly statistics in Figures 4.1 through 4.9, here we consider immediate life statistics with guarantee periods – ten years for individuals and 20 years for couples. We again focus on the joint-and-survivor annuity because most households enter retirement as married couples.

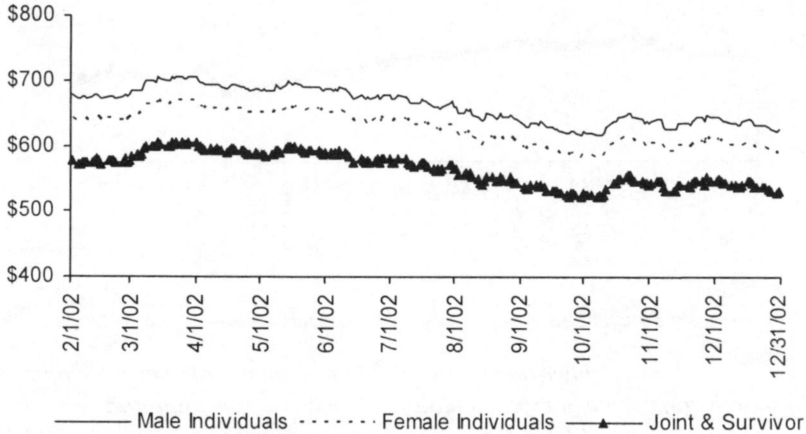

Figure 4.10 Monthly payment per $100 000 premium, nominal fixed annuity (with 120-month guarantee period for individuals, 240 months for joint-and-survivor); daily simulations, 2/1/02 to 12/31/02

In Figure 4.11, we show monthly payment rates on joint-and-survivor nominal fixed immediate life annuities actually available over the Internet issued by an AAA-rated life insurance company. Clearly rates are changed frequently, but not as often as daily (although the frequency does appear to pick up toward the end of the period), and hence volatility is somewhat lower than we have simulated. We use a money's worth calculation to judge how close our payments come to those of this particular company. Figure 4.12 shows the money's worth ratios (actual payment over simulated payment) in a relatively small band around 1.0. As interest rates increase, the money's worth ratios decline somewhat; apparently, this insurance company lags changes in interest rates slightly in its annuity pricing. A money's worth ratio so close to one is surprising because the insurance company must cover its expenses and make a profit. It is feasible here, however, because the insurance company likely invests in long-term corporate securities earning yields higher than the interest rates based on Treasury securities that we use. It is also possible that this insurance company has alternative, less conservative, mortality views than ours, which are based on the Social Security Administration's intermediate projections of improvements in life expectancy. In any case, our simulations follow the level and trend in the actual payment data very closely.

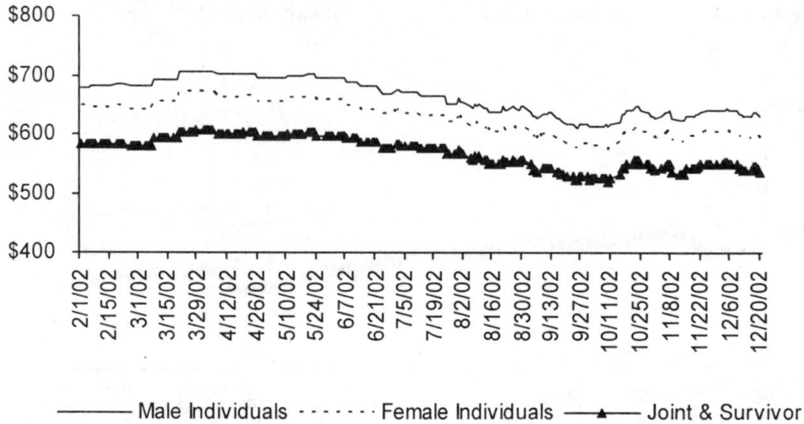

Figure 4.11 Monthly payments per $100 000 premium, nominal fixed annuity (120-month guarantee for individuals, 240 months for joint-and-survivor); daily Internet quotes, AAA-rated life insurance company, 2/1/02 to 12/20/02

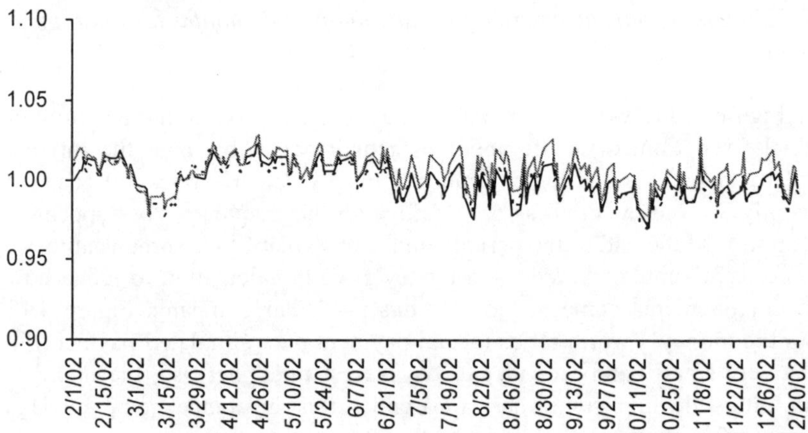

Figure 4.12 Daily money's worth ratios, nominal fixed annuity (actual payment / simulated payment), 2/1/02 to 12/20/02

4.4 STRATEGIES AND POSSIBLE POLICY IMPLICATIONS

We posed a set of questions at the beginning of this chapter, on whether the risks arising from defined contribution plans are too large, are avoidable, or are worth the trade-off for other advantages obtained. As applied to life annuities, we transposed these questions mainly in terms of the volatility of initial retirement payments, over time, produced by annuities. Clearly the volatility of fixed and increasing annuity income over the recent time horizon is generally not as large as that cited by Burtless when he compared the early 1930s and early 1980s. Nevertheless, by some measures (for example, annual differences), it can be significant. What are the options available to reduce the effect of this volatility, while still obtaining the considerable advantages of defined contribution plans?

As we saw in the prior section, because of the lower volatility of real interest rates, inflation-adjusted annuities have much lower volatility than nominal fixed and increasing annuities, and hence represent lower risk in the sense that we are discussing. In addition, these annuities have the obvious advantage of providing excellent coverage for post-retirement inflation risk. Probably an important challenge to inflation-adjusted annuities is public understanding and appreciation of the size and scope of inflation risk over a potentially extended retirement period. Another challenge to these annuities is that currently the only securities that are inflation-protected in the United States are issued by the Federal Government; owing to lower returns on government securities than yielded by private securities, annuities backed by these securities would tend to offer lower payments. This is an area worthy of further exploration by financial engineers and researchers.

Another option is to phase the purchase of fixed annuities over a short period of time. As we saw in the prior section, this smoothing of purchases reduces the volatility of initial annuity payments over time. There is presumably some increase in administrative costs and complexity from this strategy, but automation could reduce these costs substantially. It is consistent with phased retirement, an important new trend in labor force participation at older ages. Moreover, it can be implemented with the purchase of annuities with staggered deferral periods, so that payments begin all at once. A close variant of this strategy would be a one-time purchase of an immediate variable life annuity with the underlying investment pool a diversified collection of medium-term fixed income securities.

A modest step toward smoothing the volatility of initial payments could be accomplished without needing a phase-in purchase by having the insurance company smooth its immediate annuity payment rates by basing annuity prices on moving averages of long-term interest rates over short time periods, say three or four months. Although it may be difficult to require this in the individual market, where the competitive pressure to achieve the highest possible current payment rates leads to mark-to-market pricing, some modest smoothing should be possible to achieve in immediate contracts negotiated with group retirement plans, at a cost. In particular, the insurance company can pursue hedging strategies using interest rate futures and options extending three months, or alter its investment strategy appropriately. As explained in Poterba and Warshawsky (2000), the prices of annuities purchased by the Thrift Savings Plan for its beneficiaries through a bid-out group contract are based on a three-month moving average of government bond interest rates.

Additional research is warranted into other approaches to mitigate annuity risk and promote investment diversification generally. There may be a place for immediate variable annuities based on more volatile asset classes, such as equities or real estate. Of course, there is no volatility in the initial payments from immediate variable annuities, as the initial payment is based on a fixed assumed interest rate, usually 4 per cent. The volatility from such annuities occurs after the initial payment, when the underlying asset portfolio changes value, and indeed that is the advantage of fixed annuities, whether nominal or inflation-adjusted – they offer more predictability in the stream of income received during retirement.

Further research into the annuity risk and diversification properties of reverse annuity mortgages could also prove fruitful. Finally, investigation is needed into the diversification effects of other asset classes in the accumulation phase, both in the individual account held as part of the defined contribution plan, and in the household's net worth held outside of formal retirement plans, especially owner-occupied housing. In particular, it would be helpful to know more about the appropriate role of bonds and other interest-rate-sensitive investments in a dynamic investment strategy for an accumulation portfolio, as retirement is approached.

APPENDIX

We use the following formula to derive the monthly payment A from a \$100 000 premium immediate annuity:

$$A = \frac{100\,000}{\sum_{t=1}^{599} \frac{M_t}{[(1+i_t)^{1/12}]^t}} \tag{4.1}$$

where M_t is the probability that a person will live t months after exact age 65 conditional on having lived to age 65, and i_t is the interest rate in period t.

The nominal interest rates used in the annuity calculations come from a Treasury Department summary file of implied spot rates derived on a daily basis from Treasury security yield curves. The file contains rates at six-month intervals out to 30 years (we use the last rate in the series to discount after age 95) for dates beginning in late 1982. We use the rates on the last business day of the month in our calculations.

The appropriate mortality rates to use in the calculation are cohort rates for the annuitant population. Because the only published mortality tables for the annuitant population are period tables, we use the method of Mitchell et al. (1999) to convert the annuitant period tables to cohort tables. We assume that the ratio of cohort mortality risk (for the birth cohort age 65 in the reference year) to period mortality risk (in the year the individual turns 65) for a given age is the same for the annuitant population as that for the social security area population. Specifically,

$$AC_t^a = \frac{SC_t^a}{SP_{t+65}^a} AP_{t+65}^a \tag{4.2}$$

where AC is the annuitant cohort mortality, SP is the SSA period mortality, and so on, a is the age, t is the mortality table year, $65 \leq a \leq 115$, and $1918 \leq t \leq 1937$. (Note that this is equivalent to assuming that the decline in mortality risk between a person age x in year y and a person age x in year $y + (x - 65)$ will be the same in the annuitant population as projected for the social security area population). These assumed cohort annuitant mortality rates are then converted to the conditional rates found in equation (4.1).

We created annuitant period life tables for 1984–99 by linearly interpolating between the published 1983 IAM Basic period life tables and the Annuity 2000 basic tables.[6] We 'grew' annuitant tables for 2001 and 2002 from the Annuity 2000 table by applying the same change in mortality at each age as found in the SSA period tables for those years. The SSA period tables came from the background data for the 2002 Social Security Trustees' Report (TR02).[7]

Because we want the calculations to represent the price of an annuity as it would have been calculated at a particular date (that is, without the benefit of hindsight with regard to mortality outcomes), we need cohort tables that are generated from data available in the year of presumed purchase. We had cohort tables for 1935 to 1937 from the 2000 to 2002 Trustees' Reports, respectively. We created a 1927 cohort table by interpolating between 1925 and 1930 tables published in a 1992 SSA Actuarial Study. To anchor the cohort series, we created a cohort table for 1983 by first interpolating between period tables for 1980–2040 published in a 1983 SSA Actuarial Study (Faber and Wade, 1983), and then compiling the appropriate mortality rates for the 1918 (age 65 in 1983) birth year. Finally, we interpolated between the 1918, 1927 and 1935 cohort tables to fill in the missing years.

NOTES

1. These annuity payments are sometimes fixed in nominal terms or sometimes increase, usually with some measure of consumer prices.
2. A prescription for reducing the cost of adverse selection in immediate annuities is to combine Long Term Care Insurance ('LTCI') with the life annuity. The reduction in cost occurs because the integrated product attracts those individuals with lower-than-average life expectancies so that they gain access to LTCI not otherwise available to them. See Murtaugh et al. (2001) for empirical evidence on this point.
3. Our inflation forecast series uses the Blue Chip survey for 1983 through 1991Q1, the Livingston survey for 1990Q2 and 1991Q2, and the Survey of Professional Forecasters for the remainder of the time period investigated. See www.phil.frb.org/files/spf/cpie10.txt
4. Actually, for the years since 1993, the jury is still out, as we had to insert the forecasted inflation rate for quarters where we do not yet have actual experience.
5. The Thrift Savings Plan does offer US federal government employees the choice of annuities indexed to the CPI up to 3 per cent annual changes, and one major insurer issues to the public an inflation-adjusted annuity.
6. Data from Society of Actuaries web site: www.soa.org/tablemgr/tablemgr.asp
7. TR02 mortality tables include actual mortality for 1983–99 and projected mortality for 2000–2001.

REFERENCES

Ameriks, J., R. Veres and M. Warshawsky (2001), 'Making Retirement Income Last a Lifetime', *Journal of Financial Planning*, December, 60–76.

Bell, F., S. Goss, and A. Wade (1992), *Life Tables for the United States Social Security Area: 1900–2080*, Actuarial Study No. 107, Office of the Actuary, Social Security Administration.

Brown, J., O. Mitchell, J. Poterba and M. Warshawsky (2001a), *The Role of Annuity Markets in Financing Retirement*, Cambridge, MA: MIT Press.

Brown, J., O. Mitchell and J. Poterba (2001b), 'The Role of Real Annuities and Indexed Bonds in an Individual Accounts Retirement Program', in J. Campbell and M. Feldstein (eds), *Risk Aspects of Investment-Based Social Security Reform*, Chicago: University of Chicago Press for the NBER, 321–370.

Burtless, G. (2000), 'Social Security Privatization and Financial Market Risk', Center on Social and Economic Dynamics Working Paper No. 10, February.

Faber, J. and A. Wade (1983), *Life Tables for the United States: 1900–2050*, Actuarial Study No. 89, Office of the Actuary, Social Security Administration.

Mitchell, O., J. Poterba, M. Warshawsky and J. Brown (1999), 'New Evidence on the Money's Worth of Individual Annuities', *American Economic Review*, **89**(5), 1299–1318.

Murtaugh, C., B. Spillman and M. Warshawsky (2001), 'In Sickness and In Health: An Annuity Approach to Financing Long-term Care and Retirement Income', *Journal of Risk and Insurance*, **68**(2), 225–54.
Poterba, J. and M. Warshawsky (2000), 'The Costs of Annuitizing Retirement Payouts in Individual Accounts', in J. Shoven (ed.), *Administrative Aspects of Investment-Based Social Security Reform*, Chicago: University of Chicago Press for the NBER, 173–200.
President's Commission to Strengthen Social Security (2001), Report: *Strengthening Social Security and Creating Personal Wealth for All Americans*, December.

5. Pension annuitization and Social Security claiming*

Michael D. Hurd, Constantijn W.A. Panis, James P. Smith, Julie M. Zissimopoulos

5.1 INTRODUCTION

The main resources that support consumption in retirement are private savings, private pensions and Social Security. There is considerable dispute about the adequacy of these resources, but regardless of the level, how those resources are used is an important determinant of well-being, especially in advanced old age. In particular, if bequeathable wealth is used to purchase annuities, the elderly can protect themselves against outliving their resources, and, in many circumstances, consume at greater levels than otherwise.

In the US the market in privately purchased annuities is very small, and few of the elderly have any annuity income from that source. However, there are two other ways in which wealth can be annuitized, and those methods are used relatively frequently. The first involves the choice of the disposition of pension rights: many pension plans offer a retiree the choice between a lump-sum payment at retirement or an annuity stream. Lump-sum payments are available in most defined contribution (DC) plans and in about one-half of defined benefit (DB) plans. To the extent that retiring workers choose to annuitize rather than taking a lump-sum payment, they are choosing to annuitize bequeathable wealth.

The second involves the timing of the claim to Social Security retirement benefits. As pointed out by Coile et al. (2002), claiming of Social Security benefits after retirement is the same kind of decision as that involved in the purchase of annuities. Someone who retires at age 62 has the option of taking

* The authors gratefully acknowledge research support by from the Social Security Administration via a grant to RAND from the Michigan Retirement Research Center and from the Department of Labor. Additional support from the National Institute for Aging for data development at the RAND Center for the Study of Aging is gratefully acknowledged.

Social Security immediately or delaying claiming. If someone delays claiming for a year, financing consumption out of bequeathable wealth, his/her Social Security benefit will be increased by approximately 8 per cent. Thus, the delay involves the implicit marginal purchase of 8 per cent more in Social Security annuities by the expenditure of a year's Social Security benefits. The aim of the 8 per cent increase in benefit was to make the implicit purchase actuarially fair, and, as the calculations in Coile et al. show, that is approximately the case for a single male based on population life tables and a real interest rate of 3 per cent.

The objective of this chapter is to estimate the rates of annuitization of pension plans in a nationally representative sample of workers who retired in their 50s or early 60s and the rates of implicit annuitization in the US Social Security system. We will give evidence about the determinants of annuitization. Our thinking will be guided by the life-cycle model of consumption (LCM). We will find whether those factors which the LCM predicts will affect annuitization do, in fact, influence it.

5.2 THEORETICAL DETERMINANTS OF ANNUITIZATION

Under the LCM as developed by Yaari (1965) for a single retired person without a bequest motive, their lifetime utility will be increased if they annuitize all of their wealth. However, the assumptions necessary for this conclusion are rather stringent and unlikely to be satisfied in reality. For example, the interest rate that supports the annuity should be the same as the interest rate on bequeathable wealth. Yet, in any modern economy there are many interest rates, which depend on the term to maturity and the risk associated with the investment. Nonetheless the LCM provides a theoretical structure from which we can analyse actual behavior, and even if the assumptions are not strictly satisfied, the model will tell us how behavior will change when there is a departure from the assumptions. We will not derive any of the predictions of the model in this chapter; rather we will state the results and give what we hope to be an intuitive explanation.[1]

We first consider a single retiree who has no bequest motive. In the absence of any constraint the optimal consumption path will decline with age provided that the sum of mortality risk and the subjective time rate of discount is greater than the rate of return on bequeathable wealth. The rate of decline will increase in mortality risk and the subjective time rate of discount, and decrease in the rate of return on bequeathable wealth. In this situation, which is typical, should someone annuitize completely the consumption path could no longer be chosen freely, but it would be constrained to the path of annuity income. Therefore, even though annuitization increases the total lifetime resources that are available for consumption, because the time path of consumption does not follow the optimal shape, total lifetime utility is reduced from what it would be were the path to be freely chosen. The utility payoff from annuitization depends how distorted the path of consumption will be. For this discussion we will assume that the annuity payout is constant in real terms over the lifetime of an individual. This assumption is correct in the case of Social Security benefits, and it is approximately correct in a low-inflation environment in the case of private pensions or annuities.

If the subjective time rate of discount and/or mortality risk are large, the distortion in the consumption path will be substantial and the utility payoff from annuitization will be reduced. This result accords with the common-sense notion that when the time rate of discount is high individuals want to consume today, but an annuity forces them to delay consumption. Similarly, when mortality risk is high individuals want to consume today, but an annuity again forces them to delay consumption. Therefore we expect that individuals who believe their personal mortality risk is high or who have a high subjective time rate of discount will tend not to annuitize bequeathable wealth.

When the rate of return on bequeathable wealth is high the optimal consumption path is flattened, making it similar to the path of the annuity stream. Then the distortion is reduced making the utility gain from annuitization greater. This result accords with the idea that when the rate of return on alternative investments is high, people will delay consumption, which is what an annuity forces people to do. In addition to this effect on the optimal consumption path, there is a further effect from a high rate of return on alternative investments: if that rate is high enough the actual flow of income from the alternative investment could be greater than the flow of annuity income and then the investment would dominate the annuity. This was likely the case in the US during the 1980s (Hurd, 2004).

The optimal consumption path of someone who is highly risk-averse will be approximately flat, and so will not be appreciably distorted by the annuity path. Such a person will have a large utility gain from annuitization. This result accords with the notion that those who are risk-averse will want to guard against outliving their resources, and so be more likely to want to annuitize.

Typically individuals will start from some given level of bequeathable wealth and from some given level of annuitization as from Social Security, and then think of additional annuitization. The marginal value of additional annuitization will depend on the ratio of the initial level of bequeathable wealth to the initial level of annuitization: the greater this ratio the greater the utility gain from annuitization. The reasoning is that as long as bequeathable wealth is positive it can be used partially to finance consumption so that consumption need not be the same as annuity income. Therefore, high levels of bequeathable wealth mean that the consumption path can follow its optimal shape until very late in life, and make it unlikely that it will ever be constrained. We expect that high bequeathable wealth relative to annuity wealth will lead to greater annuitization.

A bequest motive implies that someone gains utility from holding bequeathable wealth. The utility gain from annuitization will be reduced by the loss in utility from the reduction of bequeathable wealth. Therefore, we would expect that a bequest motive will lead to less annuitization. The strength of a bequest motive is typically measured by the number of (adult) children. We would expect to see less annuitization as the number of children increases.

These results pertain to a single person, but they carry over qualitatively to a couple, so we will not discuss them separately (Hurd, 1999).

5.3 DATA

The Health and Retirement Study (HRS) is a biennial panel with emphasis on retirement behavior and how it is affected by health status, economic status and work incentives. At baseline in 1992 the HRS had 12 652 respondents and was nationally representative of individuals born in 1931–1941 and their spouses except for over-samples of Blacks, Hispanics and residents of Florida (Juster and Suzman, 1995). This chapter uses data from survey waves one through five fielded in 1992, 1994, 1996, 1998 and 2000. We also use restricted data on Social Security quarters of covered earnings matched with HRS respondent records from the main survey to determine whether an HRS respondent is eligible to receive Social Security benefits.[2]

According to the LCM an important determinant of the benefit from annuitization is mortality risk, or, more simply, life expectancy. Estimating the effect of life expectancy on retirement or on Social Security claiming behavior is complicated by the correlation between economic status and mortality. It is well known that those with more wealth or income tend to live longer. But because income and wealth should have independent effects on retirement, it has been very difficult to separate their direct economic effects from their correlations with mortality risk.

In the HRS, respondents were asked to give their chances of surviving to target ages of 75 and 85. These data have been the subject of considerable work, which has aimed to establish that in cross section the responses are reasonable and in panel that they predict actual mortality. Both aims have been established: in the HRS the subjective survival probabilities vary appropriately with known risk factors. For example smokers give lower probabilities and those with higher socioeconomic status give higher probabilities (Hurd and McGarry, 1995). In cross section the subjective survival probabilities aggregate well to life table levels as shown in Table 5.1. For example, a weighted average of all age-eligible responses to the target of 75 was 0.645 and a life table survival was 0.677. Thus if individuals survive with the probabilities that they state the average survival in the population will be very close to what the life table predicts.

Table 5.1 Average probabilities of surviving to 75 or 85

	All		Women		Men	
	Age 75	Age 85	Age 75	Age 85	Age 75	Age 85
HRS subjective probability*	0.645	0.427	0.663	0.460	0.622	0.388
	(0.003)	(0.003)	(0.004)	(0.004)	(0.005)	(0.005)
1990 life table, wave 1 weights	0.677	0.349	0.746	0.438	0.594	0.242

Note: * Weighted average of responses of individuals from birth years of 1931 through 1941; estimated standard errors in parentheses. 9149 observations in wave 1.

Source: Hurd and McGarry (2002).

In panel the subjective probabilities predict actual mortality. Table 5.2 shows that between waves one and two 183 HRS respondents died and they had given an average subjective survival probability to age 75 in wave 1 of 0.45. Among the survivors the average survival probability was 0.65. The predictive power of the subjective survival probability remains after controlling for a number of other risk factors (Hurd and McGarry, 2002).

*Table 5.2 Means of subjective survival probabilities by survivorship to wave 2**

	Died between waves	Lived to wave 2
Subjective survival to age 75	0.45	0.65
Subjective survival to age 85	0.28	0.43
Number of observations	*183*	*10 642*

Note: *Sample is individuals 46 to 65 in wave 1.

Source: Hurd and McGarry (2002).

These data provide an opportunity to find whether those with high subjective survival tend to annuitize even after we control for income, wealth and age.

5.4 ANNUITIZATION OF PENSIONS AT JOB CHANGE OR RETIREMENT

As shown in Table 5.3 about 64 per cent of workers in the HRS had some type of pension plan in wave 1 (1992). Defined benefit pension plans often do not have an option of a lump-sum distribution, and prior research has shown that the self-reports about its availability are unreliable. In that we want to study the choice of whether to annuitize we want to use data on those who are able to choose from the complete set of possibilities. Therefore, we exclude those with defined benefit plans only. Among those with DC plans, 90 per cent have the option of a lump sum (Table 5.4).

Table 5.3 Pension coverage rates in HRS wave 1

	Frequency	Per cent
No pension coverage	2993	36.2
IRA/Keogh only	817	9.9
Defined benefit only	1425	17.3
Defined contribution only	970	11.6
Both DB and DC plans	2055	24.9
Total	8260	100.0

Source: Authors' calculations based on HRS wave 1.

Table 5.4 Availability of lump-sum distribution option, DC plans, wave 1(excluding DK/refused and missing)(counts and percents)

	Number	Percent
Yes	2116	84.57
Partial	128	5.12
No	258	10.31
Total	2502	100.00

Source: Authors' calculations based on HRS wave 1.

The HRS asks a number of detailed questions from respondents who indicate that they separated from the job that they held at the last interview.

Among others, if they were covered by an employer-sponsored pension plan, they were asked about the status of accumulated pension rights. For our purposes, only respondents who were covered by a DC plan are relevant. DC account balances may be left to accumulate with the previous employer, rolled over into an Individual Retirement Account (IRA), converted into an annuity, cashed out into the after-tax sphere, lost, or 'other'.

Table 5.5 shows the disposition of DC plans by workers who left a job between the 1992 and 2000 waves. About 77 per cent left the assets in the plan to accumulate or transferred the assets into an IRA. In both cases a decision about whether to annuitize has been deferred.[3] About 19 per cent cashed out their pensions: they took the funds out of the tax-advantaged sector and either saved or used them for consumption. Some 64 individuals or 4.6 per cent annuitized their DC balances.

Table 5.5 Summary of reported pension plan dispositions, DC plans (counts and column percents)

Disposition	Number	Per cent
Cashed out	256	18.5
Roll into IRA	496	35.9
Leave to accumulate	566	41.0
Annuitize	64	4.6
Total	1622	100.0

Note: Table excludes 240 plans where the type of disposition could not be determined.

Source: Authors' calculations based on HRS waves 1–5.

Not all workers have the option of converting their DC balance into an annuity via an employer-sponsored plan.[4] Mitchell (1999) documents that only 27 per cent of full-time 401(k) participants had this option in 1997, down from 34 per cent in 1993. While annuitization in the context of an employer-sponsored plan may be limited, anyone can annuitize in the private market for annuities, albeit at terms that may be less favorable than in an employer-sponsored plan. Thus, in principle, there is no limitation on the availability of annuities.

Related evidence of the low annuitization rates comes from Ameriks (2002), who studied the way in which TIAA-CREF participants chose their benefit. TIAA-CREF provides pensions to faculty and staff of many higher education and research organizations in the United States. Traditionally, the only option for TIAA-CREF retirees was to take a lifelong annuity. With the introduction of alternatives in 1989, increasingly fewer participants (45.1 per cent in 2001) opted for an annuity (Ameriks, 2002).

Although the biennial rate of annuitization is low, the eventual amount of annuitization could be very much higher provided the rate of annuitization remains about the same among the 77 per cent who rolled their DC balances into an IRA or left them with the employer to accumulation. Based on HRS waves 1, 2 and 3, Hurd (2004) estimated that in steady-state about 15 per cent of DC plan balances would eventually be annuitized.[5] Nonetheless, even this level of annuitization is low relative to the predictions of the LCM.

DC balances that were converted into annuities tended to be the larger balances. Expressed in year 2000 dollars, the average annuitized balance was $90 400; the average balance that was maintained (left with the employer to accumulate or rolled over into an IRA) was $85 600, and the average cashed-out balance $20 600 (not shown).

5.4.1 Annuitization and Worker Characteristics

Annuitization rates differed somewhat by worker characteristics (Table 5.6). Generally speaking, differential propensities to annuitize are not consistent with predictions from the LCM. Annuitization was chosen more frequently by job separators that retired or became disabled: apparently those still working have deferred a choice about annuitization. An implication is that in the long run, after all workers have retired, the rate of annuitization will be higher than indicated by the average in our sample.

We will use the LCM to interpret the variation in rates of annuitization as it makes predictions about the effects of most characteristics. Because Blacks and males have a reduced life expectancy, they should annuitize at a lower rate. As the table shows, however, they do not. Education is said to be an indicator of the time rate of preference: the more highly educated deferred consumption when they received their education. The LCM would predict that more patient individuals will annuitize at a greater rate, but the table shows the least educated have the highest rate. The financial planning horizon is also taken to be a measure of the subjective time rate of discount. The resulting theoretical prediction is that those with a long time horizon will annuitize at a greater rate. We see no such pattern, and, in fact, those with the longest horizon are least likely to annuitize. With the exception of those under 50 years of age, there is a strong age gradient in the rate of annuitization. The 'annuity premium' (what the annuity pays in excess of the interest rate) increases with age, so this pattern is reasonable. Those who have never married have lower rates; there is nothing in the LCM that would explain this.

Table 5.6 Annuitization rates of DC plans

	Per cent annuitized
Subsequent work status	
Working	1.0
Retired	7.7
Disabled	6.6
Unemployed	2.5
Race	
White	4.0
Black	8.5
Other	6.3
Sex	
Female	3.1
Male	6.1
Education	
High school drop-out	6.4
High school graduate	4.8
Some college	3.7
College graduate	4.1
Age category	
Age <50	5.4
Age 50–54	1.9
Age 55–59	2.6
Age 60–64	6.0
Age >65	8.4
Marital status	
Married	4.7
Separated/divorced	4.5
Widowed	4.6
Never married	2.9
Wealth	
Bottom quartile	3.5
Second and third quartiles	4.5
Top quartile	6.8
Probability of surviving to age 75	
$p \leq 0.5$	3.6
$0.5 < p < 0.9$	4.3
$p \geq 0.9$	4.6

Table 5.6 continued

	Per cent annuitized
Probability of surviving to age 85	
$p \leq 0.2$	4.4
$0.2<p<0.75$	5.0
$p \geq 0.75$	4.4
Financial planning horizon	
A few months	4.3
1 year	5.4
A few years	5.1
5-10 years	3.6
>10 years	4.0
Probability that Social Security will become more generous	
Probably more generous	5.5
Probably less generous	3.7
Most likely less generous	3.3
Probability of double-digit inflation	
$p \leq 0.25$	4.2
$0.25<p<0.7$	5.1
$p \geq 0.7$	3.3
Self-reported health status	
Poor	7.8
Fair	4.7
Good	6.2
Very good	3.7
Excellent	3.1
Disability status	
Not disabled	4.2
Disabled	6.5
Health insurance coverage	
Not covered	1.7
Covered	4.9
Total	4.6

Source: Authors' calculations based on HRS waves 1–5.

The relationship we find between bequeathable wealth and rates of annuitization, and mortality risk and annuitization are to some extent consistent with our theoretical predictions. We classified observations by the quartile of bequeathable wealth and combined the two middle quartiles.

Those in the highest quartile annuitized at almost twice the rate of those in the lowest quartile. Under the LCM high levels of bequeathable wealth increase the utility value from annuitization, and so this pattern would be predicted by the LCM. The HRS asked respondents about survival to age 75. Those with greater subjective survival have a greater incentive to annuitize, and we find a slight tendency for that pattern. The HRS also asked about the chances of surviving to age 85; here we do not find greater annuitization among those who expect to live long.

Along with beliefs about living to age 75 or 85, HRS respondents are queried about several other expectations including Social Security benefits and inflation. As expected, those who think Social Security will become more generous are more likely to postpone claiming, i.e., to annuitize. Private annuities tend to be fixed in nominal terms. As expected, individuals who believed that double-digit inflation is quite likely over the next ten years annuitize less often.

Those in worse health have reduced life expectancies and so would be expected not to annuitize. With the exception of the 'good' category the pattern is exactly the opposite both in self-reported health status and in disability status. An interpretation of the higher rate of annuitization among those with health insurance is that they face a lower risk of unanticipated health expenditures. Large health expenditures could lead to a liquidity constraint, and an elevated probability of a constraint makes annuitization less attractive.

5.5 SOCIAL SECURITY CLAIMING

Social Security consists of a disability and a retirement component. For our purposes, disability benefits are not relevant. We are interested in the age at which retired workers claim retirement benefits under the Old-Age and Survivors Insurance (OASI) program. Workers who are insured for OASI may claim full benefits at the Normal Retirement Age, which was 65 years during the period of our data.[6] Insured workers may, however, claim benefits as early as the Early Entitlement Age of 62 years, but benefits are permanently reduced if claimed before age 65. For a worker the reduction was 6 2/3 per cent for each year before age 65, so that if taken at age 62, benefits were reduced by 20 per cent. Stated differently, if a worker delayed claiming from age 62 to 63, benefits would increase from 80 to 86 2/3 per cent of full benefits, a relative increase of 8.3 per cent. A one-year delay in benefit claiming thus amounts to the purchase of an annuity with an implicit real rate of return of 8.3 per cent. A widow(er) may claim benefits at age 60, and a spouse of an insured worker at age 62.

Based on a life-cycle model Coile et al. (2002) report that for representative single men, there is an expected utility gain from delaying claiming, and that the gain varies with bequeathable wealth. Using data from the 1982 New Beneficiary Survey, however, they report that very few individuals delay claiming. Among those who retired before the age of 62, 81 per cent claim within the first month of reaching age 62, and 91 per cent within the first year. Only 3 per cent of workers delay claiming Social Security benefits until 65, the age at which the implicit price is no longer actuarially fair. These authors conclude that '... part of the population simply claims immediately without sufficient consideration of intertemporal choice issues'. Whether early claiming is due to maximization errors by such a large fraction of the population or to observable characteristics, subjective beliefs and unobservable tastes is, in our view, an open question; but it is certainly important for public policy to establish whether substantial utility gains could be achieved by educating the population to make better choices.

The HRS offers an advance over the New Beneficiary Survey used by Coile et al. It is a panel data set so that we can observe retirement as it happens rather than in retrospect; the HRS has detailed information on pensions, which are important determinants of retirement and possibly claiming behavior; and, most importantly, it has data on the subjective survival of each respondent.

We relate the tendency to delay claiming Social Security benefits to the subjective survival probabilities. Do those with higher subjective life expectancy view the increase in benefits from delaying retirement past age 62 as generous, inducing them to delay claiming benefits?

We select individuals who are at least 62 years old in wave 2, 3, or 4. We exclude individuals who claim Disability Insurance, are widows, are ineligible for OASI benefits based on quarters of coverage, and any remaining individuals who received benefits before age 62. Our estimation is based on those who are not in the labor force at 62 years of age. We use one observation per individual and after the selections described above, our sample is 907 individuals.

Table 5.7 shows the number and per cent of retired workers who chose implicitly to annuitize by delaying claiming of Social Security to age 63. Only 17 per cent of retirees had not claimed Social Security benefits by age 63. Were they to claim at 63 their benefits would be higher by 8.3 per cent than had they claimed at 62. The table also shows the variation in the rate of implicit annuitization as it varies by personal, demographic and financial characteristics. It shows the p-value for the null hypothesis that the rates are the same across values of the characteristic. A p-value of 0.05 or less is generally considered to be statistical evidence that the characteristic has an effect.

Table 5.7 Probability of claiming of Social Security benefits after age 63 conditional on retiring before age 62

	N	Per cent delay claiming
All	906	17.2
Own subjective survival (0–100)		
0	119	18.5
1 to 49	299	15.1
50	172	14.0
51 to 99	184	15.2
100	71	19.7
p-value		*0.722*
Spouse subjective survival (0–100)		
0	71	18.3
1 to 49	197	12.7
50	132	13.6
51 to 99	141	15.6
100	53	18.9
p-value		*0.684*
Stock ownership		
Owns stock	411	13.4
Does not own stock	496	20.4
p-value		*0.006*
Pension wealth		
Has pension wealth	524	14.1
Does not have pension wealth	383	21.4
p-value		*0.004*
Pension wealth quartiles		
First	129	13.2
Second	127	10.2
Third	134	14.9
Fourth	134	17.9
p-value		*0.345*
Financial wealth quartiles		
First	230	24.3
Second	228	17.1
Third	222	10.4
Fourth	227	16.7
p-value		*0.001*
Number of children		
0	60	18.3
1	72	20.8
2,3	436	14.9
4+	339	19.2

Table 5.7 continued

	N	Per cent delay claiming
p-value		*0.355*
Marital status		
Married	777	16.7
Separated/divorced	94	20.2
Never married	35	20.0
p-value		*0.773*
Spouse age difference:		
Spouse is 5+ years older	116	15.5
Spouse is 2–4 years older	188	16.0
Spouse is 1 year older	95	17.9
Spouse is 1 year younger	84	16.7
Spouse is 2–4 years younger	190	17.4
Spouse is 5+ years younger	104	17.3
p-value		*0.996*

Source: Authors' calculations based on HRS waves 1–4.

Based on prior work we use the subjective survival probability to age 85 (P85) rather than to age 75 as our measure of subjective mortality risk.[7] The LCM predicts that those with greater survival probabilities will delay claiming. We do see that 19.7 per cent of those whose survival probability is 100 per cent had not claimed by age 63; this rate is the highest of the five groups. However, there is little systematic variation in the probability of claiming, and the rates across the groups are not statistically different from each other. Because a spouse can inherit the Social Security benefit in the case of widowing, the spouse's subjective survival probability should influence claiming qualitatively in the same way. We do not see, however, any consistent pattern or statistical significance in claiming behavior as a function of the spouse's subjective survival probability.

The relationships between stock ownership and delayed claiming, and between wealth and delayed claiming have some consistency with theory. Stock owners may view stocks as their alternative investment to increased Social Security benefits that arise through delayed claiming, and historically the returns on stocks have been high. Table 5.7 shows that stock owners delay claiming at a lower rate and that the difference is significant. Having pension wealth should lead to less utility from annuitization, and, indeed, pension wealth is associated with a seven percentage point lower rate of implicit annuitization of Social Security benefits. Conditional on having a pension, though, the pattern is not monotonic.

The LCM predicts that those with substantial bequeathable wealth will delay claiming. We find the opposite pattern. Indeed with the exception of the highest quartile the rate of claiming is increasing in financial wealth rather than decreasing. Someone with a strong bequest motive will want to claim early so as to preserve bequeathable wealth. Using number of children as a measure for the strength of a bequest motive, we find no consistent pattern in claiming behavior. Thus we find no support for a bequest motive as an explanation for the low rate of annuitization.

The structure of the US Social Security system is such that married people have an incentive to delay claiming because a widow or widower will inherit the benefit of the deceased spouse.[8] However, in Table 5.7 those who are married claim at a higher rate than those who are single.

Our conclusion from these cross-tabulations is that they offer mixed support for the LCM as an explanation for variation in claiming: for example, stock ownership and pension wealth have predictive power and the qualitative effects are in accordance with the LCM.

We now turn to a multivariate approach and estimate the probability of delayed claiming of Social Security benefits with a reduced form probit model. Table 5.8 has the average values of the right-hand variables. Table 5.9 has the estimated marginal effects on delayed Social Security claiming from a probit model of the probability of claiming after 63. We allow for non-linearities and interactions between financial wealth (less housing and business wealth) and Social Security wealth by defining three categories and their interactions. We include indicators for the amount of pension wealth. We expect high levels of prior annuitization to reduce delayed claiming because under the LCM the value of an annuity decreases with the level of annuities (Hurd, 2004). High levels of wealth should increase delayed claiming by reducing liquidity constraints and because the value of an annuity increases with the level of bequeathable wealth. The value of an annuity declines with the rate of return on alternative investments, so we include an indicator for whether the individual owns stock: stock owners may think of additional stock owning as the marginal investment.

Seventeen per cent claim after age 63. However, we can find little that differentiates between the early claimers and the late claimers. For example, in the probit just two out of 20 explanatory variables are significant at the 5 per cent level (excluding the constant and categorical variables for missing values).

We see no systematic pattern of claiming as a function of P85, and no effects are significant. The largest coefficient is that for P85=100, which is qualitatively the same as in Table 5.7. This is consistent with the LCM, but because of the lack of significance it is only suggestive.

The LCM predicts that a combination of high bequeathable wealth and low Social Security wealth will lead to delayed claiming and that low bequeathable wealth and high Social Security wealth will lead to accelerated claiming. These predictions are not based on a total wealth effect on claiming, but rather on the valuation that individuals place on annuities as a function of the mix between annuity wealth and bequeathable wealth. We do not find these effects. The LCM makes no predictions about the combination of low bequeathable and low Social Security wealth, yet this combination is associated with a rate of delayed claiming that is 16.5 percentage points greater than the reference combination (the middle two quartiles of Social Security and bequeathable wealth). We have no explanation for this result.

Table 5.8 Means and standard deviations of regression variables

	Mean	Standard deviation
Delay claiming	0.172	0.378
Survival to 85 =0	0.139	0.346
1 to 49	0.356	0.479
51 to 99	0.217	0.413
100	0.080	0.272
Missing	0.008	0.088
Financial wealth quartile lowest	0.254	0.435
Highest	0.250	0.433
Social Security wealth quartile lowest	0.252	0.435
Highest	0.256	0.437
Financial wealth low*SS wealth low	0.084	0.277
low*high	0.013	0.114
high*low	0.057	0.233
high*high	0.103	0.304
Pension wealth quartile lowest	0.142	0.349
Pension wealth quartiles 2 and 3	0.288	0.453
Pension wealth highest	0.148	0.355
Owns stock	0.453	0.498
College educated	0.388	0.488
Male	0.472	0.499
Married	0.838	0.369
Own age minus spouse age	0.312	59.881
Age difference missing	0.143	0.351
No children	0.066	0.249
Wave 2	0.322	0.467
Wave 4	0.290	0.454

Source: Authors' calculations based on HRS waves 1–4.

Table 5.9 Determinants of the probability of claiming Social Security benefits after age 63 conditional on retiring before age 62

	Change in probability	Estimated standard error	P(|Z|>0)
Survival to 85 =0	0.026	0.043	0.547
1 to 49	0.013	0.035	0.704
50 (omitted)			
51 to 99	0.016	0.038	0.670
100	0.052	0.050	0.296
Missing	0.206	0.123	0.095
Financial wealth quartile lowest	0.005	0.041	0.897
Quartiles 2 and 3 (omitted)			
Highest	0.041	0.047	0.382
Social Security wealth quartile lowest	–0.003	0.045	0.953
Quartiles 2 and 3 (omitted)			
Highest	–0.077	0.048	0.108
Financial wealth low*SS wealth low	0.165	0.065	0.011
low*high	–0.006	0.138	0.967
middle*middle (omitted)			
high*low	–0.034	0.078	0.667
high*high	0.032	0.072	0.658
Pension wealth quartile lowest	–0.071	0.039	0.071
Pension wealth quartiles 2 and 3	–0.061	0.032	0.054
Pension wealth highest	–0.005	0.038	0.903
No pension wealth (omitted)			
Owns stock	–0.053	0.031	0.084
College educated	0.065	0.027	0.018
Male	–0.034	0.029	0.241
Married	0.025	0.084	0.763
Own age minus spouse age	–0.000	0.000	0.426
Age difference missing	–0.009	0.088	0.919
No children	0.034	0.051	0.505
Wave 2	–0.055	0.031	0.077
Wave 3 (omitted)			
Wave 4	0.052	0.029	0.072
Constant	–0.242	0.093	0.009
Observed probability		*0.172*	
Predicted probability		*0.154*	
Number of observations		*907*	

Source: Authors' calculations based on HRS waves 1–4.

We find that the effects of pension wealth and stock ownership are generally consistent with theory. Pension wealth in the first three quartiles (but not at the highest) leads to a lower rate of delayed claiming relative to those lacking pension wealth. This result is in accord with theory: those who already have annuitized wealth have less to gain from further annuitization. Stock owners have a lower probability of delayed claiming. This is consistent with the view that their alternative investment return is higher than for those who do not own stocks: they do not want to leave funds in Social Security, which, in their view, has a relatively low rate of return.

5.6 CONCLUSION

The main conclusion of this chapter is that the desire to annuitize is limited. The two-year rate of annuitization of DC pensions on job separation by workers in their 50s or early 60s was about five per cent, and a rough estimate would be that about 15 per cent of DC balances would eventually be annuitized. These estimates are approximately in line with the implicit annuitization from the delayed claiming of Social Security benefits. About 17 per cent of retired workers delayed claiming Social Security benefits during the first year of eligibility, implicitly purchasing higher Social Security benefits. Thus the overall findings about the levels of annuitization are similar across the two types of data and imply that most people do not annuitize when given a choice.

This conclusion is consistent with the results reported by Ameriks (2002). TIAA-CREF participants are highly educated and likely have a better understanding of the benefits of annuitization than those in the general population, and they have much more wealth. For both of these reasons we would expect them to annuitize at a high rate. In 1988 annuitization was mandatory, so, of course, the rate was 100 per cent. Following a rule change in 1989 the rate of annuitization by those making an initial income choice has fallen continuously reaching 55.2 per cent in 1999 and 45.1 per cent in 2001 for an annual rate of decline of about five percentage points. When inertia and emulation of the choices of older retirees are important factors in deciding about annuitization, the transition to a new equilibrium can take decades. Perhaps such a transition is underway and the eventual new steady-state rate of annuitization could be even lower than it is today.

As far as the determinants of DC annuitization or Social Security claiming are concerned, we could find no consistent pattern with respect to subjective survival, which has an important role in determining the payoff from annuitization. Other theoretical determinants of annuitization had explanatory power for one of the outcomes but not for the other. For example annuitization of DC balances varied systematically with bequeathable wealth as in Table 5.6, but Social Security annuitization did not vary with bequeathable wealth. Having a college education increased the implicit annuitization in Social Security (Table 5.9) but it was not associated with annuitization of DC pensions.

The main theoretical model to explain annuitization is the LCM. In other contexts the LCM is useful and has predictive power: for example, it predicts dissaving at advanced ages and dissaving is typically found in panel data on wealth. However, the LCM had no consistent predictive power for annuitization in either analyses of this chapter. Of course, it may be that the fairly simple LCM behind our analysis neglects important aspects of the problem such as the risk of high health care expenses, which could lead to a liquidity constraint were someone to be annuitized fully. Even so, we would think that the simple version would have some predictive power because some segments of the population are well shielded from health care risk or they have sufficient resources to insure themselves against it. Therefore, we tentatively conclude that we need a new understanding of the motives for the lack of annuitization, and possibly, a new theoretical structure.

NOTES

1. Refer to Hurd (2004) for further discussions.
2. Olson (1999) and Haider and Solon (2000) studied the subsample of HRS respondents that were matched to Social Security records and concluded that failures to match occur approximately at random. See Zissimopoulos et al. (2002) for a description of Social Security beneficiaries in the HRS, their eligibility status, and characteristics of workers who take early and reduced benefits at age 62.
3. DC balances or IRAs may be held in this status until the owner is 70.5 years old. Thus, it will be some years before we know of the eventual disposition of all of these plans.
4. The HRS does not have information about whether annuitization is available for a particular DC plan.
5. This estimate is based on the assumption that the rates of annuitization and cash-out are the same for plans that are left to accumulate and for IRAs as they are for plans at job change or retirement (4.6 per cent).
6. Individuals are insured if they have at least as many credits as the number of full calendar years elapsing after age 21 and before age 62, disability or death, whichever occurs first. In our analysis sample, this implies a worker needs 40 credits to qualify for benefits. These are generally earned after ten years of labor force participation.
7. The two probabilities are highly collinear. We prefer survival to age 85 because the responses are spread more evenly than they are for survival to age 75.
8. These benefits are shown in simulation in Coile et al. (2002).

REFERENCES

Ameriks, J. (2002), 'Recent Trends in the Selection of Retirement Income Streams Among TIAA-CREF Participants', TIAA-CREF Research Dialogue (74), December.

Coile, C., P. Diamond, J. Gruber and A. Jousten (2002), 'Delays in Claiming Social Security Benefits', *Journal of Public Economics*, **84** (3), 357–85.

Haider, S. and G. Solon (2000), 'Non-Response Bias in the HRS Social Security Files', RAND Working Paper DRU-2254-NIA, February.

Hurd, M.D. (1999), 'Mortality Risk and Consumption by Couples', presented at the IFS-Bank of Portugal Conference on The Microeconomics of Saving and Consumption Growth, Lisbon, November 1995, and NBER Working paper No. 7048, March.

Hurd, M.D. (2004), Comment on 'Longevity-Insured Retirement Distributions from Pension Plans: Market and Regulatory Issues,' by J.R. Brown and M.J. Warshawsky, forthcoming in W.G. Gale, J.B. Shoven and M.J. Warshawsky (eds), *Private Pensions and Public Policies*, Washington, DC: Brookings Institution Press.

Hurd, M.D. and K. McGarry (1995), 'Evaluation of the Subjective Probabilities of Survival in the HRS', *Journal of Human Resources*, **30**, S268–S292.

Hurd, M.D. and K. McGarry (2002), 'The Predictive Validity of Subjective Probabilities of Survival', *Economic Journal*, **112**, 966–85.

Juster, F.T. and R. Suzman (1995), 'An Overview of the Health and Retirement Study', *Journal of Human Resources*, **XXX**, S7–S56.

Mitchell, O.S. (1999), 'New Trends in Pension Benefit and Retirement Provisions' NBER Working Paper No. 7381.

Olson, J. (1999), 'Linkages with Data from Social Security Administrative Records in the Health and Retirement Study', Working Paper No. 84, Washington, DC: Office of Research, Evaluation, and Statistics (ORES), Social Security Administration.

Yaari, M.E. (1965), 'Uncertain Lifetime, Life Insurance and the Theory of the Consumer', *Review of Economic Studies*, **32**, 137–50.

Zissimopoulos, J., C. Panis, and M. Hurd (2002), 'Workers Who Take Early Social Security Retirement Benefits', RAND Working Paper PM-1281-SSA, January.

6. Longevity risk in living benefits*

Ermanno Pitacco

6.1 INTRODUCTION

Recent trends in mortality lead to the use of projected survival models for pricing and reserving, where life annuities and other long-term living benefits are concerned. Several projection models have been proposed and are actually used in actuarial practice. However, the future mortality trend is random and hence, whatever kind of model is adopted, systematic deviations from the forecasted mortality may take place. Then, a 'model' (or a 'parameter') risk arises, which is clearly a non-pooling risk. Changes in the mortality pattern refer to both young and old ages. When the random mortality trend at old ages is concerned, it is usually referred to as 'longevity risk'.

Life annuities are probably the most important insurance product affected by the longevity risk. Nevertheless, this risk should be carefully considered also when dealing with other insurance covers, especially within the area of health insurance. In particular, the longevity risk affects sickness benefits for the elderly (for example, post-retirement sickness benefits) and long term care (LTC) annuities. A moving scenario in which both future mortality and future senescent disability are random, constitutes the appropriate context for pricing and reserving for LTC products.

The impact of the longevity risk on living benefits must be carefully faced. Reinsurance policies and capital allocation can provide appropriate tools to face this risk. Nevertheless, the problem of 'locating' the longevity risk via a possible sharing between the annuity provider and the annuitant should also be carefully considered.

The present chapter is mostly based on research work recently performed in the Department of Applied Mathematics of the University of Trieste. The chapter aims at providing an introduction to some important issues

* This chapter presents some results of a research work supported by the Italian MIUR.

concerning the longevity risk in the area of the insurances of the person. Albeit the longevity risk constitutes a topic of dramatic interest in the field of actuarial mathematics, the presentation follows an informal style to facilitate understanding by non-actuarial readers.

The chapter is organized as follows. Section 6.2 introduces a moving mortality scenario. Mortality trends and the consequent need for appropriate projections are illustrated. Mortality risks are then introduced, placing a particular emphasis on longevity risk.

Section 6.3 generalizes some ideas, considering future combined mortality and disability scenarios, hence paving the way for addressing longevity risk in LTC insurance products.

The impact of longevity risk on living benefits is discussed in Section 6.4. Following the description of a probabilistic approach to measure the impact of the risk itself, some numerical examples are provided, concerning various types of living benefits.

In Section 6.5 some ideas concerning the structure of life annuities are discussed. In particular, some issues concerning flexibility features of the life annuity product, aiming at adding value to the product itself, are dealt with, looking at annuities in the context of overall post-retirement income planning. The concept of 'mortality guarantee level' is then introduced, in order to express the sharing of mortality risks between the insurer and the annuitant.

Some final remarks, presented in Section 6.6, conclude the chapter.

6.2 A MOVING MORTALITY SCENARIO

This section deals with mortality trends and the need for mortality projections. Finally, the longevity risk is addressed. Recent trends in mortality are described for example by MacDonald et al. (1998) and Rüttermann (1999).

Several projection models have been proposed and are actually used in actuarial practice; the reader can refer for example to Benjamin and Soliman (1993) and CMIR (1990, 1999). Lee (2000) describes the Lee-Carter projection method, which allows for randomness in forecasted mortality. The seminal paper by Cramer and Wold (1935) provides us with one of the first examples of a rigorous approach to mortality projections; the reader can refer to this paper and the references therein for information about the earliest projection models.

The impact of the longevity risk on life insurance business is analysed by Olivieri (2001), where future mortality trends at young ages and old ages as well are considered. The paper by Riemer-Hommel and Trauth (2000) deals with longevity risk according to a risk management perspective.

A number of papers deal with the longevity risk in living benefits; some of them are referred to at the beginning of Section 6.4.

6.2.1 Trends

In many countries, mortality experience over the last decades shows some aspects affecting the shape of curves representing the mortality as a function of the attained age. Figures 6.1 and 6.2 illustrate the moving mortality scenario referring to the Italian male population, in terms of survival functions l_x (expected number of survivors as a function of the attained age x) and curves of deaths (expected number d_x of people dying as a function of x). Survival functions and curves of deaths relate to various cross-sectional mortality experiences.

Obviously, experienced trends also affect the behavior of other quantities expressing the mortality pattern, such as the life expectancy and the mortality rates. Figure 6.3 illustrates the behaviour of the life expectancy at birth, for males and females in the Italian population. In Figure 6.4, referring to Italian males, the behaviour of the life expectancy at birth, the life expectancy at age 65 and the mode of the curve of deaths (that is, the most probable dying age, also called 'Lexis point') are compared.

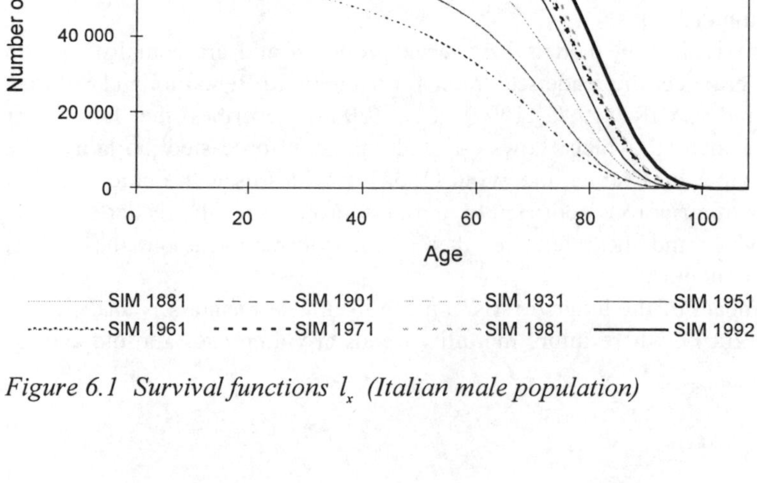

Figure 6.1 Survival functions l_x (Italian male population)

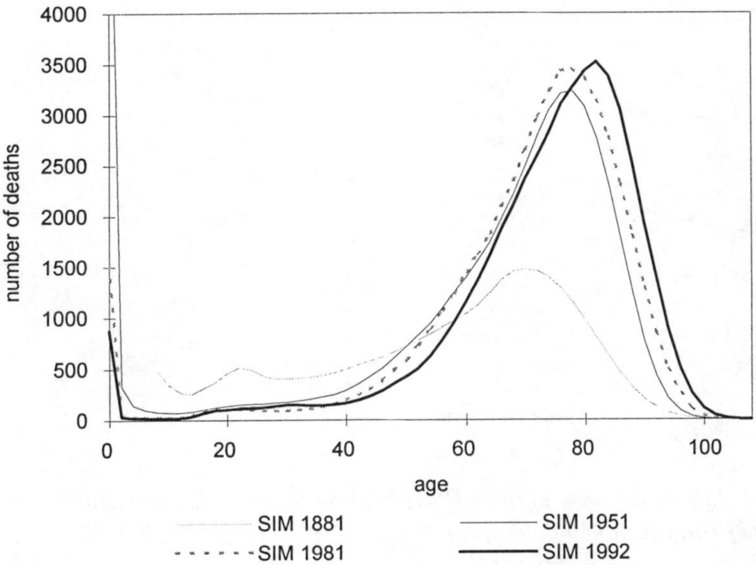

Figure 6.2 Curves of deaths d_x (Italian male population)

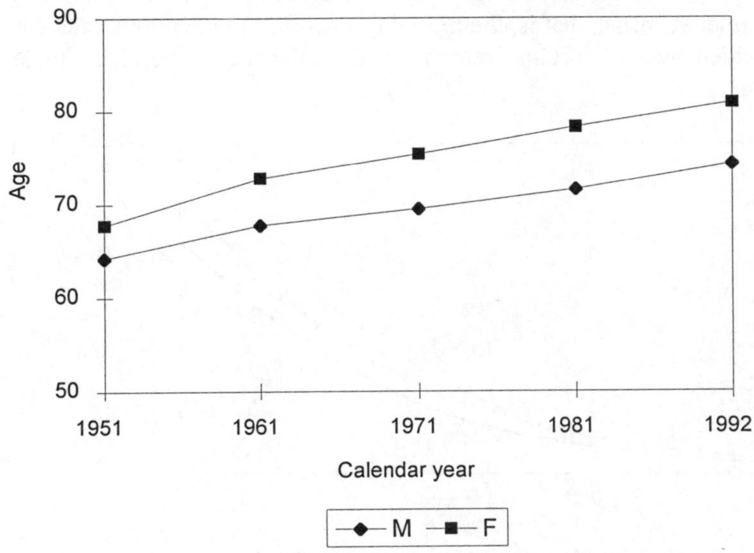

Figure 6.3 Life expectancy at birth for males [M] and females [F] (Italian population)

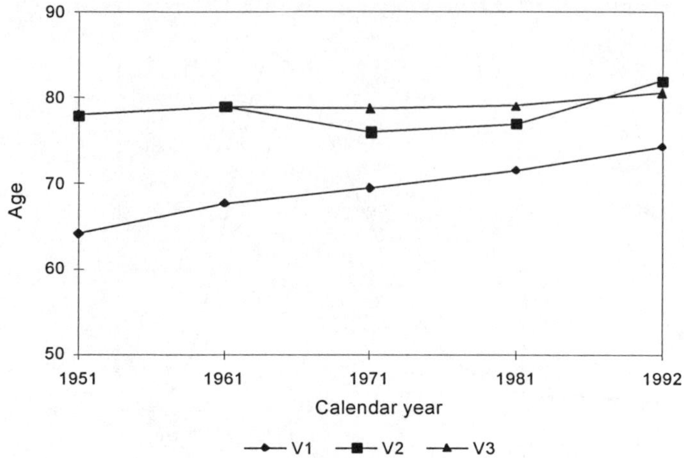

Figure 6.4 Life expectancy at birth [V1], Lexis point [V2], life expectancy at age 65 [V3] (Italian male population)

Finally, Figures 6.5 and 6.6 concern the behaviour of mortality rates. In Figure 6.5 mortality rates q_x referring to various mortality tables are plotted against the age x, while Figure 6.6 shows the so-called mortality profile at age 70 in relative terms, that is, the mortality rates $q_{70}(y)$ in various calendar year y divided by the mortality rate $q_{70}(1881)$ referring to the oldest table considered.

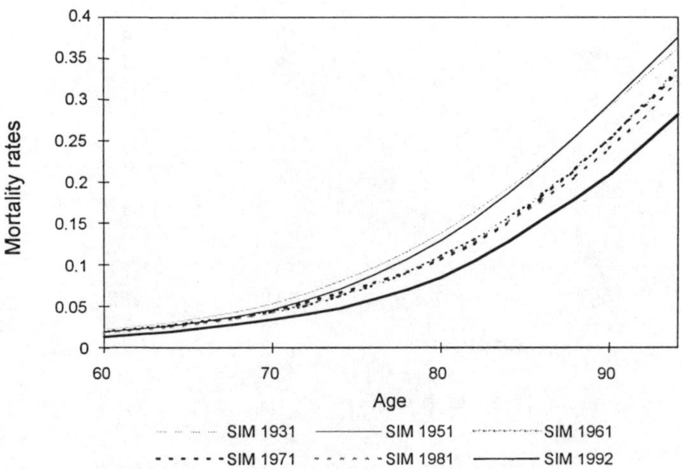

Figure 6.5 Mortality rates q_x $60 \leq x \leq 95$ (Italian male population)

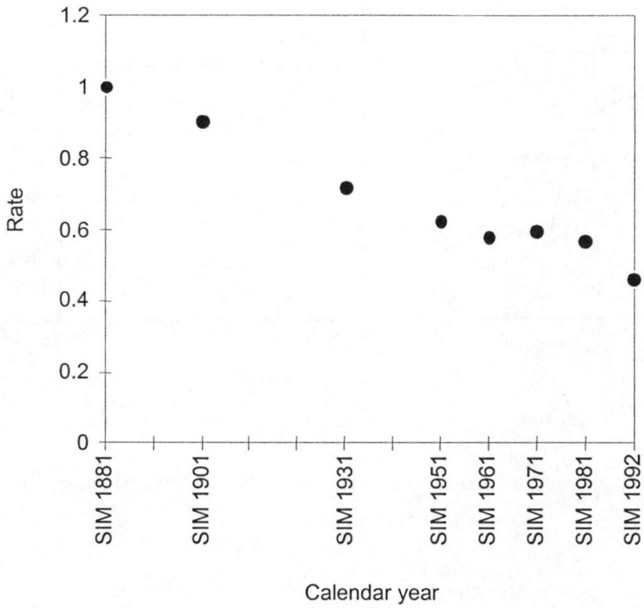

Figure 6.6 Mortality profiles $\frac{q_{70}(y)}{q_{70}(1881)}$ *(Italian male population)*

Results are self-evident. In particular the following aspects can be pointed out: an increase in the life expectancy (at birtn as well as at old ages), an overall increase in the most probable age of death, a decrease in mortality rates in particular at adult and old ages.

Turning back to the shape of the survival function and the curve of deaths, the following aspects of mortality in many countries can be singled out (for example, see Olivieri (2001)):

a. an increasing concentration of deaths around the mode (at old ages) of the curve of deaths is evident; so the survival function moves towards a rectangular shape, whence the term 'rectangularization' to denote this aspect (see Figure 6.7);
b. the mode of the curve of deaths (which, owing to the rectangularization, tends to coincide with the maximum age ω) moves towards very old ages; this aspect is called 'expansion' of the survival function (see Figure 6.8);
c. higher levels and a larger dispersion of accidental deaths at young ages (the so-called young mortality hump) have been more recently observed.

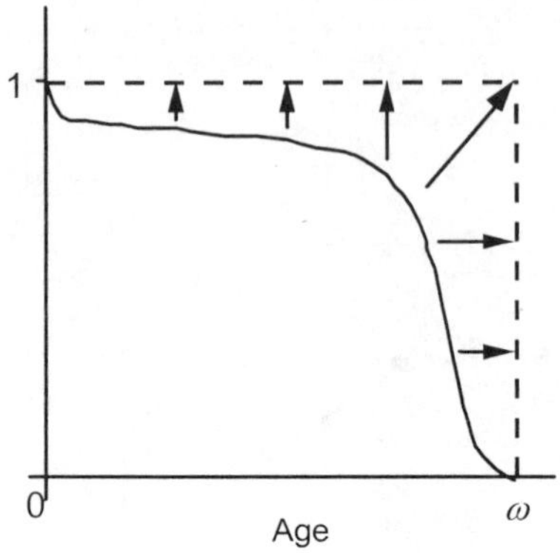

Figure 6.7 Rectangularization

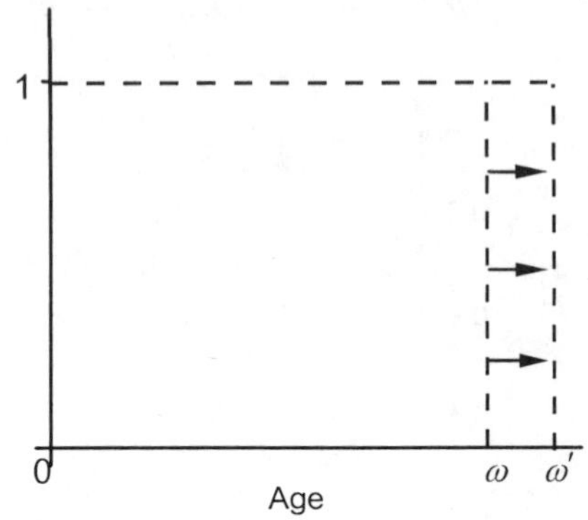

Figure 6.8 Expansion

In Section 6.3 the importance of aspects (a) and (b) in the context of mortality risk analysis is stressed.

6.2.2 Projections

Recent trends in mortality lead to the use of projected survival models for several actuarial purposes, such as for pricing and reserving for life annuities and other long-term living benefits.

When projecting mortality, the basic idea is to express the mortality itself as a function of the (future) calendar year y. If a single-figure representation of mortality is concerned, a projected mortality model is a real-valued function $\Psi(y)$. For example, the expected lifetime for a newborn, denoted by e_0 in a non-projected context, is represented by $e_0\ (y)$, a function of the calendar year y, when the future mortality trend is allowed for.

In actuarial calculations, the expression of mortality as a function of the age is needed. Then, in a projected context mortality at any age x must be considered as a function of the calendar year y. Hence, in a rather general setting, a projected mortality model is a function $\Phi(x,y)$, which may be a real-valued or a vector-valued function. The function (and, in particular, its parameters) is constructed by applying appropriate statistical procedures to past mortality experience.

In concrete terms, a real-valued function Φ may represent mortality rates, mortality odds, a force of mortality, a survival function, some transform of the survival function, and so on. A vector-valued function Φ is concerned when causes of death are allowed for.

Projection models often consist in straight extrapolation procedures of the mortality profile observed in the past (see Figure 6.9). It is worth noting that inconsistencies may emerge as a result of the extrapolations; for example we may find, for some calendar year y, $q_{x'}(y) > q_{x''}(y)$ with $x' < x''$, even at old ages. Hence, appropriate adjustments may be required.

Conversely, projection procedures based on mortality laws (say Gompertz, Makeham, Weibull, Heligman-Pollard, and so on) allow us to express the main features of the evolving scenario, such as the rectangularization and the expansion.

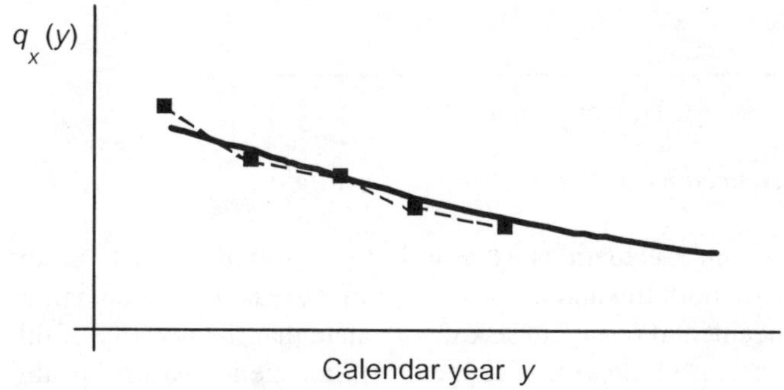

Figure 6.9 Extrapolation of the mortality profile

6.2.3 Mortality Risks: the Longevity Risk

Figures 6.10, 6.11 show projected mortality rates at a given age x (the continuous line) and two sets of possible future mortality experience (the dots). Deviations from the projected mortality rates in Figure 6.10 can be sensibly explained in terms of random fluctuations of the outcomes (the observed mortality rates) around the relevant expected values (the projected mortality rates).

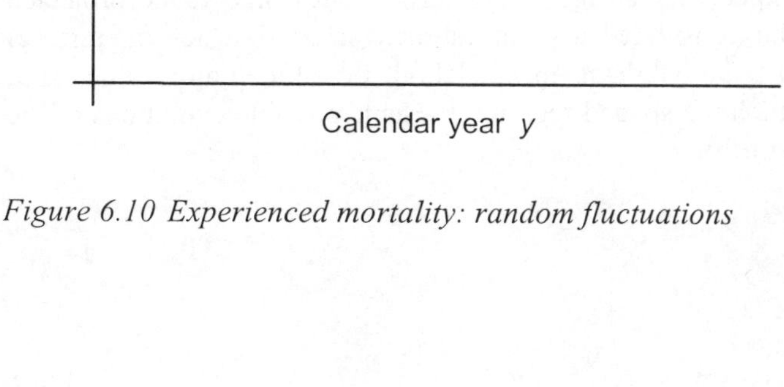

Figure 6.10 Experienced mortality: random fluctuations

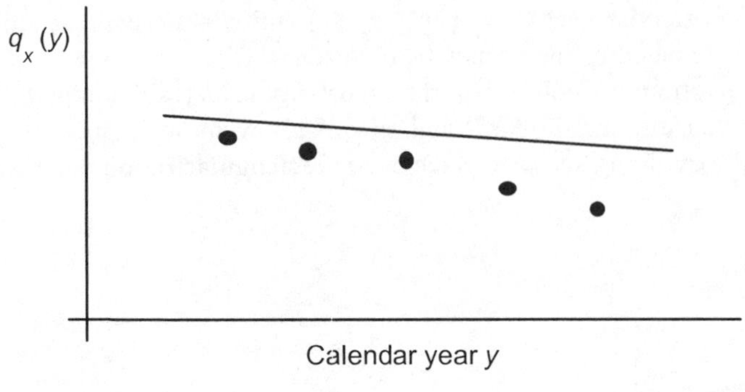

Figure 6.11 Experienced mortality: systematic deviations

The risk of random fluctuations is a well known type of risk in the insurance business, in both life and non-life insurance areas. It is often named 'process risk'. Fundamental results in risk theory state that the severity of this risk (conveniently assessed) decreases as the portfolio size increases. For this reason, random fluctuation risk is called a 'pooling risk'.

The experienced profile depicted in Figure 6.11 can hardly be attributed to random fluctuations only. Much more likely, this profile can be explained as the result of an actual mortality trend different from the forecasted one. So, systematic deviations arise. The risk of systematic deviations can be thought of as a 'model risk' or 'parameter risk', referring to the model used for projecting mortality and the relevant parameters.

The risk of systematic deviations cannot be hedged by increasing the portfolio size. On the contrary, its financial impact increases as the portfolio size increases, since deviations concern all the insured in the same direction. For this reason, the systematic deviation risk is called a 'non-pooling risk'.

It is worth stressing that future mortality is obviously random and hence, whatever kind of projection procedure is adopted, deviations from the forecasted mortality may occur.

Depending on the statistical model adopted in analysing past data and forecasting mortality, in some cases the assessment of uncertainty in future mortality constitutes an output of the statistical model itself. For simplicity, let us consider the projection of a single-figure representation of mortality, such as the life expectancy at age 0. For any (future) time y, the projected value $e_0(y)$ can be considered a point estimate, around which an interval estimate provides a probabilistic insight about possible future values (see Figure 6.12, in which the shaded region represents possible evolutions of the life expectancy at birth).

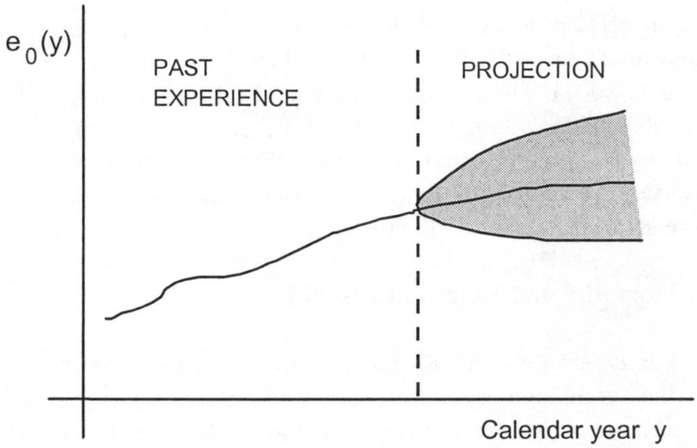

Figure 6.12 Interval estimates for forecasted life expectancy

In general terms, thus disregarding the possibility of finding a risk assessment arising from the statistical procedures adopted, in what follows we focus on possible systematic deviations from the (point) estimation of future mortality. In particular, we are interested in the consequences of this risk on valuations concerning living benefits. Restricting our attention to trends of the mortality pattern at old ages only, we will refer to this risk as the 'longevity risk'.

6.3 FUTURE MORTALITY AND DISABILITY SCENARIOS

Long term care (LTC) is care required in relation to chronic (or long-lasting) bad health conditions. LTC insurance provides income support for the insured, who needs nursing and/or medical care, in the form either of a forfeiture annuity benefit or nursing and medical expense refunding. Given the type of claim covered, LTC insurance has a lifetime duration. In what follows we focus on forfeiture annuity benefits, which represent the most common type of LTC benefit.

Where LTC annuities are concerned, combined mortality and disability scenarios constitute the natural framework for actuarial evaluations. First, it is evident that this type of living benefit is affected by the longevity risk pertaining to both healthy and disabled people. Moreover, the uncertainty in future disability inception rates (or disability prevalence rates) for the elderly should be carefully considered.

For the structure of LTC products and the relevant actuarial aspects, the reader can refer to Haberman and Pitacco (1999). Trends in disability are dealt with by Mayhew (2001). The papers by Ferri and Olivieri (2000) and Olivieri and Ferri (2003) address longevity risk in LTC covers, allowing for randomness in both mortality and disability trends. For more information about combined mortality and disability future scenarios, the reader should refer to the extensive set of references in the papers mentioned above.

6.3.1 Combining Mortality and Senescent Disability

As far as future trends are concerned, three main theories have been formulated about the combined evolution of senescent disability and mortality. The relevant scenarios are illustrated in Figure 6.13, in terms of expected lifetimes as functions of the calendar year.

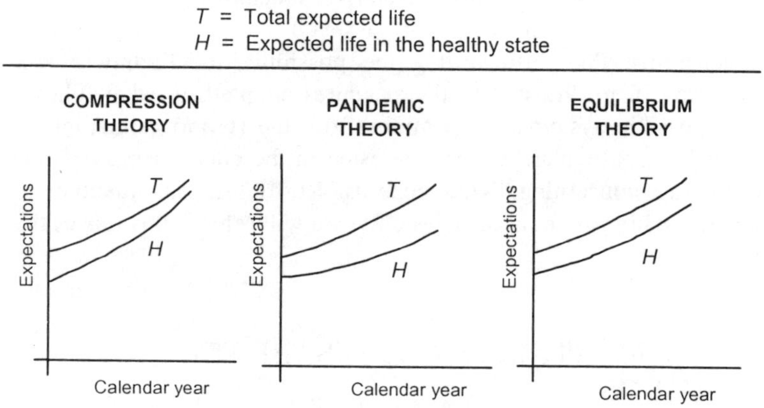

Figure 6.13 Combined mortality and senescent disability scenarios

i. 'Compression theory': chronic degenerative diseases will be postponed until the latest years of life because of medical advances. Assuming there is a maximum age, these improvements will result in a compression of the period of disability.
ii. 'Pandemic theory': the reduction in mortality rates is not accompanied by a decrease in disability rates; hence, the number of disabled people will increase steadily.
iii. 'Equilibrium theory': most of the changes in mortality are related to specific pathologies. The onset of chronic degenerative diseases and disability will be postponed and the time of death as well.

The scenarios depicted by the above mentioned theories produce different consequences for LTC insurers, as far as in-force LTC portfolios are concerned. In particular, compression theory suggests optimistic views, pandemic theory pessimistic ones. The dramatic differences among such theories imply a high level of uncertainty about the evolution of senescent disability. The adoption of projected tables for the evaluation of insured benefits seems necessary; however, since the three theories imply quite different scenarios, the mentioned uncertainty should be included in the evaluation model.

6.3.2 The Demand for LTC Insurance

LTC insurers are concerned with future combined mortality and senescent disability trends also when future acquisition of LTC policies is considered. Actually, we can imagine that trends following the compression theory would cause, at an individual level, a decreasing need for LTC and hence a decreasing demand for LTC insurance products, whilst trends following the equilibrium theory would cause a roughly constant need and demand; on the contrary, pandemic trends would imply an increasing need and demand for LTC products.

However, at a collective level, the demand depends on the size of the elderly population. Hence, assuming an increasing elderly population (as supported by population projections), we find that trends following the compression theory would cause a roughly stable demand for LTC products, while equilibrium trends would imply an increasing demand; finally, a dramatically increasing demand would be the consequence of trends following the pandemic theory.

6.4 ASSESSING AND FACING THE LONGEVITY RISK

The following problems are dealt with in this section: (a) how to express the longevity risk; (b) how to assess it; (c) how to face it.

Basic ideas underlying approaches to problem (a) are rather general and can be implemented whatever type of living benefits is concerned. Nevertheless, for the sake of simplicity we shall restrict our attention to benefits only depending on the residual lifetime, namely straight life annuities.

Problems (b) and (c) can be dealt with only by addressing specific categories of insurance products. So we shall separately consider life annuities, LTC insurance and sickness benefits for the elderly.

Ideas and results presented in this section come from the following papers. A more formal presentation can be found in Pitacco (2001). The impact of longevity risk on life annuities has been dealt with by Marocco and Pitacco (1998), where a reinsurance arrangement facing this risk is also discussed. Olivieri (2001) considers future mortality trends at young ages and old ages as well, and suggests an assessment of the impact of systematic deviations on term insurance and life annuities portfolios. The longevity risk in life annuities portfolios and pension plans and the relevant solvency requirements are dealt with by Olivieri and Pitacco (2003b), also allowing for investment risk. A joint analysis of financial and mortality risks has been proposed by Coppola et al. (2000). The paper by Olivieri and Pitacco (2002a) deals with Bayesian inference on mortality improvements. In Olivieri (2002) reinsurance arrangements for longevity risk transfer are analysed, referring to annuities portfolios.

The paper by Ferri and Olivieri (2000) and Olivieri and Ferri (2003) concern LTC benefits in a moving scenario in which both future mortality and future senescent disability are random. Olivieri and Pitacco (2001a) deal with the enhanced pension, in other words a particular LTC product; the costs for financing a proper solvency reserve, tailored to the characteristics and magnitude of the risks, and a stop-loss reinsurance arrangement are analysed.

The longevity risk affecting sickness benefits for the elderly (for example, post-retirement sickness benefits) is analysed by Olivieri and Pitacco (2002b). Finally, Biffis and Olivieri (2002), referring to pension plans, show how packaging benefits of various types can reduce the overall impact of longevity risk.

6.4.1 Future Scenarios: Deterministic vs Probabilistic Approach

The longevity risk arises from uncertainty in future mortality (and possibly disability) trends. So, when focussing our attention on the impact of this risk, first we have to choose a set of sensible future scenarios, such as a set (or 'space') of survival functions. The space of survival functions can be a discrete set (and in particular a finite one), or a continuous one (in this case survival functions should be assigned via a mathematical model, whose parameters take values in given intervals).

The choice of a set of future scenarios allows us to check the consequences of the longevity risk (for example in terms of expected numbers of surviving annuitants or expected payments by the insurer) in two ways, a deterministic and a probabilistic one. Adopting a deterministic approach, different reasonable scenarios (for example an 'optimistic' scenario, a 'medium' one, and so on) are considered and the relevant calculations are performed. Such an approach is usually called 'scenario testing'. It should be stressed that the scenario testing allows for the random fluctuation risk, whereas it provides just rough information about the longevity risk, typically through ranges for some results.

Conversely, a probabilistic approach consists in considering each scenario as a possible outcome to which some 'measure' is assigned. So, a second step in the modelling process is required, namely the expression of our degree of belief in the various scenarios; hence, a probability distribution over the set of scenarios must be assigned.

If the scenarios constitute a finite set, a probability should be assigned to each scenario, that is, to each survival function (see Figure 6.14). On the contrary, when a continuous set is concerned, a probability density function can express our degree of belief, referring for example to some parameter of the survival function. The choice of the density function can be driven by the values assumed by some projected survival functions (see Figure 6.15, where three projected survival functions are used as a starting point).

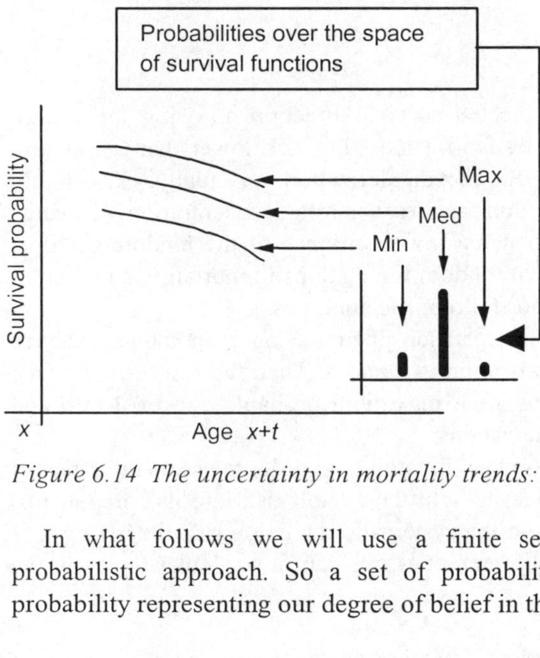

Figure 6.14 The uncertainty in mortality trends: a discrete approach

In what follows we will use a finite set of scenarios, adopting a probabilistic approach. So a set of probabilities will be assigned, each probability representing our degree of belief in the corresponding scenario.

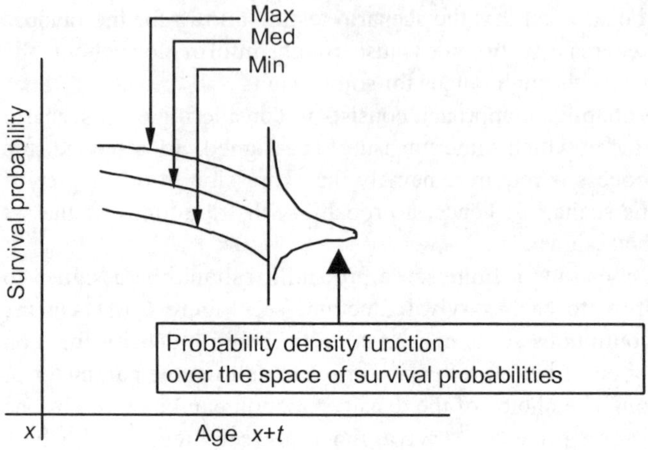

Figure 6.15 The uncertainty in mortality trends: a continuous approach

6.4.2 Life Annuities

It is worth noting that a projected survival function allowing for a high degree of rectangularization leads to a mortality risk lower than a function with a smaller degree of rectangularization. Actually, a highly rectangularized survival function implies a strong concentration of deaths around the Lexis point and hence a lower variance of the random lifetime. This results in a reduced risk of random fluctuations in mortality, and then in a reduced mortality risk in a portfolio of life annuities.

However the degree of the expansion phenomenon is unknown, whence the future location of the Lexis point is random. Then the insurer must face the risk coming from the unknown maximum probable age of death, and hence the risk of systematic deviations.

Several quantities can be used as 'functions' in order to assess the effect of mortality risks, and in particular to split the overall risk into its components, the random fluctuation risk and the systematic deviation risk. Referring to a portfolio of single premium life annuities, we can in particular focus on the following quantities:

- the variance or the standard deviation of the random present values of the insurer's future payments;
- the risk index, that is, the ratio between the standard deviation of the random present value of the insurer's future payments and its expected value;

- the percentiles of the probability distribution of the random present value of the insurer's future payments;
- the percentiles of the probability distribution of the random present value of the insurer's future payments;
- the required solvency margin, conveniently defined in order to allow for the specific risk profile of the insurer.

Here we focus on the required solvency margin, following the approach adopted by Olivieri and Pitacco (2003b).

Let us assume three projected mortality scenarios, each described by the Heligman-Pollard law, with various degrees of rectangularization and expansion. In Figure 6.16 the three scenarios, labelled [min], [med] and [max] respectively, are represented in terms of the curve of deaths, and compared with a scenario, labelled [C], assumed to represent the result of recent cross-sectional observations. The following probabilities are attributed to the projected scenarios:

$$\rho^{[\text{min}]} = 0.2; \quad \rho^{[med]} = 0.6\,; \quad \rho^{[\text{max}]} = 0.2\,.$$

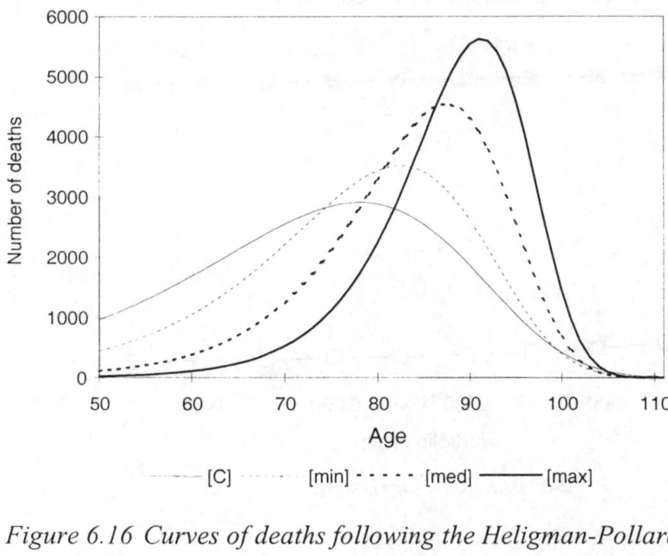

Figure 6.16 Curves of deaths following the Heligman-Pollard law

A portfolio consisting of a single cohort of annuitants has been considered. All annuitants are aged 65. The annual amount of the annuity is the same for all annuitants. Single premiums are calculated with the mortality assumption provided by the scenario [med]; the same scenario is used to evaluate the portfolio reserve. No investment risk has been considered. The following solvency criterion has been adopted.

Let $t = 0$ denote the time of solvency ascertainment. The probability that in all years, that is, at times $t = 1, 2, \ldots$, the assets allocated to the portfolio are greater or equal to the liabilities of the portfolio itself must assume an assigned value (97.5 per cent in the following numerical example). No capital allocation at times following $t = 0$ is allowed for. Hence, the insurer must allocate assets at time $t = 0$ only. These assets are partially funded by the single premium paid for the annuity purchase, while the remaining part consists of own capital.

In Figure 6.17, the (relative) required solvency margin, defined as

$$\frac{\textit{required assets} - \textit{portfolio reserve}}{\textit{portfolio reserve}}$$

(the two quantities being referred to time $t = 0$), is plotted against the size of the portfolio. Evaluations have been performed according to the deterministic approach using the scenario [med], and the probabilistic approach weighting the three scenarios with the probabilities stated above.

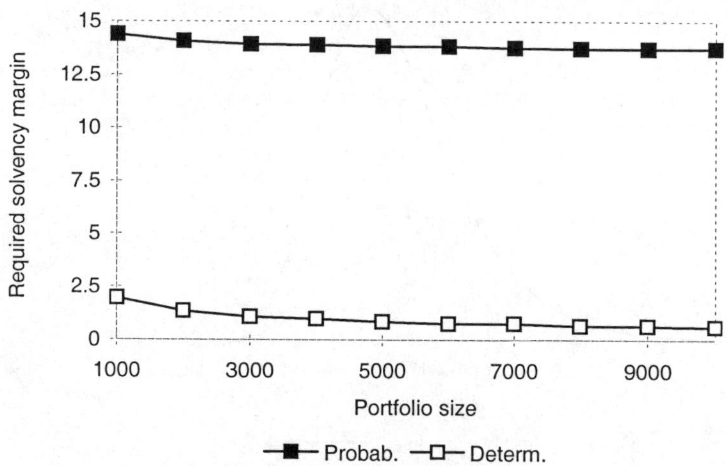

Figure 6.17 Required solvency margin (×100)

The deterministic approach only allows for the random fluctuation risk, which can be hedged by increasing the portfolio size. Actually, as shown by Figure 6.17, the required solvency margin tends to zero as the portfolio size increases. On the contrary, the probabilistic approach clearly reveals the presence of the longevity risk, resulting in a much higher solvency requirement. Moreover, the solvency requirement has a (high) positive asymptotic value witnessing the systematic component of the mortality risk, in other words the longevity risk.

In more general terms, the longevity risk can be faced by:

i. a safety loading of premiums (possibly with an annuity adjustment mechanism aiming at distribution of mortality profits to the annuitants);
ii. an adequate solvency margin (or risk-based capital);
iii. reinsurance arrangements.

Some aspects concerning point (i) are dealt with in Section 6.5.2. Here we focus our attention on some reinsurance arrangements facing the longevity risk.

Various reinsurance arrangements can be conceived, at least in principle. In particular (see Olivieri, 2002):

1. a surplus reinsurance, aiming at ceding part of high-amount annuities;
2. an XL-like reinsurance treaty, to be structured in such a way that the reinsurer pays the final part of the annuity while exceeding a given term (for example, while exceeding the age of 85; see Figure 6.18);
3. a stop-loss reinsurance, aiming at partially covering the required portfolio reserve (see Figure 6.19).

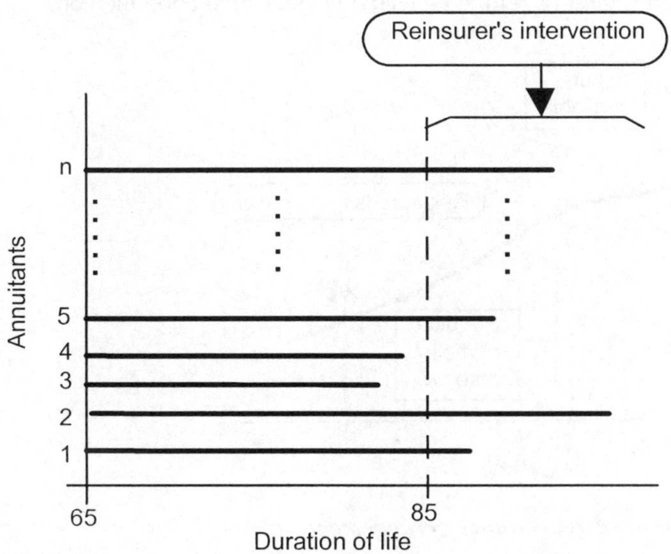

Figure 6.18 An XL reinsurance arrangement

However, in realistic terms, reinsurance arrangements defined on a short-medium period basis should be addressed, in order to avoid too high safety loadings in the reinsurance premiums. To this purpose, stop-loss arrangements could provide interesting reinsurance coverages. According to the stop-loss logic, reinsurer's interventions aim at preventing the unsolvency of the cedant, caused by mortality deviations (systematic as well as random). The effect of mortality deviations can be perceived, for example, by comparing the assets available at a given time with the portfolio reserve required to meet the insurer's obligations related to the annuitants surviving at that time (see Figure 6.19). Hence, the reinsurer's intervention can be based on this comparison. A too short period can emphasize the random deviation effects; conversely, a too long period implies a severe longevity risk for the reinsurer, and then (as mentioned above) very high reinsurance premiums.

Consistently with a stop-loss reinsurance arrangement, the assessment of the longevity risk should be based on the evaluation of the probability distributions of 'losses' meant as differences between the required portfolio reserve and the available assets. When simple portfolios are concerned (typically one-cohort portfolios) these probability distributions can be easily derived from the probability distributions of the random number of survivors. A reinsurance arrangement of the type described above was proposed by Marocco and Pitacco (1998), which the reader is referred to for some numerical examples, built up with both analytical and simulation methods.

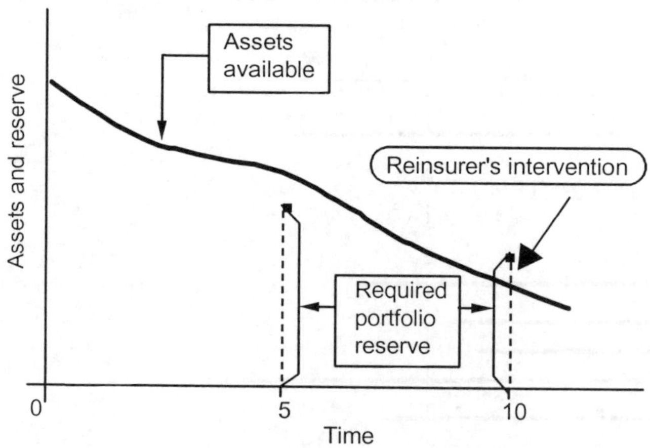

Figure 6.19 A stop-loss reinsurance arrangement

6.4.3 LTC Insurance

For the sake of brevity, we focus our attention on a particular LTC product only, the so-called enhanced pension. This product provides a straight life annuity from the retirement age on, uplifted in case the annuitant becomes disabled (according to a given definition of LTC disability).

The following hypotheses are adopted. Only one level of disability is considered. Because of the usually chronic character of LTC disability, the possibility of recovery from the LTC state is disregarded. Randomness other than the demographic one (coming from mortality and disability) is disregarded; in particular no investment risk is taken into account.

In order to appraise the risk inherent in a tariff structure for LTC covers, uncertainty of the future evolution of both mortality and senescent disability must be modelled. Following Ferri and Olivieri (2000) and Olivieri and Pitacco (2001a), different scenarios have been focused, each one including a given projection of mortality and disability trends. The scenarios have been defined in terms of the evolution of the expected time spent in the healthy state and in the disability state.

To this purpose the following quantities, referred to a person with a given age, must be considered:

- $e_{H,H}$ = expected time spent in the healthy state by a healthy person, that is, healthy life expectancy for a healthy person;
- $e_{H,LTC}$ = expected time spent in the LTC state by a healthy person, that is, disability life expectancy for a healthy person;
- e_{LTC} = life expectancy for a disabled person;
- $e_H = e_{H,H} + e_{H,LTC}$ = total life expectancy for a healthy person.

With reference to a person entering insurance in the healthy state, the three theories described in Section 6.3.1 can be expressed in terms of the evolution of life expectancies as follows:

i. when compared to past data, e_H increases with a major contribution (in relative terms) from $e_{H,H}$;
ii. e_H increases with a major contribution (in relative terms) from $e_{H,LTC}$;
iii. $e_{H,H}$ and $e_{H,LTC}$ increase at similar rates.

To express different scenarios, analytical laws for mortality and disability rates have been used in performing numerical evaluations. Mortality has been represented by a Weibull law, while disability inception rates have been modelled using a Gompertz law.

A scenario space consisting of five scenarios, $\{S_1, S_2, S_3, S_4, S_5\}$, has been considered; the five items consist of combined hypotheses about mortality and disability trends, expressed by the parameters of the analytical laws. Scenario S_C, coming from recent cross-sectional observations of mortality and disability of elderly people, has been taken as a starting-point for the construction of the five projected scenarios. Table 6.1 shows the values of the expectancies $e_{H,H}$, $e_{H,LTC}$, e_H, e_{LTC} for males aged 65 under each scenario.

Table 6.1 Life expectancies

Scenario	Life expectancy for healthy people			Life expectancy for LTC people
	in Healthy state	in LTC state	total	
	$e_{H,H}$	$e_{H,LTC}$	e_H	e_{LTC}
S_C	14.428	1.566	15.995	15.307
S_1	15.156	1.435	16.591	15.931
S_2	16.042	1.563	17.605	16.983
S_3	15.844	1.749	17.593	16.983
S_4	15.501	2.073	17.574	16.983
S_5	16.577	2.366	18.943	18.397

In the scenario construction, it has been assumed that the total life expectancy e_H will increase anyhow, as suggested by mortality trends in populations including both healthy and disabled people. As far as contributions from $e_{H,H}$ and $e_{H,LTC}$ are concerned, it is easy to deduce, comparing the results in Table 6.1, that scenario S_1 implies lower expected costs than the others, representing consequences depicted by the compression theory. On the other side, S_5 is the scenario with the highest expected costs, corresponding to the consequences of the pandemic theory. Scenario S_3 is, in some sense, intermediate between the above depicted scenarios, reflecting the equilibrium theory. Finally, S_2 and S_4 depict projections that are intermediate between scenario S_3 and the two 'extreme' scenarios.

The riskiness of the enhanced pensions has been evaluated according to a deterministic approach and a probabilistic one as well (see Section 6.4.1). In the probabilistic approach, the scenarios are weighted as follows:

$$\rho^{[1]} = 0.05\,;\ \ \rho^{[2]} = 0.15\,;\ \ \rho^{[3]} = 0.60\,;\ \ \rho^{[4]} = 0.15\,;\ \ \rho^{[5]} = 0.05\,.$$

Following Olivieri and Pitacco (2001a), here we analyse the riskiness in terms of solvency requirements. As far as the definition of solvency requirements is concerned, the approach described in Section 6.4.2 is adopted.

Figure 6.20 illustrates the behaviour of the required solvency margin. Note that small portfolio sizes have been addressed because of the type of insurance cover, actually less common than life annuity products. Again, the deterministic approach simply reveals the hedging opportunity provided by the portfolio size. On the contrary, the probabilistic approach singles out the presence of the systematic component of the demographic risk, witnessed by the high asymptotic value of the required solvency margin.

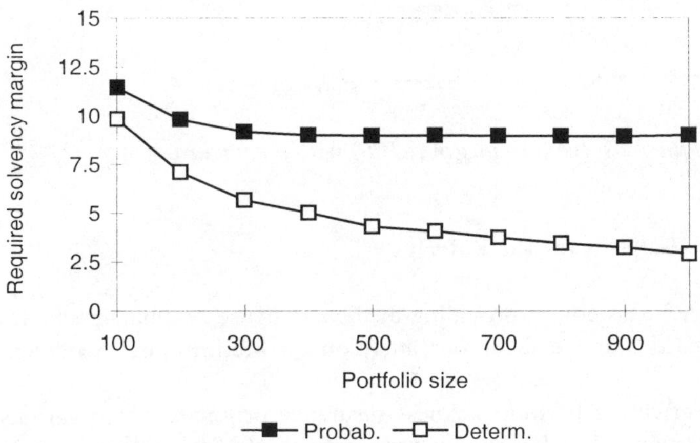

Figure 6.20 Required solvency margin (×100)

Reinsurance arrangements can help in facing the longevity risk in an LTC portfolio. Let us focus on a stop-loss reinsurance arrangement as described in Section 6.4.3, and assume that the reinsurer intervenes when the assets are less than 90 per cent of the required portfolio reserve.

In Figure 6.21 the solvency requirement in the presence of a stop-loss treaty is compared with the solvency requirement when no reinsurance works; results have been obtained adopting the probabilistic approach. It is worth noting that in the presence of a reinsurance treaty, the required solvency margin decreases as the portfolio size increases (within the range considered); this fact bears witness that a significant portion of the systematic risk moves from the cedant to the reinsurer. For more details the reader can refer to Olivieri and Pitacco (2001a).

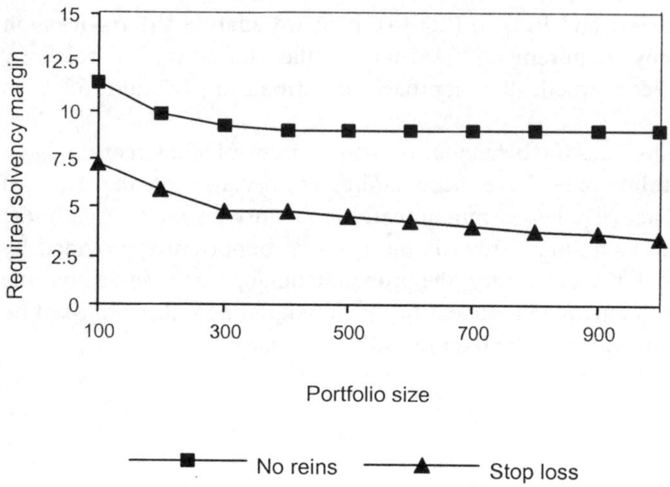

Figure 6.21 Required solvency margin (×100) with a reinsurance arrangement

6.4.4 Sickness Benefits for the Elderly

In this section sickness covers providing medical expense reimbursement are addressed. In particular we focus our attention on lifetime post-retirement sickness covers.

Uncertainty affecting lifetime sickness insurance originates from various causes. The following classification gives an insight into the randomness of a lifetime sickness cover, and can help in appreciating the role of a premium system in determining the randomness itself. Uncertainty comes from:

a. the random number of claim events in any given insured period (in particular, in each year);
b. the random amount (medical expenses refunded) relating to each claim;
c. the random duration of the life of the insured.

Note that items (a) and (b) are common to all covers in the framework of general insurance. The relevant effects can be faced by adopting appropriate premium calculation principles, and in particular by charging premiums with a convenient safety loading. However, it should be stressed that paucity of sickness data relating to very old ages increases the difficulty in assessing the randomness originating from items (a) and (b). Item (c) represents the mortality risk; its impact is strongly related with the premium system adopted.

Several premium systems can be conceived and are actually used in pricing post-retirement sickness covers. In particular:

1. a single premium at retirement age only, fully meeting the future costs of the insurer;
2. a sequence of level premiums, determined according to a given premium calculation principle;
3. a sequence of 'natural' premiums, each premium meeting the costs of the relevant year; in this case, benefits are funded on a pay-as-you-go basis;
4. mixtures of (1) and (2), that is, a single premium (partially meeting the future costs) plus a sequence of level premiums;
5. mixtures of (1) and (3), that is, a single premium (partially meeting the future costs) plus a sequence of annual premiums proportional to natural premiums (for instance, a given percentage of the natural premiums).

Each premium system leads to a different reserve accumulation process (and this implies a different exposure to the longevity risk, as mentioned below). In particular, premium system (1) requires that the whole single premium is initially reserved, while the annual expected costs are progressively funded drawing from the reserve (see Figure 6.22). Premium system (2) leads to a reserve initially increasing and finally decreasing, because of the behaviour of annual expected costs (see Figure 6.23). Premium system (3) does not require, by definition, any reserve accumulation.

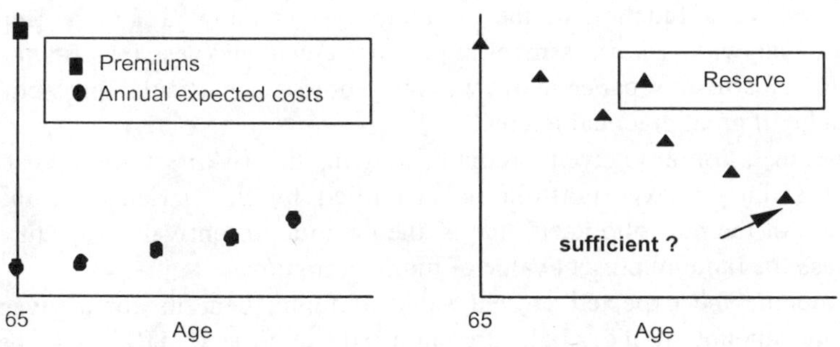

Figure 6.22 Funding sickness benefits: the case of a single premium

Each premium arrangement has interesting features from the point of view of the insurer or from the point of view of the insured. For example, a single premium (1) entirely meeting the future costs may be of great interest for the insured if a lump sum (such as a survival benefit provided by an endowment policy) becomes available at the retirement age. Conversely, a sequence of natural premiums (3) can intuitively reduce the variability of the portfolio loss and hence can be appealing for the insurer. Mixtures (4) and (5) may constitute good compromises. For example, a mixture (4) is commonly used for funding costs related to Continuous Care Retirement Communities in the US; in this case an advance fee (namely a single premium) is followed by a sequence of periodic fees (periodic premiums), possibly adjusted for inflation.

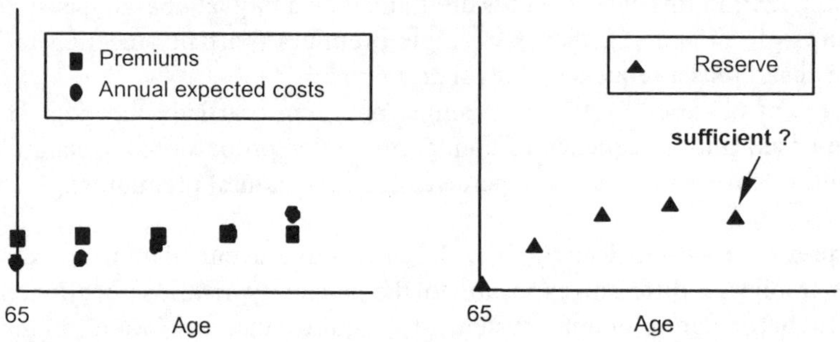

Figure 6.23 Funding sickness benefits: the case of lifetime level premiums

The problem of funding lifetime post-retirement sickness covers, in presence of the longevity risk, is analysed by Olivieri and Pitacco (2002b). The paper focuses on the mortality risk (and in particular on its longevity component), disregarding the other sources of risk, and aiming to assess the longevity risk as a function of the premium system adopted. For a deep analysis of longevity risk assessment in post-retirement sickness benefits the reader can refer to this paper. Now we only address a particular problem, which can be of great practical interest.

Assume that, for any given premium system, the riskiness of a post-retirement sickness cover portfolio is quantified by the variance of the random loss of the portfolio itself, that is, the random present value of future benefits less the random present value of future premiums.

Let E denote the expected present value of future benefits for a given policy. The amount of the single premium paid at time 0, $\Pi(\alpha)$, can be expressed in terms of E:

$$\Pi(\alpha) = \alpha E\,;$$

the annual premiums can be denoted by $\pi_k(\alpha)$, $k = 1, 2, \ldots$, and in particular by $\pi(\alpha)$ if constant.

If $\alpha = 1$ we have the case in which a single premium is only paid (case 1); if $\alpha = 0$ we find the cases in which level premiums (case 2) or natural premiums (case 3) will be paid; finally, if $0 < \alpha < 1$ a premium paid in 0 will be followed by a sequence of annual premiums (mixtures 4 and 5). Note that letting $0 \leq \alpha \leq 1$ all the premium systems can be expressed in terms of the mixtures (4) and (5).

For any given premium system, the variance of the loss function increases as the parameter α increases, because of the higher portion of benefits financed by the single premium paid in 0 and hence because of the higher level of pre-funding, which can reveal itself not sufficient to meet future costs if the actual mortality improvement is higher than the expected one.

Moreover, for any value of α (with the obvious exception of $\alpha = 1$) the variance is smaller in premium systems of type (5) than in premium systems of type (4), which means that annual premiums proportional to annual costs (that is, proportional to natural premiums) are less risky than level premiums, because of the lower reserve levels in the former case.

However, from a commercial point of view, level premiums $\pi(\alpha)$ are usually preferred. In order to design appealing premium arrangements, but aiming at limiting risk, the insurer may adopt level premiums charged with an appropriate loading.

Assume a proportional loading, so that the charged level premium is given by

$$\pi(\alpha; \lambda) = (1 + \lambda)\, \pi(\alpha) \,.$$

Properly choosing the loading parameter λ, the insurer can reduce the variance of the loss function for a premium system of type (4), possibly obtaining the variance of the corresponding system of type (5).

Table 6.2 illustrates some values for the parameter λ as a function of the parameter α which defines the premium arrangement. For each α, the parameter λ is assessed so that the variance of the level premium system coincides with the variance of the natural premium system; in case this target cannot be reached, λ is chosen so that the variance is minimized. The number of policies is denoted by N. Results are drawn from the paper by Olivieri and Pitacco (2002b), in which three future mortality scenarios are considered and weighted as described in Section 6.4.1.

Note that, for any given value of α, the requested loading decreases as the portfolio size increases. However, the asymptotic value is greater than 0, and this is clearly due to the presence of the systematic component of the mortality risk, namely the longevity risk.

Finally, it is worth stressing that the premium loading structure considered is not meant as a tool for facing longevity risk. The aim is simply to arrange premiums so that the riskiness (in terms of variance of the loss funcion) is the lowest for a given initial payment.

Table 6.2 Loading parameter λ

α	$N = 100$	$N = 1000$	$N = 10\,000$	$N = 100\,000$
0.2	0.2470	0.1933	0.1823	0.1811
0.4	0.2254	0.1891	0.1814	0.1805
0.6	0.2191	0.1877	0.1810	0.1803
0.8	0.2160	0.1871	0.1809	0.1802
1	0	0	0	0

6.4.5 Packaging Benefits to Face the Longevity Risk

Pension plans usually provide combinations of life (and possibly health) insurance benefits arranged for a given group of persons, for example the employees of a company.

For brevity, let us consider benefits depending on the duration of life only, namely old-age pensions (life annuities), lump-sum death benefits, survivor pensions and reversionary pensions. Hence, only mortality risks are involved.

Using various quantities to assess the effect of the mortality risks (such as variance, risk index and some percentiles of the distribution of the present value of pension scheme liabilities), it is possible to prove that the combination of benefits plays an important role in reducing the impact of these risks (at the same time providing the customers with a wider range of covers).

Interesting results, with numerical illustrations, can be found in Biffis and Olivieri (2002). Here we simply point out the following feature. Although combining several types of benefits can increase the overall risk, possibly because of positive correlations, in relative terms the risk decreases. This means in particular that the ratio between the amount of money required for solvency purpose and the mathematical reserve is lower when more benefits are provided. In other words, a better hedging of the mortality risk can rely on a larger overall mathematical reserve.

6.5 GENERALIZING THE STRUCTURE OF LIFE ANNUITIES

The present section aims at stimulating the debate about life annuities, meant as an important tool to provide post-retirement income. Annuity products will be addressed in the context of overall post-retirement income planning. Of course, attention will be mostly devoted to demographic issues, to keep the presentation in line with the main scope of this chapter. Nevertheless, important financial aspects should not be disregarded when assessing and comparing the various opportunities for meeting post-retirement income needs.

Here we disregard the distinction between 'pension annuities' (that is, annuities linked in some way with occupational pension schemes) and 'purchased life annuities' (that is, annuities based on an individual policy as a result of a strictly personal choice, not involving pension scheme rules). Actually, the distinction varies from country to country, also depending on specific tax rules.

Innovative ideas and proposals are presented and discussed in the reports by the Department for Work and Pensions (2002) in the UK, and the Retirement Choice Working Party (2001). The paper by Wadsworth and Findlater (2002) suggests a technical structure for a fund providing annuities. A comprehensive description of several annuities markets is provided by Cardinale et al. (2002). Various arrangements for annuities in presence of the longevity risk are dealt with, in their technical perspective, by Olivieri and Pitacco (2001b). Milevsky and Promislow (2001) analyse mortality guarantees involved by the option to annuitize. Finally, the paper by Olivieri and Pitacco (2003a) deals with the pricing of annuitization guarantees when the longevity risk is allowed for.

6.5.1 Flexibility in Financing Post-Retirement Income

We now propose a framework which can stimulate discussion and assessment of new ideas in the area of annuity design. We assume that an accumulation process takes place throughout the working period of an individual. After retirement, a decumulation process takes place and hence income requirements are met using, in some way, the accumulated fund.

Figure 6.24 illustrates the process consisting of:

1. accumulation of contributions during the working period;
2. (possible) annuitization of (part of) the accumulated fund (before or after retirement);
3. getting post-retirement income from life annuities or through income drawdown.

The annuitization of (part of) the accumulated fund consists in purchasing a deferred annuity if annuitization takes place during the accumulation period, an immediate annuity otherwise. Hence, at any time resources available for financing post-retirement income are shared between a non-annuitised fund and an annuitized one. It is sensible to assume that a higher degree of flexibility in selecting investment opportunities concerns the non-annuitized fund.

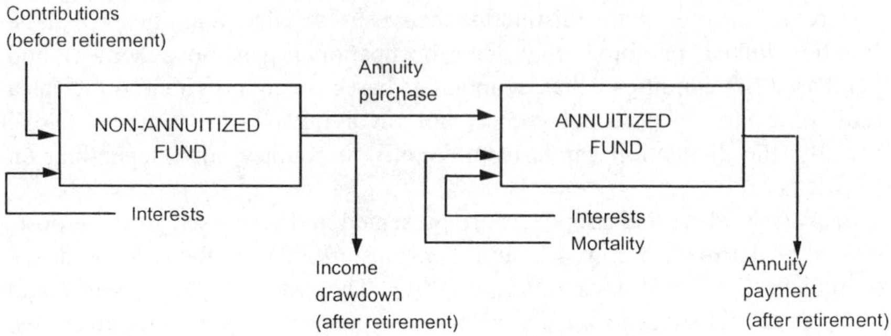

Figure 6.24 From accumulation to post-retirement income

Figures 6.25 and 6.26 illustrate the behaviour of the non-annuitized fund and the annuitized fund respectively. Effects of the annuity purchase (jumps in the processes), of income drawdown and of annuity payment are singled out.

The slope of the non-annuitized fund depends, while the fund itself is increasing, on both contributions and interests, whereas it depends on the drawdown policy while the fund is decreasing. As regards the annuitized fund, its slope depends on interests and mortality (reserves pertaining to people dying are assumed to be credited to the survivors) while it is increasing, whereas it depends on annuity payment while decreasing.

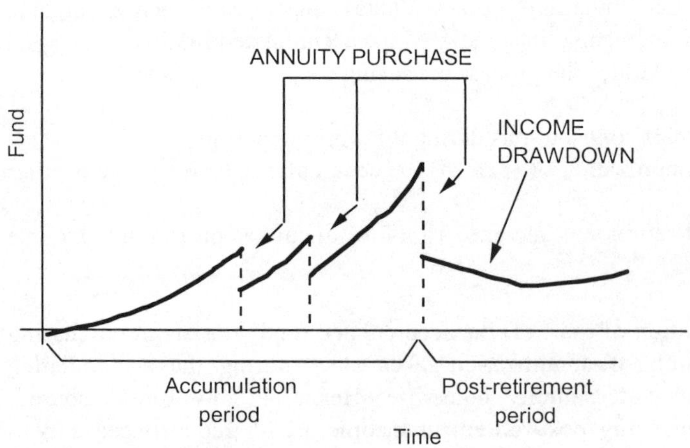

Figure 6.25 The non-annuitized fund

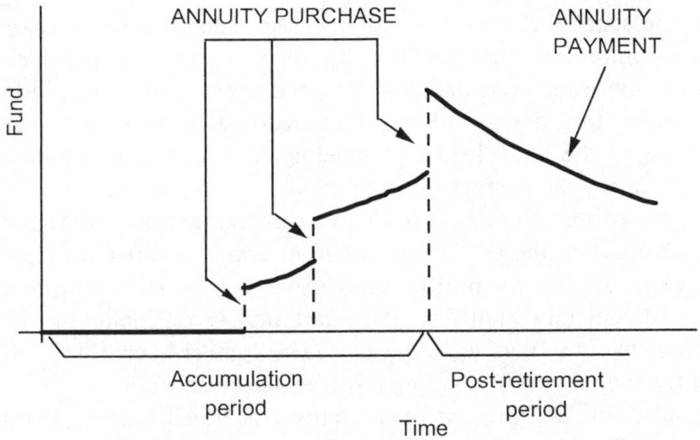

Figure 6.26 The annuitized fund

Let us denote with $F_{NA}(t)$ and $F_A(t)$ the values of the non-annuitized fund and the annuitized fund respectively, at time t. The degree of the annuitization policy can be summarized by the annuitization ratio $\mathrm{R}(t)$, defined as follows:

$$\mathrm{R}(t) = \frac{F_A(t)}{F_{NA}(t) + F_A(t)} .$$

Note that, obviously, $0 \leq \mathrm{R}(t) \leq 1$, and that $\mathrm{R}(t) = 0$ means that, up to time t, no annuity has been purchased, whilst $\mathrm{R}(t) = 1$ means that, at time t, the whole fund available consists in reserves related to purchased annuities.

Figures 6.27 to 6.30 illustrate some strategies for financing post-retirement income. In most cases, the technical tool provided by the life annuity is involved. The various strategies are described in terms of the annuitization ratio profile, thus the value of $\mathrm{R}(t)$ is plotted against time t.

To make interpretation easier, initially let us suppose that a specified mortality assumption is adopted when annuitizing (a part of) the accumulated fund and that the assumption itself cannot be replaced in relation to the purchased annuity, whatever the mortality trend might be.

Figure 6.27 illustrates two 'extreme' choices. Choice (1) consists in building up a traditional deferred annuity. In this case, each amount paid to the accumulation fund (possibly a level premium, or a single recurrent premium) is immediately converted into a deferred annuity; hence the accumulated fund is completely annuitized. Post-retirement income requirements are met by the annuity (a flat annuity or, possibly, a rising profile annuity, namely an escalating annuity or an inflation-linked annuity).

Choice (2) represents the opposite extreme. No annuitization works, whence income requirements are fulfilled by income drawdown, which implies spreading the fund accumulated at retirement, over future life expectation, according to some spreading rule. Sometimes pensioners prefer this choice because of the high degree of freedom in selecting investment opportunities even during the post-retirement period.

It should be stressed that choice (1) leads to an inflexible post-retirement income, whilst choice (2) allows the pensioner to adopt a spreading rule consistent with a specific income profile. Conversely, it is worth noting that arrangement (1) completely transfers the mortality risk (including its longevity component) to the annuity provider, whilst according to arrangement (2) the mortality risk is suffered by the pensioner only.

In more general terms, the process of mortality risk transfer depends on the annuitization profile: the portion of mortality risk transferred from the pensioner to the annuity provider increases as the annuitization ratio increases. The following arrangements constitute practical examples of how mortality risk can be transferred, as time goes on, to the annuity provider.

The annuitization of the fund at retirement date only is illustrated in Figure 6.28, which depicts the particular case of a complete annuitization. This arrangement is characterized by flexibility in the investment choice during the accumulation period; conversely it produces an inflexible post-retirement income profile.

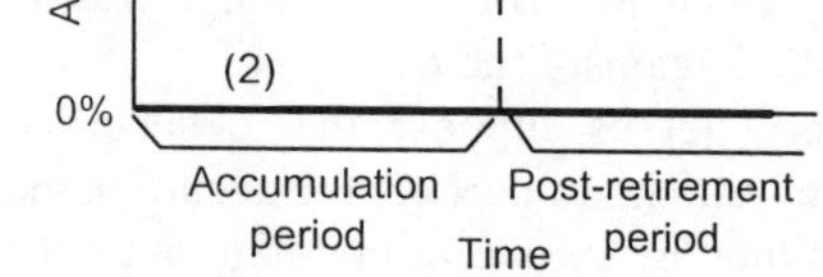

Arrangements:
1. Deferred annuity
2. Income drawdown

Figure 6.27 Staggered annuitization

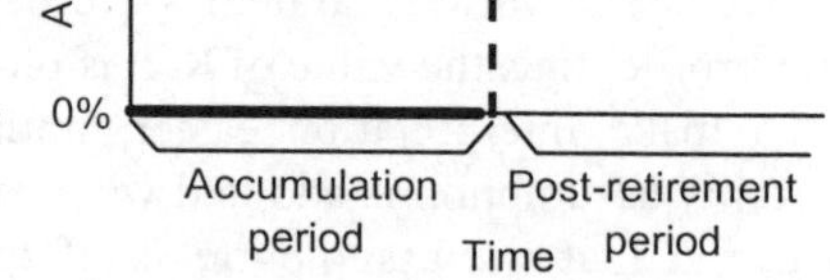

Figure 6.28 Immediate annuity

In Figure 6.29 the annuitization ratio increases during the accumulation period because of the positive jumps corresponding to the purchase of annuities with various deferment periods (which can constitute, in some contracts, the exercise of an option to annuitize). The behaviour of the annuitization ratio between jumps obviously depends on contribution and interests affecting the non-annuitized fund as well as on interests and mortality as regards the annuitized fund.

Conversely, Figure 6.30 illustrates the case in which no annuitization is made throughout the accumulation period, whereas the fund available after the retirement date is partially used to purchase annuities; such a process is sometimes called 'staggered annuitization' or 'staggered vesting'. The behavior of the ratio between jumps depends on interests and income drawdown as regards the non-annuitized fund as well as interests and mortality as regards the annuitized fund.

Arrangements like those illustrated by Figures 6.29 and 6.30 are characterized by a high degree of flexibility as regards both the post-retirement income profile and the choice of investment opportunities for the non-annuitized fund.

The framework proposed above clearly shows the wide range of choices provided by different annuitization strategies. So convenient investment and annuity products can be designed, complying with different needs and preferences of the clients.

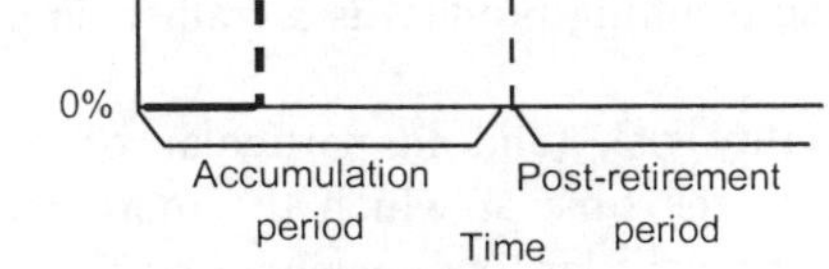

Figure 6.29 Combined annuities

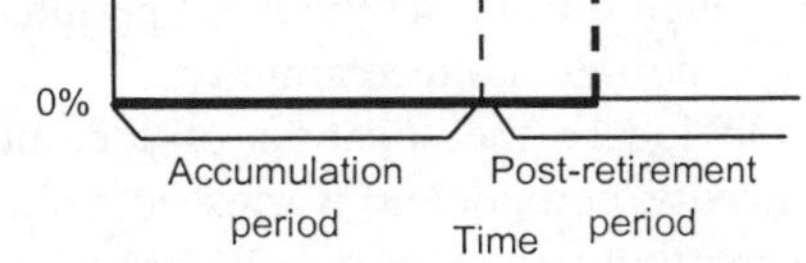

Figure 6.30 Staggered annuitization

6.5.2 Mortality Guarantees

So far we have supposed that a specified mortality assumption is adopted when (a part of) the available fund is annuitized and that, as regards the purchased annuity, the assumption itself cannot be replaced, whatever the mortality trend might be. In particular where a deferred annuity purchased during the accumulation period is concerned, this assumption leads to a very high level of mortality guarantee embedded in the annuity product, and, because of the systematic component of the mortality risk, this implies huge financial requirements in order to face the longevity risk (see Section 6.4.2).

The guarantee degree can be kept at more reasonable levels if the mortality assumption is allowed to vary throughout the deferment period, when significant deviations from the assumed mortality trend are experienced.

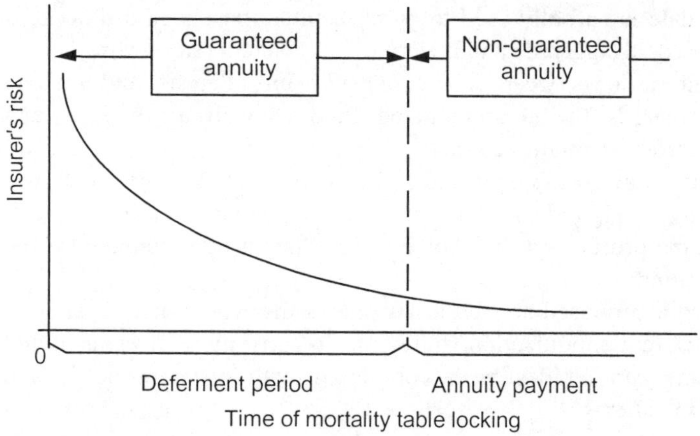

Figure 6.31 Mortality guarantee in an annuity product

It is worth noting that if the mortality assumption may be adjusted during the deferment period only, the amount of the annuity is ultimately determined at the end of this period, and the amount itself is then guaranteed for the whole lifetime. On the contrary, if the mortality assumption is allowed to vary even during the payment period, the resulting product is a (rather poor value) non-guaranteed annuity.

Obviously the location of the mortality risk (and in particular of its longevity component) varies according to the time at which the mortality assumption is locked (see Figure 6.31). In particular, the pensioner suffers a large part of the longevity risk if the mortality assumption may be adjusted at any time even during the annuity payment period.

In any case, a larger retention of longevity risk by the annuity provider should be financed by a higher premium for the annuity product. Actually, an appropriate safety loading should be calculated and applied, as the result of pricing the longevity guarantee embedded in the annuity structure. The higher premium could be justified in terms of a greater value of the annuity product. Of course, further value can be added to the product by adopting some annuity adjustment mechanism aiming at the distribution of mortality profits to annuitants.

6.6 CONCLUSIONS

The present chapter mainly aims at providing a (rather informal) introduction to the longevity risk, arising from the uncertainty in future demographical trends, and the financial requirements following the impact of the longevity risk itself on insurance covers involving living benefits (life annuities, LTC benefits, whole life sickness benefits, and so on).

From some numerical examples, the dramatic importance of the uncertainty in future demographic trends clearly emerges. In our opinion, great attention should be devoted especially to analysing possible integrations between reinsurance arrangements and capital allocation policies, in particular from a corporate point of view.

Probably, a deeper knowledge of mortality and disability trends and more actuarial research specifically dealing with this particular risk can help, in the near future, in establishing a unified approach to reinsurance arrangements, safety loadings and solvency margin requirements.

Of course, actuarial aspects must be carefully considered while designing new insurance products involving living benefits. Life annuity products provide an important example of the need for new ideas consistent with a rapidly evolving demographic scenario.

REFERENCES

Benjamin, B. and A. S. Soliman (1993), *Mortality on the move*, Oxford: The Institute of Actuaries.

Biffis, E. and A. Olivieri (2002), 'Demographic Risks in Pension Schemes with Combined Benefits', *Giornale dell'Istituto Italiano degli Attuari*: **65** (1–2), 137–74.

Cardinale M., A. Findlater and M. Orszag (2002), *Paying Out Pensions. A Review of International Annuities Markets,* Watson Wyatt research report.

CMIR (Continuous Mortality Investigation Reports) (1990), Institute of Actuaries and Faculty of Actuaries, **10**.

CMIR (Continuous Mortality Investigation Reports) (1999), Institute of Actuaries and Faculty of Actuaries, **17**.

Coppola, M., E. Di Lorenzo and M. Sibillo (2000), 'Risk Sources in a Life Annuity Portfolio: Decomposition and Measurement Tools', *Journal of Actuarial Practice*, **8**(1–2), 43–61.

Cramer, H. and H. Wold (1935), 'Mortality Variations in Sweden: a Study in Graduation and Forecasting', *Skandinavisk Aktuarietidskrift*, **18**, 161–241.

Department for Work and Pensions (2002), *Modernising Annuities*, London: Inland Revenue.

Ferri, S. and A. Olivieri (2000), 'Technical Bases for LTC Covers Including Mortality and Disability Projections', *Proceedings of the 31st ASTIN Colloquium*, Porto Cervo, Italy, 295–314.

Haberman, S. and E. Pitacco (1999), *Actuarial Models for Disability Insurance*, London: Chapman & Hall; CRC Press.

Lee, R. (2000), 'The Lee-Carter Method for Forecasting Mortality, with Various Extensions and Applications', *North American Actuarial Journal*, **4**(1), 80–93.

MacDonald, A.S., A.J.G. Cairns, P.L. Gwilt and K.A. Miller (1998), 'An International Comparison of Recent Trends in Population Mortality', *British Actuarial Journal*, **4**(I), 3–141.

Marocco, P. and E. Pitacco (1998), 'Longevity Risk and Life Annuity Reinsurance', *Transactions of the 26th International Congress of Actuaries*, Birmingham, **6**, 453–79.

Mayhew, L. (2001), 'Disability: Global Trends and International Perspectives', Paper presented to the Staple Inn Actuarial Society.

Milevsky, M.A. and S.D. Promislow (2001), 'Mortality Derivatives and the Option to Annuitise', *Insurance: Mathematics & Economics*, **29**(3), 299–318.

Olivieri, A. (2001), 'Uncertainty in Mortality Projections: an Actuarial Perspective', *Insurance: Mathematics & Economics*, **29**(2), 231–45.

Olivieri, A. (2002), 'Risk and Reinsurance in Life Annuity Portfolios', *Quaderni del Dipartimento di Matematica Applicata 'B. de Finetti'*, University of Trieste, No. 3.

Olivieri A. and S. Ferri (2003), 'Mortality and disability risks in Long Term Care insurance', IAAHS (International Actuarial Association Health Section), Online Journal, **1**: http://www.actuaries.org/members/en/IAAHS/OnlineJournal/2003-1/Mortality_and_Disability_Risks_in_Long_Term_Care_Insurance.pdf

Olivieri, A. and E. Pitacco (2001a), 'Facing LTC Risks', *Proceedings of the 23rd International ASTIN Colloquium*, Washington, http://www.actuaries.org/members/en/ASTIN/colloquia/Washington/ Olivieri_Pitacco.pdf

Olivieri, A. and E. Pitacco (2001b), 'Rendite Vitalizie: Longevity Risk, Garanzie Demografiche, Profili Tariffari', Bocconi University, Milano, CERAP Working Paper No. 22.

Olivieri, A. and E. Pitacco (2002a), 'Inference About Mortality Improvements in Life Annuity Portfolios', *Transactions of the 27th International Congress of Actuaries*, Cancun, Mexico, http://www.actuaries.org/members/en/events/congresses/Cancun/ica2002_subject/mortality/ mortality_76_olivieri_pitacco.pdf

Olivieri, A. and E. Pitacco (2002b), 'Premium Systems for Post-retirement Sickness Covers', *Belgian Actuarial Bulletin*, **2**, 15–25.

Olivieri, A. and E. Pitacco (2003a), 'Annuitisation Guarantee and Uncertainty in Mortality Trends', Bocconi University, Milano, CERAP Working Paper No. 30.

Olivieri, A. and E. Pitacco (2003b), 'Solvency Requirements for Pension Annuities', *Journal of Pension Economics and Finance,* **2**(2), 127–157.

Pitacco, E. (2001), 'Assessing and Facing the Longevity Risk. Financial Requirements', *Proceedings of the 4th Italian-Spanish Conference on Financial Mathematics*, Alghero, 528–60.

Retirement Choice Working Party (2001), 'Extending Retirement Choices. Retirement Income Options for Modern Needs', The Faculty and Institute of Actuaries.

Riemer-Hommel, P. and T. Trauth (2000), 'Challenges and Solutions for the Management of Longevity Risk', in M. Frenkel, U. Hommel and M. Rudolf (eds), *Risk management: Challenge and opportunity*, Berlin: Springer, 85–100.

Rüttermann, M. (1999), 'Mortality Trends Worldwide: Risk Insights', *General & Cologne RE*, **3**(4), 18–20.

Wadsworth, M. and A. Findlater (2002), 'Reinventing Annuities', *Transactions of the 27th International Congress of Actuaries*, Cancun, Mexico.

7. Guaranteed annuity conversion options and their valuation*

Laura Ballotta and Steven Haberman

7.1 INTRODUCTION

A guaranteed annuity option is a contract feature attached to personal (individual) pension policies, which provides the policy holder with the right to receive at retirement either a cash payment or an annuity, payable throughout the policy holder's remaining lifetime and calculated at a guaranteed rate, depending on which has the greater value. This guarantee of the conversion rate between cash and pension income was a common feature of pension policies sold in the UK during the (late) 1970s and 1980s, with more than 40 companies involved in this market.

Until recently, the UK experience has been that the cash benefit is more valuable than the guaranteed annuity payment since a higher pension could be obtained by using the cash payment to buy the best annuity rates available in the market (the so-called 'open market option'). After the reductions in market interest rates in recent years, particularly since 1998, the position has changed and the guaranteed annuity has tended to be worth more than the cash benefit; unanticipated falls in mortality rates since these policies were issued have also made the guaranteed annuity more valuable to policy holders. As a result of these two combined effects, many UK insurance companies have experienced solvency problems requiring the setting up of

* Financial support from the Society of Actuaries Committee on Knowledge Extension Research and the Actuarial Education on Research Fund is gratefully acknowledged. The authors would like to thank Prof. Gerald Rickayzen for his assistance with various C++ implementations. Earlier versions of this work have been presented at the 8th International Vilnius Conference on Probability Theory and Mathematical Statistics, 6th International Congress on Insurance: Mathematics and Economics (Cemapre, Lisbon), 37th Society of Actuaries Actuarial Research Conference (Waterloo), 2nd Conference in Actuarial Science and Finance (Samos). The authors would like to thank the participants of these conferences and in particular the following: Phelim Boyle, Andrew Cairns, Moshe Milevsky, Anton Pelsser.

extra reserves (using ad hoc methods) and leading one large mutual life insurer (Equitable Life, the world's oldest life insurance company) to be closed to new business in 2000. Although pension policies with these guarantees are no longer being sold in the UK, these are a common feature of corresponding policies in other countries, for example the US.

In this chapter, our objective is to explore a number of questions that arise from the UK experience and which are of current relevance. How should we value (and hence price) a guaranteed annuity option (GAO) in a market-consistent manner (bearing in mind the planned shift to fair valuation methodologies for insurance liabilities)? Is it possible to describe how the value of a GAO evolves over time, as the policy holder ages and as new financial information becomes available? What are the key sensitivities affecting the value of a GAO? How much of the historical problem in the UK can be explained by adverse changes in interest rates and how much by adverse changes in mortality rates? How do we allow for the uncertainty of mortality rate trends and what effect do these have on the value of a GAO?

We focus on unit-linked deferred annuity contracts purchased originally by a single premium. For simplicity, we ignore insurance company expenses, taxes, profit and pre-retirement death benefits in order to concentrate on the GAO. The analytical approach follows the financial economics literature and exploits the well known option valuation theory in order to obtain results for the pricing, reserving and hedging of the GAO. Fuller details are given in Ballotta and Haberman (2003a, 2003b). An alternative approach based on modeling the dynamics of the annuity price, rather than the underlying term structure of interest rates, has been used by Bezooyen et al. (1998), Pelsser (2002) and Yang et al. (2002). However, we argue that a methodology based on the term structure of interest rates is more sound in that it facilitates the analysis of the effect on the GAO of changes in the underlying interest rates and their term structure.

We propose an option pricing approach which is based on the similarity between the payoff structure of the contract under consideration and a call option written on a coupon-bearing bond. We use a single-factor Heath-Jarrow-Morton framework for the term structure of interest rates. This choice is justified by the need to avoid dependence of the model on the market price of interest rate risk, which usually implies an arbitrary specification of the model parameters leading to arbitrage opportunities (Heath et al., 1992). Also, single-factor models have the advantage of allowing a mathematically tractable solution to the coupon bond option pricing problem (Jamshidian, 1989). Under the additional assumption of an unsystematic mortality risk, independent of the financial risk, a general pricing framework is proposed and closed-form analytical formulae for the value of the GAO are obtained. Further, we introduce a dynamic model for the evolution of mortality rates over time which requires the use of a numerical procedure for the computation of the survival probabilities involved in the valuation of the GAO. The valuation formulae derived implicitly contain the dynamic investment strategy that replicates the contract. Numerical results are investigated and the sensitivities of the price of the option to changes in the key parameters are also analysed.

The chapter is organized as follows: Sections 7.2.1 and 7.2.2 develop the framework for the valuation of guaranteed annuity conversion options, with some of the mathematical details relegated to the Appendix. In Sections 7.2.3 and 7.2.4, we introduce different approaches to modeling mortality risk. Section 7.3 provides numerical results and a sensitivity analysis. Concluding remarks are offered in Section 7.4.

7.2 FAIR VALUATION OF GUARANTEED ANNUITY OPTIONS

7.2.1 General Framework

As noted in Section 7.1, a guaranteed annuity option provides the holder of the contract with the right to receive at retirement the greater of two choices: either a cash benefit (equal to the current value of the reference portfolio), or an annuity which would be payable throughout his/her remaining lifetime and which is calculated at a guaranteed rate, g.

Hence, if the policy holder is aged x at inception and N is the normal retirement age, the guaranteed annuity option pays out at maturity $T = N - x$:

$$\begin{aligned} C_T &= \max(gS_T a_{x+T}, S_T) \\ &= S_T + (gS_T a_{x+T} - S_T)^+ \\ &= S_T + gS_T(a_{x+T} - K)^+ , \end{aligned}$$

where S is the market value of the equity fund backing the contract, $K = 1/g$ and a_{x+T} represents the 'annuity factor', that is, the expected present value at time T of a life annuity which pays £1 throughout the remaining lifetime of the policy holder, and the notation $(v)^+$ is equivalent to $\max(v, 0)$.

Consider a competitive market with continuous trading, and assume that the market is frictionless, in other words, that there are no taxes, no transaction costs, no restrictions on borrowing or short sales, all securities are perfectly divisible, and that the price process of the equity fund S follows an adapted, càdlàg and strictly positive semimartingale. Let r_t be the stochastic short rate. Applying risk-neutral valuation,[1] the fair value at time T of the annuity can be calculated as

$$a_{x+T} = \hat{\mathbb{E}}\left[\sum_{t=0}^{w-(T+x)} e^{-\int_T^{T+t} r_u du} 1_{(\mathcal{T}_{x+T}>t)} \middle| \mathcal{F}_T\right],$$

where $\hat{\mathbb{E}}$ denotes the expectation under the risk-neutral probability measure[2] $\hat{\mathbb{P}}$, w is the largest survival age, $\mathcal{F}_T$ is the information flow at maturity and $\mathcal{T}_y$ is a random variable representing the remaining lifetime of a policy holder aged y. Assume that the mortality risk, captured in the model by the random variable $\mathcal{T}_y$, is unsystematic and independent of any source of risk existing in the financial market. Then

$$\begin{aligned} a_{x+T} &= \sum_{t=0}^{w-(T+x)} \hat{\mathbb{E}}\left[1_{(\mathcal{T}_{x+T}>t)} \middle| \mathcal{F}_T\right] \hat{\mathbb{E}}\left[e^{-\int_T^{T+t} r_u du} \middle| \mathcal{F}_T\right] \\ &= \sum_{t=0}^{w-(T+x)} \mathbb{P}\left[\mathcal{T}_{x+T} > t \middle| \mathcal{F}_T\right] P_T(T+t) \\ &= \sum_{t=0}^{w-(T+x)} {}_t p_{T+x} P_T(T+t) \end{aligned}$$

where $P_T(T+t)$ is the price a time T of a zero coupon bond with unit face value and redemption date (T+t), and ${}_t p_{T+x}$ is the t-year survival probability of a person aged (x + T). It follows that the terminal payoff of the guaranteed annuity option is:

$$C_T = S_T + gS_T \left(\sum_{t=0}^{w-(T+x)} {}_t p_{T+x} P_T(T+t) - K \right)^+ . \qquad (7.1)$$

Expressed in this way, the guaranteed annuity option contract shows a payoff structure which is analogous to that of an option written on a coupon bond, where the role of the coupon is played by the post-retirement survival probabilities.

Similarly, risk-neutral valuation implies that the value at time τ, $0 \leq \tau \leq T$, of the guaranteed annuity option contract entered by a policy holder aged x at time 0 is

$$V_x(x+\tau,\tau,T-\tau=N-x-\tau)=\hat{\mathbb{E}}\left[e^{-\int_\tau^T r_u du}C_T 1_{(T_{x+\tau}>T)}\middle|\mathcal{F}_\tau\right]$$
$$={}_{T-\tau}p_{x+\tau}\,\hat{\mathbb{E}}\left[e^{-\int_\tau^T r_u du}C_T\middle|\mathcal{F}_\tau\right] \tag{7.2}$$
$$={}_{T-\tau}p_{x+\tau}\left\{S_\tau+g\,\hat{\mathbb{E}}\left[e^{-\int_\tau^T r_u du}S_T(a_{x+T}-K)^+\middle|\mathcal{F}_\tau\right]\right\}.$$

If $\widetilde{\mathbb{P}}$ is a martingale probability measure equivalent to $\hat{\mathbb{P}}$ and defined by the density process (Geman et al., 1995)

$$\eta_T:=\left.\frac{d\widetilde{\mathbb{P}}}{d\hat{\mathbb{P}}}\right|_{\mathcal{F}_T}=e^{-\int_0^T r_u du}\frac{S_T}{S_0}, \tag{7.3}$$

then the expectation in equation (7.2) can be reduced to

$$\hat{\mathbb{E}}\left[e^{-\int_\tau^T r_u du}S_T(a_{x+T}-K)^+\middle|\mathcal{F}_\tau\right]=e^{\int_0^\tau r_u du}\,\hat{\mathbb{E}}\left[\eta_T S_0(a_{x+T}-K)^+\middle|\mathcal{F}_\tau\right]$$
$$=e^{\int_0^\tau r_u du}S_0\hat{\mathbb{E}}\left[\eta_T\middle|\mathcal{F}_\tau\right]\widetilde{\mathbb{E}}\left[(a_{x+T}-K)^+\middle|\mathcal{F}_\tau\right]$$
$$=S_\tau\widetilde{\mathbb{E}}\left[(a_{x+T}-K)^+\middle|\mathcal{F}_\tau\right],$$

where $\widetilde{\mathbb{E}}$ denotes the expectation under the stock-risk-adjusted probability measure $\widetilde{\mathbb{P}}$. Therefore, we may demonstrate that the following holds:

$$V_x(x+\tau,\tau,T-\tau)=$$
$${}_{T-\tau}p_{x+\tau}S_\tau+{}_{T-\tau}p_{x+\tau}gS_\tau\,\widetilde{\mathbb{E}}\left[\left(\sum_{t=0}^{w-(T+x)}{}_tp_{T+x}P_T(T+t)-K\right)^+\middle|\mathcal{F}_\tau\right], \tag{7.4}$$

(see Ballotta and Haberman, 2003a, 2003b, for further background).

Both equations (7.1) and (7.4) show that the fair premium that the insurer should charge for a pension plan with guaranteed annuity option feature attached is given by the current market value of the reference equity portfolio, plus the single premium for a coupon-bond-like option, weighted by the probability of the policy holder surviving till retirement. A fair premium means, in this context, that if the actual premium charged were greater than V, the customers would not receive value for money; if instead the premium were less than V, then the insurer would be offering the guarantees too cheaply. In other words, the market would not be in equilibrium and arbitrage opportunities would arise.

The two equations, (7.1) and (7.4) , also show that the guaranteed annuity option contract is affected by two sources of risk: the financial risk, in the form of the uncertainty related to future movements in both the equity fund and the market interest rate, and the mortality risk, captured by the random remaining lifetime of the policy holder. As we show in the remaining sections of this chapter, a closed analytical formula for the fair premium of the guaranteed annuity option can be obtained by modeling the financial risk within the classical Black-Scholes economy, and making use of a single-factor Heath et al. (1992) HJM framework for the term structure of interest rates. Mortality effects are taken into consideration through two approaches: (a) basing the survival probabilities on the standard mortality tables which have been adopted by UK life insurance companies (for pricing and reserving calculations); or, alternatively, (b) calculating the survival probabilities from a stochastic model for the mortality risk, which is based on the reduction factor approach for modeling the time variations in hazard rates.

7.2.2 Pricing the Guaranteed Annuity Option Allowing for Financial Risk

In the frictionless market introduced in the previous subsection, we assume that the insurer invests the single premium paid by each policy holder at the start of the contract into an equity fund, whose risk-neutral dynamic is described by the following stochastic differential equation:

$$dS_t = r_t S_t dt + \sigma_S S_t d\hat{Z}_t , \tag{7.5}$$

where $\sigma_S \in \mathbb{R}^+$ and $(\hat{Z}_t : t \geq 0)$ is a standard one-dimensional $\hat{\mathbb{P}}$-Brownian motion. Thus, S_0 is the single premium. As mentioned above, we assume that the evolution of the term structure of interest rates is given by a single-factor HJM framework and we consider the specific case in which the forward rate volatility has an exponentially decaying structure which resembles an extended form of the model of Vasicek (1977). In other words, the risk-neutral dynamic of the forward rate is given by

$$df(t,T) = \left(\sigma^2 e^{-\lambda(T-t)} \int_t^T e^{-\lambda(u-t)} du \right) dt + \sigma e^{-\lambda(T-t)} d\hat{W}_t , \tag{7.6}$$

where $(\hat{W}_t : t \geq 0)$ is a standard one-dimensional $\hat{\mathbb{P}}$-Brownian motion correlated with $\hat{Z}$, so that

$$d\hat{W}_t d\hat{Z}_t = \rho dt$$

for any $\rho \neq 0$. This implies

$$\hat{Z}_t = \rho \hat{W}_t + \sqrt{1-\rho^2}\hat{W}_t',$$

where $(\hat{W}_t' : t \geq 0)$ is a $\hat{\mathbb{P}}$-Brownian motion independent of both $\hat{W}$ and $\hat{Z}$. Hence, ρ represents the correlation coefficient between equity fund values and interest rates. In this framework:

$$r_t = \lim_{T \to t} f(t,T)$$

and

$$P_t(T) = e^{-\int_t^T f(t,u)\,du}.$$

Since we are using a single-factor model for the term structure of interest rates, and given the similarity between the guaranteed annuity option contract and a coupon bond option which we have previously observed (see equations 7.1 and 7.4), we can apply the Jamshidian (1989) decomposition and rewrite the annuity option payoff as the payoff generated by a portfolio of zero-coupon bond options with appropriate strike prices, K_t, and weights equal to the survival probabilities, ${}_t p_{T+x}$. More precisely, for $t = 0, 1, \ldots, w-(T+x)$, we find the critical value of the interest rate[3] such that

$$\sum_{t=0}^{w-(T+x)} {}_t p_{T+x} P_T(T+t) = K;$$

then we define a new 'artificial' strike price K_t as the bond price which is calculated to correspond to this critical interest rate level, that is

$$K_t = P_T^*(T+t).$$

Since the bond price is a monotonic function of the interest rate, it follows that

$$\left(\sum_{t=0}^{w-(T+x)} {}_tp_{T+x} P_T(T+t) - K\right)^+ = \sum_{t=0}^{w-(T+x)} {}_tp_{T+x} (P_T(T+t) - K_t)^+ ,$$

which implies that (7.4) can be rewritten as:

$$\begin{aligned} &V_x(x+\tau,\tau,T-\tau) \\ &= {}_{T-\tau}p_{x+\tau}S_\tau + {}_{T-\tau}p_{x+\tau}gS_\tau \sum_{t=0}^{w-(T+x)} {}_tp_{T+x}\widetilde{\mathbb{E}}\left[(P_T(T+t)-K_t)^+ \middle| \mathcal{F}_\tau\right] \\ &= {}_{T-\tau}p_{x+\tau}S_\tau \qquad\qquad (7.7) \\ &+ \frac{{}_{T-\tau}p_{x+\tau}gS_\tau}{P_\tau(T)} \sum_{t=0}^{w-(T+x)} {}_tp_{T+x} \left[P_\tau(T+t)e^{-\gamma(T,T+t)m_r(T-\tau)} N(d_t') \right. \\ &\left. - P_\tau(T)K_tN(d_t)\right] \end{aligned}$$

with

$$\begin{aligned} d_t &= \frac{\ln\dfrac{P_\tau(T+t)}{K_tP_\tau(T)} - \dfrac{1}{2}\sigma_r^2(T-\tau)\gamma^2(T,T+t) - \gamma(T,T+t)m_r(T-\tau)}{\gamma(T,T+t)\sigma_r(T-\tau)} \\ d_t' &= d_t + \gamma(T,T+t)\sigma_r(T-\tau). \end{aligned}$$

Details of the calculations that lead to equation (7.7) are provided in the Appendix.

7.2.3 Mortality Risk: Deterministic Approach

Although the procedure leading to the valuation equation (7.7) allows for stochastic mortality trends, our initial approach to the calculations is to use a set of three standard UK mortality tables for the calculation of the survival probabilities in (7.7). Each of these incorporates an element of future mortality reduction computed on a deterministic basis.

These mortality tables have been produced by the Continuous Mortality Investigation Bureau of the Institute and Faculty of Actuaries for insurance company data on male pensioner mortality. They are extensively used for the calculation of premiums and reserves. The PA90 table is based on data for the period 1967–70 projected to 1990, PMA80–C10 is based on data for the period 1979–82 projected to 2010 and PMA92–C20 is based on data for the period 1991–94 projected to 2020. Because of the declining trend in mortality rates over time, and hence the increasing trend in survival probabilities, ${}_t p_{T+x}$, the expected present value of the life annuity increases as we move the assumption from PA90 to PMA80–C10 to PMA92–C20.

7.2.4 Mortality Risk: Stochastic Approach

As an alternative to the deterministic model, we present an approximate approach to stochastic mortality. Full details are available in Ballotta and Haberman (2003b). In Section 7.2.1, we defined $\mathcal{T}_x$ to be a random variable which represents the remaining lifetime of a policy holder aged x. The survival function of this random variable, $\mathcal{T}_x$, is given by

$${}_s p_x = \mathbb{P}(\mathcal{T}_x > s),$$

where $\mathbb{P}$ is the objective probability measure. If we explicitly allow for the time dependence of the hazard rate and we define $\mu_{x+t:t}$ to be the hazard rate for an individual at time t then aged $x + t$, then it follows that

$${}_s p_x = \mathbb{E}\left[e^{-\int_0^s \mu_{x+t:t} dt}\right]. \tag{7.8}$$

A widely used actuarial model for projecting mortality rates is the reduction factor model; this has been used in the UK and US for pensioner and annuitant populations for many years; see, for example, standard tables produced by the Continuous Mortality Investigation Bureau in the UK since 1967–70 (for example CMI Bureau, 1999) and the General Annuity Valuation Tables in the US (Group Annuity Valuation Table Task Force, 1995).

Given the form of (7.8), we propose a parsimonious model for the trajectory of the hazard rate over time. Following Sithole et al. (2000), we consider a reduction factor approach based on hazard rates, so that

$$\mu_{y:t} = \mu_{y:0} RF(y,t)$$

where $\mu_{y:0}$ is the hazard rate for a person aged y in the base year (i.e. year 0) or period, and $\mu_{y:t}$ is the hazard rate for a person attaining age y in future year t (that is, as measured from the base year or period), and the reduction factor $RF(y,t)$ is the ratio of the hazard rates. Using an approach based on generalized linear models, as proposed by Renshaw et al. (1996), Sithole et al. (2000) derive a series of models appropriate to UK annuitant and pensioner populations which simplify to the following structure:

$$RF\,(y,t) = e^{(\alpha+\beta y)t}\,.$$

The parameter α represents the rate of change in the hazard rate over time on the logarithmic scale and we would expect estimates to be negative. The parameter β represents an offset term that reflects a rate of change that could differ with age y.

Hence, with $y = x + t$, we propose the following model for the time evolution of the hazard rate:

$$\mu_{x+t:t} = \mu_{x+t:0}\, e^{(\alpha+\beta x+\beta t)t+\sigma_h Y_t}, \tag{7.9}$$

where $(Y_t : t \geq 0)$ is a stochastic process on $(\Omega, \mathcal{F}, \mathbb{P})$, which is introduced to model random variations in the forecast trend, and

$$\mu_{x+t:0} = a_1 + a_2 R + e^{b_1 + b_2 R + b_3 (2R^2 - 1)}, \tag{7.10}$$

where

$$R = \frac{(x+t)-70}{50}, x \geq 50. \tag{7.11}$$

This model for $\mu_{x+t:0}$, the hazard rate for the base year, corresponds to the structure for the UK standard tables for annuitant and pensioner populations for the period 1991–94, as proposed by the CMI Bureau (1999). For numerical illustrations, we use the parameterization for the standard table for male pensioners (analysis based on lives, rather than pension amounts), and the corresponding values for α and β as estimated by Sithole et al. (2000): see Table 7.2 later.

Further, we assume that Y follows an Ornstein-Uhlenbeck process; in other words, the process Y satisfies the following:

$$\begin{cases} dY_t = -aY_t dt + dX_t \\ Y_0 = 0, \end{cases} \tag{7.12}$$

where $(X_t : t \geq 0)$ is a standard one-dimensional $\mathbb{P}$-Brownian motion, independent of the 'financial' Wiener processes, $\hat{W}$ and $\hat{Z}$ (see equations 7.5 and 7.6). This is similar to the model of Milevsky and Promislow (2001), and has the desirable property of mean reversion, with the parameter a measuring the speed of mean reversion. The solution to (7.12),

$$Y_t = \int_0^t e^{-a(t-s)} dX_s\,,$$

implies that $Y_t \sim \mathrm{N}\,(0, \xi^2(t))$, with

$$\xi^2(t) = \frac{1 - e^{-2at}}{2a}.$$

Equation (7.8) does not lead to a closed form expression principally because the sum of lognormal random variables is not itself lognormal. Hence, for computational purposes, we need a numerical approximation and adopt a simulation procedure based on the Monte Carlo technique. Thus, we subdivide the time period [0, s] into n equal subintervals of length $\Delta t = \frac{s}{n}$, and we define $t_i = \frac{i}{n} s = i\Delta t$, i=1, 2,..., n. At each step, we generate the path of the hazard rate as

$$\mu_{x+t_i:t_i} = \mu_{x+t_i:0} e^{(\alpha+\beta x+\beta t_i)t_i + \sigma_h \xi(t_i) z_i},$$

$$\mu_{x+t_i:0} = a_1 + a_2 R_i + e^{b_1 + b_2 R + b_3 (2R_i^2 - 1)}$$

$$R_i = \frac{(x+t_i) - 70}{50},$$

where z_i is a random sample from a standardized normal distribution. The integral in equation (7.8) is then approximated using the trapezoidal rule.

The model represented by equation (7.9) allows for a future mortality trend that is random. However, it is recognized in the literature that systematic deviations from the forecasted mortality rates may take place so that a parameter risk is present. When this is applied to the trend at older ages, the risk is usually referred to as 'longevity risk': see Marocco and Pitacco (1998), Olivieri (2001), Olivieri and Pitacco (2002), for example, for further discussion.

In order to incorporate longevity risk, we develop the model further by following the approach of Olivieri and Pitacco (2002), inter alia. For representing the range of possible evolutions of mortality, we consider a family of projected hazard rates, for a given age at entry x. Thus, we consider

$$\left\lfloor \mu_{x+t:t:H(x)}; H(x) \in \mathcal{H}(x) \right\rfloor,$$

where $H(x)$ is a particular hypothesis concerning the trend of mortality for individuals entering an insured group at age x and $\mathcal{H}(x)$ represents a given set of such hypotheses. In particular, if we focus on equation (7.9) where the mortality trend is expressed by a set of parameters, then we could consider

$$\left\lfloor \mu_{x+t:t:\theta(x)};\ \theta(x) \in \Theta(x) \right\rfloor \tag{7.13}$$

where $\theta(x)$ denotes a vector parameter and $\Theta(x)$ denotes the corresponding multi-dimensional parameter space. As a preliminary illustration of this methodology, we take $\theta(x) \equiv \alpha$ in equation (7.9) and consider the possible set of values for $\alpha : \Theta(x) \equiv \{-0.08, -0.05, -0.02\}$, which is shown in Table 7.1. We deal with the range of values for α by assuming that the parameter is a discrete random variable $\tilde{\alpha}$ and has the alternative probability functions shown in Table 7.1. Note that the estimate of α, $\tilde{\alpha}$, from Sithole et al. (2000), is –0.02.

Table 7.1 Parameter risk: range of values for $\tilde{\alpha}$ with corresponding probability functions

	$\tilde{\alpha}$ = with prob.	0.08	0.05	0.02
Model	1.1	0.3	0.4	0.3
	1.2	0.2	0.6	0.2
	1.3	0.1	0.8	0.1
	1.4	1/3	1/3	1/3
(symmetric distribution)				
Model	2.1	0.4	0.3	0.3
	2.2	0.6	0.2	0.2
	2.3	0.8	0.1	0.1
(asymmetric distribution)				
Model	3	$\tilde{\alpha} \sim$ U (0.08, 0.02)		

7.3 NUMERICAL RESULTS AND SENSITIVITY ANALYSIS

In this section, we use the results developed in Section 7.2.2 (namely, equation 7.7 for the GAO price), and the numerical procedures introduced in Sections 7.2.3 and 7.2.4 to carry out a full sensitivity analysis for the value of the guaranteed annuity option contract.

Precisely, we concentrate on the extra premium that the insurer should charge at inception for the coupon-bond-like option embedded in the contract, namely, referring to equation (7.7) for $\tau = 0$:

$$\frac{{}_{T-\tau}p_{x+\tau}gS_\tau}{P_\tau(T)}\sum_{t=0}^{w-(T+x)} {}_t p_{T+x}\left[P_\tau(T+t)e^{-\gamma(T,T+t)m_\tau(T-\tau)}N(d_t')-P_\tau(T)K_t N(d_t)\right].$$

For this practical example, we incorporate a common design feature and assume that the annuity has a five-year guarantee period, so that the first five annual payments of the annuity scheme would be definitely payable, providing that the policy holder survives to retirement age.

We subdivide the analysis into two sections. The first one relates to the study of the behavior of the GAO when the parameters 'imported' in the pricing formulae from the financial market are changed one at a time, *ceteris paribus*. The second set of results, instead, describes the behavior of the GAO when the mortality model parameters are changed, again individually *ceteris paribus*.

Unless otherwise stated, we use the benchmark set of parameters in Table 7.2 (and based on the stochastic mortality model of Section 7.2.4). For the stochastic mortality model, we compute the survival probabilities by simulating 10 000 paths, with each path comprising one observation per month over each year.

*Table 7.2 Set of parameters used as benchmark for the comparative statics analysis**

Parameter set for numerical analysis
Design parameters:
$g = 11.1\%;^{**}$ $x = 50;$ $T + x = N = 65.$
Financial model
$S_0 = 100;$ $\sigma_S = 20\%$ p.a.; $\rho = 1;$ $f_0 = 4\%$ p.a.; $\sigma = 0.01;$ $\lambda = 0.15$
Mortality model (stochastic)
$\alpha = 0.02;$ $\beta = 0.0001;$ $\sigma_h = 10\%$ p.a.; $a = 0.5.$
$a_1 = -\frac{0.0081}{100};$ $a_2 = -\frac{0.07}{100};$ $b_1 = -4.67509;$ $b_2 = 5.629188;$ $b_3 = -1.2.$

Notes:

* Parameters are subdivided into three blocks. The first group contains the parameters that characterize the individual policy; the second group contains the parameters representing the financial market components; the last group contains the parameters related to the mortality model.

** According to Bolton et al. (1997), g = 11.1 per cent was the common guaranteed rate used in the UK by life insurance companies.

7.3.1 GAO and the 'Financial' Parameters

In this subsection, we illustrate the main comparative statics results for the sensitivity of the GAO to the financial parameters. In particular, we look at the sensitivity with respect to the market interest rate, the entry age of the policy holder, the volatility of the equity portfolio backing the policy and its correlation to interest rates, and the volatility coefficients of the forward rate. Fuller sets of results are presented by Ballotta and Haberman (2003a), for the deterministic mortality case.

The sensitivity of the GAO to the initial redemption yield, f_0, used to calculate the initial bond prices $P_0(T)$ and $P_0(T+t)$, $t = 0,1,\ldots,w-(T+x)$, is shown in Figure 7.1. In particular, we observe a decreasing pattern due to the fact that higher current interest rates make the guaranteed annuity payments less attractive than the current rates available in the market.

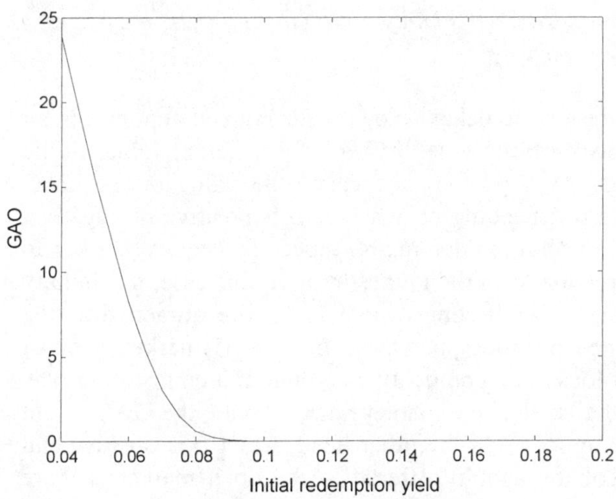

Figure 7.1 Sensitivity of the GAO to changes in the initial redemption yield used to calculate initial bonds prices

Figure 7.2 shows the GAO profile versus the age of the policy holder at inception of the contract. The observed increasing pattern is explained by the different weights attaching to the expected future annuity payments in the case of a policy holder aged 20 at inception compared to the case of a policy holder entering the contract at later ages.

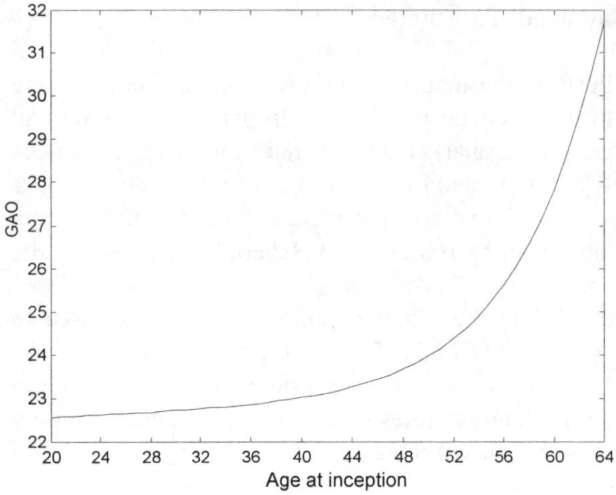

Figure 7.2 Values of the guaranteed annuity option for different entry ages and time evolution of the contract

In Figure 7.3, we represent the behavior of the guaranteed annuity option as a function of the equity portfolio volatility, σ_S, for different values of the correlation coefficient ρ. As shown by the chart, the value of the GAO presents a different pattern depending on whether ρ is positive or negative. When ρ is negative, the policy holder might expect the equity market to move in the opposite direction from the interest rate. In this case, the annuity guaranteed by the pension plan becomes more and more attractive as the volatility of the reference portfolio increases. In fact, if market rates of interest drop, the policy locks in a competitive amount at a competitive rate. In the case of a rise in the level of the market rates, instead, the GAO might simply expire out of the money. On the other hand, when ρ is positive and σ_S increases, the value of the annuity offered in the open market is more attractive, which reduces the value of the GAO. The same argument justifies the decreasing profile of the GAO as function of the correlation coefficient only (for fixed σ_S), and this may be deduced from vertical sections of the plots in Figure 7.3.

The changes in value of the GAO arising from changes in the parameters governing the volatility structure of the forward rate, and hence of the bond prices, are summarized in Figure 7.4, where the sensitivity to both the diffusion coefficient, σ, and the speed or adjustment, λ, are considered (for fixed ρ). The observed pattern finds an explanation in equations (A.3) and (A.4), which show that the short rate volatility, σ_r, is a function which is increasing with σ and decreasing with λ. This means that if the interest rates are very volatile, the expected present value of the annuity payments falls. So the policy holder seems to prefer not to exercise the option, but to take the cash payment instead and reinvest it at more favorable market conditions.

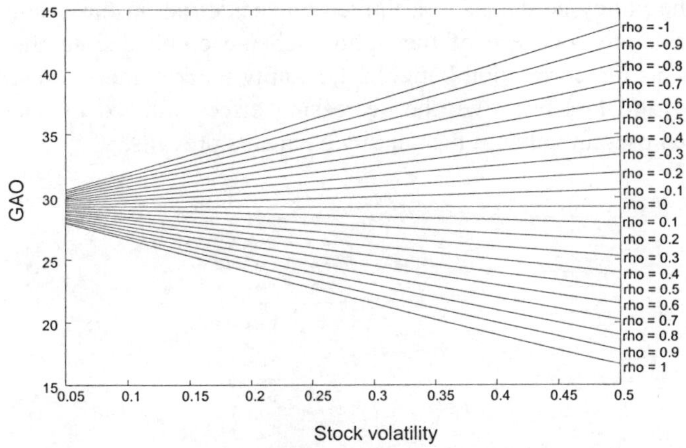

Figure 7.3 GAO vs volatility of the equity fund backing the policy, for different values of the correlation coefficient between equity and interest rates

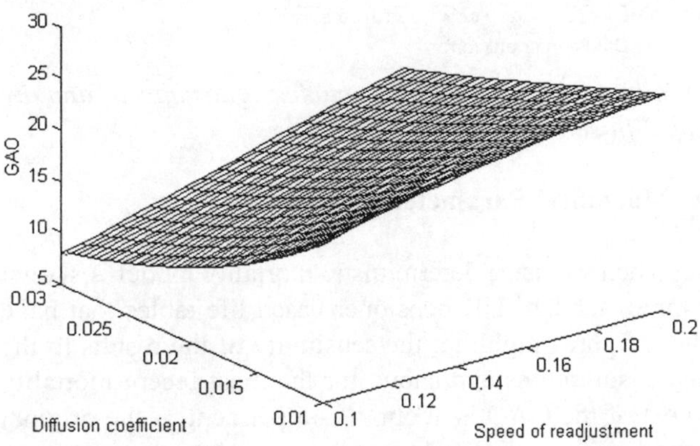

Figure 7.4 Sensitivity of the GAO value to the parameters governing the forward rate volatility

The sensitivity of the value of the GAO to changes in the diffusion coefficient, σ, and the correlation coefficient, ρ, is shown in Figure 7.5. As noted above, as σ increases, the present value of the annuity payments falls. When ρ is close to -1, this effect is offset by the attractiveness of the guarantee. Thus, as the volatility σ increases, the chance that interest rates will perform very well or very badly increases. The policy holder may benefit from falls in interest rates since the guaranteed payment appears more competitive; but the policy holder faces a limited downside risk in the event of a rise in interest rates because of the option scheme embedded in the contract. However, as the correlation between the equity market and interest rates becomes less and less negative, the decreasing effect induced by the drop in the expected present value of the annuity payments prevails.

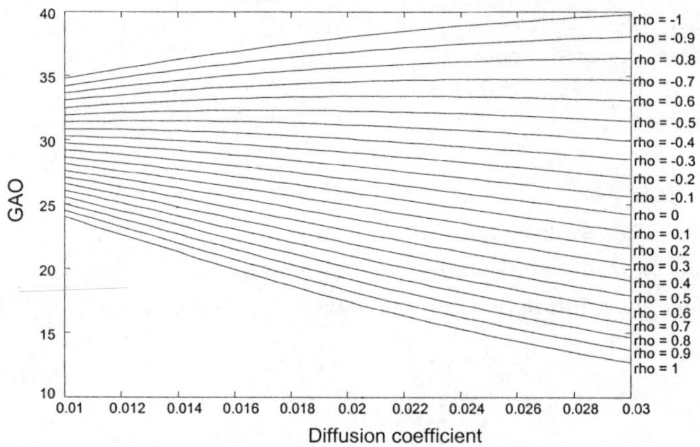

Figure 7.5 Exponentially decaying volatility model: guaranteed annuity option sensitivity to the diffusion term

7.3.2 GAO and the 'Mortality' Parameters

The value of the GAO when we use a deterministic mortality model is shown in Table 7.3, for the three standard UK pensioner-based life tables that have been investigated. These figures highlight the sensitivity of the results to the choice of the mortality assumptions and show, for the most recent mortality table, that the initial cost of the GAO is about 40–45 per cent of the original initial premium, S_0, paid by the policy holder at the outset (for the parameter values shown). The limiting case of $\lambda \to 0$ corresponds to a constant volatility model, which is discussed more fully by Ballotta and Haberman (2003a).

Table 7.3 Price of the guaranteed annuity option. Parameter set: $S_0=100$; $\sigma_S=0.2$; $\rho=1$; $g=11.1$ *per cent;* $f_0=0.04$; $x=50$; $N=65$.

	Price of the GAO		
Life table	$\sigma=0.01, \lambda=0.15$ (the benchmark case)	$\sigma=0.001, \lambda=0.001$	$\sigma_f=0.001, \lambda\to 0$
PMA92-C20	42.0175	45.8667	45.8083
PMA80-C10	26.5497	29.7971	29.7541
PA90	13.7925	16.3651	16.3342

We now consider the impact on GAO values of changes in mortality trends, when survival probabilities are computed using the model described in Section 7.2.4 and summarized by equations (7.9)–(7.12). Figure 7.6 shows the impact on GAO values of the parameters related to the 'deterministic' part of the model, that is, the logarithmic rate of change in the hazard rate over time, α, and its offset term β. As α becomes more negative, so the downward trend in mortality rates becomes stronger. The final effect is then an improvement in survival probabilities and, as a consequence, the GAO value contract rises in value. On the other hand, the value of the GAO decreases as β increases. This is consistent with the nature of this parameter, which is to mitigate the rate of decline in the mortality trend.

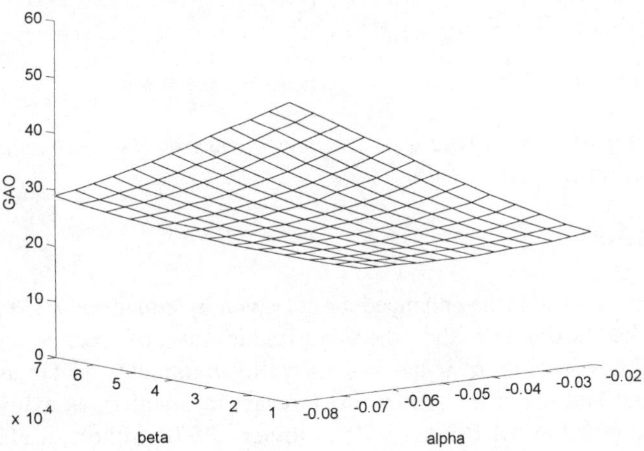

Figure 7.6 Effects on the guaranteed annuity option produced by the rate of change in mortality trends

Figure 7.7 shows the behavior of the GAO value as a function of the parameters related to the stochastic component of the model for the hazard rate. We observe that the value of the contract is an increasing function of the speed of convergence to the long-run mean, *a*. In particular, for small values of the diffusion parameter σ_h, the GAO is almost insensitive to changes in the parameter *a*. This means that the convergence of the random noise to its long-run mean is faster, the less 'amplified' is the noise in the mortality process. We also observe that the GAO values decrease as σ_h increases; in other words, as uncertainty increases in the mortality trends, survival probabilities deteriorate and the contract value reduces consequently. However, as the mean-reversion effect becomes stronger, the effect of σ_h becomes almost negligible.

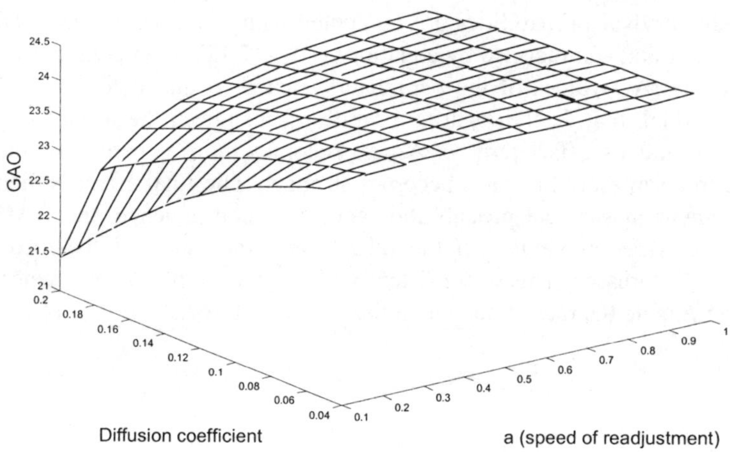

Figure 7.7 Sensitivity of the GAO to the parameters governing the stochastic component of the mortality model

7.3.3 Longevity Risk

In this subsection, we consider the enhanced model given by equation (7.13), where we relax the assumption that the logarithmic rate of decline in mortality rates, α, is constant. α is the key mortality parameter as far as trends are concerned and has been difficult to forecast in practice, as many commentators have noted (CMI Bureau, 1998, Olivieri, 2001, Sithole et al., 2000). We reflect on this feature by assuming that this parameter is random. We use the specific distributions of Table 7.1 in order to illustrate the effect on the value of the GAO of allowing for this feature. In this discussion, we make the underlying assumption that $\tilde{\alpha}$ is independent of the other sources of randomness present in the model.

Table 7.4 thus shows the effect on the value of the GAO of allowing for parameter error in α. We firstly consider four symmetric distributions for $\tilde{\alpha}$ and the uniform distribution case, each with mean –0.05. Relative to the case with constant α, the results indicate that the presence of parameter error leads to a reduction in the GAO value and that increased uncertainty (measured by Var ($\tilde{\alpha}$)) leads to larger reductions. Given the one-sided option-like nature of C_T , the presence of symmetric uncertainty in $\tilde{\alpha}$ would be expected to lead to this result, which is comparable to the sensitivities with respect to σ_h (shown in Figure 7.7). The three asymmetric cases indicate the effect of underestimating the size of α on the value of the GAO – the comparison with the deterministic benchmark values at the foot of Table 7.4 shows again that the presence of uncertainty leads to a marginal reduction in the value of the GAO (see Section 7.3.2).

Table 7.4 Sensitivity of the values of the GAO to the parameter error in the logarithmic rate of decline of hazard rates over time (α)

Model	GAO	$\mathbb{E}(\tilde{\alpha})$	Var ($\tilde{\alpha}$)
Symmetric distribution case			
1.1	35.55	0.05	0.00054
1.2	36.1314	0.05	0.00036
1.3	36.9628	0.05	0.00018
1.4	35.1092	0.05	0.0006
Asymmetric distribution case			
2.1	36.4207	0.053	0.000621
2.2	40.9213	0.062	0.000576
2.3	46.5424	0.071	0.000369
Uniform distribution case			
$\tilde{\alpha} \sim U($ 0.08, 0.02)	36.4237	0.05	0.0003
3			
The benchmark			
$\tilde{\alpha} =$ 0.05	37.8578		
$\tilde{\alpha} =$ 0.06	43.1731		
$\tilde{\alpha} =$ 0.07	48.5634		

7.3.4 UK Historical Analysis

In this subsection, we use the valuation formulae obtained above to understand how much of the GAO solvency problem experienced in the UK has been attributable to reductions in interest rates and how much to the reductions in mortality rates. The analysis carried out is an extension of a similar study performed by Ballotta and Haberman (2003a) and is based on

Ballotta and Haberman (2003b). We start with a hypothetical contract issued in 1970 to a policy holder then aged 20, and follow the evolution of the value of this contract over time up to the present day. Thus, we use the annual average of retail banks' base rates (Bank of England, 2002) for the initial term structure of interest rates. For convenience, the pre-retirement survival probability is computed using a fixed (life insurance-based) mortality table, namely the AM92 mortality table. Post-retirement survival probabilities are computed using the stochastic mortality model (thereby allowing for post-mortality improvements) implemented in Section 7.2.4. Results are presented in Figure 7.8. In Figure 7.9, we present the evolution over time of the implied guaranteed rate, i.e. the rate of interest such that the expected present value of the guaranteed annuity equals the principal amount, or

$$gS_T a_{x+T} = S_T . \tag{7.14}$$

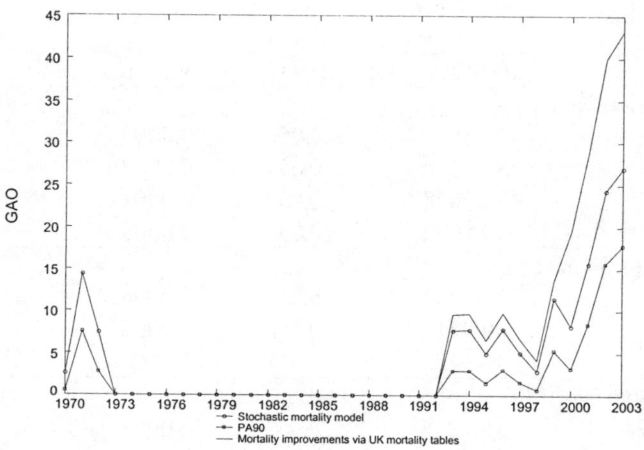

Figure 7.8 'Historical evolution' of a guaranteed annuity option contract issued in 1970 to a policy holder aged 20 for different specifications of the mortality model

Figure 7.9 shows that, between 1970 and 1972, the implied guaranteed rate of the hypothetical contract, for the chosen set of parameters, was 7.93 per cent while the market interest rates were oscillating between 5 per cent and 7 per cent. Hence, the guaranteed annuity option was 'in the money'. After 1973, the market interest rate increased up to a maximum level of 15.50 per cent in 1980; while the implied guaranteed rate of 7.93 per cent was not competitive at all, and thus the guaranteed annuity option contract was far 'out of the money'. However, in 1993, market rates of interest dramatically decreased from 12 per cent to 6 per cent, which brought the GAO contract back 'in the money'. In the following years, market interest rates have fallen further to the current minimum value level of 3.75 per cent, and the consequence has been a continuous rise in the value of the GAO. These results are confirmed by the trends in Figure 7.8.

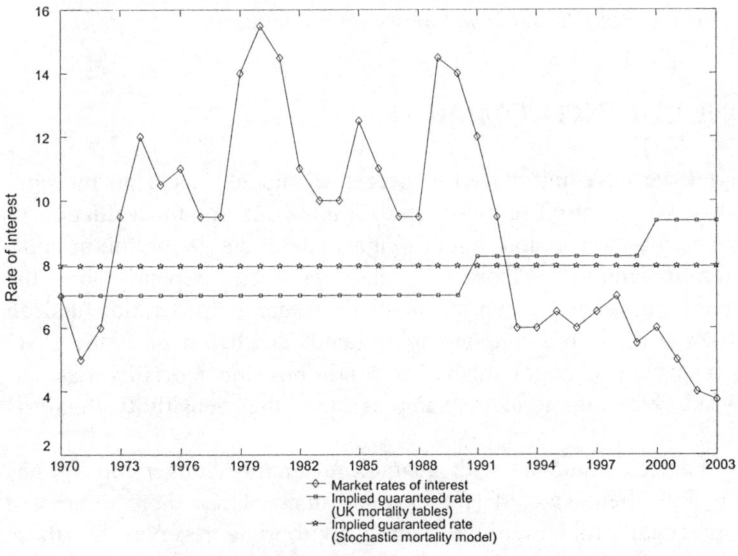

Figure 7.9 'Historical evolution' of the implied guaranteed rate for different specifications of the mortality model (equation 7.14)

Figures 7.8 and 7.9 show the historical evolution of the GAO value for the case in which mortality is modeled as described in Section 7.2.4. Also shown, for comparison purposes, are the trends generated by the model in which the survival probabilities are computed using UK standard mortality tables (as described in Section 7.2.3). Two such alternative models are analysed. Firstly, we consider the case in which post-retirement survival probabilities are calculated using the PA90 mortality table only, as was the practice during the 1970s. The results are compared to those obtained for the case in which mortality improvements are incorporated by 'switching' to more up-to-date mortality tables as these become available. Hence, when the valuation is performed during the period 1991–99, the PMA80–C10 life table is used, while from the year 2000 onward, the PMA92–C20 life table is used.[4]

The model based on the PA90 life table only provides a useful benchmark for distinguishing the effect of changing interest rates on the GAO values from the effect generated by improvements in mortality trends. This is because no mortality improvements (beyond 1990) are captured since a single fixed mortality table is used for valuation throughout the entire lifetime of the contract. Thus, neglecting improvements in mortality rates leads to an underpricing of the guaranteed annuity option of about 60 per cent in year 2002 with respect to the values obtained using the model based on the three mortality tables. The corresponding level of underpricing is about 40 per cent with respect to the stochastic mortality model used.

7.4 CONCLUDING COMMENTS

In this chapter we have introduced a theoretical model, based on the one-factor Heath-Jarrow-Morton term structure framework, for the valuation of guaranteed annuity conversion options attached to single premium unit-linked deferred annuity contracts. The approach depends on the correspondence between the contingent claim under consideration and an option contract written on a coupon-paying bond. The behavior of the GAO value with respect to changes in market conditions and mortality risk has been analysed with numerical examples and the sensitivity analysis presented.

Although pension contracts with guaranteed annuity conversion options may no longer be being issued (for example in the UK), there remains a significant practical problem of estimating appropriate reserves for those contracts sold in the past and where the option has not yet been exercised (Bolton et al., 1997). Thus, we believe that the above results (see equation 7.7) will be of considerable assistance to insurance companies for estimating such reserves, and for reporting and regulatory purposes.

Equation (7.7) provides some guidance as to the theoretical hedging strategy which should be employed. In fact, according to the valuation formula, the guaranteed annuity option can be seen as a portfolio consisting of a long position in the $(T + t)$-zero-coupon bond which has to be funded by a short position in the T-zero-coupon bond. However, we recognize that there are practical considerations to take into account, for example, the question of the availability of $(T + t)$-zero-coupon bonds for such long maturities as the ones implied by the contract.

We have seen that the inclusion of stochastic mortality, through fluctuations around a trend, or longevity risk, leads to a reduction in the expected value of the GAO. However, we would advise some caution in the application of this result. Our valuation formula for V_x, equation (7.7), relates to an expected present value obtained using risk-neutral valuation methods. However, an insurer might also be interested, for example for reserving purposes, in the full distribution of the random present value and, in particular, in upper tail values. These percentiles are likely to depend more directly on the stochastic mortality parameters introduced in the above models.

7.A APPENDIX: VALUATION FORMULA FOR A GUARANTEED ANNUITY OPTION

The purpose of this Appendix is to show the derivation of the valuation formula (7.7) presented in Section 7.2.1. Given the complexity of the terminal payoff of the guaranteed annuity option, we subdivide the calculations into three parts. In the first part, we give a quick overview of the market setup in the HJM framework; on the basis of this setup we price zero-coupon bonds, and finally we use this preliminary set of results to complete the valuation process for the guaranteed annuity option.

7.A.1 The Financial Model

The market framework is described in Section 7.2.1 and 7.2.2.

Consider the stock risk-adjusted probability measure $\widetilde{\mathbb{P}}$ defined in (7.3) by

$$\eta_T = e^{-\int_0^T r_u du} \frac{S_T}{S_0} = e^{-\frac{\sigma_S^2}{2}T + \sigma_S \hat{Z}_T}$$
$$= e^{-\rho^2 \frac{\sigma_S^2}{2}T - (1-\rho^2)\frac{\sigma_S^2}{2}T + \sigma_S \rho \hat{W}_T + \sigma_S \sqrt{1-\rho^2}\, \hat{W}_t'}.$$

Since the Girsanov theorem implies that

$$\widetilde{W}_t \ :=\hat{W}_t - \rho\sigma_S t$$
$$\widetilde{W}_t' \ :=\hat{W}_t' - \sigma_S\sqrt{1-\rho^2}\,t$$

are $\widetilde{\mathbb{P}}$-standard Brownian motions, the $\widetilde{\mathbb{P}}$-dynamic of the forward rate is then

$$df(t,T) = \left(\sigma e^{-\lambda(T-t)}\left(\sigma \int_t^T e^{-\lambda(u-t)} du + \rho\sigma_S\right)\right) dt + \sigma e^{-\lambda(T-t)} d\widetilde{W}_t .$$

Under these assumptions, it follows that the short rate process is

$$r_t = f(0,t) + \int_0^t \widetilde{\mu}_f(v,t)\,dv + \sigma \int_0^t e^{-\lambda(t-v)} d\widetilde{W}_v \,,$$

where

$$\widetilde{\mu}_f(v,t) = \sigma e^{-\lambda(t-v)} \left(\sigma \int_v^t e^{-\lambda(x-v)} dx + \rho\sigma_S \right)$$
$$= \sigma e^{-\lambda(t-v)} \left[\frac{\sigma}{\lambda}(1 - e^{-\lambda(t-v)}) + \rho\sigma_S \right].$$

Therefore

$$r_t = f(0,t) + (1 - e^{-\lambda t}) \left[\frac{\sigma^2}{2\lambda^2}(1 - e^{-\lambda t}) + \frac{\rho\sigma\sigma_S}{\lambda} \right] + \sigma \int_0^t e^{-\lambda(t-v)} d\widetilde{W}_v \,. \qquad \text{(A1)}$$

As the last equation shows, the exponentially decaying structure of the forward rate volatility leads to a mean-reverting form of the short rate that closely resembles an extended version of the Vasicek (1977) model. Although equation (A1) is similar to the expressions derived by Vasicek (1977), it differs in the fact that it is obtained taking the initial term structure as exogenous, while for the Vasicek model the initial term structure is endogenous. According to (A1), under $\widetilde{\mathbb{P}}$

$$(r_t - f(0,t)) \sim N(m_r(t), \sigma_r^2(t)) \qquad \text{(A2)}$$

where

$$m_r(t) = (1 - e^{-\lambda t}) \left[\frac{\sigma^2}{2\lambda^2}(1 - e^{-\lambda t}) + \frac{\rho\sigma\sigma_S}{\lambda} \right]$$

and

$$\sigma_r^2(t) = \sigma^2 \left(\frac{1 - e^{-2\lambda t}}{2\lambda} \right). \qquad \text{(A3)}$$

Therefore we can show that

$$P_t(T) = \frac{P_0(T)}{P_0(t)} e^{-\frac{1}{2}\gamma^2(t,T)\sigma_r^2(t) - \gamma(t,T)(r_t - f(0,t))}, \qquad \text{(A4)}$$

where

$$\gamma(t,T)=\left(\frac{1-e^{-\lambda(T-t)}}{\lambda}\right).$$

7.A.2 Bond Pricing

Let

$$F_\tau(T+t,T):=\frac{P_\tau(T+t)}{P_\tau(T)}$$

be the forward price at time $\tau \le T$ for delivery at time T of a zero-coupon bond expiring at time (T + t), written as F_τ for short. From the HJM model, it follows that under $\hat{\mathbb{P}}$ the forward price satisfies the following stochastic differential equation:

$$dF_\tau = -\sigma_P(\tau,T)\,C_\tau(T,T+t)\,F_\tau d\tau + C_\tau(T,T+t)\,F_\tau\, d\hat{W}_\tau\,,$$

where

$$\sigma_P(\tau,T) = -\int_\tau^T \sigma e^{-\lambda(s-\tau)}ds = \frac{\sigma}{\lambda}\left(e^{-\lambda(T-\tau)}-1\right)$$

is the volatility of a T-zero-coupon bond price process, and

$$\begin{aligned} C_\tau(T,T+t) &= \sigma_P(\tau,T+t) - \sigma_P(\tau,T) \\ &= \frac{\sigma}{\lambda}e^{-\lambda(T-\tau)}(e^{-\lambda t}-1)\,; \end{aligned}$$

so that

$$C_\tau\,(T,T+t) = -\sigma e^{-\lambda(T-\tau)}\gamma(T,T+t)\,. \tag{A5}$$

Hence, under $\widetilde{\mathbb{P}}$

$$\begin{aligned} dF_\tau &= -\sigma_P(\tau,T)\,C_\tau(T,T+t)\,F_\tau d\tau + C_\tau(T,T+t)\,F_\tau\,(d\widetilde{W}_\tau + \rho\sigma_S d\tau) \\ &= C_\tau(T,T+t)(-\sigma_P(\tau,T)+\rho\sigma_S)\,F_\tau d\tau + C_\tau(T,T+t)\,F_\tau d\widetilde{W}_\tau \\ &= A_\tau(T,T+t)\,F_\tau d\tau + C_\tau(T,T+t)\,F_\tau d\widetilde{W}_\tau\,, \end{aligned}$$

with

$$A_\tau(T,T+t)=C_\tau(T,T+t)(-\sigma_P(\tau,T)+\rho\sigma_S),$$

or

$$A_\tau(T,T+t)=\gamma(T,T+t)e^{-\lambda(T-\tau)}\left[\frac{\sigma^2}{\lambda}(e^{-\lambda(T-\tau)}-1)-\rho\sigma\sigma_S\right]. \quad \text{(A6)}$$

Note that the forward price $F_\tau(T+t,T)$ admits the following representation under $\widetilde{\mathbb{P}}$:

$$F_\tau(T+t,T)=F_0 e^{\int_0^\tau\left(A_v(T,T+t)-\frac{C_v(T,T+t)^2}{2}\right)dv+\int_0^\tau C_v(T,T+t)d\widetilde{W}_v}.$$

In particular, consider $F_\tau(T+t,T)=P_T(T+t)$, then

$$\begin{aligned}F_\tau(T+t,T)&=F_0\, e^{\int_0^T\left(A_v(T,T+t)-\frac{C_v(T,T+t)^2}{2}\right)dv+\int_0^T C_v(T,T+t)d\widetilde{W}_v}\\&=F_\tau e^{\int_\tau^T\left(A_v(T,T+t)-\frac{C_v(T,T+t)^2}{2}\right)dv+\int_\tau^T C_v(T,T+t)d\widetilde{W}_v}\\&=F_\tau e^{X_\tau(T)},\end{aligned}$$

with

$$X_\tau(T)=\int_\tau^T\left(A_v(T,T+t)-\frac{C_v(T,T+t)^2}{2}\right)dv+\int_\tau^T C_v(T,T+t)\,d\widetilde{W}_v. \quad \text{(A7)}$$

Equations A5 and A6 imply that:

$$\begin{aligned}\int_\tau^T C_v(T,T+t)^2\,dv&=\sigma^2\gamma^2(T,T+t)\int_\tau^T e^{-2\lambda(T-v)}dv\\&=\gamma^2(T,T+t)\sigma^2\left(\frac{1-e^{-2\lambda(T-\tau)}}{2\lambda}\right)\\&=\gamma^2(T,T+t)\sigma_r^2(T-\tau);\end{aligned}$$

and

$$\int_\tau^T A_v(T,T+t)\,dv = \gamma(T,T+t)\frac{\sigma^2}{\lambda}\int_\tau^T e^{-\lambda(T-v)}(e^{-\lambda(T-v)}-1)\,dv$$
$$-\gamma(T,T+t)\rho\sigma\sigma_S\int_\tau^T e^{-\lambda(T-v)}dv$$
$$=\gamma(T,T+t)\frac{\sigma^2}{\lambda}I_1-\gamma(T,T+t)\rho\sigma\sigma_S I_2.$$

The integrals I_1 and I_2 can be evaluated thus:

$$I_1=\int_\tau^T e^{-\lambda(T-v)}(e^{-\lambda(T-v)}-1)\,dv$$
$$=-\frac{1}{2\lambda}(1-e^{-\lambda(T-\tau)})^2;$$
$$I_2=\int_\tau^T e^{-\lambda(T-v)}dv$$
$$=\frac{1}{\lambda}(1-e^{-\lambda(T-\tau)}).$$

Therefore

$$\int_\tau^T A_v(T,T+t)\,dv=-\gamma(T,T+t)\frac{\sigma^2}{2\lambda^2}(1-e^{-\lambda(T-\tau)})^2-\gamma(T,T+t)\frac{\rho\sigma\sigma_S}{\lambda}(1-e^{-\lambda(T-\tau)})$$
$$=-\gamma(T,T+t)(1-e^{-\lambda(T-\tau)})\left[\frac{\sigma^2}{2\lambda^2}(1-e^{-\lambda(T-\tau)})+\frac{\rho\sigma\sigma_S}{\lambda}\right]$$
$$=-\gamma(T,T+t)\,m_r(T-\tau).$$

Hence, from (A7) it follows that

$$X_\tau(T)=-\gamma(T,T+t)m_r(T-\tau)-\frac{1}{2}\gamma^2(T,T+t)\sigma_r^2(T-\tau)-\sigma\gamma(T,T+t)\int_\tau^T e^{-\lambda(T-v)}d\widetilde{W}_v.$$

This implies that:

$$X_\tau(T)\sim N\left(-\gamma(T,T+t)m_r(T-\tau)-\frac{1}{2}\gamma^2(T,T+t)\sigma_r^2(T-\tau),\gamma^2(T,T+t)\sigma_r^2(T-\tau)\right).$$

7.A.3 Pricing the Guaranteed Annuity Option

In Section 7.2.1, we showed that the valuation formula for the guaranteed annuity option is

$$V_x(x+\tau,\tau,T-\tau)$$

$$= {}_{T-\tau}p_{x+\tau}S_\tau + {}_{T-\tau}p_{x+\tau}gS_\tau \sum_{t=0}^{w-(T+x)} {}_tp_{T+x}\,\widetilde{\mathbb{E}}\left[(P_T(T+t)-K_t)^+ \mid \mathcal{F}_\tau\right].$$

Therefore, in order to determine a closed analytical formula for the option contract, we need to solve the following expectation:

$$\widetilde{\mathbb{E}}\left[(P_T(T+t)-K_t)^+ \mid \mathcal{F}_\tau\right],$$

where $\widetilde{\mathbb{E}}$ denotes the expectation under the stock risk-adjusted probability measure $\widetilde{\mathbb{P}}$ and

$$K_t = P_T^*(T+t)$$

is the artificial strike price calculated as the bond price such that

$$\sum_{t=0}^{w-(T+x)} {}_tp_{T+x}P_T(T+t) = K.$$

The expectation under consideration can be solved using the results obtained in the previous subsections. In fact, it can be rewritten as:

$$\widetilde{\mathbb{E}}\left[(P_T(T+t)-K_t)^+ \mid \mathcal{F}_\tau\right]$$
$$= \widetilde{\mathbb{E}}\left[(F_T(T+t,T)-K_t)^+ \mid \mathcal{F}_\tau\right]$$
$$= \int_{-d_t}^{\infty} \left(F_\tau e^{-\frac{1}{2}\gamma^2(T,T+t)\sigma_r^2(T-\tau)-\gamma(T,T+t)(m_r(T-\tau)-\sigma_r(T-\tau)y)} - K_t\right)\frac{1}{\sqrt{2\pi}}e^{-\frac{y^2}{2}}dy$$

where $y \sim N(0,1)$ and

$$d_t = \frac{\ln\dfrac{P_\tau(T+t)}{K_tP_\tau(T)} - \dfrac{1}{2}\sigma_r^2(T-\tau)\gamma^2(T,T+t) - \gamma(T,T+t)m_r(T-\tau)}{\gamma(T,T+t)\sigma_r(T-\tau)}.$$

Therefore

$$\widetilde{\mathbb{E}}\left[(P_T(T+t)-K_t)^+\right]$$

$$= F_\tau e^{-\frac{1}{2}\gamma^2(T,T+t)\sigma_r^2(T-\tau)-\gamma(T,T+t)(m_r(T-\tau)} \int_{-\infty}^{d_t} \frac{1}{\sqrt{2\pi}} e^{-\frac{1}{2}(y^2-2\gamma(T,T+t)\sigma_r(T-\tau)y)} dy$$

$$- K_t \int_{-\infty}^{d_t} \frac{1}{\sqrt{2\pi}} e^{-\frac{y^2}{2}} dy$$

$$= F_\tau e^{-\gamma(T,T+t)m_r(T-\tau)} \int_{-\infty}^{d_t} \frac{1}{\sqrt{2\pi}} e^{-\frac{1}{2}(y-\gamma(T,T+t)\sigma_r(T-\tau))^2} dy - K_t N(d_t)$$

$$= F_\tau e^{-\gamma(T,T+t)m_r(T-\tau)} N(d_t') - K_t N(d_t)$$

$$= \frac{P_\tau(T+t)}{P_\tau(T)} e^{-\gamma(T,T+t)m_r(T-\tau)} N(d_t') - K_t N(d_t)$$

where

$$d_t' = d_t + \gamma(T,T+t)\sigma_r(T-\tau)$$

$$= \frac{\ln \frac{P_\tau(T+t)}{K_t P_\tau(T)} - \frac{1}{2}\sigma_r^2(T-\tau)\gamma^2(T,T+t) - \gamma(T,T+t)m_r(T-\tau)}{\gamma(T,T+t)\sigma_r(T)},$$

which leads to equation (7.7) .

NOTES

1. We notice that the assumptions made about the market behavior guarantee the existence of a market equilibrium, which rules out the existence of arbitrage opportunities.
2. Here we implicitly assume that the market is complete, in other words that any contingent claim is attainable and therefore that the risk-neutral equivalent martingale measure is unique. The financial market described in the following Section 7.2.2, in fact, is complete. We notice though that the pricing argument leading to the valuation equation (7.2) holds also in the more general case of incomplete markets, although in this case the risk-neutral probability measure is not unique.
3. Equation (A4) in the Appendix shows that

$$P_t(T) = \frac{P_0(T)}{P_0(t)} e^{-\frac{1}{2}\gamma^2(t,T)\sigma_r^2(t)-\gamma(t,T)(r_t - f(0,t))}.$$

Hence, the above described procedure is implemented looking for the critical value r^* such that

$$\sum_{t=0}^{w-(T+x)} {}_t p_{T+x} \frac{P_0(T+t)}{P_0(t)} e^{-\frac{1}{2}\gamma^2(T,T+t)\sigma_r^2(T)-\gamma(T,T+t)(r_T-f(0,T))} = K,$$

so that

$$K_t = \frac{P_0(T+t)}{P_0(T)} e^{-\frac{1}{2}\gamma^2(T,T+t)\sigma_r^2(T)-\gamma(T,T+t)(r_T^*-f(0,T))}.$$

4. We note that each of these standard life tables is a 'single-entry' table with extrapolation up to a single future time point. Hence, they differ in character fundamentally from the stochastic model represented by equation (7.9) which allows for explicit projection of the hazard rate over each future potential survival period.

REFERENCES

Ballotta, L. and S. Haberman (2003a), 'Valuation of Guaranteed Annuity Conversion Options', *Insurance: Mathematics and Economics*, **33**(1), 87–108.

Ballotta, L. and S. Haberman (2003b), 'The Fair Valuation Problem of Guaranteed Annuity Options: the Stochastic Mortality Case', under review.

Bank of England (2002), *Annual Statistical Abstract*, Part 1, September 2001, updated to February 2002, London: Bank of England.

Bezooyen, J.T.S., C.J.E. Exley and S.J.B. Mehta (1998), 'Valuing and Hedging Guaranteed Annuity Options', Paper presented to Institute and Faculty of Actuaries Investment Conference, September 1998, University of Cambridge.

Bolton, M. J., D.H. Carr, P.A. Collis et al. (1997), *Reserving for Annuity Guarantees – The Report of the Annuity Guarantees Working Party*, London: Institute of Actuaries.

Continuous Mortality Investigation Bureau (1998), *The Mortality of Pensioners in Insured Group Pension Schemes 1991–94*, Continuous Mortality Investigation Report N° 16, The Institute and Faculty of Actuaries, UK.

Continuous Mortality Investigation Bureau (1999), *Standard Tables of Mortality Based on the 1991–94 Experiences*, Continuous Mortality Investigation Report No. 17, The Institute and Faculty of Actuaries, UK.

Geman, H., N. El Karoui and J.C. Rochet (1995), 'Changes of Numeraire, Changes of Probability Measure and Option Pricing', *Journal of Applied Probability*, **32**, 443–58.

Group Annuity Valuation Task Force (1995), '1994 Group Annuity Mortality and Annuity Reserving Tables', *Transactions of the Society of Actuaries*, **47**, 865–913.

Heath, D., R.A. Jarrow and A. Morton (1992), 'Bond Pricing and the Term Structure of Interest Rates: a New Methodology for Contingent Claims Valuation', *Econometrica*, **60**, 77–105.

Jamshidian, F. (1989), 'An Exact Bond Option Formula', *The Journal of Finance*, **44**(1), 205–209.

Marocco, P. and E. Pitacco (1998), 'Longevity Risk and Life Annuity Reinsurance', *Transactions of the 26th International Congress of Actuaries*, **6**, 453–79.

Milevsky, M.A. and S.D. Promislow (2001), 'Mortality Derivatives and the Option to Annuitise', *Insurance: Mathematics and Economics*, **29**, 299–318.

Olivieri, A. (2001), 'Uncertainty in Mortality Projections: an Actuarial Perspective', *Insurance: Mathematics and Economics*, **29**, 231–45.

Olivieri, A. and E. Pitacco (2002), 'Inference about Mortality Improvements in Life Annuity Portfolios', Paper presented to 27th International Congress of Actuaries, Cancun, Mexico.

Pelsser, A. (2002), 'Pricing and Hedging Guaranteed Annuity Options via Static Option Replication', Discussion Paper 02-037/2, Tinbergen Institute.

Renshaw, A., S. Haberman and P. Hatzoupoulos (1996), 'The Modelling of Recent Mortality Trends in United Kingdom Male Assure Lives', *British Actuarial Journal*, **2**, 449–77.

Sithole, T.Z., S. Haberman and R.J. Verrall (2000), 'An Investigation into Parametric Models for Mortality Projections, with Applications to Immediate Annuitants' and Life Office Pensioners' Data', *Insurance: Mathematics and Economics*, **27**, 285–312.

Vasicek, O. (1977), 'An Equilibrium Characterization of the Term Structure', *Journal of Financial Economics*, **5**, 177–88.

Yang, S., H.R. Waters and A.D. Wilkie (2002), 'Hedging for Guaranteed Annuity Options', *Conference proceedings of the 6th International Congress on Insurance: Mathematics and Economics.*

8. The behavior of UK annuity prices from 1972 to 2002*

Edmund Cannon and Ian Tonks

8.1 INTRODUCTION

Although pensions are not usually considered the most interesting of topics, there has been considerable discussion in the British press (for example: the *Sun* 5 March 2002, the *Observer* 17 February 2002) about supposedly low rates of return on annuities and the legislative compulsion to devote 75 per cent of one's pension fund to the purchase of such an annuity by the age of 75. The government has become so concerned about the functioning of the annuities market in the UK that it issued a consultation paper[1] in February 2002. In this chapter we consider a variety of potential criticisms of both the legal requirements and the way that annuities operate.

We first start by noting that at least part of this discussion seems to be based upon a misapprehension. This is that where the money is paid towards an annuity by annuitants who then die relatively young, their wealth is received by the life insurer because any implicit capital available at the point of death is not paid to the deceased annuitant's estate. In fact, however, this money is used to subsidize those people who live for a relatively long time and who receive considerably more money from their annuity than they actually paid in. This is a key component of the idea of an annuity: it insures people against uncertain lifetimes by redistributing from those who die relatively young to those who die relatively old. The risk insured is the possibility that one might live too long, or, if that seems an odd thing to avoid, the possibility that one might live for a longer time than one has assets to finance. Criticism of annuity markets on this basis is clearly faulty and it is a matter of educating the public (or perhaps the press) as to the true state of

* This research was funded by the ESRC 'Understanding the Evolving Macroeconomy' Programme under grant L138 25 1031. We should like to thank Becca Fell and Sally Lane for entering the data and *Pensions World* for assistance in obtaining back copies.

the matter. It is noteworthy that analyses of the UK annuity market by Murthi et al. (1999) and Finkelstein and Poterba (2002) suggest that the market is approximately efficient and that annuities are not actuarially mispriced.

An alternative interpretation of the critique that annuities fail to pay back any capital is that some individuals do not wish to use the pension fund to finance their retirement income at all, but wish to preserve the wealth (which has been accumulated tax-free) to pass on to the heirs. For this reason, London and Colonial have issued a form of annuity which does involve a component of wealth being paid to the estate of an annuitant at the point of death. There are two problems with allowing annuity markets to develop in this way. The first is definitional. If pensioners are to be allowed to preserve their capital indefinitely, then this means that they are effectively being allowed to buy infinite-dated financial instruments, or 'Consols', in other words an asset which is not an annuity. While one might accept that financial intermediaries and Humpty Dumpty may choose what words mean, using the word 'annuity' to describe a 'Consol' is likely to lead to more confusion rather than less. (For a discussion see Quinton, 2001). The second problem is that allowing financial instruments such as that of London and Colonial has significant tax implications, both for revenue and distribution. Most individuals in the UK have a pension fund of less than £50 000, corresponding to a pension income of at most £4250 per year at current annuity rates compared with an annual income of £2300 which could be earned from Consols. Given the current level of the UK state pension, such pensioners will need to annuitize their whole pension fund to obtain a satisfactory income. Those individuals who will most wish to avoid annuitizing their pension fund will be rich people using their pension plan as a way to avoid tax.

A more promising criticism of the current annuity rules is that annuity rates are unusually low. It is certainly true that annuity rates have fallen from about 15 per cent to about 8 per cent over the last ten years. Part of the explanation for this is that longevity has increased. As people live longer, a given sum of money paid for an annuity has to finance a longer stream of income and so income per year has had to fall. This reduction in annuity rates is unavoidable. However, the fall in annuity rates over the last ten years is clearly far too large to be due to changes in longevity alone.

Another important contributory factor is that all interest rates have fallen as can be seen in Figure 8.1, which illustrates the time series behavior of the annuity rate alongside that of the Consol rate. The question that this chapter addresses is whether the fall in annuity rates is larger than justified by the fundamental changes in interest rates and longevity. However, even if low annuity rates are in some sense 'justified' it is still reasonable to ask whether pensioners should be forced to purchase annuities at such low rates. To do so appears to make pensioners particularly susceptible to annuity rate risk. Apart from the effects this has on people retiring now, it may also influence potential saving behavior of people who will retire in the future. Blundell and Stoker (1999) have shown that the timing of risk may be significant in determining agents' savings decisions and that even quite small future risks may influence current savings behavior.

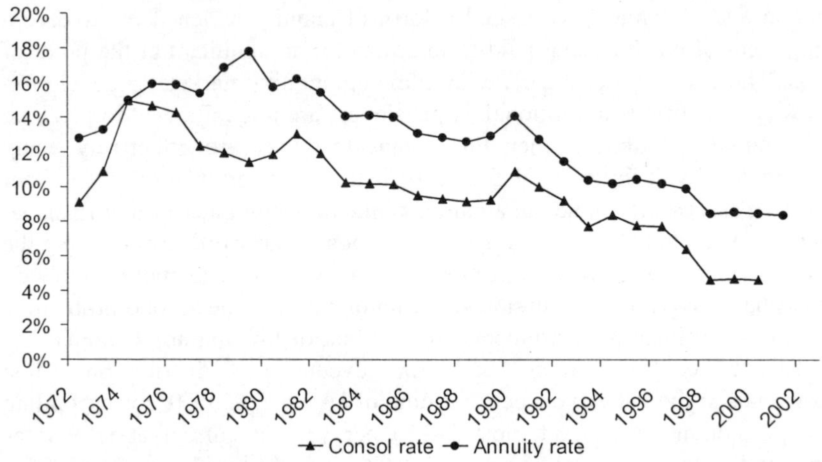

Figure 8.1 Annuity rates (male, 65, five-year guarantee) and long-term interest rates

To answer this question we need to consider the effects of two additional factors on people's pensions. The first is the interaction of government legislation with the national debt and the second is the behavior of the stock market.

Because annuities are relatively long-lived financial liabilities from the point of view of an insurance company, it has been common practice to match these with long-lived assets such as long-dated government debt. A series of government regulations following on from the Maxwell pension scandal has led many pension funds also to hold significant quantities of such assets to match the liabilities of those pensions currently being paid out. Unfortunately, this increased demand for long-dated government debt coincides with a reduction in the size of the national debt through a series of budget surpluses or very small deficits, as well as the large transfer to the government of the money raised in the 3G telecommunications auction. This has led to very high prices of long-dated government debt and relatively low yields, to the point where the yield curve is now perversely shaped, that is, downward sloping, at the long end. Thus, although low annuity rates merely reflect low long-term interest rates, this may be because long-term interest rates themselves have been artificially distorted. This phenomenon has led to calls for pension funds to be able to hold a wider variety of assets and this alone might allow annuity rates to rise. According to this line of argument (which relies upon a preferred-habitat view of the term structure), there is a major distortion of all long-term interest rates which has a corresponding effect on annuity prices.

On the other hand, there is good reason to believe that low annuity *rates* in themselves are irrelevant. If the annuity rate is A and the value of a pension fund at the point of retirement is V, then the value of a pension that can be purchased is AV. For a pension fund invested predominantly in the stock market, V effectively represents the stock market index, which tends to be negatively correlated with interest rates. Thus it is quite possible for the annuity rate, A, to be relatively low while AV is close to its long-run value. For this reason, no discussion of annuity rates can be divorced from a wider discussion of financial markets.

The rest of this chapter is organized as follows: in the next section we present an annuity rate for the last 30 years for the UK and discuss its relationship with the long-term interest rates. We then calculate the net present value of such an annuity over this period, a figure sometimes referred to as the 'money's worth'. To relate the decumulation phase of a pension to the accumulation phase we then conduct a simple analysis of the relationship of annuity rates and the stock market before concluding.

8.2 ANNUITY RATES AND LONG-TERM INTEREST RATES

There is a paucity of time series data on annuity rates in the United Kingdom, contrasting with the historical analysis of the US by Warshawsky (1988). Our data are taken from bi-monthly or monthly figures published in *Pensions World* from September 1972 to November 1977 and monthly data from April 1980 to May 1998. During these periods *Pensions World* published a consistent series of data of non-escalating purchase annuities guaranteed for five years, for both men and women of different ages from a variety of different annuity providers. The gaps in the series are filled with data from *Money Management* and *Money Facts*. More details can be found in Appendix A. One concern with using non-escalating annuities is that these are the forms of annuity most at risk from inflation, apart from the fact that they fail to keep pace with secular increases in average earnings. However, from the point of view of analysing the UK annuity markets they are appropriate, since most annuities which are purchased are of this form. An additional consideration is that data for index-linked or escalating annuities are not available for much of the period.

Our data for annuities for males, aged 65, are illustrated in Figure 8.1: lest there be any confusion, the annuity prices are usually quoted in the form of an annuity of £600 per £10 000 purchased, which we would represent as 6 per cent on our graph. For comparison with other interest rates we also plot the Consol rate. Theoretically these two series should be linked because they are both long-term assets: if longevity were constant and the short-term rate were not particularly variable then the two would differ on average only by a constant.

Descriptive statistics are presented in Table 8.1 below. As can be seen from the graph, the series are highly correlated (the correlation between the two series is 0.906). Given a 5 per cent critical value of 3.59, it is impossible to reject the null hypotheses that the they each have unit roots,[2] but it is possible to reject the null of a unit root in the difference between the two variables, suggesting that the series are cointegrated.

Table 8.1 Descriptive statistics for annuity and Consol rates

	Annuity rate	Consol rate	Annuity rate – Consol rate
Mean	13.06 %	9.85 %	3.21 %
St. dev.	2.64 %	2.76 %	1.18 %
ADF test for unit root 5% critical value = 3.59	3.31	2.87	3.89

Multivariate analysis of the two series is hazardous with so few observations and so further analysis of the cointegration properties of the two variables is suggestive rather than conclusive. In a bivariate model of the two series whose residuals seem well behaved[3] it is possible to reject the null of two unit roots with a trace statistic of 26.2 (p-value 0.43), but it is possible to reject the null hypothesis that the cointegrating vector is simply the difference of the annuity and Consol rates but for a linear trend (the test for the homogeneity restriction is $\chi_1^2 = 12.8$).

Thus we conclude that there is sufficient statistical evidence to confirm what is visible by eye, namely that the annuity and Consol rates have behaved similarly over the last 30 years, but insufficient statistical evidence to specify the relationship closely. For this reason we turn to a more theoretically based analysis of the annuity rate.

8.3 NET PRESENT VALUE CALCULATIONS

There are two ways to compare the value of annuities with other assets. The simplest way to calculate the value of an annuity is to use the measure called the 'money's worth', which is simply the ratio of the expected present value of the flow of payments made by an annuity to the money paid for an annuity. This procedure has been used by Mitchell et al. (1999) to analyze the annuities market in the USA and by Murthi et al. (1999) and Finkelstein and Poterba (2002) to analyse the UK annuity market: in this collection McCarthy and Mitchell (Chapter 2) use the approach to compare annuity markets in different countries. These three papers all analyse a cross-section of annuity rates offered by different firms and also consider how the money's worth depends upon the type of annuity purchased: the evidence suggests that annuities purchased by older annuitants yield a lower money's worth. A detailed description of the method can be found in the references cited: for a general discussion see the Introduction to the collection of papers in Brown et al. (2001).

The alternative way to compare the value of annuities with other assets is to consider the internal rate of return implied by an annuity rate. The advantage of the latter approach is that it is necessary only to project life expectancies, whereas the money's worth approach requires assumptions about expectations of future interest rates as well. However, since the results we obtain by the two approaches are consistent, we relegate our results from the internal rate of return approach to Appendix C.

Returning to the money's worth approach: define the annuity rate $A_{t,65}$ as the payment made per year of an annuity which cost £1 to buy in year t for someone aged 65. The money's worth for a level five-year guaranteed annuity can be written as

$$A_{t,65}\left\{\sum_{k=66}^{70}\prod_{j=1}^{k-65}\left(1+r_{t+j}\right)^{-1}+\sum_{k=71}^{\infty}\pi_{t,k,65}\prod_{j=1}^{k-65}\left(1+r_{t+j}\right)^{-1}\right\} \tag{8.1}$$

where r_{t+j} is the interest rate in period $t+j$ and $\pi_{t,k,65}$ is the probability of someone born in year t-65 surviving to age k having reached age 65.[4]

We estimate expectations of future interest rates from the term structure of interest rates. This means that the 1988 interest rate used to value an annuity sold in 1980 is the implicit rate in 1980 yield curve. We choose to use this interest rate rather than the ex post interest rate because it provides a consistent series of interest rates for us to use over the whole period. Apart from consistency across time, the approach has the advantage that it can be compared directly with Mitchell et al. (1999), Murthi et al. (1999) and

Finkelstein and Poterba (2002), as well as giving an idea of the profits anticipated by life assurers at the time of selling the annuity, rather than the ex post realization.

It is, of course, well known that the term structure is rather a mediocre predictor of future interest rates. According to theories where there is a liquidity or term premium or according to preferred-habitat theories, it may be a biased predictor. Most discussion assumes that longer rates are higher because of a term premium, in which case the interest rates we infer from the yield curve will be biased upwards and the money's worth biased downwards. Since we shall be arguing that the money's worth is quite high, this bias will be against our argument and in fact strengthen our conclusions.

As mentioned in our introduction, however, there may be some reason to believe that long-term interest rates are currently biased downwards, in which case we would be overestimating the money's worth. We shall partially address this problem in the following section where we discuss the value of pensions.

To implement equation (8.1) we also need to infer expected survival probabilities. Ideally we should use a panel of ex ante survival probabilities. However, because of data constraints we have used the ex post realized probabilities where they are available, which can be justified on the basis that these move relatively slowly and are less prone to severe misprediction. Where we do need to project survival probabilities into the future we do so using a simple model quadratic in time and age, described more fully in Appendix B. We use two estimates: one is relatively conservative and assumes longevity will only increase slowly, whereas the other assumes faster increases in longevity. In the Appendix we discuss the possibility that our estimates of survival probabilities based on mortality rates as a whole will provide a further downward bias to our estimates of the money's worth.

The money's worth under these two assumptions is illustrated in Figure 8.2. The observations for 2001 and 2002 are not perfectly comparable with previous years, since not all of the relevant mortality data are available, and not all of the yield curve data are yet published: the 2002 observation is based on the first quarter only. The money's worth in 2000 was between 89 pence and £1.01, falling to a range of 85–96 pence for the first few months of 2002.

Figure 8.2 illustrates that the money's worth is not particularly poor at the moment. Certainly there have been times when it was worse, notably the 1970s. In addition to the money's worth being lower in that decade, a fixed nominal payment may have been worth less then because it was more quickly eroded by the high inflation. Of course, if long-term interest rates had fully incorporated correct expectations of inflation during that period, then the existence of high inflation would have had no effect on the value of an annuity, but there is considerable evidence in the economic literature of the term structure that expectations fail to incorporate inflation fully.

Furthermore the money's worth only appears poor if one assumes that future life expectancy will be relatively low: using the higher estimate of life expectancy leads to money's worth estimates that still appear high by comparison with the last 30 years.

These results are very similar to the cross-sectional analysis of Finkelstein and Poterba (2002) and Murthi et al. (1999). The former found the money's worth to be 90 pence and the latter 93.2 pence in 1998, comparing with our figure of 93 pence based on a smaller increase in life expectancy. Murthi et al. (1999) also provide estimates of 99.6 pence in 1990 and 92.1 pence in 1994: our analogous figures are 99 pence and 84 pence.

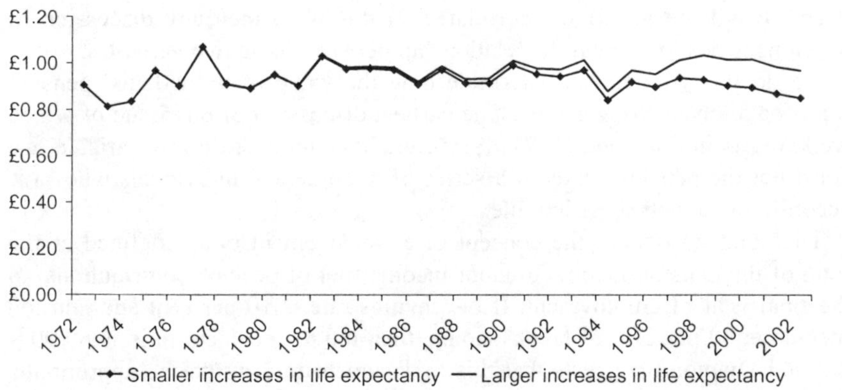

Figure 8.2 'Money's worth' or the present value of annuity income stream purchased with £1 (male, 65, five-year guarantee)

This section has illustrated that using the money's worth criterion, annuity rates appear competitive compared with the last 30 years. This result depends to a considerable extent on the yield curve being a valid source of information for the calculation of the money's worth. As we have noted, however, this may not be valid if, as would be the case in preferred-habitat theories, the long-term interest rate is itself artificially low: the fact that there is efficient arbitrage between annuity markets and bond markets is of little comfort if all financial markets are distorted. We address this question indirectly in the next section by asking how much pension an annuity can buy at the present time.

8.4 VALUE OF PENSION FUNDS

The previous discussion centers on the actuarial fairness of annuity contracts. Perhaps more important to the actual annuitant is the pension that he/she receive, regardless of how long he/she lives. This means that we need to consider both the accumulation of pension fund and the annuity rate together. The value of the pension received by a pensioner is AV, where A is the annuity rate and V is the value of the pension fund at the point of retirement (assuming that all of the pension fund is annuitized). It is a well known empirical regularity that the value of assets is negatively correlated with interest rates. This is theoretically unsurprising, since the formula for the value (strictly speaking net present value) of an asset is negatively related to the discount rate. Thus there is very good reason to believe that the variables A and V will be negatively correlated. If this is so then any discussion of pensions needs to address the relationship between these two variables.

To do this we need to determine how the value of individuals' pension funds have changed over time. The earliest discussion of this issue of which we know is in Diamond (1977). Since we have no data on this variable, we construct the pension funds of a series of hypothetical individuals who save according to a well specified rule.

Diamond introduces the concept of a 'replacement ratio', defined as the ratio of the pension income to labor income (net of pension contributions) in the final year of employment. If the savings rate is 10 per cent and pension income is 60 per cent of labor income, then the replacement ratio is 60/90 = 2/3 and Diamond suggests that this replacement ratio might be appropriate. Empirically such replacement ratios are common in UK company pension schemes where employees have completed their full set of contributions.

The optimal value of the replacement ratio is unclear. In a simple utility maximization framework where agents only wish to smooth consumption flows, the optimal ratio would be one. However, this result does not follow if agents also obtain utility from leisure and utility is not additively separable in consumption and leisure: because leisure discontinuously increases at the point of retirement we should also expect consumption to discontinuously fall. We might note that there are at least two reasons for consumers' expenditure to change upon retirement: the elimination of work-related expenditure (commuting, and so on) and variation in expenditure on leisure activities.

Consider the pension fund of someone retiring at time t, who has contributed a proportion s of their income y_{t-i} in year $t-i$ to a fund for the last R years. Each year $t-j$ the entire value of the fund (including previous years' returns which are re-invested) earns a rate of return r_{t-j}. Then the value of the fund at retirement is

$$V = s\sum_{i=0}^{R-1} y_{t-i}\prod_{j=0}^{i}\left(1+r_{t-j}\right).$$

(We assume that interest is earned on the last year's contribution.)

Note that this rule underlies the so-called '60:40:20:10:5:2 rule'. With a constant rate of return r and with constant income growth so that $y_s = y_0\left(1+g\right)^s$, the formula for the value of the fund at retirement simplifies to

$$V = sy_t\sum_{i=0}^{R-1}\left(1+g\right)^{-i}\left(1+r\right)^{i+1}.$$

This fund can then be converted into an annuity over the expected retirement life of the individual. Manipulation of the formula leads to the surprisingly tidy result that: if one wants one's pension to be 60 per cent of one's final salary and one works for 40 years followed by 20 years of retirement, then it is sufficient to save just 10 per cent of one's income every year, so long as the real rate of return (on both investments and annuities) is 5 per cent per year and real wages are growing at 2 per cent per year. Again, this rule implies a replacement ratio of 2/3.

Rather than assume a constant rate of return and labor income growth, we use actual data to calculate possible pension fund values. We consider a series of hypothetical individuals whose labor income is proportional to the UK average earnings index in each year of their life. From the age of 26 to 65, they save 10 per cent of their labor income and invest it in the stock market: all dividends are reinvested. To account for charges, we assume that there is a 5 per cent charge for purchasing shares, so that the effective savings rate is 9.5 per cent instead of 10 per cent, that there is a 2 per cent charge every year on the capital invested, and that the bid-offer spread on equity is zero. These charges are consistent with the estimates of charges found by Chapman (1999). At 65 the agents purchase an annuity at the prevailing annuity rate.[5]

Figure 8.3 shows the replacement ratio, A_tV_t / y_t, under these assumptions. This replacement ratio may appear very high, averaging a little under one, whereas the typical defined benefit company pension yields a replacement ratio closer to 2/3 (often consisting of an annual income of half final salary and a lump sum). However, defined benefit company pensions are not level pensions but usually index-linked and they also usually contain a reduced pension for any spouse who survives the principle pensioner. Direct comparison is thus impossible. We are currently attempting to gain additional data on indexed pensions and joint pensions to see how these replacement ratios compare, but back-of-envelope calculations suggest that if appropriate reductions were made then the resulting replacement ratio would be lower at about 2/3 as we should expect.[6]

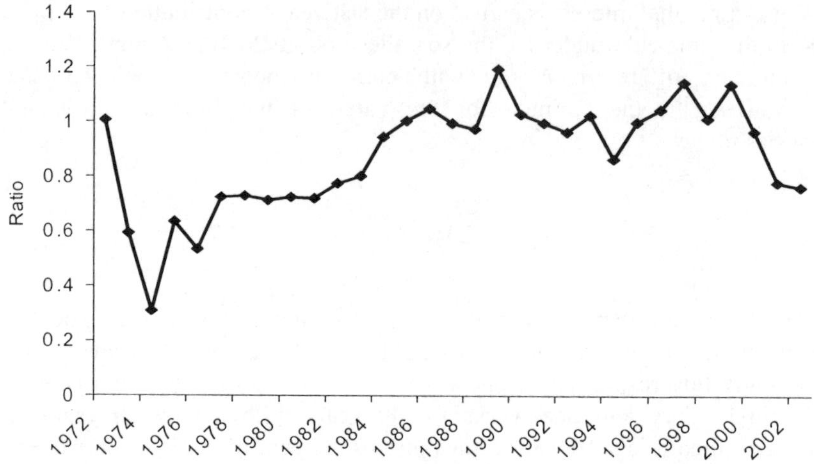

Figure 8.3 The replacement ratio – how the ratio of pension income to labor income has varied over the last 30 years (annuity purchased is male, 65, five-year guarantee)

It is clear from the graph that the last two years have been less favorable times to retire than 1999, when the stock market was at its peak. But even after the fall in stock market prices, the replacement ratio does not appear particularly bad, certainly not as bad as the mid-1970s. Even compared with the period 1982–2000, when the replacement ratio averaged just over unity, the replacement ratio does not appear disastrously low.

The reason for this is that there has been a strong negative correlation between stock markets and annuity rates since then. As we have argued above, both empirically and theoretically low interest rates (and hence annuity rates) tend to be correlated with high asset prices (and hence equity prices). However, the value of the stock market at any point in time is a poor indicator of the value of pension funds of people retiring at that time, since the pension fund is a function of stock returns and wage rates over a long period of time. For illustrative purposes we plot the annuity rate, A_t, against the ratio of pension fund to final salary V_t / y_t in Figure 8.4: the value of V_t / y_t shows the value of pension funds controlling for economic growth, that is, it is suitably detrended. There is a clear negative relationship between the annuity rate and the pension fund values which we have calculated. We have labeled the points for 2001 and 2002 and, although these do lie below the curve, they do not do so very much. This graph illustrates that over the last 30 years there has been a negative correlation between the value of a pension fund and the annuity rate and this explains why lower annuity rates in recent years have been consistent with replacement ratios that are not much different from the average.

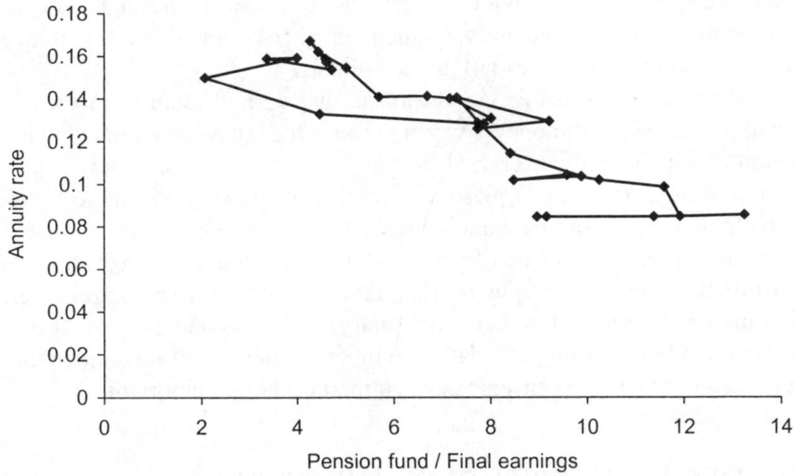

Figure 8.4 Correlation of annuity rate and pension fund

It should be noted that the replacement ratio since 1980 is steady despite increases in longevity over the last 20 years, and we have ignored the issue of longevity in this section. Thus individuals retiring in 2002 on the same replacement ratio as people 20 years earlier are, in some sense, better off, since they live longer and have a similar annual income.

8.5 CONCLUSION

In this chapter we have constructed a time series of annuity prices since 1972. This is considerably longer than the only other time series that we know to have been published, in Murthi et al. (1999), which included a graph of the best annuity rate for the period 1988–98.

Using this series we answer two questions: are annuity rates unfairly low and does it matter that they are low?

In answer to the first question we find no evidence that the average annuity rate is unfairly low. Depending on the assumptions we make about future longevity, the present value of an annuity is of the order of between 90 per cent and 100 per cent of the purchase price. Compared with the typical costs of buying financial services this figure looks suspiciously good: annuity providers must earn a profit and cover the real resource costs of annuity provision. Perhaps even more worrying is the fact that annuity providers appear to have no cushion if longevity rises as fast as our more liberal projections allow. The insurance provided by annuity markets is to smooth longevity risk between individuals, but there is an additional risk of misestimating average longevity, which is faced either by insurance companies or, if the companies fail, the annuitants.

A possible response to this conclusion is that current annuity rates may appear to provide a good money's worth because the latter is calculated using interest rates which are themselves distorted.

In answer to our second question, we find no reason to suggest that individuals are worse off by annuity rates being low, since this has been offset by increases in the value of pension funds over the last 30 years. Even apart from the fact that people retiring today expect to live longer, their pension income (compared to their final salary) looks as good as ever. This is *prima facie* evidence to suggest that government policy is not misguided and that any distortions of the pensions or bond markets are unimportant.

APPENDIX A: DISCUSSION OF THE DATA

The majority of our data are taken from bi-monthly or monthly figures published in *Pensions World* from September 1972 to November 1977 and monthly data from April 1980 to May 1998. During these periods *Pensions World* published a consistent series of data of non-escalating purchase annuities guaranteed for five years, for both men and women of different ages from a variety of different annuity providers.

Because the *Pensions World* series is incomplete, we have also used data from *Money Management* and *Money Facts* to fill in the missing periods from 1978–80 and 1998–2001 respectively. A consequence is that there are a total of three problems in aggregating these data: changing composition of annuity providers, stale prices and inconsistent series. We discuss how we overcome these problems in turn.

The first problem that we have is that the composition of annuity providers changes over time even within *Pensions World*. To overcome this we have analysed several different measures: the mean of all prices quoted, the median of all prices quoted, the best price quoted, the mean of prices from a relatively constant subset of companies and the median from the same subset.

The second problem is that some companies appear to keep their prices exactly constant for long periods of time, during which time they are often quite uncompetitive. This may be because the price in the data source is stale, being just rolled over from the previous month, or it may be because the company was not actively seeking to gain custom, in which case the annuity price may be unrepresentative of annuities which were actually purchased at that time. To overcome this situation we have also considered using only those prices of firms which have changed since the previous month. With the possible exception of 1974 this makes little difference: in that year there is some evidence that annuity rates of firms whose prices had changed were systematically 1 per cent better than all annuity rates, consistent with some stale prices during a period of rising prices. For the purposes of our annual analysis, the difference is so small (and only affects one observation), that this makes virtually no difference.

The resulting monthly series is illustrated in Figure 8.5. These are the raw data, with no adjustment made for changes in definition.

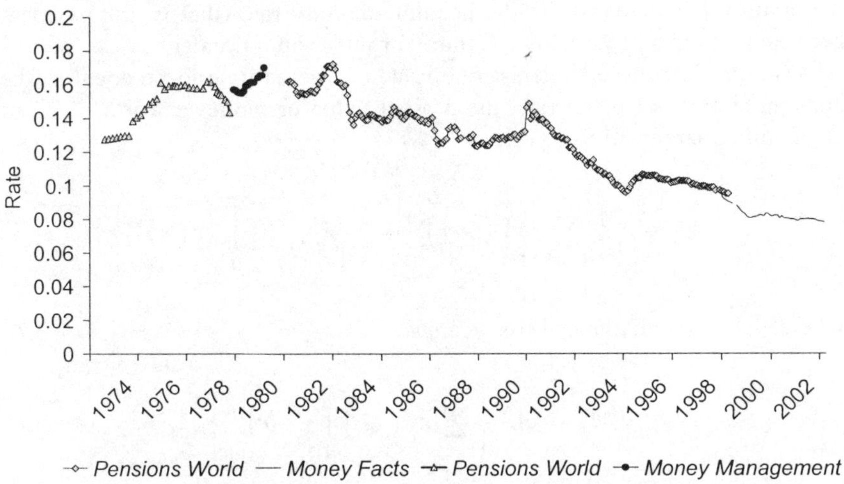

Figure 8.5 Monthly annuity rates (male 65) – inconsistent series

This brings us to our third problem of maintaining consistency between the data in *Pensions World* and the data in the other two sources. The data in *Money Management* are for annuities paid half-yearly in arrears and not guaranteed, whereas the data in *Pensions World* are for annuities paid monthly in advance, guaranteed for five years.

Because of the inconsistency in type of annuity, we provide two sets of numbers for this period. In our own analysis we prefer to use the raw data and amend our analysis to allow for the change in definition. In our analysis above we perform money's worth calculations on annual data using the original data for years 1978 and 1979 and the appropriately different definition of money's worth for a non-guaranteed annuity. However, where the objective is to have a consistent time series (perhaps to be graphed for illustrative purposes), we infer a monthly guaranteed rate from the *Money Management* data.

Our inference to correct for this definitional difference is based on some simple actuarial calculations: recall that we make this correction only on our annual data series. To make the series compatible we performed a calculation in two steps. Annuities paid half-yearly in arrears result in payments being paid on average a quarter of a year later, so we subtracted one-quarter of the then prevailing Consol rate (actually 11.5 per cent) to effect the increased discount given to payments made further in the future.

The probabilities of dying for a man between the age of 65 and the ages of 66–70 can be written $1-\pi_{t,66,65}$, $1-\pi_{t,67,65}$, *etc.*, where $\pi_{t,k,65}$, is the probability of someone aged 65 in year t living to age k (and hence receiving the annuity payment). Write the headline annuity rate (that is, the payment per year) as A per £1 paid to the annuity provider on retirement.

Assuming a constant interest rate r, which we assume to be equal to the contemporaneous Consol rate, the present value or money's worth, M_t, of an annuity guaranteed five years is:

$$M_t \equiv A_t \left\{ \sum_{k=66}^{70} \prod_{j=1}^{k-65} (1+r)^{-1} + \sum_{k=71}^{\infty} \pi_{t,k,65} \prod_{j=1}^{k-65} (1+r)^{-1} \right\}$$

whereas that not guaranteed five years is

$$M_t^N \equiv A_t^N \left\{ \sum_{k=66}^{\infty} \pi_{t,k,65} \prod_{j=1}^{k-65} (1+r)^{-1} \right\}.$$

Finkelstein and Poterba (2002) have argued that the money's worth for the two types of annuities will differ because of adverse selection effects: individuals with private information that they are likely to be shorter-lived self-select into annuities guaranteed five years and thus the true money's worth for the guaranteed annuity should be based on lower survival probabilities. Since we are unable to identify the true survival probabilities the money's worth appears to be higher. Then, assuming a constant interest rate,

$$\frac{M_t}{A_t} - \frac{M_t^N}{A_t^N} = \sum_{k=66}^{70} \left(1 - \pi_{t,k,65}\right)\left(1 + r\right)^{65-k} \approx 0.37$$

where the number 0.37 arises from the data for a male aged 65 and the interest rates prevailing at that time. Rearranging this expression we obtain

$$A_t = \frac{M_t}{M_t^N / A_t^N + 0.37}.$$

In the absence of any data on the money's worth values for the relevant years, we use those calculated by Finkelstein and Poterba (2002, Table 5, p. 46) for annuities sold in 1998, which are reproduced in Table 8.2:

Table 8.2 Comparative annuity rates with and without guarantee periods

	No guarantee	Guaranteed 5 years
Male 65	0.862	0.865
Male 70	0.833	0.844
Female 65	0.854	0.857

It is this estimate of the annuity rate that we use (for illustrative purposes only) in Figure 8.1: analogous adjustments are possible for males aged 70 and females aged 65.

The data in *Money Facts* are defined similarly to those in *Pensions World*, but are drawn from a different list of companies. More worrying, the annuity rates for the subset of companies in both sources are different. We have contacted the relevant annuity providers to seek an explanation for this and have been told that it arises due to different commission charges being included in the two quotes (for instance, one included a commission of 1 per cent and the other a commission of 1.3 per cent). To overcome this difference we have spliced the series together using a shift factor derived from the overlap period of four months (January–April 1998), which turns out to be 0.38 per cent, comfortably close to the figure we might expect given the commission charges quoted.

APPENDIX B: ESTIMATION OF LONGEVITY

To calculate the money's worth or the internal rate of return it is necessary to have estimates of the probabilities of the annuitant living to a given age. Back-of-envelope calculations regarding the money's worth can be conducted using life expectancy alone and assuming that annuity payments are made for the same period as the money's worth: this is the simplification used in Diamond (1977) and in 60:40:20:10:5:2 rule. However, this is a very crude method because there is considerable variability of actual age of death around life expectancy; it will also introduce biases over time since the patterns of mortality are changing (see for example, Craig, 1998).

To discuss the issue of the pattern of mortality we introduce the concept of the hazard, or probability, of dying at a given age. We use data on cross-sectional hazards for the population in the UK life tables to construct a series of cohort hazards, ie the probability of dying at any given age for individuals born in a specific year.

It is these mortality rates that are needed to determine the money's worth of an annuity. However, we are interested not so much in the probability of dying as the probability of surviving (and hence receiving an annuity payment). Write the hazard rate for someone age i born in period $t-i$ as h_{it}. The probability of someone aged j at time t being alive at age k is then

$$\pi_{t,jk} = \prod_{i=j+1}^{k} 1 - h_{it} \, .$$

We now turn to the calculation of these survival probabilities in practice.

Mitchell et al. (1999) note that purchasers of annuities tend to be longer-lived than typical agents of the same age. This merely reflects the adverse selection problem faced by insurers, that agents who choose to buy annuities are self-selected to be those who will benefit most. Comparative data for annuitant and population mortality are illustrated on pp. 18–19 of Brown et al. (2001).

The estimates of the money's worth in this chapter are based on population mortality figures rather than annuitants' mortality figures. Unless there have been systematic changes in the relative life expectancies of the two groups, using population mortality figures will make no difference to our comparison of money's worth over time. Regarding the absolute size of error in our estimates of the money's worth, it should be noted that the bias in our estimates of the money's worth is *downwards*, since annuitants tend to live longer than the population as a whole. As we are arguing that the money's worth is relatively *high,* the bias will lead us to *understate* our case that annuities are not underpriced.

Hazard rates are published in 'life tables' based on census and other data. Because there are sometimes relatively few people of a given age (especially for the very elderly), the raw data are usually smoothed to ensure that sampling error is minimized (see for example, Haberman, 1997). However, English life tables are only published every ten years (No. 15 was published in 1997, based on the 1991 census). Because we wanted annually available data we have constructed our own life tables using data for death rates in *Population Trends* for ten-year groups (45–54; 55–64, and so on) and log-linearly interpolating to obtain an annual panel of hazards for every year of age.

To project these survival probabilities into the future we fitted two possible relationships between survival probability, cohort effect and age:

$$1-h_{it}=\alpha_0+\alpha_1 i+\alpha_2 i^2+\alpha_3(t-i)+\alpha_4(t-i)^2$$

and

$$1-h_{it}=\alpha_0+\alpha_1 i+\alpha_2 i^2+\alpha_3(t-i)+\alpha_4(t-i)^2+\alpha_5(t-i)i\,.$$

The first of these regressions restricts the 'survival probability curve' to be the same shape and allows it to shift up over time. We use a quadratic to allow for the very slight curvature in the empirical curve. The second regression allows the curve to change shape in that it can become gradually flatter.

The projected survival probabilities from the second of the two equations are considerably larger and we thus refer to these estimates as the 'larger life expectancy', whereas the former relationship is the 'smaller life expectancy' case. Although these projections are econometrically rather crude, they provide a useful interval of life expectancies. The historical record of life expectancy projections is that they tend to underestimate increases in life expectancy (Cox, 1975), suggesting considerable room for error: this is another reason for considering a range of possibilities.

APPENDIX C: INTERNAL RATES OF RETURN

An alternative method of evaluating annuity rates is to look at the internal rate of return of an annuity instead of the money's worth. The advantage of this approach is that it is not necessary to have expectations about future interest rates, although it is still necessary to have information on survival probabilities.

The internal rate of return for an annuity ρ for a male aged 65 guaranteed five years is defined implicitly from the equation

$$1 = A_t \left\{ \sum_{k=66}^{70} (1+\rho)^{65-k} + \sum_{k=71}^{\infty} \pi_{t,k,65} (1+\rho)^{65-k} \right\}.$$

We calculate ρ numerically in Excel to obtain a series which is illustrated in Figure 8.6: we calculate the series using the two different projections of survival probabilities used in calculating the money's worth and plot the Consol rate for comparison. In the mid-1970s, and to a smaller extent in the mid-1990s, Consol rates are considerably higher than the internal rate of return on annuities, whereas for the rest of the period Consol rates move closely with the internal rate of return. As with the money's worth calculations, the projection with the larger increase in life expectancy leads to firms being unprofitable: internal rates of return on annuities (that is a cost to the firm as these are payments) are higher than the long-run interest rate.

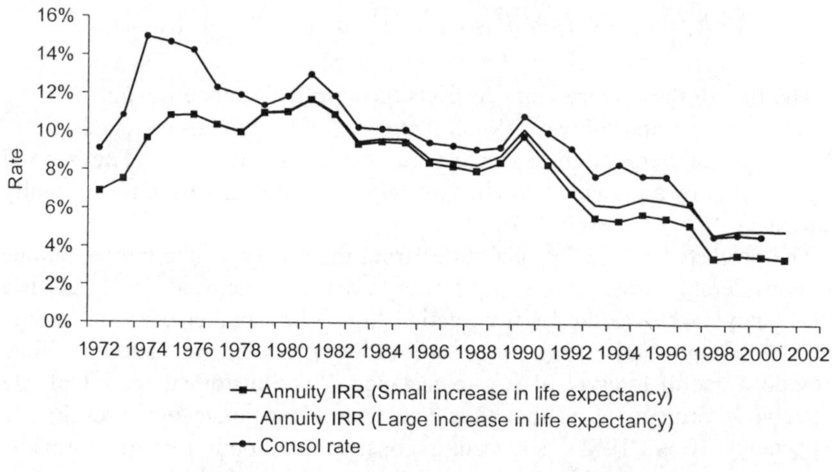

Figure 8.6 Comparative rates of return (male, 65, five-year guarantee)

NOTES

1. Department for Work and Pensions and Inland Revenue, 'Modernising Annuities: A Consultative Document', February 2002.

2. Data are 1973–2000. The unit root tests are based on a regression involving a constant and a trend, since both series are trending downwards over the period, and include two lags. Alternative specifications yielded very similar results.
3. Our cointegration analysis was based upon one lag of the variables concerned with a linear trend restricted to be within the cointegration space. Apart from the fact that it was statistically significant, the trend was included as a crude proxy for any possible convergence between the two rates over the period due to increased longevity (as life expectancy rises, the length of time for which an annuity pays out increases and hence it becomes 'more similar' to a Consol). However, since the annuity and Consol rates are themselves trending down, the inclusion of a trend is itself problematic. Its exclusion makes it impossible to reject the null hypothesis of no cointegration between the two series.
4. This assumes that no (fraudulent) payments are made to the annuitant or his/her estate after the point of death (disregarding payments made in the guaranteed five-year period). Evidence from the Audit Commission (2002) suggests that such fraud may not be insignificant: £24 million of fraudulent payments were discovered for 2000, despite relatively few pensions providers taking part. While such payments may not be of major concern to the annuitant, they obviously affect the profitability of the annuity provider and hence are a further reason for the money's worth to be low.
5. These assumptions about the accumulation of pension funds are not fully realistic, since agents would hold some of their wealth in bonds and might change the proportions of bonds and equities over their life. Consideration of this issue is the subject of ongoing research.
6. In January 2002 Legal and General is quoted in *Pensions World* as being the 5th best provider of annuities for male aged 65 level, no guarantee (being only 0.2 per cent behind the best provider, Friends Provident) and as the best provider of joint annuities for male aged 65, wife aged 63, escalating 3 per cent, no guarantee. The annuity rates are respectively 8.32 per cent and 5.13 per cent, so the escalating annuity with income for spouse is just over 3/5 the level annuity with no income for spouse.

REFERENCES

Audit Commission (2002), *Match Winner: Report of the 2000 National Fraud Initiative,* London: Audit Commission.

Blundell, R. and T.M. Stoker (1999), 'Consumption and the Timing of Income Risk', *European Economic Review,* **43**, 475–507.

Brown, J.R., O.S. Mitchell, J.M. Poterba and M.J. Warshawsky (2001), *The Role of Annuity Markets in Financing Retirement*, Cambridge, MA: MIT Press.

Chapman, J. (1999), 'Persistency and Charges: Exposing the Big Hitters', *Money Management,* January, 72–5.

Cox, P.R. (1975), 'Life Tables: the Measure of Mortality', and 'Life Tables: (2) Wider Applications,' *Population Trends,* **1**, 13–15 and **2**, 19–21.

Craig, J. (1998), 'To Be Or Not To Be – What Are the Odds?', *Population Trends,* **92**, 42–50.

Diamond, P.A. (1977), 'A Framework for Social Security Analysis', *Journal of Public Economics,* **8**, 275–98.

Finkelstein, A. and J.M. Poterba (2002), 'Selection Effects in the United Kingdom Individual Annuities Market', *Economic Journal,* **112** (476), 28–50.

Haberman, S. (1997), 'Smoothing Spline Graduation of the Crude Data for the English Life Tables No. 15', English Life Tables No. 15, London: The Stationery Office.

McCarthy, D. and O.S. Mitchell (2003), 'Annuities for an Ageing World', Chapter 2 in this volume.

Mitchell, O.S., J.M. Poterba, M.J. Warshawsky and J.R. Brown (1999), 'New Evidence on the Money's Worth of Individual Annuities', *American Economic Review,* **89**, 1299–1318, reprinted in Brown et al. (2001), 71–6.

Murthi, M., J.M. Orszag, and P.R. Orszag (1999), 'The Value for Money of Annuities in the UK: Theory, Experience and Policy', discussion paper, Birkbeck College, London.

Quinton, P. (2001), 'Rule bending may lead to wrong advice for retirees', *Investment Adviser*, 12 August.

Warshawsky, M.J. (1988), 'Private Annuity Markets in the United States: 1919–1984', *Journal of Risk and Insurance,* **55**(3), 518–28, reprinted in Brown et al. (2001), 57–70.

9. Private annuities and public pensions in Germany

Reinhold Schnabel

9.1 INTRODUCTION

During the past decades, public pensions have been the dominant source of retirement income in Germany. They provide an annuity income that is indexed to average earnings. In addition to old-age pensions the pension system also provides survivor pensions and disability pensions. Occupational pensions have – on average – played only a minor role. The majority of occupational pensions are of the defined benefit type and are usually paid out as indexed annuities. Private savings are a third source of retirement income. However, only a negligible part of the individual funds available to retirees has been annuitized in the past.[1] As a consequence, the market for private annuities is still small in Germany compared to other countries. Moreover, average elderly households did not use their private wealth for consumption. The average (mean or median) elderly households consume less than their current pension income that is derived from the first and second pillars.

The demand for individual or occupational pension plans is very likely to increase during the next few years. First, due to the pension reform of 2001, the replacement rate of public pensions is bound to be reduced from 70 to 64 per cent. Given the mounting problems in financing the public pension system, further cuts are inevitable even in the short run. This reduction in the annuitization may spur the demand for private annuity plans. Second, the pension reform of 2001 has tried to strengthen the private provision of retirement income in order to compensate for the reduction in public pensions. This was done by new subsidies and tax incentives for investment in formal (second or third pillar) pension plans, the Riester-plans, named after the former minister of labor and social affairs. Moreover, employers have to offer some kind of occupational pension plan from 2002 on, into which the employees can make their own contributions. Deferred taxation and regulation of the new pension plans discourage lump-sum withdrawals, thus supporting annuities or other regular withdrawal schemes. However, given the traditionally high household savings rates in Germany, it is not clear whether all this will lead to higher aggregate savings. Also, the heavy regulation of the Riester-plans may turn out to be an obstacle to saving for retirement.

This chapter starts by presenting the basic empirical facts on public and private pension provision in Germany with special attention to annuities. The current situation and challenges due to population ageing that motivated the reforms of 1992 and 2001 are presented. Then, the main steps of the recent pension reform are analysed with respect to their relevance for private retirement provision and private annuities. Finally, first empirical evidence on the impact of the 2001 reform on the savings behavior of private households is presented. The chapter concludes with a tentative outlook on the development of private pensions and annuity markets in Germany.

9.2 PUBLIC AND PRIVATE PENSIONS IN GERMANY

9.2.1 Public Pensions and Replacement Rates

The pay-as-you-go social security system is by far the most important part of the German pension system. It covers about 85 per cent of the labor force and is financed by payroll contributions and by general taxes. Civil servants are covered by a special system, which is completely financed out of general revenues and grants more generous pensions. The self-employed (about 10 per cent of the labor force) are usually exempt from mandatory contributions. However, almost all self-employed workers have contributed to the social security system at some point in their working career. Total public pension expenditures have increased steadily during the last decade. In the year 2002 public pension expenditures reached 275 billion € and exceeded 13 per cent of GDP.[2] A driving force of this recent rise in the pension bill was a considerable increase of the old-age dependency ratio since 1993. The old-age dependency ratio is expected to grow dramatically during the next 40 years. Without further changes in the pension system, the share of GDP that is required to finance public pensions will tend towards 20 per cent around the year 2040. Despite contribution rate increases, the deficit of the social security system has already widened during the last decade. The contribution rate in the social security system reached 19.5 per cent in the year 2003 and covers barely two-thirds of expenditures. Some 35 per cent of expenditures are covered by the federal subsidy in 2002 with a rising tendency.[3] A contribution rate of 29 per cent would have been required in 2002 in order to finance the social security system exclusively through payroll contributions.

Since the mid 1970s, the *net replacement rates* of the social security system have been around 70 per cent.[4] This net replacement rate is based on the hypothetical pension received by a person with 45 years of average gross earnings (*base pensioner* or 'Eckrentner'). The replacement rate is calculated as the ratio of this *net pension* in the year of retirement over the economy-wide average *net earnings* in that same year. Due to the exceptional increases of earnings combined with an increasing generosity of the PAYG system, the indexation of pensions led to particularly fast-rising pensions in the 1970s. This in turn led to much higher effective replacement rates as compared to the initial replacement rate in the year of retirement. For cohorts born around the year 1910 who retired around 1970 the effective replacement in 1980 (that is, after ten years in retirement) came close to 100 per cent of their former net wage in 1970 (Schnabel, 2001b). After 1980, the wage increases were smaller and the pensions stayed more or less constant in real terms.

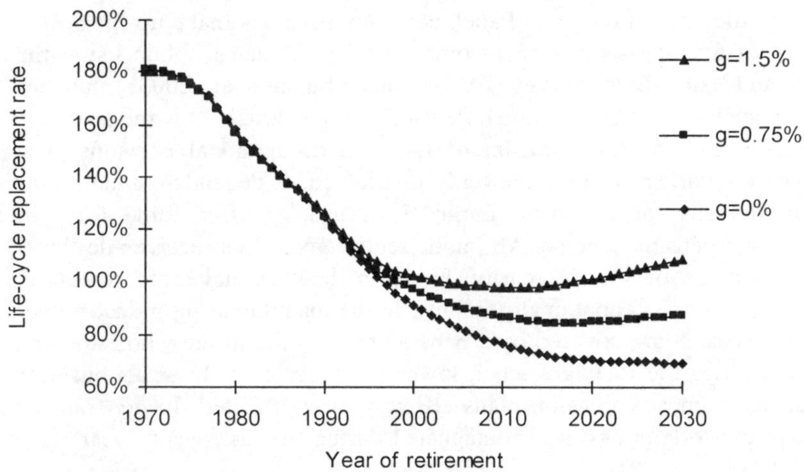

Note: The life-cycle replacement rate is calculated as the 'average' social security pensions divided by the 'average' life time wage of a pensioner with a 45 year work history, who retires in year *t*.

Sources: Own computations based on VDR 2003. Calculations are done for different future growth rates of gross wages (*g*=0.5 per cent to *g*=1.5 per cent) and are based on the pension rules of the status quo ante 2001. The reform of 2001 will reduce the relative pension by roughly 9 per cent. Note also that the average growth rate of the German economy was below 1.5 per cent during the years 1993–2003.

Figure 9.1 Life-cycle replacement rates of social security pensions

Taking a life-cycle view, one may compare public pensions to 'average' earnings over the work career. As Figure 9.1 shows, this replacement rate, defined relative to the life-cycle average wage, exceeded 100 per cent for all cohorts that retired before the year 2000.[5] For a worker born in 1935 who retired in, say, 2000 after 45 years of work, the social security pensions are still as high as the average wage over his/her life-cycle. Thus, the annuitization of retirement income is high relative to the labor income. For younger cohorts, the replacement rates relative to their lifetime earnings will fall below 100 per cent if the real growth rate of the economy is less than 1.5 per cent in the long run. Note that annuitization through the social security system has declined and will further decline due to lower macroeconomic growth rates. This is true even in the absence of population ageing and cuts in the pensions system.

9.2.2 Occupational Pensions (Second Pillar)

According to estimates by Börsch-Supan and Schnabel (1998) using micro data from the Socio-Economic Panel, company pensions make up for only 5 per cent of average retirement income. Similar estimates obtain using the Income and Expenditure Survey (EVS) (Börsch-Supan et al., 2003). Statistics by the Association of Occupational Pensions (ABA, 2002) show the coverage of workers and the total amount of funds in occupational pensions. The coverage of workers is very unevenly distributed. It depends on the sector and on the size of the firm. Large firms usually offer some form of occupational pension scheme. All public sector employees receive additional pensions on top of social security. Firms in the financial sector regularly provide extensive occupational pensions. In the manufacturing industry two-thirds of workers are covered by a pension plan, while in the wholesale and retail industries the rates are much lower at 25 per cent. In small business enterprises, company pension plans are very rarely offered. In general, the coverage of workers has at best stagnated during the last twenty years (see Figure 9.2).

The capital stock of occupational pension plans in the year 2000 is estimated at 331 billion €, exactly one sixth of the German GDP of 2 trillion € (ABA, 2002). Note that public pensions exceeded 250 billion € in the year 2000. The majority of the funds are still held in the form of book reserves and are typically defined benefit plans (see Figure 9.3). The default risk is covered by a mandatory pension insurance in the case of bankruptcy of the firm.[6] The 'Support funds' are very similar but have a slightly different institutional setting. In Germany these two types of pension plans are called 'internal plans', because the capital is under the control of the firm. Consequently, the other types of pension plans are called 'external', since their capital stock is held outside the firm in a separate financial institution (insurance company, Pensionskasse). A Pensionskasse is basically a special type of insurance company that is set up for the specific purpose of providing pensions, is subject to similar regulations, and may offer occupational pensions for a number of firms. It is important to stress that the traditional occupational pension schemes have a lot of discretion about how to pay out the capital. The statute of a plan usually offers several ways, strict annuities being only one. Clearly, progressive income taxation discourages lump-sum withdrawals in many instances.

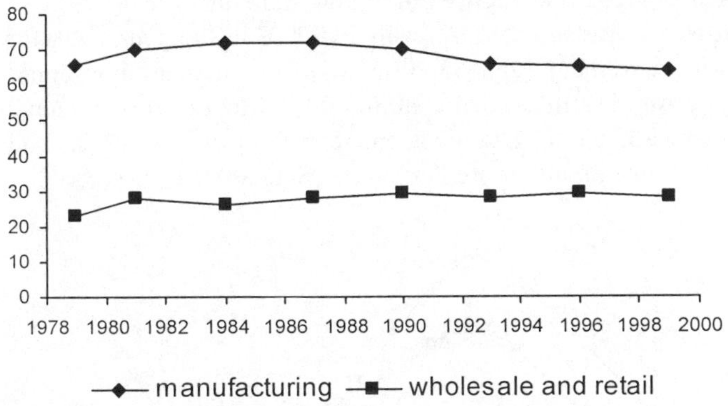

Source: ABA, 2002.

Figure 9.2 Coverage of employees (selected sectors, West Germany, 1979–99)

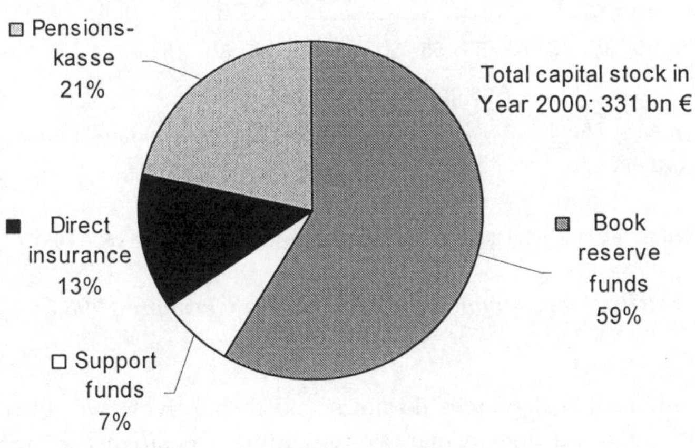

Source: ABA, 2002.

Figure 9.3 Distribution of funds across pension vehicles in 2000

9.2.3 Private Savings and Wealth (Third Pillar)

Private savings are about 10 per cent of disposable income of private households (much higher than in the 1980s). A large part of savings is due to the acquisition of private homes (saving for down payment and paying back the principal). Home ownership ratios are increasing strongly over the life-cycle until age 60; these rates have also increased across cohorts. As a result, *housing wealth* makes up the lion's share of the average portfolio of German households. Two-thirds of German households enter retirement as homeowners with an average housing wealth of 280 000 € in 1998.[7]

Mean financial wealth is estimated to reach 53 000 € in the year 1998 for households prior to retirement (age 55–59).[8] *Median* financial household wealth for this age group is still estimated at 30 000 €. Most of this financial wealth is kept in bequeathable form (bank accounts, life insurance, stocks and bonds). In contrast, private annuities are negligible (Schnabel, 1999).

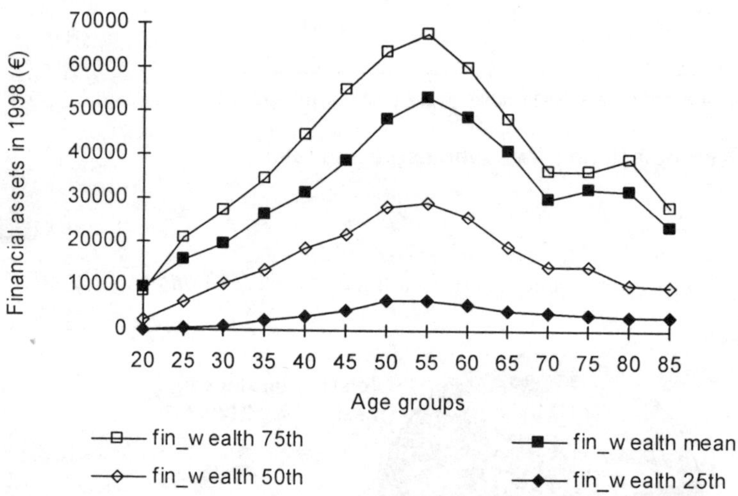

Source: Own computations based on the Income and Expenditure Survey 1998 (EVS, 1998).

Figure 9.4 Age distribution of financial wealth in West Germany 1998 by percentile

It is well documented that retirees do not spend their private wealth for consumption. Instead mean and median savings remain positive (or zero) after retirement. The households of the elderly also devote about 7 per cent of disposable income to private transfers. All this seems to indicate that the demand for private annuities used to be low – given the high replacement rates of the public pension systems and the small – though not negligible – company pensions. In fact, since the majority of company pensions are currently of the defined benefit form they also represent a kind of annuity income. However, the generosity of the public pension system is about to change due to the pension reforms of 1992 and 2001. These reforms will inevitably reduce the public pension-annuitization of future cohorts. At the same time, the incentives to save in second or third pillar pension products that provide annuities are increased.

9.3 REFORMS OF PUBLIC PENSIONS AND POPULATION AGING

9.3.1 The Pension Reform of 1992

The generosity of the public pension system was steadily extended until the late 1970s. The landmark pension reform of 1992 (actually enacted before German reunification in the year 1989) was the first attempt to limit the expenditures of the pension system in a systematic way (Börsch-Supan et al., 2004). The pension reform of 1992 introduced an explicit net-wage indexation of public pensions. This effectively conserved the 'statutory' replacement rate at 70 per cent. The reform also introduced adjustment factors for early retirement at a rate of 3.6 per cent for each year prior to the statutory retirement age of 65. However, this rule has been phased in slowly and will take full effect after 2004. Together with some other minor measures this will reduce the *effective* replacement rates considerably, if individuals do not postpone retirement. Econometric estimates suggest that the introduction of the adjustment factors will increase average retirement age by 1 to 2 years (that is from 60 to 62 at best). Persons who retire at 62 will then have to accept a 10.6 per cent reduction of their pension. Four percentage points of this gap are offset by the effect on the pension level of working 2 years longer. Clearly, the annuitization provided by public pensions is going to be reduced compared to older cohorts.

9.3.2 The Pension Reform of 2001

The pension reform of 2001 claimed to secure the solvency of the public pension system. A central measure of this reform is the reduction of the statutory net replacement rate of the social security system from 70 to 64 percentage points during the next two decades.[9] According to government projections (published in 2001) based on overly optimistic assumptions, contribution rates were estimated to drop below 19 per cent and to reach 20 per cent in 2020 and 22 per cent in 2030. Given that the old-age dependency ratio is going to double over the next 40 years[10] these projections are simply wishful thinking given the relatively small changes in the pension system that were enacted in 2001.

According to several independent projections the pension cut enacted by the 2001 reform has to be considered as a first step in aligning expenditures and revenues in the long run. However, the government – like all its predecessors – maintains that the recent reform will secure solvency. Moreover, the government conceals the magnitude of the replacement rate cut by a cosmetic redefinition of the replacement rate. This policy is counterproductive since it weakens the willingness of households to save for retirement – either in the form of individual savings or firm pension plans.

9.3.3 Continuing Rise of Contributions or Pension Cuts

Despite the reforms of 1992 and 2001, the expenditures of the PAYG public pension systems exceeded 13 per cent of GDP in 2002. This is in part due to an unexpectedly strong shift in life expectancy. Envisaging a dramatic population aging during the next 40 years, the current system is clearly unsustainable. Schnabel (2001a) shows that the contribution rates would have to increase to at least 25 per cent using a *medium* scenario that is slightly less optimistic than the government scenario. Moreover, the government projection stops in the year 2030 although the old-age burden will keep on rising after 2030, with contribution rates reaching 27 per cent in the year 2050. In this medium scenario, total public PAYG pensions would amount to 17 per cent of GDP in 2030 and to 18.4 per cent in 2050 with a replacement of 64 per cent. In order to limit the contribution rate to 22 per cent (as envisaged by the government), the replacement rate has to be reduced to 56 per cent by the year 2030 and to about 52 per cent by the year 2050.

9.3.4 Resulting Pension Gaps

For each percentage-point reduction of the replacement rate the annual pension gap is going to increase by 3.75 billion €. This is the value at constant prices under the assumption of zero real economic growth. With a real annual growth of 1.5 per cent and a replacement rate of 56 per cent in 2030, the annual pension gap relative to the current 70 per cent replacement rate will reach 75 billion € in 2030. In order to fill that gap, a large capital stock is required. Its size depends on several factors such as the real interest rate, life expectancy, and the degree of annuitization of private pension wealth. With full annuitization, a capital stock of 750 billion € might suffice. However, if Germans stick to their traditional strategy of holding bequeathable wealth, far more than 1000 billion € will be required. Given the heavy demographic burden, it may be helpful to develop the annuity market in order to make an efficient use of the capital stock of the elderly.

9.4 THE PENSION REFORM OF 2001 AND PRIVATE PENSIONS

While the pension reform of 2001 reduces the level of public pensions relative to wages, it tries to strengthen second and third pillar retirement provision. This is done by subsidies or tax incentives, and by other measures that may encourage private saving in pension plans in general and annuitization in particular. Subsidies and tax incentives are conditioned on a number of rules. The following subsections describe this new framework.

9.4.1 Subsidies and Tax Incentives

The pension reform of 2001, also called *Riester-Reform* after the Minister of Labor and Social Affairs Walter Riester, has introduced a new preferential treatment of individual and occupational pension plans. In order to be eligible the plan and the beneficiary have to meet certain conditions (see below, Section 9.4.3). If contributions to a pension plan (either individual or occupational) are eligible for the subsidy or tax relief, the plan is often called 'Riester-Plan'.

The preferential treatment is available either in the form of a subsidy or in the form of a tax advantage. The subsidy depends on the amount invested and on the number of children; it is thus independent of income. If the tax advantage in a given year turns out to be higher than the subsidy, then the difference is paid out to the beneficiary. Hereafter, we simply call this the 'Riester subsidy' although it may entail an additional tax advantage. There is also no capital gains taxation during the savings phase. Since all benefits are taxed during retirement, it is basically a deferred taxation scheme (EET).

Only three out of five legal types of occupational pension plans are eligible for this new preferential treatment. The Riester subsidy adds to the already existing two types of tax treatments of occupational pensions. Third pillar pension plans (provided they meet the conditions in Section 9.4.3) are also eligible for the subsidy. The Riester subsidy also adds to the TEE-type taxation of individual (third pillar) life and pension insurance that has been available for decades.

Four available types of tax treatments

1. Contributions of employer or employee to occupational pension plans are exempt from income taxation. The upper limit is 4 per cent of the social security ceiling (appr. 50 000 €). Until 2008 the contributions are also exempt from payroll deductions (42 per cent of gross wages in 2003). Interest and capital gains are not taxed. Withdrawals (either lump sum or pensions) are fully taxed (that is, deferred taxation, EET).
2. It is also possible to choose income taxation of contributions at the flat rate of 20 per cent. This option is limited to contributions of 1700 € per year. As in option (1) no payroll contributions have to be paid until 2008. Neither interest and capital gains nor lump-sum withdrawal are subject to income taxation. If an annuity is chosen it is taxed the same way as in option (1).
3. In order to be eligible for the Riester subsidy, the contribution has to be paid out of net income after income *and* payroll taxes. The maximum amount eligible for the subsidy is 525 € in the years 2002 and 2003 and will eventually reach 2100 € in the year 2008. The Riester subsidy is paid directly into the plan by a newly founded federal administration. Contributions are tax deductible and the amount exceeding the subsidy is credited. Although payroll contributions have to be paid, the Riester subsidy may be more profitable than option (1) if the income tax rate is sufficiently low. This will be the case for low or middle income earners with many children. For a full-time worker, the tax treatments (1) and (2) will be more profitable until 2009, the year in which the payroll tax exemption for (1) and (2) will expire.
4. Contributions to individual life insurance or individual pension plans have to be paid out of taxed income. If the maturity of the policy is 12 years or longer, capital gains, interest and lump-sum withdrawal are tax free. This tax treatment is only available for insurance policies, not for mutual funds. If an annuity is chosen, a certain fraction of the annuity is considered as interest income and is counted as taxable income. A table in the German tax code determines the 'interest part' of the annuity depending on the age of the annuitant when the annuity starts. Life insurance policies are the single most important vehicle of financial savings. In the past, the vast majority of the elderly have withdrawn the whole capital as one lump sum. There is also a limited tax allowance for insurance contributions which is usually exhausted by the compulsory social security contributions of employees. The self-employed, however, who usually do not contribute to social security, can use this tax allowance to make tax free contributions to life insurance or pension plans.[11]

Type (4) can only be used with insurance policies (life insurance or pension plans). Types (1) and (2) are only applicable to occupational pension plans. The new Riester subsidy (3) is available for individual pension plans and for three out of five occupational pension vehicles. It is also possible to cumulate (1), (2), and (3) in one or two occupational pension plans. If all three ways are exploited, it is possible to save up to 4500 € per year in 2002–03; this will rise to roughly 6000 € in 2008. Compared to an average annual social security wage of about 30 000 € this is more than enough to provide funds for retirement for an average household. Table 9.1 summarizes the central features of tax treatments in occupational pension plans.

Table 9.1 Pension vehicles and tax treatments of employee contributions

	Up to 2100 € of earnings: - out of untaxed income, - no payroll taxes, - full taxation of withdrawals (lump sum or annuity).	Up to 1700 € - flat income tax 20%, - no payroll taxes, - no taxation of lump-sum withdrawal.	Up to 525 € (2008: 2100 €) - Riester subsidy or tax advantage, - full payroll tax, - full taxation of withdrawal.
Book reserve funds	Yes	No	No
Support funds	Yes	No	No
Direct insurance	No	Yes	Yes
Pensionskasse	Yes	Yes	Yes
Pension funds	Yes	No	Yes

Notes: 'Yes' means that the specific tax treatment is available for that particular pension vehicle. No taxation of capital gains and interest during the accumulation phase. Payroll taxes for social security are currently about 42 per cent of gross wage, and are split between worker and employer. The no-payroll tax privilege expires in 2009. 2100 € is 4 per cent of the social security upper ceiling. The employer can contribute to book reserve and support funds in excess of 2100 €.

9.4.2 Regulation of Individual and Company Pension Plans

The Riester-plans have to be certified by a federal institution that is part of the insurance supervision authority. The most important rules are:

- A minimum return guarantee of zero per cent (nominal capital guarantee) is required for the end of the accumulation phase. The capital guarantee is also required during the pension phase.

- If the capital is taken out before the age of 60, a penalty has to be paid that exceeds the received subsidies and tax benefits. The same applies if the capital is withdrawn after retirement as a lump sum.
- The subsidies and tax benefits have to be paid back if Germany is left 'permanently'. This is of great importance to foreign workers who return to their home countries and also to Germans who want to move after retirement. This also applies, if a worker or pensioner moves within the European Union. This rule will probably be overthrown by Common Market Law.
- As a rule, the capital stock has to be annuitized. However, up to 20 per cent can be taken out as a lump sum upon retirement, provided that the remaining capital stock for annuitization is at least as large as the sum of contributions and state subsidies. Moreover, up to 20 per cent can be converted to a 'flexible pension' before the age of 85.

The new Riester-plans are more heavily regulated than the traditional pension plans. For instance, lump-sum payments are easily possible with the 20 per cent flat rate tax scheme (2). Pension plans that use the tax deduction (1) can use flexible payout schemes and are not limited to annuities. The payout scheme is usually regulated in the statute of the pension plan and usually allows for several different ways of withdrawal.

9.4.3 Other Important Reform Steps

Pension funds

The pension reform of 2001 also introduced pension funds as a fifth vehicle of occupational pensions. However, pension funds have to meet additional requirements that make investment in a pension fund relatively unattractive compared to the other pension vehicles.

- Pension funds are subject to the same *life-insurance* supervision as the direct insurance and the Pensionskassen. In addition, pension funds and employers have to guarantee the nominal capital. The employer has to pay contributions to the 'Pension Insurance Fund', which will have to pay the guarantee if the pension fund performs badly and the employer goes bankrupt. This is similar to the regulation of the book reserve funds and the support funds. However, those are not regulated by the life insurance supervision. This additional requirement may make the German pension funds more expensive than the other four pension vehicles.[12]
- Pension funds also have to annuitize the capital, even if they are not used in combination with the Riester subsidy. Thus, pension funds

become less flexible than the other pension vehicles in the pension phase. Very recently, a provision has been added that allows for a 20 per cent lump-sum withdrawal.
- Each pension fund has to report annually whether and how *ethical, social, and ecological* aspects have been considered in the investment decisions. A certain percentage of ethical investment may be mandated by government in the future.

Entitlement to a firm pension plan
From 2002 on, each employee has the right to demand that some kind of occupational pension vehicle be made available. If the employer does not offer either a Pensionskasse or a pension fund, direct insurance becomes the default option. This provision may turn out to become the most powerful reform step with respect to private pensions. It will force small and medium firms to offer pension plans. Collective agreements (at the industry or firm level) that provide new standards have recently been finalized. For millions of workers, this opens the opportunity to contribute to tax-advantaged pension schemes.

Transferability
All contributions of workers into pension plans have to be transferable from the beginning. Contributions of employers become transferable after a minimum tenure of five years.

Discouraging investment in the old DB plans
The reform tries to discourage the two pension vehicles which usually have been organized as defined benefit plans: 'Direktzusage' (book reserve funds) and 'Unterstützungkasse' (support funds). These types will not be eligible for Riester subsidies. The government also introduced the possibility to transfer the pension claims to a *pension fund* without losing the tax advantage embedded in the book reserves or support funds. However, the internal vehicles are still very attractive since employers' contributions are fully deductible and no payroll taxes have to be paid.

9.5 PRELIMINARY EMPIRICAL EVIDENCE ON PARTICIPATION IN ANNUITY PLANS

The insurance companies were the first to market private pension plans of the Riester type. Retail banks and mutual funds followed much later, since it took longer to set up the new product and get the certification for 'Riester-eligibility'. About three million individual Riester-products were sold by insurance firms until the end of 2002. The market share of banks and mutual funds remains very small at about 10 per cent of the third pillar market. During the year 2002 the first Riester-type occupational pension plans became certified and started to market their products. Demand for individual pension products has been declining after the initial boom. At the end of 2002, a total of two million occupational pension plans were reported.[13] The market share of occupational Riester-plans has been fairly stable at 40 per cent since the previous survey in September. However, there is evidence that this number may also contain old pension plan contracts that were relabeled after obtaining the Riester certificate.

The average annual contribution of employees was 175 € in the market of life insurance products. Together with the subsidy of roughly 120 €, the average gross contribution is about 300 €. This is 1 per cent of the average gross earnings and thus exactly matches the minimum requirement for the full subsidy. Employees who have bought into a Riester-plan apparently contribute only the minimum amount in order to receive the maximum possible subsidy.

Some 16 per cent of respondents reported having a Riester-plan, while another 16 per cent are contemplating doing so in the near future. In the most relevant age groups, 20 to 45 years, 21 per cent have a Riester-plan. About two-thirds of employees report that they do not plan to contribute to a private Riester-plan. However, this does not mean that they refuse to contribute to other occupational pension plans, since the number of employees who consider occupational pensions is increasing. The vast majority of respondents (84 per cent of the age group 18 to 65) think that private savings are required to guarantee a sufficient standard of living. However, they do not feel that this should be done with a Riester-plan. People rightly assume (or know) that there are other ways of providing for private retirement income.

The survey also reveals that a large fraction of workers is badly informed about pension products in general, tax treatment, and personal eligibility. Many employees, who – by definition of their labor market status – are eligible to receive a Riester subsidy, think that they are not. Moreover, a large fraction also has the subjective feeling of being not well informed. Given that the newly introduced Riester-plans have significant disadvantages (see above) and are not well understood by a large part of the working population, the ratio of 21 per cent Riester contracts in the relevant age group is quite surprising. The results on participation in the new pension products do not imply that participating workers will increase their saving. Given that the average savings rate is already high in Germany, it is very plausible that the middle class will substitute the subsidized forms of savings for other forms of private savings (such as traditional life insurance).

However, the survey shows that compared to October 2001, the number of respondents who think that private savings are necessary has increased. At the same time the confidence in the public pension system has declined. This may be a much more important driving force behind private savings than subsidized contributions to formal pension plans.

The degree of annuitization in occupational pension plans depends very much on the products that are offered by the employer. The traditional pension plans usually offer annuities, though this is not mandated by law. Direct insurance – usually in the form of a life insurance contract – offers the possibility of lump-sum withdrawals without a tax penalty. Depending on their specific charter Pensionskassen may also offer flexible withdrawal schemes. The annuitization of Riester-plans and of pension funds is mandatory – with the exception mentioned above. Thus, a wide range of (more or less) tax-preferred pension vehicles is available. Large firms usually offer a number of products so that the employee has some discretion with respect to the degree of annuitization of his or her occupational pension.

At the moment it is too early to speculate about the steady state market share of the different pension vehicles. It is also too early to make quantitative predictions about the future role of annuities. However, the experience during the first year after the 2001 reform shows that there is a considerable market for individual, annuitized pension products (individual Riester-plans). This will increase the availability of private annuities in Germany. Whether this is driven by individual preferences or purely by tax considerations remains open to debate. Occupational pension plans (be it the Riester type or one of the other varieties) are becoming more important than in the past and probably more important than the individual plans due to cost considerations. It seems safe to predict that the annuitization of private wealth will increase during the next decade, while public pensions (that is, public annuities) are going to decline in importance.

NOTES

1. See Börsch-Supan et al. (2003) for a detailed description of income sources of retirees.
2. Own calculations based on VDR (2003), and BMF (2002).
3. This subsidy to the social security system absorbs 30 per cent of the federal budget.
4. The net replacement rates of civil servants with a full working career are far higher than 70 per cent, since their pension is 75 per cent of their *last gross earnings*. Other public sector employees enjoy similar pension benefits that are financed by additional contributions (6.5 per cent of the payroll in 2003) on top of the regular social security contributions. The total public sector work force makes up for about 15 per cent of the total.
5. See Schnabel (2001b) for details of the estimation.
6. This protection is of limited value. First, the pension claims may be reduced in order to prevent bankruptcy (in other words to protect existing jobs). Second, in case of bankruptcy

the insurance does not fully cover all occupational pensions. Due to the dramatic increase of bankruptcy rates, the insurance premia have also risen markedly during the last years.
7. Own estimates based on the Income and Expenditure Surveys (EVS), years 1978–98.
8. These are very conservative estimates. Compared to aggregate figures based on the banking statistics of the Bundesbank, underreporting of financial wealth by a factor of 50 per cent is likely. In this case, the average numbers would have to be inflated by a factor of 2. Another indicator for underreporting of financial wealth is the high level of saving in financial assets in the EVS. Integrating annual savings also leads to much higher wealth levels.
9. Similar reductions have been legislated for the pensions of civil servants.
10. See Schnabel (2001a) for more details on the projection of demographic and economic dependency ratios, and on projections of contribution rates.
11. In this case, the income is untaxed. This will most probably be changed in the near future.
12. The official justification for this 'double burden' is that pension funds are more risky than the other vehicles and thus require a tougher protection!
13. This estimate is calculated from survey data, see DIA (2003).

REFERENCES

ABA – Arbeitsgemeinschaft für betriebliche Altersvorsorge (2002), www.aba-online.de

BMF – Bundesministerium für Finanzen (2002), *Finanzplan des Bundes 2002 bis 2006*, Berlin.

Börsch-Supan, A., A. Reil-Held and R. Schnabel (2003), 'Household Saving in Germany', in A. Börsch-Supan (ed.), *Life-cycle Savings and Public Policy*, New York: Academic Press.

Börsch-Supan, A. and R. Schnabel (1998), 'Social Security and Retirement in Germany', in J. Gruber und D. Wise (eds), *Social Security and Retirement Around the World*, Chicago: University of Chicago Press.

Börsch-Supan, A., R. Schnabel, S. Kohnz and G. Mastrobuoni (2004), 'Micro Modeling of Retirement Decisions in Germany', in J. Gruber and D. Wise (eds), *Social Security Programs and Retirement around the World: Micro-Estimation*, Chicago: University of Chicago Press.

DIA – Deutsches Institut für Altersvorsorge (2003), *Rentenbarometer*, Cologne, February.

EVS (1998), *Einkommens- und Verbrauchsstichprobe 1998*, Statistisches Bundesamt, Wiesbaden, 1998.

Schnabel, R. (1999), 'Vermögen und Ersparnis im Lebenszyklus in Westdeutschland', SFB 504 Discussion Paper 899–43, Mannheim.

Schnabel, R. (2001a), 'Die Rentenreform 2001 – Gutachten zur Rentabilität, Generationengerechtigkeit und den wirtschaftlichen Annahmen der Regierung', Deutsches Institut für Altersvorsorge, Cologne.

Schnabel, R. (2001b), 'The Golden Years of Social Security – Life-cycle Income, Pensions and Savings in Germany', SFB 504 Discussion Paper, University of Mannheim.

VDR – Verband Deutscher Rentenversicherungsträger (2003), *Rentenversicherung in Zeitreihen*, Frankfurt am Main.

10. Mandated annuities in Switzerland*

Monika Bütler

10.1 INTRODUCTION

Probably the most important role annuities will play in the decades to come is within mandated fully funded pension schemes. Designing and regulating a so-called second pillar pension system is an ambitious task and requires careful evaluations of different policy options. As of today, only limited long-term experience on mandated fully funded pension plans is available. A notable and much cited example is Switzerland. Total accumulated capital stock amounted to approximately 120 per cent of GDP (see Figure 10.1) in 2000. Already today occupational pensions make up for approximately 40 per cent of publicly provided or regulated transfer income during retirement. This percentage is anticipated to be higher for current contributors.

During the last 20 years Switzerland's first pillar AHV/AVS[1] has suffered a substantial loss of reputation and public confidence due to ongoing and anticipated demographic changes and their impact on the financial viability of the plan. The second pillar, on the other hand, had been considered a safe and reliable provider of income in old age until very recently. Occupational pension plans had also played an important role in a traditionally tight labor market, with firms offering better pension plans attracting and keeping the better workers. Increases in life expectancy and the recent fall in stock market prices have turned the model pupil into the problem child of Swiss politics.

In this ongoing crisis, it turned out that forward-looking strategies of reserves management were rare at best. Few companies had accumulated enough reserves to cover the losses associated with a decrease in the market

* I am very grateful to Urs Birchler, Jürg Blum, Federica Teppa and the conference participants at Moncalieri for many valuable comments and interesting discussions. Olivia Popa provided very able and efficient research assistance. Most importantly I would like to thank CeRP, especially Elsa Fornero and Silvia Maero, for their hospitality and support (which made it possible for me to attend the conference with a small baby). This work was supported in part by a grant from the Swiss National Science Foundation (grant N.1214-67875.02).

return. But the crisis is also a consequence of an inflexible regulation that is neither indexed to general economic conditions nor to demographic changes. The episode shows that it is inherently difficult to plan and regulate a system involving contracts spanning several decades.

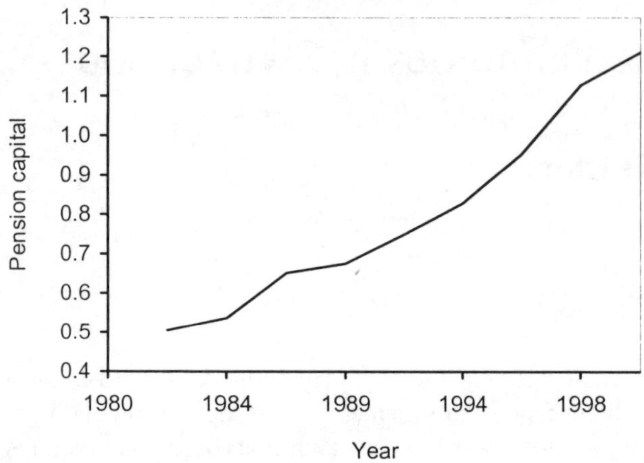

Figure 10.1 Accumulated pension capital as a fraction of GDP in Switzerland

An area for which the Swiss second pillar provides valuable insights is the design of payout options. Mandated pension schemes are implemented primarily to prevent old-age poverty that may result from short-sighted planning or from the absence of adequate market saving instruments. From an economic efficiency point of view, this goal should be achieved without distorting optimal individual decisions too much. By law, Swiss second pillar annuities are joint annuities even for individuals without potential survivors. This may lead to a substantial redistribution from single to, on average more affluent, married beneficiaries. On the other hand, pension providers can (and often do) offer the option to withdraw the entire accumulated retirement assets as a lump sum. The combination of the two features is hardly optimal from both an equity and an efficiency perspective. The case of Switzerland thus shows that the design of payout options during the decumulation phase is of crucial importance in mandated annuity plans.

This chapter provides a short overview of the Swiss pension system with a particular emphasis on the second pillar in Section 10.2. The importance of prudential regulation and supervision is demonstrated in Section 10.3, which describes the recent crisis of the Swiss second pillar in more detail. Some illustrative evidence for the importance of payout options drawn from the Swiss case is provided in Section 10.4. Section 10.5 concludes.

10.2 THE SWISS OLD-AGE INSURANCE SYSTEM

Switzerland has been the first OECD country that has mandated an occupational pension scheme as the second pillar to complement a pay-as-you-go (PAYG) system. The reliance on a multi-pillar approach has triggered considerable interest in the Swiss system. This section provides a short overview of the system, with an emphasis on the second pillar with its merits and problems.

10.2.1 The System in a Nutshell

The core of Switzerland's pension system, also summarized in Table 10.1, is composed of three pillars, of which the first and second are of approximately equal importance. The first pillar, AHV/AVS, is a predominantly PAYG system. It was introduced after a very successful referendum in 1948. The second pillar is a mandatory, employer-based, fully funded occupational pension scheme (as described in more detail below). The so-called BVG/LPP[2] became mandatory in 1985, but had been a very important source of retirement for many Swiss employees long before the first pillar was set up. The first and second pillars are complemented by a voluntary third pillar of individual tax-favored saving for retirement.

In 2000, on average, approximately 40 per cent (50 per cent) of publicly mandated retirement income was paid out by the second (first) pillar. This understates the importance of the occupational pension system, however, as contributing agents today can expect more than half of their combined first and second pillar income to come from the second. The third pillar predominantly covers self-employed workers, but is also used as a tax-saving device for upper middle and high income earners. The capital accumulated in the third pillar is almost always paid out as a lump sum due to the already high degree of annuitization by the first and second pillars.

10.2.2 The First Pillar

The first pillar aims at providing a basic subsistence level of income to all retired residents in Switzerland. Its structure has changed considerably in ten so-called revisions during the last 50 years. However, since a large increase in the size of the program in the late 1960s and early 1970s (in which period both payroll tax and pension benefits approximately doubled), the payroll tax rate has remained unchanged, and the ratio between average pension benefits and average *per capita* wages has remained almost constant.

The main features of the first pillar can be described as follows. Although there is a small trust fund, the public pension system is a pay-as-you-go

*Table 10.1 Switzerland's two pillars of income support during retirement**

	1. Pillar: 'AHV/AVS'	2. Pillar: 'BVG/LPP'
Goal	Subsistence	Living standard
Financing principle	Pay-as-you-go	Fully funded
Financing sources	Labor income (≈ 70%) General taxation (20%) VAT (≈ 10%)	Labor income
Employee / Employer	50% / 50%	≤ 50% / ≥ 50%
Contribution rate (payroll)	8.4%	7–18%
Provision / Organization	Government	Frms and insurance companies
Administration costs (as % of contributions)	≈ 0.33%	≈ 8%
Tax–benefit linkage	Weak, DB (relatively flat)	Proportional, DC (some DB)
Form of benefits	Individual annuity	Joint annuity or lump sum
Universality	Universal coverage	Restricted coverage
Accounts	None	Collective
Redistribution:		
– Intergenerational	+ older generations	+ older generations
– Intragen. explicit	+ poor, (+ women)	+ married individuals
– Intragen. implicit	+ women	+ rich, –single men
Insurance also for:	Survivors	Survivors, disabled
Reinsurance	Government	Security Fund, (government?)

*Note:** There is considerable variation among second pillar institutions, however. A + (–) before a subgroup of the population denotes a redistribution in favor (at the expense) of the respective group. Implicit redistribution in favor of women will end with the next revision of social security law.

system, in which the current young have to finance the pensions of the current old. The system is financed mainly with a proportional payroll tax on all labor income (that is, without a cap), and an earmarked fraction of the consumption tax (value added tax). By law, 20 per cent of total expenditures has to be financed out of general federal government revenues. Pension benefits are paid out after the legal retirement age, regardless of whether the agent leaves the workforce or not.

There is a limited tax-benefit linkage in Switzerland, but the benefit scheme is relatively flat in reality. More important for the determination of future benefits is the number of contribution years including those granted for child care.[3] A majority of retirees qualify for a pension close or equal to the maximum benefit level. As in most other countries, the first pillar offers some explicit and implicit redistribution within and between generations and insurance against various contingencies.[4] Apart from the regular pension benefits, AHV/AVS also avails means-tested supplemental benefits. The combination of a relatively flat benefit structure and supplementary benefits have led to a low poverty rate among the elderly in Switzerland,[5] although there are still gaps for low-income earners.

Recent and ongoing revisions of the first pillar have led to a number of important structural changes although the contribution rate and total expenditures have remained basically unchanged. First, family/household benefits have been replaced by individual benefits. Married couples' entitlements are capped at 150 per cent of a single benefit. This reduction takes into account that *per capita* expenses are considerably lower in a two-person than in a single household. Married couples, on the other hand, benefit from AHV/AVS's survivor insurance (in favor of widows only!) during the working period. The redistribution between single and married individuals is thus small. Second, individuals with responsibilities for children aged up to 16 years or other dependants are now entitled to (child-)care credits. Third, contributions during marriage, including child-care credits, are split between the spouses. This change led to a substantial improvement for divorced women, but reduced the entitlements of couples with a non-working spouse and few or no children. Fourth, the legal retirement age for women will be raised stepwise from 62 to 64 years, and most probably to 65.

For a very long time, the first pillar has been viewed as very stable, efficient (at reducing poverty in old age) and cheap (due to very low administration costs of $\approx$ 0.33 per cent of benefits). But like most PAYG systems in Europe, the Swiss first pillar is plagued by unfavorable demographics due to lower mortality and fertility rates which have led to a strong increase in the old-age dependency ratio.[6] If current levels of contributions and benefits are left unchanged, the present value of future contributions falls short of the present value of future claims by about a third.

There are virtually no reserves – the AHV/AVS trust fund makes up for less than one year's worth of benefits – to cushion the anticipated population ageing. There is no consensus in current political debate as to how to fix the financing problem apart from an increase in the earmarked VAT. It is important to note that policy makers face strong political constraints on potential reforms. Any change of the law can be (and usually is) challenged by an optional referendum. The public thus possesses veto power for all reform of the current social security system. This is crucial as the median voter, who is approximately 48 today, is anticipated to have an age of 52 by the year 2020.

The retirement age observed in reality is below the statutory retirement age albeit to a somewhat lesser degree than in other European countries. According to a recent SAKE/ESPA study,[7] a majority of Swiss men (53 per cent) and 44 per cent of Swiss women retire before the legal retirement age of 65 for men or 62 for women. The outcome is striking in view of the fact that the first pillar does not yet offer early retirement. Many of those (predominantly middle and high-income) beneficiaries have received generous early retirement packages from their occupational pension provider, often with additional benefits until age 65–62 to bridge the time to the legal retirement age. Figure 10.2 shows the distribution of retirement ages collected from ten Swiss occupational pension funds. The data exhibit a wide variety of retirement ages, with a triple-peak profile for men and a double-peak profile for women at ages 60, 62, and (for men only) 65. The peaks at 60 and 62 correspond to the lowest age for which early retirement packages are offered at relatively favorable conditions in occupational pension funds.

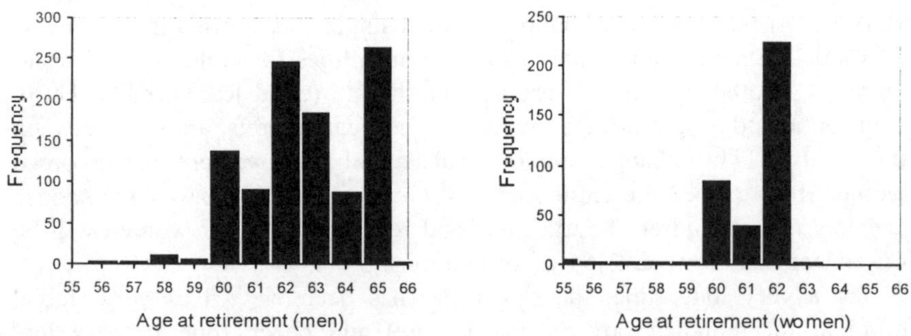

Source: Pilot study on Swiss pension funds as described in Bütler and Teppa (2002).

Figure 10.2 Distributions of age at retirement for men and women

10.2.3 The Second Pillar: Occupational Pension Plans

The Swiss second pillar, after a long history as a private occupational pension system, became mandatory in 1985. As Figure 10.3 shows, a sizeable fraction of the working force had been covered already before such plans were mandated by law. Although Figure 10.3 overstates the true coverage rate due to some double-counting, the numbers convey a relatively high coverage especially for male workers.

The second pillar's main goal is to maintain the pre-retirement living standard together with the benefits stemming from the first pillar. Apart from retirement income, the second pillar also provides insurance for disability and survivors of insured men (but not of women) during the accumulation period. A detailed description of all aspects of the second pillar is thus beyond the scope of this chapter. The interested reader is referred to Queissar and Vittas (2000), especially concerning institutional details and the official publications of the Swiss *Bundesamt für Statistik* (2002).

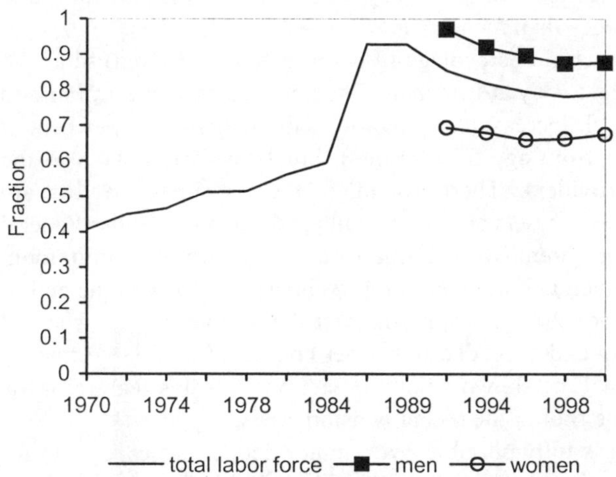

Note: The numbers are somewhat overestimated due to double-counting of insured individuals.

Figure 10.3 Workers covered by an occupational pension plan as a fraction of the active population since 1970

Organization and financing

Occupational pension plans are organized, in general, by the employer. The employer can choose several forms of organization, the two polar cases being an autonomous pension fund, on the one hand, and a contract with an insurer, on the other hand. As a consequence (and also for historical reasons), the system is very segmented. There are more than 10 000 funds, though this number is decreasing rapidly. When occupational pension plans were mandated, all schemes had to be defined benefits (DB). By now, and after an early change in the law, more than 75 per cent are defined contributions (DC). Administration costs are low by international standards, approximately 8 per cent of benefits, but high compared to AHV/AVS.

The second pillar is designed to be integrated with the first pillar. As the latter provides a basic level of income, the BVG/LPP only insures income above a certain threshold level, the so-called coordination offset which is equal to a yearly maximum single AHV/AVS pension (in 2003: 25 320 CHF ≈ 17 000 € ≈ 18 500 $). There is, in principle, also a maximum insured earning which is equal to three times the maximum single AHV/AVS benefit. Pension providers are free to offer insurance for income below or above the two threshold levels. While most do for income greater than the maximum – many companies do not even have an upper level – very few do for income below the threshold level. This lower threshold explains the much lower coverage for female workers (Figure 10.3), who often work part-time and have lower average wages than men.

Contributions are a certain percentage of coordinated (= insured) salary of which the employer has to pay at least half. The law also mandates minimum contribution rates, which increase considerably with age (from 7 per cent at age 25 to 18 per cent from age 55 onwards), but leaves the details to the individual pension providers. These so-called age retirement credits are accumulated as retirement assets and bear an interest rate. The Swiss Federal Council determines the (nominal!) minimum rate of return. This minimum rate requirement remained at 4 per cent for 17 years (from 1985 to the end of 2002, 3.25 per cent since 2003), despite the fact that market returns showed considerable variability and exceeded this 4 per cent level by a large margin most of the time. As will be shown below in Section 10.3 this feature of the Swiss system was at the root of the recent pension crisis.

The accrued capital is fully portable (with minor deductions especially for short employment spells) when the insured individual changes their employer. By law, an employee changing firms gets the accumulated total contributions accrued at the minimum interest rate. The law is silent as to how accumulated reserves have to be distributed. In practice this meant that job changers got less than their fair share during the high return episodes. This feature was considered an important obstacle to mobility on the Swiss labor market in the 1990s. With the present low market returns and widespread underfunding of pension providers, on the other hand, the requirement could potentially induce employees to flee an underfunded pension provider, in other words, an employer attached to such a provider.

Insured benefits

Upon attainment of retirement age, the accumulated capital can be withdrawn either as a monthly lifelong annuity or as a lump sum provided the pension fund allows for this option.[8] Old-age pension benefits are strictly proportional to the accumulated retirement assets (retirement credits plus accrued interest). The accumulated capital K is translated into a yearly pension B using the conversion factor γ:

$$B = \gamma K$$

This conversion also applies to DB plans; the fund has to make sure that enough capital is accumulated to cover the claims made based on previous income. Benefits are fixed annuities in principle, but the law states that pension providers have to adjust current old age benefits to inflation within the scope of their financial possibilities.

The conversion factor presently amounts to 7.2 per cent and is determined by the Swiss Federal Council. This number was constructed using a (technical) interest rate of 4 per cent (the legal minimum requirement for 17 years) and somewhat optimistic – from the pension provider's perspective – mortality tables that underestimate average longevity. As Table 10.2 demonstrates – using most recent mortality tables – this factor together with a market interest rate of 4 per cent delivers an average money's worth ratio (MWR) close to one. With this presently unrealistically high discount factor, there is no room for increases (such as inflation adjustments) in the yearly benefit for already retired individuals. It is thus not surprising that the private market for annuities in Switzerland is relatively thin. Private insurers are simply unable to offer the same deal to their customers, especially if they are bound to face adverse selection due to information asymmetries with respect to mortality rates.

The BVG/LPP mandates joint annuities; the conversion factor is the same for everybody irrespective of gender, family status or income. Children under age 18 (or under age 25 if still dependent) of retired persons get an additional pension of 20 per cent of the main claimant's benefit. When a retired man dies, his widow receives a benefit amounting to 60 per cent of the previous pension, his dependent children a benefit of 20 per cent each. As is obvious from Table 10.2 this leads to sizeable differences in the MWR, as will be explained in more detail in Section 10.4 below.

When given the choice between an annuity and a lump sum,[9] most individuals choose the former although lump-sum withdrawals enjoy a preferential tax treatment – the present value of taxes can be up to three times higher with the annuity, depending on the canton of residence. This is presumably also a consequence of the very high MWR offered by the second pillar.

Table 10.2 Money's worth ratios as a function of marital status and retirement age (=RA) that qualifies for full benefits

Gender	Marital	R.A.	$r = .04$ $g = 0$	$r = .04$ $g = .01$	$r = \text{EJ}$ $g = 0$	$r = \text{EJ}$ $g = .01$
Male	Single	65	0.73	0.79	0.82	0.89
Male	Married (–3)	65	1.01	1.11	1.16	1.28
Female	Single	65	0.95	1.04	1.08	1.19
Female	Married (no)	65	0.98	1.08	1.12	1.24
Female	Married (+3)	65	1.02	1.13	1.18	1.31
Male	Single	62	0.80	0.87	0.90	0.98
Male	Married (–3)	62	1.08	1.20	1.25	1.40
Female	Single	62	1.02	1.14	1.18	1.31
Female	Married (no)	62	1.05	1.17	1.22	1.36
Female	Married (+3)	62	1.10	1.23	1.27	1.42

Note: For married individuals, the number in parentheses denotes the age difference between the spouses, or indicates the case in which no survivor benefit is available (this is the standard option for married women). As mortality differences are small between divorced, widowed and single agents, only single is reported. See Section 10.4 for details.

Regulation and supervision

The Swiss second pillar is heavily regulated in both the accumulation and the decumulation phase. Apart from the above mentioned requirements concerning the minimum rate, the contribution rates and the survivor benefits, the BVG/LPP and its amendments also put limits on possible asset structures. These limits on investment, which are also a function of a fund's asset and liability structure, have been relaxed considerably, however, so that they hardly ever bind in practice.

In the payout phase, the pension fund's hands are tied as well. The conversion factor can only be relaxed in extraordinary circumstances and in general only for the part exceeding the upper coordination limit. Pensions of current retired beneficiaries cannot be reduced unless the law is changed. While this constraint provides a high degree of security in old age, the grandfathering of existing pensioners potentially goes at the expense of future generations as will be argued below.

Most importantly, by law, *the pension provider must guarantee that it can fulfill its obligations at all times.* The law states that the pension institution must regulate its systems for contributions and funding in such a way that the benefits can be paid when due, but does not specify more precise requirements.

Other aspects of regulation concern the organization and the administration of the pension fund, impose accounting standards and specify audit requirements.

Supervision of occupational pension institutions is overseen by the Swiss Federal Council. Pension institutions without national or international importance are supervised by cantonal supervisory authorities.[10] The Federal Office for Social Insurance supervises the cantonal supervisory authorities as well as pension providers of national or international importance. The different layers and the large segmentation of the supervisory authority potentially reduce the quality and transparency of supervision.

The Federal Office for Social Insurance is also in charge of the so-called Suppletory Institution,[11] and even more importantly, of the BVG/LPP *Security Fund*. The Security Fund's most important task is to act as a reinsurance institution, that is, to secure benefits in accordance with the rules for the beneficiaries of insolvent pension providers. In contrast to what may be expected of such an institution, the fund does not primarily accumulate reserves,[12] but is financed on a pay-as-you-go basis, with a contribution rate of 0.1 per cent of the coordinated earnings at present. To cover its obligations in bad times the Security Fund will have to increase the contribution rate when the individual funds face greater difficulties financing their primary obligations. Given that occupational pensions are mandated by law, an important question is whether the government has the moral obligation to guarantee the benefits when the Security Fund is unable to do so. Another question is whether an employer can afford to let their fund go bust.

Up to now, little emphasis has been placed on transparency. The pension providers have to inform the insured about their anticipated benefits in old age or when disabled, but do not have to inform them about their financial situation. The lack of transparency has two important aspects. First, the insurance companies may be insufficiently supervised and may decide on investment/contribution strategies that are detrimental to the interest of the insured worker. Second, individuals that are not aware of potential financial shortfalls of their fund, may find out only at a time when they do not have much time left to make up for the losses.

A short appraisal of the system

The long history of the scheme is reflected in the large capital stock accumulated to date. The capital stock amounts to approximately 120 per cent of GDP. Although coverage is restricted, the second pillar insures a relatively high percentage of the labor force.

In contrast to the first pillar, the BVG/LPP is based on outdated models of the labor market and the family structure. The coordination offset is not reduced for part-time employment. Widowers can usually not claim a benefit after the death of an insured married female individual even when the wife had been the main bread winner of the family. The structure of the BVG/LPP thus has an important catch. When Queissar and Vittas (2000) conclude that the second pillar is 'remarkably well integrated' with the first, this is again only true for a male married single earner. The system does not take account of the many cohabiting unmarried parents with children, part-time workers or job sharers as well as homosexual couples, who all get a much lower degree of insurance for their contributions than married men.

Money's worth ratios of the Swiss occupational pension system are very high except for single men.[13] A constant discount factor of 4 per cent – this corresponds to the minimum rate requirement – together with a non-increasing pension delivers an average MWR only marginally smaller than one. If one adds a moderate growth of pension benefits of 1 per cent annually, the MWR is already close to 1.1. Taking the term structure of interest rates reported in James and Song (2001),[14] the picture looks even more favorable for the pensioners – and worse for the insurers.

As will be argued below in Section 10.3, overly generous pension and survivor benefits together with opaque rules of regulation and supervision pose a serious threat to the second pillar.

10.3 THE RECENT (AND ONGOING) SWISS PENSION CRISIS

The Swiss pension system has had a long successful history and has enjoyed considerable international praise from both the academic and the political side. Fundamental changes to the system have been rare and contributions and replacement rates have basically stayed constant for many decades. Consequently public awareness of potential shortcomings of the fully funded part was weak at best, reinforced by the fact that little emphasis had been put on sufficient information and transparency.

10.3.1 An Overview of the Crisis

Market returns on both the bond and stock market had been markedly above the minimum rate of 4 per cent during the early and mid 1990s. Average bond and stock returns from 1990 to the end of 2001 amounted to 5.5 per cent and 12 per cent, respectively (see Figure 10.4). In 2002, however, Swiss pension providers suffered a loss of approximately 10 per cent on average. But even when one includes the recent downturn of the stock market, the average return on stocks since 1990 was still 8.4 per cent to the end of 2002.

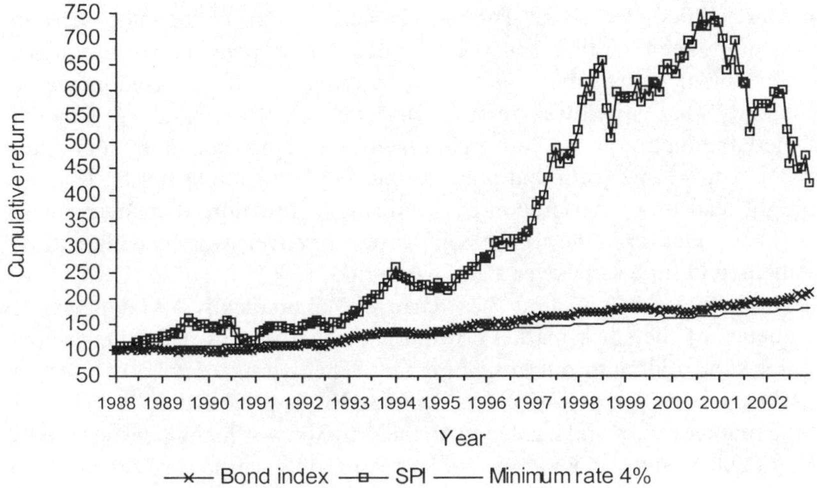

Note: SPI = Swiss Performance Index.

Figure 10.4 Cumulated bond and stock returns since 1988 in comparison with a 4 per cent interest rate

'Excess returns' in good times were often spent on adjusting pension benefits not only to inflation but also to wage growth or on financing generous early retirement packages. Another way to distribute high returns was a reduction of contribution rates. Many pension funds did not even collect contributions for some period of time or reimbursed employees and employer at the end of the year. Recommendations to accumulate higher reserves for rainy days were left as unheard as claims to adjust the minimum rate to the high market returns. The few advocates of prudential reserve management were not really taken seriously.

The public woke up when the problem-ridden airline company Swissair announced that it reclaimed several million Swiss francs of paid contributions out of the fund. The former CEO of SAir group argued that 'two thirds of the contributions are paid by the employer. Thus also a part of the fund's reserves belongs to the employer.'[15] The justification of this claim was that reserves do not belong to the fund, but to the contributors, that is, the employees and the employer. In fact Swissair's claim was nothing more than what had been considered common practice during the 1990s. But by then financial prospects were less favorable (the market return had already started to fall), and – more importantly for the public perception – it involved a firm with huge financial difficulties.

In March 2000, the Swiss Federal Council announced that the pension funds would need more resources to fulfil future pension requirements. However, this need was motivated rather by realized and projected increases in longevity than by lower returns. In fact, the Swiss Federal Council suggested a reduction in the conversion factor or an increase in the minimum rate from 4 to 4.8 per cent, but realized that the latter might not be feasible and might lead to a deterioration of the financial situation of many pension funds. The reduction in the conversion factor, moreover, was scheduled to be implemented in little steps over a 20-year period.

Since 2000, the situation has changed dramatically. Mainly as a consequence of the stock market downturn, market returns had fallen below the 4 per cent minimum return requirement. The average degree of funding obligations of pension providers has decreased to approximately 90 per cent with the market return and has led to an underfunding of many pension funds. In mid 2002 and under the guidance of the company Swiss Life (Rentenanstalt), the life insurers (which predominantly organize pension plans for smaller and medium enterprises) requested a reduction of the minimum return to 3 per cent or less. After what was publicly perceived to be an unprecedented lobbying act of the life insurers, the Swiss Federal Council conceded to this request and announced that it would reduce the minimum return requirement to 3.25 per cent as of 1 January 2003.

This announcement caused a public outcry that went far beyond the usual level of indignation in Switzerland. Life insurers were accused of attempted 'theft' of pension benefits (*Rentenklau*). Observers attributed the strong reaction not primarily to a lack of comprehension of the measure taken, but to other factors. One factor was scandals that concerned two well known pension providers.[16] The more important reason, however, was an almost complete absence of transparency and the fact that potentially huge profits during the 1990s that should have been used to accumulate reserves seemed to have disappeared. As Figure 10.4 demonstrates it would have been easy for pension companies to cushion a fall in the market interest rate – at least for a certain time.[17]

The debate is going on. A minimum rate equal to or slightly below the market return guarantees that the pension provider can accumulate retirement assets at the rate mandated by the law. But not only the accumulation, but also the decumulation phase is affected by a change in the prevailing market return. Regardless of any minimum rate requirements, the market cannot always generate a return on accumulated retirement assets that would be necessary to maintain the mandated pension benefits from a given capital stock, especially as Swiss MWRs are very high. A lower minimum rate thus only solves part of the financial problem in low return periods as will be argued below.

A further reduction of the minimum return below the 3.25 per cent as well as a reduction of the conversion factor, and possibly even of benefits of already retired individuals are still open issues. Politically a reduction in the conversion factor (and even more so of current pension benefits) seems difficult to achieve, however. Contributors and current pensioners are not willing to make what is generally perceived as yet another sacrifice.

10.3.2 Minimum Rate Requirement and the Conversion Factor: A Simple Analysis

The market return has two major implications for a fully funded pension plan. Firstly, the higher the return the faster the retirement capital will accumulate, and a lower contribution rate is needed to achieve a certain capital stock at retirement. Secondly, the higher the return, the higher the annuity that can be paid out from a given level of retirement assets. This section provides a simple formal analysis of how a permanent reduction in the market return affects MWRs for different generations under the current Swiss regulatory setup. Recall that the minimum rate at which pension providers have to accumulate retirement is fixed by law, and that retirement benefits are a fixed fraction (the conversion factor) of accumulated retirement assets upon retirement.

To simplify the analysis, I assume that the fall in the interest rate is permanent and that the conversion factor and current pension benefits are left unchanged.[18] I also assume that the previous market interest rate had been equal to the minimum return of 4 per cent, and that the new market interest rate is 3 per cent. Contributions are assumed to grow at 2 per cent annually accounting for wage growth and increasing contribution rates with age.

Figure 10.5 shows the MWRs for an 'average' individual over the life cycle for various combinations of market and mandated interest rates.[19] For younger individuals the numbers reported in Figure 10.5 are MWR for deferred annuities, with the payout period starting at age 62. When the market interest rate is equal to the minimum rate of 4 per cent, the MWR is equal to one for all ages, and the pension providers break even in the absence of administration costs.

Let us now consider a permanent fall in the market interest rate to 3 per cent. Taking this value to discount pension payments and retirement credits, Figure 10.5 reveals that the resulting MWR is considerably above one, as the present value of future pension benefits exceeds the capital at retirement by approximately 10 per cent. If the minimum rate stays above the market rate (solid line and stars in Figure 10.5), this effect is reinforced by the fact that pension providers have to credit a higher interest rate than the market interest rate during the contribution period. This would lead to an insolvency of the pension provider sooner or later even in the presence of reserves.

But even if the minimum rate is reduced to the new market return (dashed line in Figure 10.5), MWRs exceed one for all ages. The reason is that the present value of pension benefits at retirement is considerably above the capital stock (on which the benefits are based) at retirement. Thus if retirement benefits are to be left untouched, the pension providers need an additional margin to finance their liabilities.

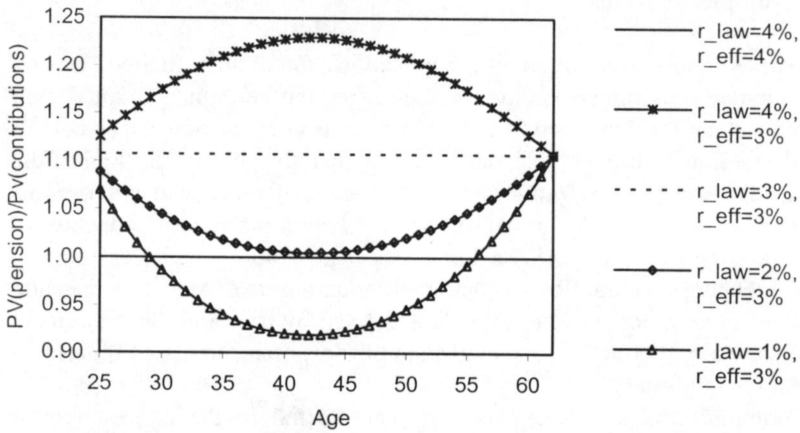

Note: r_law and *r_eff* denote the legal minimum return requirement and the prevailing market interest rate, respectively. Contributions are assumed to grow at 2 per cent annually.

Figure 10.5 Money's worth ratio for a deferred annuity with a fixed conversion factor (γ=7.2 per cent) as a function of age and applicable interest rates in a riskless setting

If the conversion factor cannot be adjusted, the solvency of the pension fund can only be restored by an interest rate on retirement credits considerably below the market interest rate. A fraction of the potential return on the working generation's capital stock will then be diverted to finance the claims of the retired individuals. A sufficient funding can, therefore, only be achieved with a sizeable redistribution between living generations as is reflected in Figure 10.5. The effect on the MWRs is largest for middle-aged individuals. These contributors see their already accumulated pension capital and their retirement credits grow at too low a rate. The accumulation deficit due to the forgone return on accumulated retirement credits exceeds the potential benefit of too high a conversion factor upon retirement for the current middle-aged. For younger individuals the trade-off is more favorable as contributions are concentrated towards the end of working life. As a consequence, the present value of the accumulation deficit due to too low a return on retirement credits is smaller for them. The closer to retirement age, on the other hand, the more important in present value terms is the favorable conversion between accumulated retirement credits and pension benefits.

10.3.3 Preliminary Lessons from the Crisis

Fluctuations in the market return are one of the main challenges pension providers and regulators face. There are two polar ways to deal with these fluctuations from an ex ante perspective. The first would be to let individuals bear the market risk, leading to a relatively transparent pension environment, but jeopardizing the goal of providing sufficient insurance in old age. The second would be to aim at a stable contribution-benefit regime, transferring investment risks to pension providers and across generations (as well as potentially the government as a reinsurer of last resort). If the emphasis is on stability of acquired claims at least to a certain degree, fluctuation reserves must be sheltered from political pressure. The fundamental trade-off the regulatory authority has to take a stand on is thus between flexibility and insurance of pension claims.

The Swiss second pillar has relied greatly on a stability of acquired claims, requiring a minimum return which seemed realistic at least in the medium run. In retrospect, the financial problems of many Swiss pension providers could have been avoided at least temporarily by an accumulation of sufficient reserves. But the system left the management of 'excess returns' basically at the discretion of pension providers, while no real precautions were prescribed for the downside risk. The requirement to accumulate enough reserves remained opaque. Many pension providers failed to accumulate enough reserves to cushion fluctuations in the market return on their own account, while the regulatory authority remained silent.

The definition of property rights in the Swiss second pillar has been fuzzy; the link between residual control rights and residual claims is very weak. The Swiss basically have relied on the political process as a complement to incomplete contracts. But as experience has demonstrated, discretionary policy changes can lead to a piecemeal regulation that may be detrimental to both the efficiency and the viability of the system. A lesson that can be drawn from the recent crisis is that transparent adjustment rules should avail for potential crisis. Under pressure, it is more difficult to recognize that various components of the regulatory setup – such as the conversion factor and the minimum rate requirement in the Swiss case – are affected by the same underlying market forces. Most likely, crisis management under time pressure also leads to a one-sided distribution of the rescue burden at the expense of certain groups of insured individuals.

Even if the system emphasizes insurance of pension claims, regulation should be able to take account of *permanent* changes in the underlying parameters, notably the market returns (ageing of baby-boomers) and changes in mortality rates. In the long run, the very high MWRs the Swiss system currently offers will not be sustainable as the financial margin for pension providers is simply too small.

Inadequate regulation and supervision are often closely related to insufficient transparency. Given that it is inherently difficult to assess the financial situation of a fund even for experts, the regulators should aim at the highest degree of transparency possible. It seems as if – in the absence of sufficient information – Swiss insured individuals have trusted the regulatory setup and have not found it worth the effort to acquire additional information. Information asymmetry is thus somewhat endogenous.

The Swiss episode also highlights political economy considerations of pension fund regulation. The first is an important asymmetry in the political process if adjustments are not rule-based. Claims to increase the minimum return during high-return episodes had been ignored while the fall in the market rate led to a (for Swiss standards) almost immediate adjustment. The second consideration is that long-term planning (and regulation) are difficult in the presence of political pressure to increase benefits when capital reserves are high.

10.4 THE DESIGN OF PAYOUT OPTIONS

The design of payout options as well as the degree of flexibility offered to pensioners in a fully funded pension system are crucial questions policy makers face. The two most important payout options in a fully funded pension plan are usually the choice between a lump sum and an annuity, as well as the choice between single and joint annuities. Many Swiss pension plans (notably a majority of DC plans) offer at least a partial choice between a lump sum and an annuity. Provided the individual chooses to annuitize upon retirement, however, there is no choice in Switzerland; the benefit comes in the form of a joint-and-survivor annuity without a compensating increase in benefits for those without potential eligible survivors. Below, I will explore these two features of the Swiss system in turn.

10.4.1 Joint Annuities – But Not for All

The Swiss second pillar insists on joint-and-survivor annuities *for married men*, but *not for women* or non-married couples. Given a certain capital stock upon retirement, the resulting pension benefit is independent of gender, marital status or the age difference between eligible spouses. Thus single individuals and married women do not get higher benefits to compensate for the absence of eligible survivors.[20]

The most popular rationale for joint annuities is to prevent poverty among elderly widows. On the other hand, the prevalence of joint annuities even before the second pillar became mandatory in Switzerland hints at the fact that the 'normal' insured worker had been male and married until well into the 1970s. Legislation in 1985 just continued what had been common practice before although the situation had already started to change by then. At present, the single-earner model is no longer valid for a majority of Swiss families, with the divorce rate climbing to more than 40 per cent and Switzerland having a relatively high female labor market participation.

To investigate the impact of this joint-annuity requirement I have computed money's worth ratios as a function of gender, marital status and the age difference between spouses based on the most recent population mortality tables. Survival probabilities depend on gender and marital status, and the joint probability of survival is obviously a function of the age difference d between the spouses. For expositional reasons, both the discount rate ρ and the yearly increase in the benefit level g are assumed constant.

For a married individual with an eligible spouse, the present value (PV) of all future benefits from retirement age on can be written as

$$\mathrm{PV} = \sum_{t=J}^{\infty}\left(\frac{1+g}{1+\rho}\right)^{t-J} B\times\begin{cases} \Pr\left[M\ alive, S\ alive\right](t) \\ +\ \Pr\left[M\ alive, S\ dead\right](t) \\ +\ \Pr\left[M\ dead, S\ alive\right](t)\times\lambda \end{cases}$$

where Pr[·, ·](t) denotes the probability of a benefit inducing marital status at age t, conditional on the main claimant being alive and married at age J.[21] The parameter λ denotes the fraction of the main claimant's pension the surviving spouse gets after the death of the former. For non-married individuals the computation is similar.

As the yearly benefit is $B = \gamma K$ the money's worth ratio (which is equal to PV/K) is simply

$$\mathrm{MWR} = \gamma\times\sum_{t=J}^{\infty}\left(\frac{1+g}{1+\rho}\right)^{t-J}\begin{cases} \Pr\left[M\ alive, S\ alive\right](t) \\ +\ \Pr\left[M\ alive, S\ dead\right](t) \\ +\ \Pr\left[M\ dead, S\ alive\right](t)\times\lambda \end{cases}$$

The resulting MWRs are reported in Table 10.2 and Figure 10.6. For married individuals in Table 10.2 it is assumed that the wife is three years younger than the husband as is approximately the case in reality. As mortality differences between single, widowed and divorced agents above age 65 are very similar, MWRs are only reported for single men and women in Table 10.2. I have also abstracted from the (very small) probability of (re)marriage after age 65.

Note: The figure is drawn for a retirement age of 62, a discount rate of 4 per cent and a constant annuity; negative numbers mean that spouse is younger.

Figure 10.6 Money's worth ratio as a function of gender and the age difference between spouses

As is obvious from Table 10.2, MWRs differ considerably across marital status and gender. The difference between married and single men is mainly driven by the present value of widow benefits which make up nearly 20 per cent of total expected benefits. The rest, 8 to 10 per cent, can be explained by differences in life expectancy. Differential mortality is relatively unimportant for women. The discussed introduction of a widower benefit would increase the MWR for married women by approximately 4 per cent. This low increase is due to longevity differences between men and women and the fact that husbands are generally older than their wives. Taking present labor market participation and wages of married women, a widower pension would increase pension funds' expenditures by less than half a per cent on average.

The fact that widow benefits make up for a relatively large fraction of anticipated pension benefits for married men also explains the sensitivity of the MWR with respect to the age difference between spouses as demonstrated in Figure 10.6.[22]

The reported numbers can only convey an incomplete picture of the variation of MWR across different groups of the population. In this context, two important aspects are worth mentioning. Firstly, potentially *eligible children* are not included in the analysis. The reported numbers thus underestimate the true MWR for married men. Although women may also claim child benefits in theory, the probability of them doing so is very small for obvious reasons. Secondly, *differential mortality* is only accounted for with respect to marital status, but not with respect to income. This effect increases the variation of MWR especially among men.[23] Note that richer men are more likely to be married, and if married, are more likely to be married to a younger woman and have eligible children upon retirement.

10.4.2 The Choice between a Lump Sum and an Annuity

The choice between a lump-sum capital payment upon retirement or a lifelong annuity is offered by many DC pension plans in Switzerland. As a consequence of the high fragmentation of the second pillar reliable information on individual decisions is difficult to obtain. We do have, however, some data from a limited pilot study, analysed in Bütler and Teppa (2002).[24]

The expected return for each of these two options depends crucially on an agent's gender, his/her expected lifetime and marital status (see also Table 10.2), the presence of children under 18 (for which a substantial supplementary benefit is due), as well as his/her perceived ability to manage the assets in case of a one-time capital payment.

Present value considerations would predict the following patterns: because (single and married) women live longer than single men on average, the former should choose an annuity, and the latter a lump-sum capital payment. Married men, like women, should also prefer an annuity due to the high value of the provided survivor insurance. As the expected lifespan is correlated with wealth (differential mortality), richer pensioners should opt for an annuity, and poorer for a one-time capital payment. Richer agents, however, also benefit more from the preferential tax treatment of capital payments,[25] and are potentially more capable of managing a large fund. Together with the desire to leave bequests,[26] these factors may offset the advantage of an annuity for the more affluent to a certain degree.

Despite data limitations, a number of interesting results can be drawn from the database. Most importantly, the data analysed clearly exhibit an 'acquiescence bias', meaning that a large majority of retirees chooses the standard option upon retirement, despite sizeable differences across different plans.[27] As in most plans, the standard option is the annuity, only 23 per cent (13 per cent) withdraw their accumulated retirement assets entirely (partially) in the form of a lump sum.

We also find that those who do deviate from the standard option generally do so as expected from theory. Not surprisingly, married men with children always choose the annuity. The probability of taking the capital lump-sum option shows a U-shaped dependence on total capital at retirement. For low levels of accumulated capital the likelihood of withdrawing it is decreasing. The most plausible reasons are differential mortality and magnitude effects. The latter effect is well documented in the literature (Shane et al., 2002). A relatively small amount of money is more likely to be withdrawn in the form of a lump sum, as it would only guarantee a low annuity. For higher levels of accumulated capital the attractiveness of (partially) withdrawing the capital as a lump sum is again increasing. This can be well explained by the preferential tax treatment, investment opportunities, and the desire to leave bequests.

At first sight the findings contradict James and Song (2001) who conclude that people frequently prioritize investment choice over longevity assurance. Almost two-thirds of Swiss pensioners fully annuitize their retirement assets although the first pillar provides a subsistence level of annuitization and although the tax on lump-sum withdrawals is up to three times smaller. The main reason for this finding – apart from the above mentioned acquiescence bias – probably lies in the very high money's worth ratios (still) offered by the system.

10.5 CONCLUSIONS

One of the most important lessons to be drawn from the recent developments in Switzerland has been that a high degree of confidence in a fully funded pension system, even when it had been built up over many decades, can be shattered in a very short time span. The ongoing crisis demonstrates not only the notoriously difficult long-term planning and regulation but also the importance of transparency and adequate information given to the public. As pension contracts spanning several decades are mandated by law, property rights need to be well defined and high standards of regulation and supervision are indispensable. The Swiss case has shown that there is considerable political pressure to rescue underfunded pension companies. The system should, therefore, also avail reinsurance, especially for benefits covering basic needs in old age.

As a consequence of the recent crisis, other interesting aspects of the Swiss system are likely to be ignored. The second pillar in Switzerland usually provides pension benefits not only in an intermediate income range, but also for high incomes. This means that basically the same rules for (survivor) benefits apply regardless of income, potentially leading to substantial (regressive) redistribution not intended by law. The factual non-separation of mandatory and non-mandatory parts of income provision in old age also potentially impedes the restructuring of a fund in financial difficulties. On the other hand, if the aim is to prevent poverty in old age (as much as poverty among widows), it is indispensable to open up second pillar pension plans for low-income earners and part-time workers.

Another important feature of a fully funded pension system is the design of payout options in the decumulation phase. The combination of mandated joint annuities with an (in general unlimited) choice between a lump-sum withdrawal and an annuity in Switzerland is certainly not optimal. The former, introduced to prevent poverty among widows, today reinforces the redistribution from single to, on average more affluent, married beneficiaries. The lump-sum option, on the other hand, potentially undermines the insurance of longevity. The system should thus be flexible enough to take into account socioeconomic changes. Options that satisfy the requirements today might not be the ones that do so when the current contributors retire.

NOTES

1. AHV = Alters- und Hinterbliebenen-Versicherung; AVS = Assurance Vieillesse et Survivants.
2. BVG = Bundesgesetz über die berufliche Alters-, Hinterlassenen- und Invalidenvorsorge, LPP = Loi fédérale sur la prévoyance professionnelle vieillesse, survivants et invalidité.
3. The linkage between pre-retirement earnings and the benefit level has become considerably weaker in the last two decades. A large majority of (potential) beneficiaries with a full contribution period are entitled to maximum benefits, so that earnings history only matters for people with low average wages and/or contribution gaps. In 1998, for example, an average married couple received more than 92 per cent of maximum benefits.
4. See Bütler (2002) and Table 10.1 for more details.
5. The last comprehensive poverty study in Switzerland dates back to 1992 (Leu et al., 1997). It reports a poverty rate of 5.6 per cent for the whole population, and of only 3.6 per cent for people beyond the legal retirement age. Recent numbers suggest that the general picture has remained unchanged.
6. Foreign immigrants, who make up approximately 20 per cent of the workforce, are net contributors at present. An increase in immigration is not really considered an option due to political resistance and the fact that the fertility rate of second-generation immigrants is very close to that of Swiss citizens.
7. SAKE/ESPA is a longitudinal (rolling panel) study of the Swiss labor market, but also covers individuals beyond the retirement age.
8. Focusing on annuities I again abstract from benefits (disability/survivor) during the accumulation period.
9. See also Section 10.4 for more details.

10. The 26 cantons are the Swiss states. They enjoy a considerable independence from the confederation in many important areas such as tax setting, schooling, and regulation.
11. The Suppletory Institution covers voluntary insured individuals as well as employees if the employer has not affiliated with an occupational pension provider despite legal provisions.
12. In the past, its reserves have always been less than 1/10 of the total accumulated retirement assets in Switzerland, and were even negative at times.
13. This fact has already been pointed out by other authors. See, for example, James and Song (2001) and Davis (2004).
14. James and Song (2001) argue that the used term structure of interest rates is probably too conservative, in other words too low. But since Swiss real interest rates have traditionally been considerably below European and US real interest rates (the difference is of the order of 1.5 per cent), discounting interest rates below 4 per cent seems very plausible.
15. The citation (originally in German) is taken from the weekly Swiss journal *Cash* (5 May 2000): 'Zwei Drittel der Beiträge stammen von den Arbeitgebern. Demzufolge gehören auch die Reserven zu einem Teil dem Arbeitgeber.'
16. Top managers of a big life insurer were reported to have borrowed large amounts of company money at very favorable conditions to invest in an investment found resulting in large purely private profits. Two former CEOs of an international firm allegedly used the company's pension fund to process huge golden parachute payments in order to benefit from a very favorable tax treatment.
17. This, of course, does not apply to pension providers entering the market (or new plans offered) after mid 2000. This fact had been used as an argument in favor of a decrease in the minimum rate.
18. As argued above, a reduction in the conversion factor is more difficult politically than a reduction in the minimum return as it affects vested claims more directly.
19. To do this, I pooled mortality and survival rates for male/female and married/single individuals. As the resulting MWR for a market interest rate equal to a mandated interest rate of 4 per cent is very close to one, the numbers in Figure 10.5 are normalized to 1 for this scenario.
20. As mentioned above, the second pillar also pays out benefits to widows and (semi-) orphans before the insured individual reaches retirement age. This section abstracts from this possibility. It is important to mention, however, that survivor benefits before retirement increase the intragenerational distribution in favor of married men.
21. This implies that Pr[M *alive*, S *alive*](J) = 1, and that for any $t \geq J$, Pr[M *alive*, S *alive*](t) + Pr[M *alive*, S *dead*](t) + Pr[M *dead*, S *alive*](t) + Pr[M *dead*, S *dead*](t) = 1 .
22. The analysis neglects the fact that couples usually coordinate their retirement decision. See Falkinger et al. (1996) for a nice illustration of this effect.
23. There are no detailed studies of differential mortality with respect to income in Switzerland. The situation is likely to be very close to countries like the Netherlands (Nelissen, 1999) and Germany (Reil-Held, 2001).
24. The data also contain some information concerning early retirement. The corresponding findings, however, are even more preliminary than for the choice between an annuity and a lump sum as the data are contaminated by various factors. Nevertheless, two results stand out as robust. The first is that early retirement seems to be *the* dominant option regardless of individual characteristics. If early retirement is possible, most people opt for it. The second result is that within the analysed plans, the 'rich', i.e., pensioners with higher levels of accumulated pension capital, often retire earlier than the 'poor'.
25. In Switzerland, there is clearly a tax advantage in withdrawing the accumulated pension wealth in the form of a lump sum. This effect is much stronger for high and very high levels of capital.
26. The higher the annuity, the lower the marginal utility of consumption. People might prefer to hold their pension wealth in the form of capital to be able to bequeath it to their children.
27. For further references concerning the acquiescence bias and other choice anomalies in funded pension plans see Benartzi and Thaler (2001) and Hurd (1999).

REFERENCES

Benartzi, S. and R.H. Thaler (2001), 'Naive Diversification Strategies in Defined Contribution Saving Plans', *American Economic Review*, **91**(1), 79–98.

Bundesamt für Statistik – Office fédéral de la statistique (2002), *Pensionskassenstatistik 2000: Die berufliche Vorsorge in der Schweiz*, Neuchâtel; more information is available on its webpage: www.bfs.admin.ch

Bütler, M. (2002), 'Flexibility and Redistribution in Old Age Insurance', *Swiss Journal of Economics and Statistics*, **138**(4), 427–37.

Bütler, M. and F. Teppa (2002), 'The Personal Discount Rate: Evidence from Swiss Pension Funds', Working Paper, CentER Tilburg and DEEP-HEC, University of Lausanne.

Davis, E.P. (2004), 'Issues in the regulation of annuities markets', Chapter 3 in this volume.

Cash (5 May 2000), 'Auf zum Kassenkampf'.

Falkinger, J., R.W. Ebmer and J. Zweimüller (1996), 'Joint Retirement of Spouses and Social Security Reform', *European Economic Review*, **40**, 449–72.

Hurd, M. (1999), 'Anchoring and Acquiescence Bias in Measuring Assets in Household Surveys', *Journal of Risk and Uncertainty*, **19**(1–3), 111–36.

James, E. and X. Song (2001), *Annuities Markets Around the World: Money's Worth and Risk Intermediation*, www.estellejames.com/downloads/aea_annuitites.pdf

Leu, R.E., S. Burri and P. Johnsons (1997), *Lebensqualität und Armut in der Schweiz*, Berne: Paul Haupt.

Nelissen, J.H.M. (1999), 'Mortality Differences Related to Socioeconomic Status and Progressivity of Old-age Pensions and Health Insurance: The Netherlands', *European Journal of Population*, **15**, 77–97.

Queisser, M. and D. Vittas (2000), 'The Swiss Multi-Pillar Pension System: Triumph of Common Sense', Working paper, The World Bank.

Reil-Held, A. (2001), *Einkommen und Sterblichkeit in Deutschland: Leben Reiche länger?*, Sonderforschungsbereich 504, University of Mannheim.

Shane, F., G. Loewenstein and T. O'Donoghue (2002), 'Time Discounting: A Critical Review', *Journal of Economic Literature*, **40**, 351–401.

11. The market for annuities in Italy: reality or chimera?*

Margherita Borella, Elsa Fornero and Giacomo Ponzetto

11.1 THE BUILDING OF A PENSION MARKET

As a counterbalance to the 1990s reforms directed at strengthening the long-term sustainability of the social security system – and therefore at reducing its overall generosity – Italy witnessed, during the same period, an intense, although not very effective, legislative action aimed at developing supplementary private pensions.[1]

While a certain number of company schemes already existed, in particular in the financial sector, in macroeconomic terms they were of very limited weight, and operated out of any regulatory framework. In 1993 the government set out to change this situation with a first law[2] establishing and supporting *occupational pension funds*. According to the new rules, these funds – also called 'closed' because participation is, for each of them, restricted to a predefined category of workers – are voluntary, fully-funded defined contribution schemes. They are created and managed jointly by employers' and employees' representatives of an entire industry or region, and they constitute separate legal entities, which cannot be owned, nor directly managed, by the sponsoring companies.[3]

A subsequent law[4] introduced *individual pension plans*, in the form of either 'open' pension funds established by financial and insurance companies or specific annuity policies offered by the latter (generally known by the acronym PIP). These third pillar products are basically tax-advantaged long-term saving plans, very similar respectively to mutual funds and traditional life insurance policies, but with mandated restrictions on capital withdrawals.

* Financial support by MIUR (Italian Ministry for Education, University and Research) is gratefully acknowledged.

Between these two main laws, a few other interventions have tried to pave the way for what was considered (and still is) a missing element of the Italian economy, that is, a non-negligible funded component of pension wealth, viewed as a crucial factor not only for the pension system but also for the privatisation process and the development of financial and insurance markets. A unified consistent design of supplementary pensions is however still lacking.[5] The various laws enacted in the last few years instead constitute a complicated series of piecemeal interventions, partly based on misconceptions and 'illusions', such as the somewhat artificial distinction between employees and independent workers and the expectation of easy financing through already available resources.

On the one hand, the current setup is centered on the provision of supplementary pensions for employees, particularly private employees, and rests on the assumption that these workers deserve more *paternalistic protection* than other categories. They are thus strongly encouraged to enroll in the more heavily regulated occupational pension funds – governed by representatives of trade unions and firms – and discouraged from taking too much personal responsibility for their pension wealth. Such a conception, however, seems based on outdated models of the labor market: it is debatable that employees as a whole are currently a weaker and financially less educated group than the self-employed, and it is also evident that the least protected category is made up of a large number of 'non-typical' workers, employed part-time or on short-term contracts, with a much lower payroll tax rate for public pensions and with little possibility of financing their own private pension. Moreover, even occupational pension funds, like individual pension plans, put all the risks on the workers, so that they are quite different from the so-called second pillar, which typically provides pensions on a defined benefit basis.

On the other hand, the financing of supplementary pensions has always been left scarce room because the reforms of the first pillar have reduced future benefits but not the contribution rates, which will continue to be as high as 33 per cent for employees.[6] Given the high replacement rates still granted by the public system in the long transition towards the new regime, even a relatively generous tax treatment would perhaps have had limited effectiveness in determining either a diversion of already existing saving flows or an increase in savings. The normative 'solution' to this problem was to identify, as the ideal candidate to finance supplementary pensions, the annual flow of contributions destined for the accumulation of severance pay (TFR for *Trattamento di fine rapporto*), amounting to almost 7 per cent of the wage bill. TFR and pension fund assets proved, however, to be very imperfect substitutes in the workers' choices.

11.2 THE FINANCING OF PRIVATE PENSIONS: THE TFR DEVOLUTION

TFR is a form of severance pay which private sector employees receive when employment is, for whatever reason, terminated.[7] As such, it acts as a sort of unemployment insurance, but also as a source of liquidity when the worker voluntarily resigns or retires. Moreover, after eight years of continuous employment, workers can obtain an advance of up to 70 per cent of the accumulated fund, provided the sum is used to pay for health expenditures or as a down payment in the purchase of a house. Financially, TFR is fuelled by a deduction of 6.91 per cent of gross wages, earns a legal interest rate of 1.5 per cent plus 3/4 of the inflation rate and 'accumulates' as book reserves, representing a liability in the balance sheet of the employer.

TFR has always been prominent in the attempts to build a funded pension component in Italy. As a *stock*, it represents, on the one hand, a significant asset in the Italian households' portfolios, amounting to about 10 per cent of GDP;[8] on the other, a very important source of low-cost financing for companies, especially for small and medium-sized firms (which are very important in the Italian economy). In the light of the last consideration the transfer to pension funds of the stock was ruled out, while that of the annual flow – still representing a costly switch from the accrual of a liability to a negative cash flow – was at the heart of the government attempts to promote pension funds, with the provision of both fiscal incentives and a rather byzantine system of TFR '*securitization*'.

As for workers, they were not expected to be particularly reluctant to divert their TFR flows, since its legal return, being lower than the cost of financing for companies, was also supposed to be lower than expected returns to be earned by pension funds in the financial markets. At any rate, the government chose to earmark the TFR flow as the main source of pension savings by conditioning the tax allowances on its diversion: employees can only make tax-exempt contributions to a pension plan up to twice the amount of the transferred TFR flow.[9] However, irrespective of the outdated and inefficient features of TFR as an instrument to allocate credit[10] and of the fiscal incentives to divert the annual flows, this diversion has taken place only on a very small scale, thus limiting the development of supplementary pensions.

From an economic point of view, this evolution is not too surprising, for TFR was not meant to be a form of retirement savings in the first place, having rather the role of precautionary savings against spells of unemployment, or the possibility of liquidity constraints when purchasing a house, or unpredictable shocks during retirement.[11]

The problem of the low substitutability between the two forms of savings was explicitly recognized only in 1999, when the same liquidity options applying to TFR were introduced for pension plans, in terms of: advances; of possible withdrawals at job termination; of choosing a lump sum up to 50 per cent of the accumulated assets at retirement.[12]

If the liquidity aspects have thus been tackled,[13] the risk-return profile of pension funds and TFR remains starkly different: the latter has a guaranteed return, defined partly in nominal terms and partly as an inflation adjustment; the former, on the contrary, expose participants to the full risk, as well as the opportunities, of financial markets. The issue is relevant not only with reference to the capitalized value available at retirement, but also with respect to the amount that the worker may need, during the accumulation phase, precisely to overcome liquidity constraints.

The trade-off between precautionary savings and pension savings manifests itself here in the likelihood of different planning horizons and, consequently, different asset allocations. A first concern is that mandating the substitution of the two forms of savings may by itself introduce undesirable distortions, since pension fund participants are prohibited from segmenting their pension portfolio into separate sub-accounts.[14] As a matter of fact, a majority of occupational pension funds have chosen the legal TFR return as a benchmark, and as a result they are investing heavily in the money market, contrary to theoretical predictions. Moreover, a conservative short-term investment strategy, while possibly unsuited to pension savings, does not even represent a perfect match for the chosen benchmark, since the latter includes partial inflation adjustment, while even short-term interest rates sometimes fail to make up for the full impact of future inflation. Although companies are supposed to be eager to issue debt at an interest rate equal to the legal TFR return, none has so far done so, presumably out of the conviction that no pension fund would buy such securities because of credit risk. Inflation-indexed government bonds, which have been considered but not issued by the Italian government, would obviously be a safer investment.[15]

Financial guarantees, however, are not in general developed in the Italian pensions market: financial engineering and the use of hedging and derivatives seem to be currently non-existent, presumably due to the requirement that pension fund assets be constantly marked to market and available for withdrawal at any time.[16] Open pension funds do routinely offer nominal guarantees, with occupational funds expected to follow suit in the future; but these guarantees invariably accompany conservative money market and bond investments, and are simply set at a level of average return which is apparently considered a credible floor for future government bond yields, ranging from zero to 2.5 per cent.[17] Insurers have greater room for manoeuvre, as they are not bound to mark assets to market: traditional with-profit annuities rely on book value, and about half the existing PIPs have adopted this structure.[18] Companies set up a separate investment account and guarantee a minimum annual return which is 'locked in' at the end of the year, instead of an average return over the whole duration of the policy. However, the guarantee is essentially similar to those offered by pension funds.[19] The assets backing the policies are almost exclusively bonds, with a prevalence of Italian government securities, and the guaranteed rate currently ranges from 1 to 2.5 per cent, being also subject to a legal ceiling of the lower between 3 per cent and 60 per cent of the average yield of long-term government bonds.

Proposals have been mooted to allow pension plans to offer guaranteed returns and simultaneously pursue more aggressive investment strategies, by entering into expressly tailored insurance contracts. These would exploit the exemption from market valuation and harness the considerable experience which insurers acquired in the past by predicting TFR outflows when selling specific policies to individual companies.

Nevertheless, several important issues need to be worked out before such a solution can become operational. To begin with, pension funds are prohibited from relinquishing ownership of assets and buying insurance policies, for the sake of transparency and liquidity.[20] Moreover, the law seems to allow only nominal guarantees, and not the arguably more valuable real variety which would be possible given sufficient depth of the Euro inflation-indexed securities market. Finally and most important, although insurers are legally permitted to apply book valuation not only to securities but also to riskier and higher-yielding asset classes, such as equities, caution has always led them to avoid experimenting with such strategies.

11.3 THE TAX REGIME

In most countries, preferential tax treatment is the main incentive to contribute to a voluntary private pension scheme. Pension saving is encouraged firstly as a long-term commitment, and secondly as a means of financing old-age consumption through a life-insured distribution, namely an annuity: it follows that tax advantages are, at least partially, conditional on annuitization of the accumulated funds.

Italy is no exception to this general rule, yet its tax system is different from most others in that the annual investment income earned on pension assets is taxed, albeit at a favourable rate. This contrasts with the widespread adoption of a pure expenditure taxation, which taxes only pension income (in so-called EET schemes) or, less frequently, only contributions (TEE schemes). The Italian system technically has an ETT structure, since pension annuities are also taxed; yet such a classification risks being profoundly misleading, because the regime does not fit into any of the standard schemes. In fact, payouts are only partially subject to the regular income tax: the share resulting from investment income already taxed during the accumulation phase is tax-exempt. Therefore, the system actually lies between ETT and an exceptionally generous ETE.[21] This rather complicated structure reflects both the desire of the fiscal authorities not to postpone taxes too much, and the principle of no double taxation.

From the households' point of view, the real advantage is that pension plan participants are allowed to earn investment income on deferred income taxes;[22] in other words, to defer taxes, perhaps by decades, without increasing their nominal amount.[23] The resulting overall tax rate is lower than the personal income tax rate, leading to a greater tax advantage than that of a classical EET scheme, irrespective of the anticipated levy on investment income.[24]

Yet it should also be remarked that this fiscal regime (see Box 1) has two arguably undesirable effects: first, it reduces the progressivity of the tax system, by granting a greater advantage to wealthier people whose income tax rate is higher; second, it might encourage riskier investments, since it reduces the volatility of net asset returns. Of course, both effects actually constitute a reduction in distortions caused by traditional taxation, probably unintentionally in so far as return volatility is concerned.

11.4 MARKET SEGMENTATION

In addition to being the crucial source of pension savings and a prerequisite for tax advantages, TFR devolution is also the cornerstone of a complex set of distinctions illustrated in Figure 11.1 below.

On the demand side, different modes of participation ought to mirror the distinction between the second and the third pillar. However, it is actually very difficult to discern in the Italian framework any significant element distinguishing the two: collective participation seems to be little more than a formal condition for TFR diversion, effectively precluding employees from participating in tax-advantaged individual pension plans. On the supply side, on the contrary, the distinction between various kinds of pension schemes has more substantial implications, particularly with regards to costs, as will be shown in the following section.

The separation of the two pillars should arguably relate first and foremost to risk aspects. Even if the classification is not completely scientific, it is widely understood that occupational pensions in an international context are epitomized by the defined benefit (DB) company plan: managed more or less directly by the employer, such a plan is usually mandatory, characterized by risk sharing between employer and employees, and by elements of redistribution among workers; as such, the scheme is fully integrated within the employment contract, and it acquires a crucial role as an incentive device in labor relations.[25]

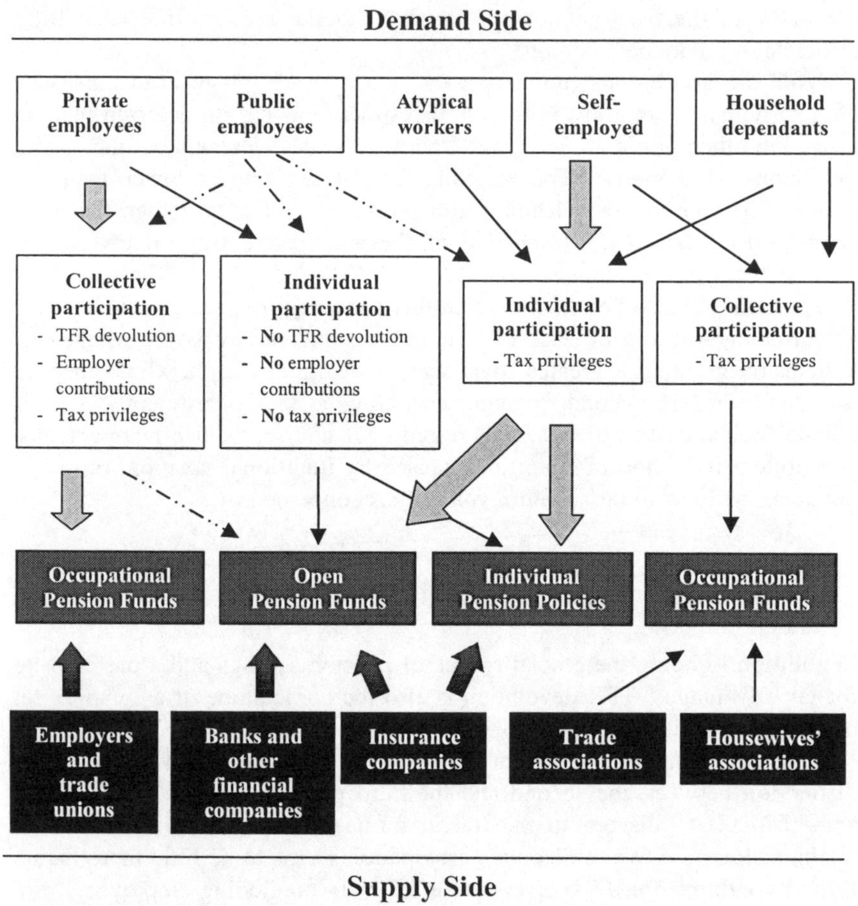

Figure 11.1 The structure of the Italian market for private pensions

On the contrary, in Italy all private pension plans share the structure of voluntary defined contribution (DC) schemes, with financial and longevity risks borne by participants during the accumulation phase, and with annuity provision aiming at actuarial fairness rather than *ex ante* redistribution. This choice can be justified both by the major role played by social security and in the light of labor market trends showing a world-wide shift from DB to DC plans; yet it also warrants the doubt that a single private pillar actually exists in Italy.

In fact, on the one hand, 'occupational' pension funds also exist for the self-employed and for housewives, who are free to join them under the same rules governing individual participation in an open pension fund or the purchase of an annuity. On the other hand, collective participation in a pension fund by employees is required for TFR devolution, employer contribution and tax advantages, but it seems to entail simply that trade unions and employers, rather than the individual worker, choose the fund and set the contribution rate.[26]

The relevance of fund selection derives from the fact that, although either a closed or an open pension fund could theoretically be selected, a number of legal hurdles have been created effectively preventing the choice of the latter. This segmentation is questionable from a theoretical point of view, and various arguments support a level playing field for all pension funds. Yet, from an empirical perspective a defense of the status quo can also be made (as it has been by the trade unions) based on the premise that occupational funds are safer and more efficient than other retirement saving vehicles.[27]

A skepticism on market capacity to deliver good pensions undoubtedly underpins part of the preference accorded to occupational pension funds. At the same time, there does exist an apparent progression of institutional guarantees protecting pension plan participants.

As we have seen, a closed pension fund is a legal entity with a board of directors composed of employers' and employees' representatives; the board has to delegate portfolio management to professional managers, but the fund retains ownership of all assets. An open pension fund, on the contrary, is owned by the sponsoring financial company, although the fund is legally separated from the assets of the company, and not only must it be professionally managed in the sole interest of participants, but it is also protected from appropriation by the sponsoring company as well as from any claims of its creditors.[28]

These differences suggest that the main peculiarity of occupational pension funds belongs to the realm of corporate governance, since they are the only financial instrument where voting rights resulting from stock ownership are not necessarily exercised by professional managers. In so far as investor protection is concerned, however, open and closed pension funds are subject to fairly homogeneous rules, as well as being supervised by the same authority.[29]

BOX 1 FOCUS ON THE FISCAL REGIME

Contributions are tax-exempt up to a yearly ceiling of 12 per cent of income, or 5165€ if lower; moreover, as already seen, contributions from the labor income of private sector employees are only exempt up to a limit of twice the amount of TFR flows diverted to the pension scheme.

Investment income, including interest and capital gains net of past losses, earned in the accumulation phase is taxed yearly at a favorable rate of 11 per cent, compared to a regular rate of 12.5 per cent.

At retirement, annuitization of at least half the accumulated capital is mandatory, but the fiscal treatment strongly discourages lump-sum withdrawals of more than one third of assets.

Private pensions are divided into:

- the share corresponding to investment income earned after retirement, which is taxed at the 12.5 per cent rate;
- the share corresponding to previously tax-exempt contributions, which is taxed at the regular income tax rate;
- the share corresponding to investment income earned before retirement, which is not taxed, having already been taxed (at the favorable 11 per cent rate) during the accumulation phase.

Lump-sum capital withdrawal options are subject to a rather complex tax treatment, aimed at creating a hierarchy of more or less favored alternatives. They are granted the same advantages if up to one third of assets is taken out as advances and retirement lump sum combined: the sum of past contributions is taxed at the average rate of income tax calculated over the previous five years, and no tax is due on the rest of the withdrawn capital. If the limit is exceeded, on the contrary, the full withdrawn amount, instead of the sum of original contributions, is taxed at the average income tax rate, unless the total accumulated funds provide a pension lower than 75 per cent of the social allowance (that is, 3328.5€). Finally, during the accumulation phase, if plan participation is terminated because the worker voluntarily left his/her job, the sum of past contributions is taxed at the marginal, instead of the average, income tax rate.

Unsurprisingly, institutional guarantees are negatively correlated with contractual commitments. It has already been mentioned that insurers, not being required to mark assets to market, can offer a yearly return guarantee, while pension funds can only guarantee an average return over longer periods (so far only open funds have done so). The difference is even more pronounced when demographic instead of financial risks are considered. Pension funds are largely untouched by this issue: they simply negotiate on behalf of retiring participants a group immediate annuity contract at favorable rates. PIPs are allowed to act in the same way, by defining mortality tables only when annuity payments begin; but they can also choose to sell deferred annuities with annuity rates locked in at the time of purchase, possibly up to 40 years in advance.

Such a guarantee should logically be valuable for workers, even if there is no evidence that they are currently willing to pay for it, since those contracts offering it are not on average costlier than the others. This is also a ground for some concern, since it underlines the difficulties in properly pricing demographic guarantees, while it is well known that predetermining annuity rates based on uncertain mortality forecasts represents a significant risk for insurance companies.

11.5 THE COST OF PRIVATE PENSIONS

A common argument in favor of the second pillar is its lower costs, deriving from its predefined area of demand, which allows both a significant reduction of marketing and sales costs and substantial economies of scale in asset management.

This argument is also borne out by empirical evidence, as summarized by a recent European Union report: 'in Italy overall management costs of closed pension funds were estimated at 0.57 per cent of the value of assets – which represents a significant reduction in real returns. Open funds incur considerably higher costs, but not as high as private pension schemes operating through life insurance policies.'[30] The latest figures computed by the regulator present an average cost/assets ratio of 0.61 per cent for the 14 completely operational closed pension funds, compared to an estimated annual charge over a 35-year period of 1.3 per cent for open pension funds, and 1.8 per cent for PIPs.[31]

A comparison with the costs of actively managed investment vehicles shows that Italian pension funds are broadly in line with international standards: for instance, James et al. (2001) report an average cost/assets ratio of 1.52 per cent for actively managed US mutual funds, and 0.81 per cent for institutional funds such as occupational pension schemes. PIPs are costlier, but the higher cost might be imputed to financial and demographic guarantees or to the greater portfolio choice which can be offered to plan participants. A more detailed analysis of costs provides nonetheless some interesting insights.

For third-pillar schemes, management charges are predetermined and specified in the contractual documents: on this basis, the cost of these products may be estimated by a simple simulation model.[32] Of course, as with any long-term financial product, costs cannot be measured at any point in time, but only over the whole duration of plan membership, since charges are levied in a number of different ways.

The results presented in Table 11.1 are based on a simple set of stylised assumptions.[33] Quarterly contributions are supposed to be proportional to earnings, with the contribution rate growing in time up to a maximum of 10 per cent at the end of working life; earnings are derived from estimates of the income profile of the median private sector employee. Three scenarios are considered, with a common retirement age set at 65 years: a 50-year-old worker choosing a bond portfolio with a constant annual nominal return of 4 per cent; a 40-year-old choosing a balanced portfolio with a return of 5 per cent; and a 30-year-old choosing an equity portfolio with a return of 6 per cent. A constant inflation rate of 2 per cent is always assumed.

A final hypothesis concerns indirect charges levied by PIPs. In fact, these can and usually do invest in mutual funds and similar financial products, whose charges are then added to those paid to the insurance company itself.[34] The contracts specify an admissible range for these costs, and simulation results are presented considering both the minimum and the average value.

After computing the accumulated capital at retirement, two comprehensive charge measures are proposed: the equivalent annual fee and the equivalent front-loaded fee. The former is defined as the yearly management charge proportional to assets which would lead to the same final capital in the absence of other fees: in other words, it is the reduction in yield due to management costs.[35] The latter is analogously defined as the percentage levy on contributions which would lead to the same final capital in the absence of other fees: namely the charge ratio (or premium loading) due to management costs.

The analysis is based on a sample of the 34 open pension funds sponsored by the ten most important groups, with an overall market share of more than 80 per cent, and 25 equally representative PIPs.[36]

The main and most striking result is the substantial difference between open pension funds and PIPs: under the hypothesis of average indirect charges, insurance products are approximately twice as costly.

This result is clearly sensitive to assumptions regarding indirect charges: if these are set at a lower level, overall cost estimates also fall. However,

Table 11.1 Equivalent fees of individual pension plans

	15 years – 4% return		25 years – 5% return		35 years – 6% return	
	Annual	Front-loaded	Annual	Front-loaded	Annual	Front-loaded
Open pension funds:						
Average[a]	1.00 %	7.19 %	1.24 %	14.03 %	1.46 %	21.66 %
Minimum	0.60 %	4.39 %	0.60 %	7.14 %	0.60 %	9.68 %
Maximum	1.69 %	11.81 %	1.87 %	20.28 %	2.15 %	29.90 %
Market leaders[b]	0.81 %	5.90 %	1.15 %	13.13 %	1.42 %	21.20 %
PIPs:						
average indirect charges						
Average[a]	2.08 %	14.23 %	2.42 %	25.23 %	2.52 %	33.80 %
Minimum	1.01 %	7.26 %	1.22 %	13.91 %	1.20 %	18.21 %
Maximum	3.15 %	20.60 %	3.30 %	32.41 %	3.81 %	45.43 %
Market leaders[c]	2.48 %	16.71 %	2.47 %	25.71 %	2.70 %	35.63 %
PIPs:						
minimum indirect charges						
Average[a]	1.84 %	12.75 %	1.97 %	21.20 %	2.04 %	28.67 %
Minimum	1.01 %	7.26 %	1.19 %	13.61 %	1.20 %	18.21 %
Maximum	2.90 %	19.13 %	2.81 %	28.57 %	3.73 %	44.84 %
Market leaders[c]	2.02 %	13.88 %	1.58 %	17.55 %	1.81 %	25.93 %

Notes:

a. Unweighted arithmetic average

b. Average of the 11 open pension funds sponsored by the two most important groups

c. For the 15-year scenario: average of the two products with the largest market shares, one a with-profits annuity and the other a unit-linked policy; for the longer scenarios only the unit-linked policy is considered.

insurers are not forced to avoid costly mutual fund investments, and they might even have a perverse incentive to choose them to generate a profit for asset managers in their same group.[37]

Moreover, as shown by the data above and confirmed by the estimates of the COVIP, even with lower indirect charges PIPs still have equivalent annual fees on average more than 50 basis points higher than pension funds, a difference hardly motivated by differences in guarantees. Demographic guarantees have little impact on price, and if anything reduce it.[38] As for financial guarantees, Table 11.2 below shows that with-profits annuities with a minimum guaranteed yearly return have lower average charges than bond accounts in unit-linked policies, although a large part of the discrepancy is due to indirect charges.

Table 11.2 Comparison between the equivalent fees of the two kinds of pension annuity policy – 15 years – 4 per cent return

	With-profits annuities		**Unit-linked annuities average indirect charges**		**Unit-linked annuities minimum indirect charges**	
	Annual	Front-loaded	Annual	Front-loaded	Annual	Front-loaded
Average	1.74 %	12.12 %	2.42 %	16.33 %	1.94 %	13.37 %
Minimum	1.01 %	7.26 %	1.30 %	9.19 %	1.18 %	8.43 %
Maximum	2.59 %	17.36 %	3.15 %	20.60 %	2.90 %	19.13 %
Market leader	2.59 %	17.36 %	2.38 %	16.07 %	1.48 %	10.39 %

While these data refer to preliminary evidence, they warrant the doubt that some personal pension providers might rather pursue a short-sighted strategy than aim at consolidating the market in the long run, possibly with a convergence toward the level of efficiency already attained by a small minority of PIPs. Room to reduce open pension fund costs also exists, even if their average is already aligned with international standards.[39]

The comparison with closed pension funds is not straightforward, since these do not have contractually predefined charges, so that their costs can only be computed *ex post*. For the year 2001, only eight closed pension funds were fully operational, and the ratio of costs to average assets[40] ranged from 0.58 per cent to 2.39 per cent, with an unweighted average of 1.08 per cent. However, these figures reflect mainly administrative costs, with asset management charges reaching a maximum of 0.31 per cent; therefore, there should be ample room for economies of scale, a view which is borne out both by the value of the asset-weighted average cost, amounting only to 0.70 per cent, and by the ongoing reduction of cost ratios.[41] In the long term, a credible estimate of average charges lies in an interval from 50 to 100 basis points.

The tentative conclusion may be reached that the conventional wisdom on the lower costs of the second pillar compared to the third is confirmed by Italian experience; but also that the gap between PIPs and open pension funds is at least as great, and possibly more significant, than the one between the latter and closed pension funds.

A final point could be made concerning annuitization, which is eventually mandatory with few exceptions. So far, no annuities are being paid out by private pension plans, so that any discussion of pricing is purely hypothetical. Closed pension funds have not even yet finalized the required partnership with insurance companies, and thus have not declared prospective annuity rates. Individual plans have, but their rates are still susceptible to change, as has already been mentioned. As a rule, annuity rates are based on the RG48 projected annuitant mortality tables, expressly developed by the insurers' association (*Associazione Nazionale tra le Imprese Assicuratrici* or ANIA) from government mortality forecasts and British selection factors.[42]

Moreover, approximately uniform pricing is expected, since participants are effectively offered an 'open market option', given that they may switch from one plan to another at retirement. This rule is particularly relevant in that it applies to occupational funds as well: since the accumulation phase is over, TFR devolution and the entailed tax advantage no longer limit mobility between the second and the third pillar. As the regulator observes, this precludes closed pension funds from choosing unisex mortality tables, given that individual plans employ instead mortality assumptions differentiated by gender.[43]

11.6 HOW THE CHANGES IN INSTITUTIONAL FRAMEWORK ALTERED HOUSEHOLDS' ATTITUDES TOWARDS ANNUITIES

During the 1990s the percentage of Italian families owning private pensions and life insurance contracts increased substantially, although it remains lower than in other EU countries. The determinants of this trend can be found in the substantial reform process undergone by the Italian social security system in the same period, which reduced average pension entitlements – especially for younger worker cohorts – and sought to provide incentives for the private demand for old-age benefits.[44] This section investigates whether the reforms of the social security system and the subsequent reduction in public pension wealth held by families have led to an increase in 'contractual' savings, that is, savings for retirement in the form of either private pensions or life insurance contracts.[45]

The analysis is conducted using a sample drawn from the Bank of Italy Survey of Household Income and Wealth (SHIW). The data show, during the 1990s, a significant increase in the percentage of families owning private pensions and/or life insurance contracts, as already documented, for example, by Guiso and Jappelli (2001). As shown in the descriptive analysis, private pension and life insurance owners are typically younger, better educated and wealthier than non-owners.

A reduced-form approach is followed to identify the determinants of the probability of a household to own a private pension or a life insurance contract. As the reforms of the social security system changed the expected value of public pension wealth in different ways for different groups of people, we use this variation to identify the effect of public pension wealth on the probability of buying a private pension or a life insurance contract.[46]

The results show that both life insurance and private pension demand are increasing in income, financial wealth, and education. Public pension wealth reduces the probability of purchasing private pensions at younger ages, while its effect tends to zero in the age range of 40–50. As for life insurance, the estimate of the effect of public pension wealth is negative, but small and not significantly different from zero.[47]

11.6.1 Data and Sample Selection

The sample used in the analysis has been drawn from six waves of the Bank of Italy Survey of Household Income and Wealth (SHIW), covering the period from 1989 to 2000.[48] The SHIW is the most comprehensive survey of individual data in Italy. It contains detailed information on household members' demographic characteristics, labor supply variables as well as financial and real wealth.[49] Crucial information about ownership of private pensions and life insurance contracts was collected in the survey at the family level until 1993; since 1995 the information collected is more detailed and at the individual level, and can be used to analyse the sample in a deeper investigation. For estimation purposes, however, the years up to 1993 are crucial to identify the effect of public pension wealth on the probability of owning a private pension or a life insurance contract. For this reason, estimation is carried out over the whole sample from 1989 to 2000 and only family-level information is used.

An important issue concerns the definition of 'private pensions' as distinct from 'life insurance contracts' in the SHIW data collection questionnaire. The section on *Insurance* contains a first subsection on *Life insurance contracts* asking if the household owns life insurance, and a second one on

Private (supplementary) pensions, annuities and other forms of insurance savings, asking if the household 'has contributed to a private (or supplementary) pension, an annuity or even an endowment policy'. It follows that term and whole-life insurance is necessarily reported in the first subsection, while private pensions which are not sold by insurance companies belong to the second. Deferred annuities and endowment policies, which constitute the bulk of life insurance contracts sold in Italy, could, however, be recorded in either section: as mixed life insurance in the first or as insurance savings in the second. The deciding factor seems to be the perception of the respondent: contracts reported under the label of private pensions are bound to be perceived as a long-term commitment and in particular as contractual retirement savings, while those reported as life insurance are more likely to represent precautionary savings.

It should be noted that, in any case, a large majority of private pensions recorded in our sample are life insurance contracts. The data show that only a small fraction of private pension owners were enrolled in group schemes: 10 per cent in the year 2000. COVIP (2001) reports that in the same year open (that is, individual) pension funds had 223 032 participants, compared to 1 569 546 for occupational funds. Therefore, we estimate that about 1.4 per cent of private pensions reported in the SHIW took the form of participation in an open pension plan. Since PIPs could not be sold before 2001, it follows that almost 90 per cent of private pensions were in fact traditional (with-profits or unit-linked) insurance policies.

Sample selection has been carried out as follows. Households whose head was born before 1925 and after 1964 have been selected out. In addition, households whose head is self-employed have been excluded due to the extreme difficulty of computing their public pension wealth: they represent a heterogeneous group to which quite different pension rules apply. It is nonetheless important to report that the percentage of families owning a private pension or life insurance contract is almost double among the self-employed.

After applying these selection criteria, the whole sample consists of 21 856 households, observed from 1989 to 2000. On average, in the selected sample, buyers are younger, better educated and wealthier than non buyers (Table 11.3). For each individual, gross public pension wealth has been calculated as the present value (computed at the year of the interview) of future pension entitlements; net pension wealth is equal to gross PPW minus the present value of future contributions to be paid. Both net and gross PPW have been computed for the head of the household and, when present, for the spouse, and then aggregated.[50] While both net and gross PPW are higher for life insurance and private pension buyers than for non-buyers, the lower value of net PPW of private pension owners compared to life insurance owners reflects the fact that on average the former are younger.[51]

Table 11.3 Head and household characteristics

	Life insurance	Private pension	LI+PP	Total
Head age	46.96	45.28	46.67	50.26
Head married	88%	85%	87%	83%
Head male	86%	85%	86%	84%
Head higher education	55%	60%	55%	38%
No. of income recipients	1.91	1.93	1.91	1.81
No. HH components	3.43	3.21	3.38	3.17
No. of children	1.22	1.05	1.18	0.99
Resident in the South	31%	12%	27%	33%
Disposable income	34.07	35.96	34.07	27.79
Total assets	160.73	160.63	158.71	120.78
Gross PPW	345.35	345.27	344.14	302.44
Net PPW	260.79	245.64	257.51	240.07
No. of observations	4344	1317	5300	21 856

Note: monetary values are expressed in thousands of € at constant prices (year 2000).

Source: selected sample from SHIW (1989–2000).

Exploiting the time dimension of the data, Table 11.4 reports the percentages of families owning private pensions or life insurance contracts by year. Participation increased over the observed period for both assets, from 15.4 per cent in 1989 to 22.5 per cent in 2000 for life insurance contracts, and from 4.9 per cent in 1989 to 8.6 per cent in 2000 for private pensions.

Table 11.4 Percentage of households participating in the market, by year

	1989	1991	1993	1995	1998	2000	Overall
Life insurance							
% participants	15.42	18.64	21.97	19.07	21.12	22.47	19.88
Private pension							
% participants	4.86	4.99	6.64	5.32	5.41	8.60	6.03
No. of families	3333	3590	3568	3780	3584	4001	21 856

Source: selected sample from SHIW (1989–2000).

11.6.2 Model Specification

Probit models have been estimated to study the probability of ownership for both life insurance contracts and private pensions. It is expected that the reduction in future pension entitlements which occurred during the 1990s boosted the demand for contractual savings, especially for those households who experienced a substantial reduction in their pension wealth and still had time to save for their retirement, that is for younger households. Therefore, in order to capture the effect of public pension wealth on ownership at different ages, the specification includes the variable PPW interacted with a polynomial in the age of the household's head.[52] Other characteristics included are wealth, household disposable income, level of education of the household's head and some demographic variables expected to influence the decision to buy a life insurance contract or a private pension, such as the number of children and the number of earners. In order to control for aggregate effects and for fixed group effects, year and cohort dummies are also included.[53]

11.6.3 Estimation Results

Tables 11.5 and 11.6 report the estimates of the probability of life insurance and private pension ownership respectively. For life insurance ownership, the public pension wealth variable has been interacted with age only, as the interaction with higher powers of age did not yield different results: although the effect of pension wealth is negative, especially at younger ages, the coefficients are not precisely estimated and are not statistically different from zero. The probability of investing in life insurance contracts is increasing with income and wealth. The effect of an increase in income is substantial: raising it from about 17 to 35 thousand € (that is from the 25th to the 75th percentile of the income distribution) raises the predicted probability by 8.7 percentage points. Raising wealth from 8 to 162 thousand € (again, moving from the 25th to the 75th percentile of the distribution) raises the predicted probability by 14.5 percentage points. Being resident in Central Italy raises the probability of ownership by approximately 4 percentage points, as does having a higher education. The number of children also raises the predicted probability, while being a male, being married, and being a pensioner or a private employee (rather than a public sector employee – the excluded category) do not have an effect statistically different from zero. Being resident in Northern Italy is not statistically different from being resident in the South (the excluded category). The number of income recipients in the household is, *ceteris paribus*, negatively correlated with life insurance ownership, which could indicate that risk sharing occurs in the family. The dummy variables for year indicate that the probability of owning increased over time, with a spike in 1993.

Turning to private pension ownership, public pension wealth interacted with a third-degree polynomial in age is estimated to have an effect statistically different from zero and to be quantitatively important. The marginal effect by age, computed at the sample means, is plotted in Figure 11.2: this is negative and quantitatively important at the beginning of the life cycle, and subsequently increases, reaching zero at around age 40–50. At age 30, for example, average pension wealth is equal to about 115 000 €; increasing it by 1 percentage point would lower the probability of buying a private pension by about 1 percentage point.

Disposable income has a positive effect on the predicted probability, raising it by 2.9 percentage points when moving from the 25th to the 75th percentile of the income distribution (approximately from 17 to 35 thousand €); wealth raises the probability of owning a private pension by 4 per cent when moving from the 25th to the 75th percentile of the distribution (that is, from about 8 to 162 thousand €). The number of income recipients has a negative effect on the probability of ownership, while being resident in Northern (Central) Italy increases the probability by 5.6 (4.9) percentage points with respect to being resident in the South. Private employees, *ceteris paribus*, as well as better educated heads of households, are more likely to invest in private pensions, with a marginal effect equal to 1.7 and 1.6 percentage points respectively.

In conclusion, we have found that the decrease in public pension wealth faced by Italian families during the 1990s does help in explaining the increase in the share of households owning private pensions, as defined above, while it seems to have no significant effect on the percentage of families owning other kinds of life insurance contracts. In other words, the analysis warrants the deduction that Italians are increasingly aware of the need for private pension provision. However, the number of families actually engaged in contractual saving schemes is still quite low up to 2000, the last available year of data. Furthermore, the use of occupational schemes and pension funds in general as a vehicle for retirement savings was extremely limited. This could be a consequence of inadequate incentives; indeed, it should be borne in mind that tax advantages for pension funds only came into effect in 2001.

Whether these will suffice to promote the growth of dedicated pension plans remains to be seen: for the time being, similar schemes still represent no more than a small fraction of the assets of Italian households.[54]

Table 11.5 Probability of owning: life insurance

	Coef.	Std. err.	P>|z|	dF/dx
PPW	–0.00016	0.000459	0.729	–4.1E–05
PPW*age	5.45E–06	8.14E–06	0.503	1.40E–06
Family income	0.026778	0.002862	0	0.006879
Family income^2/10	–0.00148	0.000261	0	–0.00038
Financial wealth	0.0009	0.000169	0	0.000231
Financial wealth^2/10	–6.57E–07	1.74E–07	0	–1.69E–07
Married	–0.02697	0.042252	0.523	–0.00699
No. of income recipients	–0.03428	0.019462	0.078	–0.00881
No. of children	0.058236	0.014429	0	0.01496
North	–0.00261	0.031684	0.934	–0.00067
Centre	0.155051	0.035437	0	0.041484
Male	0.058703	0.039146	0.134	0.0148
Private employee	–0.02007	0.031279	0.521	–0.00514
Pensioner	–0.04903	0.049116	0.318	–0.01254
Higher education	0.154539	0.02876	0	0.040368
Year 91	0.152966	0.035498	0	0.04117
Year 93	0.262192	0.037299	0	0.072825
Year 95	0.159841	0.038702	0	0.043055
Year 98	0.187268	0.040562	0	0.050912
Year 00	0.264743	0.04209	0	0.07326
Cohort dummies	yes			
Log likelihood	–9902.68			
No. of observations	21 856			

Table 11.6 Probability of owning: private pensions

	Coef.	Std. err.	P>|z|	dF/dx
PPW	–0.01671	0.00728	0.022	–0.00139
PPW*age	0.000969	0.000435	0.026	8.09E–05
PPW*age^2/100	–0.00182	0.000854	0.033	–0.00015
PPW*age^3/1000	0.00011	5.53E-05	0.047	9.16E–-06
Family income	0.031489	0.004744	0	0.002627
Family income^2/10	–0.00188	0.000474	0	–0.00016
Financial wealth	0.000423	0.000228	0.064	3.53E–05
Financial wealth^2/10	–4.77E–07	2.57E–07	0.063	–3.98E–08
Married	–0.05842	0.055329	0.291	–0.00505
No. of income recipients	–0.0698	0.026696	0.009	–0.00582
No. of children	–0.01921	0.01956	0.326	–0.0016
North	0.620218	0.047196	0	0.056202
Centre	0.462186	0.053243	0	0.049092
Male	0.033181	0.051458	0.519	0.002715
Private employee	0.19548	0.04007	0	0.017281
Pensioner	0.0335	0.070045	0.632	0.002811
Higher education	0.18034	0.037552	0	0.015663
Year 91	0.026852	0.053666	0.617	0.002277
Year 93	0.144642	0.05451	0.008	0.013162
Year 95	0.01247	0.058216	0.83	0.001048
Year 98	–0.00225	0.062533	0.971	–0.00019
Year 00	0.260029	0.061567	0	0.025147
Cohort dummies	yes			
Log likelihood	–4342.13			
No. of observations	21 856			

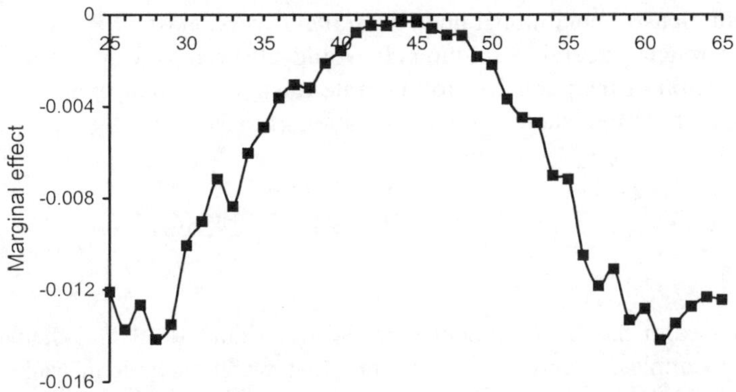

Figure 11.2 Estimated marginal effect of PPW on the probability of owning a private pension, by age, evaluated at sample means

11.7 CONCLUSION

The building of a market for private pensions in Italy has proved very difficult. New attempts by the government under way in 2003, in the form of a new delegation bill, are meant to sustain the long awaited take-off. In our view, this bill does not properly tackle the true obstacles preventing the development of supplementary pensions. On the one hand, the law rightly aims at creating a level playing-field on the supply side for the several types of private pension schemes, in order to foster competition in the sector and improve its overall performance. On the other hand, however, it does not address the question of accessible forms of guarantees, leaving a dangerous gap between the present guaranteed severance pay funds and the risky defined contribution pension plans. Moreover, irrespective of this gap, a shortcut is proposed in order to overcome the low propensity of workers to accumulate private pension wealth, by forcing them to divert the TFR flows to pension schemes.

This compulsory approach is hardly consistent with the aim of promoting competition by equalizing, on the supply side, the conditions of access to different products. On the other hand, although the reforms of the first pillar have reduced future benefits especially for younger generations, as long as the payroll tax rate remains as high as 33 per cent, little room will be left for a different accumulation of pension wealth. Indeed, our estimates, conducted on Italian micro-data, show that the decrease in public pension wealth faced by Italian families during the 1990s does help in explaining the observed increase in participation in the market for contractual saving for retirement.

An opting-out clause[55] conditional upon a parallel diversion of TFR flows appears to be a much preferable solution. It would allow new workers to transfer the reduction of the public payroll tax rate to supplementary pension products, granting them free choice in the destination of these resources.

APPENDIX: COMPUTATION OF PUBLIC PENSION WEALTH

Public pension wealth has been computed at the individual level and then aggregated over couples, according to the rules that were relevant in each year considered in the analysis. Along with the relevant legislation, the ingredients needed to compute the future pension benefit for an individual who is still active in the labor market are a projection of future gross earnings up to the age of retirement, the number of working years and the age at retirement. Gross earnings profiles, used for the projection, have been estimated using the SHIW 1989–2000 sample for different groups of the population, defined on gender, date of birth, occupation, education and area. Age at entry into the labor market and expected age at retirement are recorded in the data for each individual, and this information is used in order to compute the future pension entitlement (assuming continuous careers and point expectations). The individual gross public pension wealth is then defined as the present value of future (or actual, for pensioners) pension entitlements; the net measure of public pension wealth is defined as gross pension wealth minus the present value of the payroll tax that still has to be paid to the system (by both the employee and the employer). Both quantities are valued at the year of the interview, assuming a subjective discount rate equal to 2 per cent. Individual net pension wealth is then aggregated over couples (when a spouse is present) and this quantity is used in the estimates presented in the text.

Table 11.7 shows net public pension wealth for both individuals and couples in the various years considered in the analysis; year of birth groups have been formed so that in the last column (that is, individuals born 1955–64) appear mainly individuals who had been active in the labor market for less than 15 years in 1992, and therefore faced a substantial change in the benefit computation formula both after the 1992 and after the 1995 reform. All individuals (including pensioners) faced a change in the indexation rule of the benefit, linked (although not completely) to earnings growth before 1992, and only to prices since that date. The effect of the 1992 reform is mainly evident for the older age groups (first two columns in Table 11.7) who were on average accumulating (net) pension wealth at a high rate between 1989 and 1991; the 1995 reform, whose effect should be visible in the years 1998 and 2000, did not hit these cohorts, but it applied to individuals who had been active in the labor market for less than 18 years in 1995. The youngest group of individuals was hit both by the 1992 reform (which resulted in a lower rate of growth of pension wealth across 1991 and 1993) and by the 1995 reform, which resulted in zero growth of public pension wealth between 1995 and 1998.

Table 11.7 Net public pension wealth for different cohorts (thousands of €)

		Year of birth	
Year	**1935–44**	**1945–54**	**1955–64**
1989			
PPW	228.9	158.6	102.2
PPW-couple	276.0	210.0	137.3
Nr. of obs	703	1150	776
1991			
PPW	257.1	174.2	104.2
PPW-couple	307.6	231.4	137.5
No. of obs	749	1153	767
1993			
PPW	244.8	170.4	106.9
PPW-couple	297.8	230.8	138.0
No. of obs	712	1073	742
1995			
PPW	258.1	177.2	111.4
PPW-couple	325.7	237.8	143.9
No. of obs	825	1075	794
1998			
PPW	260.0	196.4	110.7
PPW-couple	336.7	261.2	145.3
No.of obs	826	1054	811
2000			
PPW	261.8	218.0	122.3
PPW-couple	341.3	283.0	160.9
No.of obs	1007	1070	939

From another perspective, it is interesting to follow the evolution of public pension wealth for given age classes over time: in Table 11.8 individuals aged 35–44 in 1989 are the same group of individuals born between 1945 and 1954 displayed in Table 11.7, with individual pension wealth approximately equal to 159 000 €. Some 11 years later, the same age group (only approximately – as data are not available for 1999 – the group of individuals born between 1955 and 1964 in Table 11.7) holds pension wealth that amounts to only 119 thousand €. With some caution, due to the sometimes small cell sample size, a substantial reduction in public pension wealth is observed for all the age classes considered.

Table 11.8 Net public pension wealth for different age groups (thousands of €)

	Age class			
Year	**25–34**	**35–44**	**45–54**	**55–65**
1989				
PPW	102.2	158.6	228.9	
PPW-couple	137.3	210.0	276.0	
No. of obs	776	1150	703	
1991				
PPW	96.3	158.5	237.4	320.8
PPW-couple	128.5	209.3	295.1	351.5
No. of obs	569	1108	903	89
1993				
PPW	95.7	143.3	216.8	255.9
PPW-couple	122.3	193.3	275.1	309.8
No. of obs	397	974	945	211
1995				
PPW	92.2	132.5	213.1	265.8
PPW-couple	115.6	174.1	282.2	330.6
No. of obs	271	913	1052	458
1998				
PPW	75.8	117.7	207.1	258.1
PPW-couple	104.7	155.0	272.2	336.9
No. of obs	76	822	1055	738
2000				
PPW		119.2	207.9	261.3
PPW-couple		156.3	269.6	341.3
No. of obs		842	1063	1111

NOTES

1. For a description of the reform of the public pension system in Italy, see Brugiavini and Fornero (2001), Fornero and Castellino (2001) and Franco (2003).
2. Legislative Decree 124/1993.
3. Pre-existing plans are supposed to adapt to the new discipline, although most have not yet done so.
4. Legislative Decree 47/2000.

5. A new bill, which would enable the government to promulgate a single act on pensions (*Testo unico in materia previdenziale*), is precisely directed at giving a definite start to supplementary pension schemes, through the compulsory diversion of the severance pay flows. However, its political fate (as of Spring 2004, after almost 2 years and a half in Parliament) is still uncertain.
6. Nineteen per cent for independent workers. Both rates are insufficient to pay for projected pension benefits, the equilibrium payroll tax rates for employees being something like 10 percentage points higher for the next three decades.
7. Since 1995 this system should have been extended to public employees as well, but so far the old rules on civil servants' severance pay (*Indennità di buonuscita*) still apply in most cases.
8. Fornero (1999), p. 181.
9. It should be noted that employees are also entitled to tax-exempt contributions proportional to their non-labor income, and that anyway the TFR devolution rule does not apply to contributions made by the head of a household for dependent family members. Both exceptions seem to be practically irrelevant, although the latter theoretically offers a perfect loophole for married single earners wishing to have both their TFR and a private pension, so long as the spouse can be relied upon to select a joint-and-survivor pension.
10. For instance, its mechanism privileges large and static firms over small and more dynamic ones.
11. It can be remarked that there is no evidence that TFR has ever been annuitized by retirees.
12. Even the whole capital if the accumulated funds are so small that the resulting annuity is lower than the annual 'social allowance' (*assegno sociale*, equal to 4438 € in 2003).
13. Nevertheless, pension plans are still more constrained than TFR: to begin with, annuitization at retirement is the rule, waived only partly or in exceptional cases. Furthermore, there are strong tax penalties weighing on advances and eventual lump-sum withdrawals totaling more than one third of assets.
14. This practice is allowed, on the contrary, in pension annuity policies.
15. An interesting, albeit largely unexploited, opportunity thus seems to be provided by the French OAT€Is, coupon-bearing bonds indexed to the European Harmonised Index of Consumer Prices (HICP): these currently exist with two maturities, namely 2012 and 2032, and they are also theoretically available for stripping, even if the feasibility of the operation would be debatable. Remarkably, so long as the real yield on these instruments remains above 1.5 per cent (the real coupon yield is 3 per cent and 3.15 per cent respectively for the two issues) they can also conceivably be used for option-based investment strategies guaranteeing no less than the legal TFR return while still offering upside potential.
16. From the point of view of the pension fund, of course: workers have limited liquidity options, as discussed above.
17. An examination of the ten largest providers of open pension funds (for a total of 34 pension funds and a market share of over 80 per cent) also shows that only one, albeit implicitly, prices the guarantee, by setting a higher yearly charge for participants selecting the guaranteed investment line; on the contrary, in all the other funds the guaranteed line is also the least costly one.
18. The rest are unit-linked policies, which can offer guarantees analogous to those of pension funds. A with-profit structure is also the only choice currently offered for annuities, including private pensions, during the payout phase.
19. The importance of the 'locking in' feature is mainly related to the smoothing of benefit flows in the payout phase, when the annuity profile can thus be guaranteed to be non-decreasing.
20. Although they can choose an insurance company as an asset manager.
21. We are referring here to the rules applying since 2001; they changed quite substantially a former fiscal treatment that, when considering the TFR diversion, was in fact penalizing participation.
22. Of course, this is advantageous because investment income is always taxed at a lower rate than personal income.

23. More precisely, without increasing the nominal amount of the tax base: uncertainty remains regarding future movements in the income tax rate.
24. On the whole, the regime can be very generous: in a stylized example with constant nominal returns of 4 per cent, constant nominal contribution growth of 3 per cent and a constant income tax rate of 30 per cent, it is equivalent to an EET scheme with a reduced income tax rate of 22.6 per cent, while the regular ETT taxation of non-pension savings in Italy leads to an equivalent rate of 38.9 per cent. This corresponds to an effective tax cut of 42 per cent.
25. The most typical, although by no means the only, incentive is towards low worker turnover, favored by back-loaded pension formulae.
26. The latter point is questionable, for a single rate is determined for all workers in the same industry-wide contract, while life cycle theory normally implies that, given positive wage growth during a worker's career, the optimal rate should be lower for younger workers and rise in time.
27. Which somehow questions the optimality of a system where the best pension funds are closed, thus becoming a privilege for specific groups of workers.
28. PIPs, on the other hand, expose participants to the albeit remote risk of insurance company bankruptcy.
29. The Commissione di Vigilanza sui Fondi Pensione (COVIP). In addition, open pension funds also have to conform to the regulation on the marketing of financial products set by the financial market regulator, CONSOB. Occupational funds are exempt from this scrutiny because they are not directly sold to individual customers. Annuities, on the other hand, only have to comply with the regulation imposed by the insurance supervisor, the Istituto per la Vigilanza sulle Assicurazioni Private e di Interesse Collettivo (ISVAP).
30. European Commission (2003), p. 84.
31. The headline figure for closed funds is 0.53 per cent, computed as the ratio of expenses to final assets. The value of 0.61 per cent is obtained by considering average assets, which seems more suitable for comparison with the charges levied by individual pension plans. Cf. COVIP (2003).
32. Costs other than management charges actually exist, but they appear to be negligible. The possibility of changes in the terms of the contract is also disregarded.
33. Cf. Fornero et al. (forthcoming).
34. In the case of open pension funds, on the contrary, indirect charges (when present) are paid by the sponsoring company and not by participants.
35. A further reduction in yield is due to the taxation of pension plan investment income.
36. Detailed market shares for insurance products are not available, but concentration is very high, with two policies accounting for two-thirds of total capital in 2001 and half in 2002.
37. Theoretically, competitive pressure should discourage such behavior, but preliminary evidence suggests that this is not happening in Italy: price dispersion is quite high and extremely aggressive sales techniques were widely used until the intervention of the regulator in October 2002. The two leading policies have an extremely complex and front-loaded charge system, with higher-than-average costs even in the longer term. This seems to confirm the dictum that insurance is sold rather than bought, as well as the intuition that pricing is not the main selling point.
38. For instance, in each simulation the most expensive product lacks them, while the least costly includes them.
39. Three of the products considered stand out from the sample: they all have an annual management charge of less than 1 per cent of assets, even for equity investments, and no other recurring cost. However, none of these is a major market player and each is sponsored by a group offering other, more expensive and more successful pension funds, possibly because the most efficient products aim at collective rather than individual participation.
40. Computed as the average of assets at the beginning and at the end of the year.
41. In particular, the outlying value of 2.39 per cent was almost halved in 2002, with the same fund having a ratio of 1.27 per cent.

42. Remarkably, though, the impact on money's worth ratios of assumed annuitant selection is lower in Italy than abroad, as noted for example by McCarthy and Mitchell (this volume, Chapter 2).
43. COVIP (2003), pp. 76–7.
44. See Note 1.
45. The focus is on whole and endowment life insurance contracts, which are payable at the death of the insured or on a specified maturity date if the insured is alive. They are virtually never annuitized in Italy; nevertheless, together with private pension plans, they can be seen as part of the savings of families for their retirement.
46. This approach, which is an application of the difference-in-difference estimator, has been previously followed by Attanasio and Brugiavini (1996) to estimate the elasticity of savings to public pension wealth.
47. Due to questionnaire design, the SHIW data only allow a somewhat blurred distinction between life insurance and private pensions contracts. See Section 11.6.1 for details.
48. The available waves (since 1989) are those relative to the years 1989, 1991, 1993, 1995, 1998 and 2000.
49. See Brandolini and Cannari (1994) for a detailed description of the data and a comparison with macroeconomic data.
50. See Appendix for more details. The effect of the social security reforms on individuals' public pension wealth has been studied for example in Brugiavini (1999), Brugiavini and Fornero (2001) and Forni and Giordano (2001).
51. The distinction between life insurance and private pension is the largely psychological one outlined above.
52. Attanasio and Brugiavini (1996) specify a similar model to estimate the elasticity of saving to changes in public pension wealth.
53. It would also be possible to control for the tax incentives/disincentives that hit different groups of the population that decided to invest in life insurance during the 1990s. Such an experiment has been performed by Jappelli and Pistaferri (2003); as the authors did not find a significant effect of tax treatment on the demand for life insurance, here we ignore this issue.
54. Banca d'Italia (2002); COVIP (2003).
55. The opting out proposal advanced by CeRP is described in Fornero and Castellino (2001).

REFERENCES

Attanasio, O.P. and A. Brugiavini (1996), 'L'effetto della riforma Amato sul risparmio delle famiglie italiane', University of Venice, WP 96.05.

Banca d'Italia (2002), 'Aggregati monetari e creditizi dell'area dell'euro: le componenti italiane', supplement to Statistical Bulletin Nr. 46: *Indicatori monetari e finanziari Aggregati monetari e creditizi dell'area dell'euro.*

Brandolini, A. and L. Cannari (1994), 'Methodological Appendix', in A. Ando, L. Guiso and I. Visco (eds), *Saving and the Accumulation of Wealth,* Cambridge: Cambridge University Press.

Brugiavini, A. (1999), 'Social Security and Retirement in Italy', in J. Gruber and D. Wise (eds), *Social Security and Retirement around the World*, Chicago: University of Chicago Press, 181–237.

Brugiavini, A. and E. Fornero (2001), 'Pension Provision in Italy', in R. Disney and P. Johnson (eds), *Pension Systems and Retirement Incomes across OECD Countries*, Cheltenham and Northampton, MA: Edward Elgar, 197–235.

COVIP (2001), *Relazione per l'anno 2000.*

COVIP (2003), *Relazione per l'anno 2002.*

European Commission (2003), *Joint Report by the Commission and the Council on Adequate and Sustainable Pensions.*

Fornero, E. (1999), *L'Economia dei Fondi Pensione. Potenzialità e Limiti della Previdenza Privata in Italia,* Bologna: Il Mulino.

Fornero, E. and O. Castellino (2001), *La Riforma del Sistema Previdenziale Italiano*, Bologna: Il Mulino (an English summary of this report can be found at http://cerp.unito.it/Pubblicazioni/archivio/OTHER/English/SUMMARY_report.pdf).

Fornero, E., C. Fugazza and G. Ponzetto, forthcoming, 'Analisi comparativa dell'onerosità dei prodotti previdenziali individuali', *Mercato Concorrenza Regole.*

Forni, L. and R. Giordano (2001), 'Funding a PAYG Pension System: the Case of Italy', *Fiscal Studies*, **22**(4), 487–526.

Franco, D. (2003), 'Italy: the Search for a Sustainable PAYG Pension System', in N. Takayama (ed.), *Taste of Pie: Searching for Better Pension Provisions in Developed Countries*, Tokyo: Maruzen Co.

Guiso, L. and T. Jappelli (2001), 'Household Portfolios in Italy', in H. Guiso and T. Jappelli (eds), *Household Portfolios*, Cambridge, MA: MIT Press, 251–90.

Jappelli, T. and L. Pistaferri (2003), 'Tax Incentives and the Demand for Life Insurance: Evidence from Italy', *Journal of Public Economics,* **87**, June, 1779–99.

James, E., J. Smalhout and D. Vittas (2001), 'Administrative Costs and the Organization of Individual Account Systems: A Comparative Perspective', in R. Holzmann and J. Stiglitz (eds), *New Ideas About Old Age Security*, Washington, DC: World Bank; revised version published in *Private Pension Systems: Administrative Costs and Reform,* Paris: OECD, 2001.

Index